Jeanne Devereaux,
Prima Ballerina
of Vaudeville and Broadway

Jeanne Devereaux, Prima Ballerina of Vaudeville and Broadway

"She Ran Between the Raindrops"

KATHLEEN MENZIE LESKO

Foreword by Anthony Slide

McFarland & Company, Inc., Publishers
Jefferson, North Carolina

LIBRARY OF CONGRESS CATALOGUING-IN-PUBLICATION DATA

Names: Lesko, Kathleen M., editor.
Title: Jeanne Devereaux, prima ballerina of vaudeville and Broadway : "she ran between the raindrops" / Kathleen Menzie Lesko ; foreword by Anthony Slide.
Description: Jefferson, North Carolina : McFarland & Company, Inc., Publishers, 2017. | Includes bibliographical references and index.
Identifiers: LCCN 2017009574 | ISBN 9781476666945 (softcover : acid free paper) ∞
Subjects: LCSH: Devereaux, Jeanne, 1912–2011. | Dancers—United States—Biography. | Vaudeville—United States—History.
Classification: LCC GV1785.D45 L47 2017 | DDC 792.802/8092 [B] —dc23
LC record available at https://lccn.loc.gov/2017009574

BRITISH LIBRARY CATALOGUING DATA ARE AVAILABLE

ISBN (print) 978-1-4766-6694-5
ISBN (ebook) 978-1-4766-2749-6

© 2017 Kathleen Menzie Lesko. All rights reserved

No part of this book may be reproduced or transmitted in any form or by any means, electronic or mechanical, including photocopying or recording, or by any information storage and retrieval system, without permission in writing from the publisher.

Front cover photograph of Jeanne Devereaux from the Jeanne Devereaux Perkins Collection

Printed in the United States of America

*McFarland & Company, Inc., Publishers
Box 611, Jefferson, North Carolina 28640
www.mcfarlandpub.com*

To my friend Jeanne for sharing her life.
To the memory of my mother Anne, who dreamed of being
a movie star, and of my brother David, who loved history.
And especially to my husband Bob
who inspired me with his intelligence and artistry.

Table of Contents

Acknowledgments ix
Foreword by Anthony Slide 1
A Note on the Text 4
Prologue 5
Introduction 7

1 • Family Life in St. Louis, Missouri 11
2 • The Making of a Ballerina 20
3 • New York and the Circuits 32
4 • Hollywood, a Fanchon and Marco Tour and Pasadena 45
5 • The Roxy and the Circuits 57
6 • The London Palladium 69
7 • A Royal Command Performance and a European and North African Tour 83
8 • Touring the British Provinces with *George Ahoy!* 93
9 • International Casino and a Royal Performance in Paris 105
10 • Radio City, Brazil and Lean Times 119
11 • Aunt Lenore's Dream House and Performing at the St. Louis Muny 133
12 • Touring with *Earl Carroll's Vanities* 143
13 • Radio City and Clifford C. Fisher's *Folies Bergère* 154
14 • Hollywood and Summer Operettas 171
15 • A USO Camp Shows Tour to Japan 180
16 • Radio City, Summer Operettas and the Milton Berle Television Show 194

17 • Final Year in New York	211
18 • Marriage and Four More Careers	222
Epilogue	243
Afterword by Jeanne Devereaux Perkins	246
Appendix One: Sample of Jeanne's Poetry	248
Appendix Two: Jeanne's World War II Legacy	250
Appendix Three: Jeanne's Research on Grace Nicholson	251
Appendix Four: Sarkis Badalyan's Commemorative Poem Written for Jeanne's Celebration of Life at the Huntington Library, October 2011	254
Chapter Notes	255
Bibliography	262
Index	265

Acknowledgments

Many people contributed to making this biography a reality. I want to thank all the wonderful people who were interviewed along with Jeanne and Tom Perkins, with some of them also providing key documents and photographs: Christopher Adde, Peggy Almquist, Aida Cervata, Virginia Elwood-Akers, Katherine Murray-Morse, Ginger Paul, Kay Bennett Paul, Martha Perkins, Patrick Purdy, Kathleen Seabury, Elly van Dijk, Marlene Voskian, and Robert Winter. I am particularly grateful to Christopher Adde, manager of the General Collection at the Huntington, for his enduring friendship with Jeanne and Tom, his enthusiastic support of this biography from its inception, and for alerting me to the materials about Jeanne in the Huntington Library's newly-acquired Fanchon and Marco collection. As the executor of the Perkins estate, Chris also discovered Jeanne's personal diary for the mid–1930s as well as additional family letters.

I greatly appreciate the librarians and curators who patiently took my calls and answered my questions—Diane Jaust, the archivist at Radio City Music Hall, Alexa Potter, the historian at the Library of Congress' Veterans Oral History Project, and Yolanda Garrett, the communications coordinator at the USO. While conducting research at the New York Public Library for the Performing Arts at Lincoln Center, I had the good fortune to meet with Linda Murray, curator of the Jerome Robbins Dance Division, and Doug Reside, curator of the Billy Rose Theatre Division.

I am extremely thankful to all my generous colleagues and friends—Denise Cavanaugh, Jill Cogen, Virginia Elwood-Akers, Deborah Payne, Elizabeth Pomeroy, Anthony Slide, Emma Lewis Thomas, Susan Shalgos Wolsfeld, and June Vayo—who carefully read my drafts and provided excellent criticisms and insights. Jill Cogen's suggestions for cutting an early draft made the difference between an unwieldy manuscript to one more tightly structured. Virginia Elwood-Akers' meticulous copyediting skills and innate sense of narrative style made my writing less academic and more reader friendly. Deborah Payne made cogent suggestions that took my writing to a new level, and Anthony Slide not only validated the show business context for Jeanne's performances but offered many stylistic improvements. My talented and experienced editor June Vayo helped me to reduce my voluminous manuscript to a marketable size, and recommended revisions that would make a reader love Jeanne from the outset and eager to read her biography. I also acknowledge with admiration all the celebrity photographers who recorded Jeanne's dancing career for posterity, as well as Dario Marquez of Cantu Graphics who meticulously prepared the photographs.

I want to thank John T. Dooley, former president and CEO of the USO San Diego

Center, and his project team for enthusiastically archiving and exhibiting Jeanne's surviving green army trench coat and hat bearing the "USO Camp Shows, Inc." red, white, and blue insignia, as well as interpretive printed materials describing her USO tour to Japan. My appreciation is also extended to special members of the Huntington staff—Sarkis Badalyan and Patricia Vanley—who so warmly greeted Jeanne each day over the years as she checked into the Rothenberg Reading Room and personally befriended her, as well as Leslie Jobsky, a library assistant who was a regular member of Jeanne's teatime group in the Footnote Lounge. A special thanks to my husband Bob, who read my manuscript with his artistic eye, nurtured me through my crises of confidence, and never wavered in supporting my multi-year writing projects. Last but not least, thank you to Jeanne for trusting me.

Foreword by Anthony Slide

As she has done since 1978, a striking elderly lady sits in the Reading Room of the elegant and prestigious Huntington Library in San Marino, California. She is researching the life and career of Pasadena resident Grace Nicholson, a collector of Native American and later Asian art, whose Chinese Treasure House of Oriental and Western Art was to become the Pasadena Art Museum. The researcher is named Jeanne Devereaux (married name Jeanne Devereaux Perkins), and both she and Grace Nicholson are formidable ladies in terms of their very different careers. Both are forgotten, both have been brought together thanks to the Huntington, and it is thanks to another Huntington researcher, or "Reader," as they are identified, Dr. Kathleen Menzie Lesko, that the current volume exists.

I find it ironic, and also curiously appealing, that Jeanne Devereaux, whose career very much belongs in the world of American popular culture, should be saved from anonymity thanks to Kathleen Lesko and thanks indirectly to the Huntington Library, which is really about as far removed from the world of entertainment as it is possible to be (and that despite being the repository of a collection of radio and television scripts relating to *Gunsmoke*, together with the papers of two prominent female screenwriters, Zoe Akins and Sonya Levien).

Indeed, it is quite fascinating to read here how Jeanne and a boyfriend visited the Huntington and its famous Botanical Gardens back in December 1940. How could she have known then what an important role it was to play in her life?

Kathleen Lesko, like so many other scholars at the Huntington, befriended Jeanne Devereaux, socialized with her at the Huntington's Rose Garden Café, and happily it was Kathleen who decided that her biography needed to be recorded for future historians, students, researchers, and scholars.

It is equally ironic that thanks to the friends she made at the Huntington that Jeanne Devereaux was better known in that prestigious establishment than she is remembered in outside society as a major exponent of classical dance on the vaudeville stage and in the world of musical comedy and revue. She belonged to a unique band of brothers and sisters who survived a perilous, financially fraught career on the vaudeville stage, in revues, musical comedies, and operettas, barely existing at a time when America's taste in popular entertainment was changing. Jeanne Devereaux was not the typical performer of her day. She wasn't a comedienne or female stooge (in the tradition of Gracie Allen or Eve Sully), she wasn't a singer with a distinctive style (such as Trixie Friganza or Sophie Tucker), she wasn't a member of an acrobatic troupe, she wasn't a showgirl, and she certainly wasn't a freak act. It seems a harsh description, but she was perhaps what was described as a "dumb" act, a performer or performers an audience didn't need to actually listen to.

Jeanne Devereaux was what was identified as a toe dancer, and she billed herself as a prima ballerina. She danced "en pointe," with her full body weight supported on the tips of her toes, and she did it not just once a night but in multiple shows a day in vaudeville and revue. Her act was every bit as sophisticated and as strenuous as the work accomplished by dancers in the world of classical ballet, but it was generally influenced by the demands of her audience. As she explained, being a toe dancer in vaudeville "was more creative and rewarding than being in a company." Jeanne Devereaux, a diminutive creature with big brown eyes and a winning smile, was not an anonymous pair of feet in *Swan Lake* or *La Sylphide*, but rather a headliner in the spotlight for many years.

She didn't dance nude, but she did dance with a balloon, probably with far less sauce but far more sophistication than did Sally Rand, who specialized not only in balloons but also fans. Like the strippers in burlesque who understood the need for a patriotic finale, Jeanne Devereaux was every bit as patriotic with her flag dance, which she featured when America was both at war and at peace.

It was vaudeville that made Jeanne Devereaux a headliner, but as that medium lost its appeal with the American public, she was able to move on, working with such famous names as George White, Florence Ziegfeld, and Earl Carroll, so closely associated with revue, as well as the West Coast producers Fanchon and Marco. Beginning with the Christmas 1938 show, she was frequently featured at New York's Radio City Music Hall, and later a staple with various Civic Light Opera companies across the United States. With the outbreak of World War II, she went on USO tours, and with the increasing popularity of television in the late 1940s, she found employment working for its first major star, Milton Berle, who, appropriately enough, like her came from the vaudeville stage. How fascinating that early television variety—and how I wish it existed today—could blend such diverse entertainment as stand-up comedy and classical dance with consummate ease, proof if proof is needed that vaudeville was still alive.

She was not only a dancer, but also a choreographer and relatively early in her career also a ballet mistress, responsible for a chorus of one hundred boys and girls. Jeanne Devereaux was there at the opening of New York's Roxy Theatre, working with the dancers who were later to become the Rockettes. She took herself, her mother and her act abroad, appearing in August 1935 at the London Palladium—the prestigious flagship for British vaudeville just as New York's Palace Theatre was the flagship for American vaudeville—and proving that American entertainment had more to offer than singers or comics.

Considering that Jeanne Devereaux is so completely forgotten today, it is amazing to discover thanks to Kathleen Lesko's work that not only did she appear before a general British audience, she also performed in front of King George V and Queen Mary in October 1935 at the Royal Command Performance, hosted by the London Palladium. She was the first American prima ballerina to be asked to appear at such a prestigious event. I am amused that another American was on that same bill, Will Mahoney, whose act featured his tap dancing on a xylophone, striking the instrument with his feet rather than a pair of wooden mallets; it is too bad the two did not appear on stage in the same act, with one dancing en pointe and the other dancing en xylophone!

It is a fascinating biography, and we have to thank Kathleen Lesko for bringing it to life. She is a scholar who knows how to use the resources at hand, including her subject's own remembrances, her diaries and correspondence, and what is obviously an extensive archive. Quite frankly, we don't usually come across a biography such as this, discussing someone who, in many respects, is outside of the mainstream of popular entertainment. That is not to say that Jeanne Devereaux was a minor performer, but rather she is someone who is not readily identifiable as a major "name" in any of the various areas of American entertainment with which she was associated.

With a scholar's touch but a human sympathy, Kathleen Lesko has put together a volume that documents in great detail all aspects of the life of a woman who might carelessly be identified as a typical American stage entertainer, an individual not associated with the motion picture (which is not to imply that Jeanne Devereaux would not have been happy to embrace a screen career). It is all here, from her childhood in St. Louis, the beginning of her dance training at the age of seven. We read of the troubled family background, with mother Lillian and father Bill basically (and certainly physically) separated as the former travels with her daughter initially as a chaperone and then as general assistant and wardrobe woman, while her father stays on in St. Louis, living most of his life at the YMCA. It is a life of financial uncertainty, with Jeanne's appeal obviously in decline after World War II.

As already noted, I would not pretend that Jeanne Devereaux is remembered today. She was a trouper who worked long and hard, rehearsing and nurturing her act to fit the times and the venues, almost unperturbed by the poor accommodations that she and her mother were forced to rent, surviving on a diet—cottage cheese and radishes—that is so unappealing to the reader that starvation seems almost preferable, and buoyed perhaps by publicity stories and reviews, but always aware that the impact of such coverage was transitory and ultimately meant nothing.

Earlier I questioned if Jeanne Devereaux was a typical American entertainer. It is a difficult question to answer. Typical or atypical, Jeanne Devereaux's life and career are worthy of recognition and examination. How she prospered while, arguably, never quite realizing her full potential, and how she later survived, is a narrative within American popular culture that is difficult to comprehend and generally difficult to document. In that sense Kathleen Lesko's book is important on many levels. It is about one performer, but it might well be about countless similar entertainers of the first half of the 20th century.

Jeanne Devereaux retired from active research at the Huntington Library in September 2008, giving up the scholar's desk of which she had proved to be a worthy occupant. She said, "Cheery pip!" (a condensation of "Cheerio" and "Pip pip") to her life as a Huntington Library scholar, just as in the last century, she had said, "Cheery pip!" to her stage career.

Hopefully, Kathleen Menzie Lesko's book will help expand Jeanne Devereaux' fame and bring her back to the stature that she once enjoyed, as the many press comments from the 1930s and 1940s included here testify. We close the book with a sense of fulfillment at having learned so very much and equally with a feeling of sadness that the book and the life are over. Cheery pip, Jeanne Devereaux.

Historian Anthony Slide is the author or editor of more than 200 books on all aspects of popular entertainment. In 1990 he was awarded an honorary doctorate of letters by Bowling Green State University in recognition of his work on the history of popular culture.

A Note on the Text

I have retained all the orthography and punctuation of the original documents except for hyphens that have been replaced with dashes. I have added [*sic*] only when a misspelled word is distracting or confusing. I have included most of the documentation directly in the text to reduce the chapter notes, and to allow the reader to follow closely the chronology of Jeanne's dancing career and personal life.

Prologue

In 2004, when I arrived as a scholar at the Huntington Library, Art Collections, and Botanical Gardens in San Marino, California, I noticed a short, elegant woman seated on a cushioned chair at her desk in the library's Rothenberg Reading Room. She wore a long dress and beaded sweater, with her reading glasses perched low on the bridge of her nose and her gray hair pulled back and anchored with sparkling hair clips. She had an exquisitely shaped head, wrinkled but luminescent skin, and youthful, impish eyes. She was ninety-two years old with only an eighth grade education and very intriguing. Her desk was piled high with stacks of books and magazines and bits of paper; a porcelain English teacup was placed prominently on the corner. Her glitter, glamour, and clutter stood out in the sea of scholars around her.

Little did I realize that this diminutive woman had been an international vaudeville and Broadway prima ballerina from 1923 to 1952. She had danced in more than 6,000 performances for more than fifty million people on the best stages in America and in Europe. She had danced before royalty more than any of her peers. She had been accompanied by her indomitable mother Lillian—her constant companion and manager. She had been a headlining star in show business and now indulged her passion for research and writing in the quiet ambience of the Rothenberg Reading Room.

The Huntington was the perfect venue for Jeanne in her twilight years. Always driven by a passionate desire for excellence and an insatiable curiosity about people and places, she surrounded herself with stimulating people in books or in person. Jeanne and her husband Tom lunched every weekday at the Huntington's Rose Garden Café, seated at a table next to the entrance where, like a persistent siren, she would invite scholars and staff to join them for lunch and engaging conversation. She continued those conversations in the afternoon at her tea table in the Huntington's Footnote lounge. Whenever she spoke I would hear echoes of her visiting with her fellow performers backstage in the theatre wings, in her dressing room, and in the automats and diners where she and her mother often would eat at midnight after the last show.

Jeanne always intended to write her autobiography. After several beginnings and many random notes other projects intervened, so she put down her pen and waited. When I suggested writing an article about her extraordinary life, she was excited and eager to cooperate. She shared her treasured leather scrapbook containing clippings and programs of some of the best of thousands of performances she had given as a prima ballerina in the prime of her career from 1935 to 1947. She also shared many documents in boxes and paper bags scattered in her American Craftsman house in Pasadena, California.

I was seduced by this extensive documentation. When Jeanne shared her professional photographs and personal letters to her mentally ill father, I knew that my article was a biography. Over the next few years I conducted oral interviews with Jeanne and her husband Tom, her remaining friends, her few relatives, and her former ballet students. Later Jeanne found the love letters that she had written her fiancé while she was still living in New York, and the executor of her estate discovered her personal diary for the mid–1930s. It is my hope that all of these primary sources—printed, visual, and oral—will be archived in an appropriate library.

Jeanne's dancer's feet, once bound in satin toe shoes laced with crisscrossed ribbons, were now red and swollen, and her neck and shoulders slightly bent. She shrouded herself in flowing dresses. Her twinkling eyes were sometimes dulled by the glare of her thick reading glasses. Jeanne, however, retained her natural *joie de vivre* and lived each day to the fullest. When she retired from the Huntington Library in 2008, her friends and colleagues remembered her hunched over her desk in the Rothenberg Reading Room, poring over books and indecipherable old manuscripts, and missed her intelligent and witty conversation. Even in her late nineties Jeanne's stride was still elegant and strong, though she walked with a cane; her mind was active and curious despite being sometimes forgetful and fatigued; and her spirit was stubborn and optimistic, even when she occasionally reflected on her mortality.

Jeanne outlasted the hundreds of satin toe shoes she had worn out during her dancing career. The passion and self-discipline that had defined her carried over into her four subsequent careers. Every morning in Pasadena when she woke up and planned her day either at the Huntington or later in her home office, the curtain went up, and she put on one of her long dresses and beaded sweaters. She secured her hair with sparkling hair clips, applied her makeup, and waited for her cue to make her grand entrance onto the stage of yet another challenging, productive day in her memorable life. In Jeanne's words, "Yesterday was history. Tomorrow is a mystery, and Today is [a] gift called the Present."

Introduction

When petite, slightly chubby Jean Helman, later known professionally as Jeanne Devereaux, entered show business at age eleven in 1923 in her hometown, St. Louis, Missouri, she could not have envisioned the dreams she would eventually realize during her long life of nearly ninety-nine years. She left St. Louis and her mentally ill father for New York City in early 1927, accompanied by her indomitable mother, to become a ballerina in popular entertainment. She joined the thousands of performers, called troupers, who performed in the strictly vaudeville theatres, the palatial presentation houses that combined vaudeville with feature films, the outdoor summer operetta stages, nightclub and casino cabarets, fancy hotel floor shows, and Broadway musical comedies and spectacular revues featuring themes and showgirls. Her professional dancing career also included stardom in Europe, a trailblazing USO Camp Shows tour, several movies and television appearances, and hundreds of free benefit performances. As one of the last vaudevillians alive in the second decade of the twenty-first century, Jeanne's unique voice speaks for thousands of forgotten troupers, particularly dancers, whose careers ended in the 1940s because they did not make the transition to radio, film, or television.

Like other troupers of her era she was the sole support of her family, which meant she had to delay marriage and forego a traditional family life with children. Child performers in public entertainment in the vaudeville era were constantly traveling on trains and living in hotels, so most were chaperoned and managed by their mothers. Jeanne was no exception. Lillian Lane Helman was a quintessential stage mother—vigilant companion, business manager, seamstress, dresser, general troubleshooter, and shareholder in her daughter's net profits. In Jeanne's words, her mother was the "boss" and Jeanne was the "star"; she was the "mother hen" and Jeanne was the "little chick." Jeanne endured the constant stress of her financial exploitation; she loved and admired her ambitious, authoritative but unaffectionate mother and idealized and pitied her mentally ill father. Living with mothers, however, could be difficult, especially for young people, and Jeanne often felt an acute loneliness and need for companions closer to her age. Over the years Lillian would look at Jeanne and say, "*She* ran between the raindrops," but more often she meant "*We*," for theirs was an inseparable partnership that spanned Jeanne's professional dancing career only ending with her mother's death in 1972. Running the treacherous obstacle course of popular entertainment, they were sprinkled but never soaked; they stumbled but never sank; they flirted with disaster but never succumbed. They kept running or they would starve.

The vaudeville era of live popular entertainment in America flourished between the years 1883–1932 and limped along during the Great Depression and World War II until it was overshadowed by radio, film, and television. While vaudeville's peak years were from 1905 to 1925, most of the stars in popular show business from 1925 through the 1960s began their careers in vaudeville. Sime Silverman, the founder and editor of the trade newspaper *Variety*, signaled vaudeville's decline when in 1925 he moved the vaudeville news from the front to the back of his influential publication. Most vaudevillians date the death of big-time two-a-day vaudeville to 1932 when the Palace Theatre, the flagship of the RKO circuit in New York's Times Square, re-opened with programs, called bills, alternating five-a-day live stage acts with talking films until it eliminated the vaudeville acts three years later. Over the next two decades it periodically revived two-a-day vaudeville, culminating in the early 1950s with Judy Garland's famous solo shows. Other vaudevillians, however, date the end of vaudeville to 1947 when the palatial Loew's State Theatre on Times Square presented its last vaudeville bill. Despite these benchmarks for its official death, vaudeville lived on through the 1960s in film, television variety shows and situation comedies, and avant-garde live theatre. Today's television reality talent contest shows are direct descendants of vaudeville.

When Jeanne arrived with her mother in New York City in early 1927 to break into show business she focused on creating a specialty act that would attract the agents and bookers and sell in the large vaudeville theatres and movie presentation houses. To be a star in vaudeville, which consisted of a succession of acts, and in order to derive her income exclusively from her bookings, she needed to be unique and sensational. She needed to distinguish herself on a vaudeville bill filled with acts that entertained an audience of thousands seated even in the upper rows of theaters. Toe dancers were expected to dazzle vaudeville audiences with their gracefulness, technical virtuosity, acrobatics, and glamorous costumes. "Mother pushed me hard to be outstanding," said Jeanne, because "if you were not outstanding you wouldn't be competitive with hundreds of other dancers." To thrill her audiences Jeanne combined classical ballet training with awe-inspiring technical virtuosity to create spectacular balletic moves like her lightening fast turns called pirouettes, her record-setting triple spin turns called fouettés, and her flexible vertical arabesques. She realized from the beginning that her profession required an incredible combination of artistry and athleticism and extraordinary mental, emotional, and physical discipline. While shows in vaudeville theatres and movie presentation houses often featured scantily clad and semi-nude chorus girls, Jeanne maintained her artistic integrity by including in her contracts a clause that specified no nude dancing.

Over a professional career spanning twenty-nine years Jeanne promoted herself as a "prima ballerina." She gave more than 6,000 paid and 500 benefit performances for nearly fifty million people, playing at least seven times and more on all of the vaudeville circuits that combined live stage shows and films in America's cities. When Jeanne entered show business at age eleven, the big-time two-a-day vaudeville associated with the impresarios B. F. Keith and Edward R. Albee existed in only a few theatres. As a trouper she performed primarily in the small-time vaudeville theatres combining live acts with feature films originated by William Fox and Marcus Loew and in the palatial movie presentation houses seating thousands built by the film studios in the 1920s and

'30s. Along with the famous movie palaces in Times Square such as the Palace and the Lowe's State, most large American cities had Fox, Paramount, Orpheum, and Loew's theatres. During the mid–1930s she starred at famous music hall theatres in Europe, where vaudeville was still called "variety," and danced seven times before royalty. From the late 1930s through the 1940s she was a soloist at Radio City Music Hall, one of the last palatial presentation houses that survived the decline of vaudeville. She led a landmark USO Camp Shows tour to Japan in 1945–46. In the final years of her career she appeared on Milton Berle's famous television show *The Texaco Star Theatre.*

Jeanne loved seeing her name as a headliner in a prominent position in the theatre playbills and programs and in lights on the outdoor marquees. The vaudeville acts were carefully scheduled on the bill, which was not officially locked in until the Monday matinees, keeping the performers in suspense until opening night. In the small-time vaudeville theatres and movie presentation houses the big-time bill of more than ten specialty acts performed twice nightly was reduced to bills of five to six acts complementing feature films. This combination of live acts and film often played continuously four or five times a day into the night. Eventually the stage shows had a master of ceremonies, scenery, and a modest storyline. They were often organized into traveling units showcasing music, dancing, and spectacle that could play in all the theatres on a circuit. The bill typically began with a mighty Wurlitzer organ recital, followed by the orchestra's overture, a short newsreel, the stage show, and the feature film. During the Depression years of the 1930s, when vaudeville was in decline in America, many performers worked in Europe, where vaudeville acts, there called variety acts, were flourishing.

Jeanne shared the vaudeville bill with singers, comedians, acrobats, jugglers, magicians and even animals. Performers avoided being the opening act in front of the curtain while the audience was still taking their seats, called performing "in one," as well as the dreaded deuce spot also performed "in one" while the audience settled down. Other acts followed until the coveted next-to-closing act that starred a headliner. The final act might feature live animals, acrobats or another headliner. Jeanne emphasized that she was never in the dreaded opener or deuce spots; as her career progressed, she was always a featured soloist in a favorable spot on the bill.

Jeanne claimed that she did not regret becoming a toe dancer in popular entertainment instead of becoming a member of the corps de ballet in Broadway musicals or opera houses or in one of the fledging elite ballet companies. In fact, today's established companies—the New York City Ballet and the American Ballet Theatre—had under different names only begun to thrive in the late 1930s. Ballerinas in these early companies complained about their meager salaries, Spartan lifestyles, and being limited to the corps de ballet. Famous company ballet dancers would perform in vaudeville when they were forced to earn real money. When she had the opportunity of joining the Ballet Russe de Monte Carlo, a European touring company existing from 1932 to 1962, she declined and remained a well-paid soloist with star billing in popular entertainment, since she needed to earn a decent living for her family. She admits in some of her personal letters, however, that when she was struggling to make a living in a depressed vaudeville market, she would have welcomed a temporary membership in a low paying ballet company. In her interviews Jeanne was adamant that "ballet is an art form, like music and painting; it is not a company." Being a toe dancer in vaudeville "was more creative and rewarding than being in a company," since she was able to be a soloist, choose her own music, create her own choreography, and design her own costumes.

As a vaudevillian Jeanne lived a life of uncertainty and constant travel. Unless she were performing in a long run in New York or London or in the summer operettas, like other troupers she traveled for months at a time, first by train and later by automobile, for weeklong engagements in the major cities and also split weeks, requiring exhausting "jumps" from one venue to another, from one small town to another on the vaudeville circuits. Most of her tours originated in New York, where all the troupers met at Grand Central Station, renewing old friendships before boarding their trains. They rarely had any leisure time to tour the city or town where they were performing, so their education about America came from reading books and looking out the train window. Arriving at the theatres, dancers like Jeanne immediately inspected the stage floors, since one too slick, uneven, or splintered could affect performance and cause injuries. She particularly disliked the raked stages that were angled up from the edge of the stage toward the back, making it difficult for the dancer to maintain balance and speed. Each theatre had its own musical director, so having the correct music and enough rehearsal time for her dances was a top priority for Jeanne. She carried her musical orchestrations by hand on the trains to the next town so that she was ready to rehearse the following morning.

During her dancing career Jeanne was usually able to support her family from her earnings. When she was broke, she and her mother lived with her maternal grandparents in Pasadena, California, and she performed in the Los Angeles area. They lived on a frugal budget from paycheck to paycheck, and her constant financial outlays for dance lessons, rehearsal halls, pianists, costumes, travel, hotel rent, publicity, commissions for agents, and weekly tips to doormen, call boys, and stage managers greatly reduced her net profits. At her zenith in 1940 Jeanne was capable of earning $250 to $300 a week—not in the thousands like some of the famous headlining comedians and singers—but a very respectable income for a dancer at that time.

Stoic in the face of adversity, Jeanne was adamant that it was the quality of the performance that really mattered to her as an artist. "You worked for a weekly wage," she said, and "approval by the audience as they applauded and shouted 'Bravo!' ... Each time you took a bow that was your reward. Everything was centered on a good performance; life offstage was an interlude." The socializing, shopping, and touring in between and after shows, during layoffs, and when unemployed were only temporary diversions from the work. Not one to be defined by her financial worries or the physical rigors of the vaudeville grind of four to five shows a day, Jeanne preferred to remember her unique opportunity to create art and beauty and her lifelong passion for reading and learning. In 2005, when she commenced the task of working with her first biographer, she recalled her memories stretching over nearly an entire century, beginning as a small child in her hometown of St. Louis, Missouri, who dreamed of becoming a world-class ballerina, and ending with a new life beyond the footlights.

1

Family Life in St. Louis, Missouri

From her first breath Jean Eleanor Helman was tough, both physically and mentally. When she began piano lessons at an early age, she was incapable of sitting still and needed the athletic challenge of dance. A diminutive girl, only five feet, two and three-quarters inches, with big brown eyes and a winning smile, Jeanne always emphasized to the press how important that last three quarters of an inch was to her self-image. Prone to chubbiness, Jeanne was always on a diet, and during her dancing career her weight ranged between ninety-five to 118 pounds, with 105 pounds being the norm. As the *St. Louis Times*, July 10, 1940, observed: "This, you should remember, was the girl who was known among her classmates at the Bryan Mullanphy School and her playmates around the Tower Grove-Shaw's Garden area as one who could lick twice her weight in neighborhood bullies any day of the week." In an interview Jeanne described with great flair the day she had defeated the school bully Monkey Unger, who was about to steal her bike, and chased him up on a lawn, pinning him face down on the ground by using her strong ballet legs to tuck her ankles under his legs until he apologized. None of the school bullies ever bothered her again.

Born in St. Louis on Halloween, October 31, 1912, Jean Helman was an only child who was extremely close to her parents. During her early childhood she had a relatively normal home life in St. Louis, Missouri, living in an apartment with her loving parents without a radio or television, attending the neighborhood school, taking ballet lessons, performing in dance recitals, enjoying her dog Laddie, and taking long vacations with her parents around the country. Jeanne went to sleep every night in her Tower Grove apartment listening to the distant whistles of the trains whizzing along the tracks down the block next to the Missouri Botanical Garden and to her mother playing classical music on her Mason and Hamlin concert grand piano.

Jeanne wistfully remembered many of her early childhood experiences. Although she was less than two years old, she claimed to have fleeting memories of when her tonsils were removed without any anesthetic. Jeanne's first introduction to theatre was at the age of four-and-a-half when she went with her parents in St. Louis to see the opera *Pagliacci*, and she was captivated by the fantasy of the theater. She "watched with fascination when the clowns did acrobatics in their Harlequin costumes & neck ruffs. The spotlight followed them and the man who sang wearing orange satin. When it was over I rode up the aisle on my dad's shoulder looking down at the crowd of people." That same year she had a near fatal ride "down a very steep hill on a sled after the older boy fell off. When the sled hit a stone wall & I hit the wall head on." Her injured nose caused her breathing problems, and years later had to be cosmetically fixed.

When she was in elementary school her mischievous father would pick her up at her classroom, telling the teacher that she had a dental appointment, and after they were safely outside he would give her a little wink, revealing that the family was taking a ride out to the country to have a picnic and view nature in full bloom. "I felt such joy but carefully controlled my sharing of the joke until I had retrieved my coat & lunchbox from the cloakroom," she later wrote. The family spent the afternoon "riding around the countryside seeing blossoming trees & wild flowers—& eating lunch beside a sparkling stream." Her childhood was a blend of "city experience & nature."

The loving family of three traveled extensively in their open-air Dodge touring car. At age four-and-a-half during one of Bill's business trips to company headquarters in upstate New York Jeanne had seen most of the eastern part of the country. At age eight in 1920, the year of women's suffrage, she remembered riding from town to town with her mother in the back seat of the family touring car with a canvas top. Bill also drove the car in a celebratory parade while she and her mother sat in the back seat banging on a pipe that Bill had lowered from the roof on ropes. By age nine during a six-month trip with her parents on the national unpaved highways Jeanne had seen the West all the way north to the Canadian border. Unable to afford hotels, the family mostly camped along the way, sleeping in a special tent that Bill had designed to protect them from mosquitoes and roving animals. Jeanne appreciated this aspect of her childhood as one "of changing scenes & foods & people—exposure to every interest."

Jeanne's lifelong fascination with Native American arts and crafts was also related to early childhood experiences. At age seven, when she attended an exhibition of Native American basketry in St. Louis by Dat so Lali, one of the finest weavers in America, she sat in the lap of this famous artist, who let her hold a basket the size of a finger tip. She always remembered the beauty of Dat so Lali's woven baskets. On the family trip in the West when she was nine her father encountered a Hopi chief in Taos, New Mexico, who complained about his tribe's dire poverty and the unfairness of the local United States agent. Bill went to the tribal retail store and noted the low prices on the beautiful native baskets and rugs for sale. He offered to sell some of the Native American rugs for a better price in St. Louis. His lunch group in St. Louis purchased the best rugs at an excellent price, and he returned all of the proceeds to the Hopi chief. As an expression of his gratitude, the Hopi chief sent Jeanne a wampum necklace, made of turquoise and sea shells. In later years whenever Jeanne was asked her about her most valuable piece of jewelry, she replied, "The wampum necklace."

Jeanne was proud of her family ancestry that followed the same pattern as many early American immigrants in the nineteenth century. Her parents came from families who had migrated west from their early roots in New England. Both were raised in Protestant churches, but later rejected organized religion and lived according to strong, secular ethical values that they passed along to Jeanne. Neither Jeanne nor her mother drank alcohol, and they maintained a Victorian code of ethics while living a life in show business. Emigrating from England, Lillian's ancestors came to Connecticut, with each succeeding generation moved farther west to affordable land. When he wanted to purchase a bigger farm in 1885, Lillian's father moved the family to Doniphan, Nebraska, where many of Jeanne's relatives remained after her grandparents retired in 1918 to Pasadena, California. Bill's family had migrated from Alsace Lorraine to French Canada, eventually moving down the Mississippi River to French New Orleans. Jeanne's grandfather Helman eventually moved his family to Memphis, Tennessee, where he sold cotton to Northern mills and had his own wine distillery. Years after the Civil War he gathered up his family in two carriages and embarked on a Mississippi River boat bound for St. Louis, where the family permanently settled.

Jeanne's father, William "Bill" Douglas Helman, was born in Memphis, Tennessee, on June 12, 1879. An avid reader, sportsman, historian, explorer, inventor, musician, calligrapher, and philatelist, Bill Helman in Jeanne's eyes epitomized a Renaissance man. In spite of later family tensions and tragedies, Jeanne idolized her charming, brilliant, mentally ill father. He made bows and arrows, played golf and tennis, and strummed the guitar while singing around the campfire on family canoe trips. Jeanne and her father were both philatelists, so the stamps on their letters were put to good use; she shared the rare U.S. stamps with fellow philatelists, such as the stage manager's twelve-year-old son in Scotland, the youngest chorus girl, an agent's stenographer in Paris, and an Italian drummer in the orchestra when she performed in Tripoli, who had asked for the stamps through pantomime since he did not speak English.

Bill took the family on camping adventures on the banks of the rivers that fed into the Mississippi River. Jeanne described the surrounding shores of the nearby rivers as "a fairy land of unspoiled nature." After Bill had acquired his first canoe at age thirteen, he explored with his best friend Bert Loewnstein the caverns, caves, and burial mounds along these rivers. Bill's "canoe group" had a shack at Valley Park on the Merrimac River

William Douglas "Bill" Helman with Jeanne's dog Laddie in his canoe, ca. 1920s. When Jeanne left for New York City in 1927 she left her beloved Laddie behind. Laddie symbolized all the comforts of a secure home that she had to sacrifice for her itinerant life as a vaudevillian prima ballerina. Courtesy Jeanne Devereaux Perkins Collection.

for storing their canoes, which had a simple kitchen, sleeping quarters, and an outdoor privy for day trips and short family vacations. Jeanne recalled when her heroic Dad rescued six swimmers caught in the creek's rapids and crying for help. It was at Valley Park where Jeanne picked magnificent violets, her favorite flower, in the fields, and caught baby frogs on the creek's bank. Jeanne described the shack as "a cabin dwarfed by giant virgin forest trees of enormous girth situated above a creek that joined the Merrimac River a few hundred feet away." Her father identified the trees as "Hickory, Elm, Sycamore, Black Walnut, Persimmon, as we slowly moved upstream in our canoe 'Nenemousha.' ... The river was both peaceful & teeming with life & peril." "Nenemousha" was the name of two lakes in the Algonquin Park Forest in Ontario, Canada, known for its canoe routes. On these canoe trips, among the eight or ten people who shared the shack clubhouse, Jeanne was the only child, and was nicknamed "Little River Rat and allowed to wear a turkey feather in a headband." While camping along the banks of the rivers, Jeanne wrote that the group enjoyed "'season watching' & evenings of spontaneous, unorganized self created entertainment."

Although finances were always tight, Bill insisted on having the finest quality Abercrombie and Fitch camping equipment and designed his own tent and storing containers. In the evenings Bill would serenade them around the campfire with his guitar, singing all the songs he knew. Bill was also a clever wordsmith. He taught Jeanne the tongue-twisting names of all the prehistoric animals. When Jeanne was six she accompanied her father, who was a "spelunker," a cave investigator, to the caves in St. James, Missouri, where he pointed out to her the difference between stalactites and stalagmites. He taught her the names of exotic colors like magenta, chartreuse, ochre, cobalt, sapphire, and cerulean. Throughout her life Jeanne enjoyed these fine distinctions between words and things; she credited her sense of humor and passion for learning to her intelligent, gregarious, charming, and witty father.

Bill worked in sales as an independent contractor for the American Manufacturing Concern in Falconer, New York, the world's largest manufacturer of advertising specialties of wood, and for other companies who also produced corporate gifts used for advertising. He was one of the American Manufacturing Concern's star salesmen, as well as their official representative for the vast region west of the Mississippi River. Before magazine advertising most companies promoted their goods and services by using well-designed tangible objects as gifts to clients and employees. Jeanne credited her father with improving these advertising objects like the simple ruler: Bill figured out how to add a steel edge to the wooden ruler to increase accurate measuring and drawing. He also designed a ruler in the shape of a wooden letter opener, a memento that Jeanne loved to give as presents to her friends, and created the logos for Red Goose and Buster Brown school shoes. When the world of advertising moved to print media with colorful pages in popular magazines, Bill failed to change with the times. Lillian warned him that he needed to reinvent himself professionally, but he was incapable of change and prone to bouts of depression.

Born on January 28, 1885, in Doniphan, Nebraska, Jeanne's mother, Amanda Lillian Lane, was attracted to the performing arts. She was a trained musician with professional aspirations of her own. Although Lillian had graduated from the Chicago Conservatory of Music with the goal of becoming a concert pianist, her dream was never fully realized.

After graduation she worked at the famous Aeolian music store in Chicago, Illinois, and then taught music at Carlton College for Women in Beaumont, Texas, soon becoming the Head of the Music Department. She left teaching to tour the Midwest with a concert group, but their manager absconded with their concert proceeds, leaving them stranded and nearly broke. Lillian had just enough money to buy a ticket to St. Louis, Missouri, but not home to Nebraska. In St. Louis she looked for a job at the Thebes Stirling music store, and was hired after her new employer learned that she had worked at the Aeolian. The female elite of St. Louis would come to Thebes Stirling in search of the latest and most sophisticated phonograph records, and would invite the knowledgeable and charming Lillian out to their mansions to advise them on what they needed to enhance their record collections. Lillian was a great musical resource to these sophisticated ladies and later to her talented daughter Jeanne.

Lillian was a beautiful woman with liquid blue eyes, porcelain skin, and thick, dark hair. When Bill Helman walked into Thebes Stirling one day in late 1910 and feasted his eyes on Lillian selling records, for him it was love at first sight. Perhaps he first admired that glorious head of hair, which she wore pulled back and cascading down her back. The surviving photographs of the young couple capture Bill's dark good looks and brooding charisma and Lillian's beauty and intelligent gaze. They were married on January 28, 1911, also Lillian's birthday. Jeanne was born the following year.

When Lillian's industrious parents, Eldoras and Jeanette Lane, retired in 1918 to California from Nebraska, they kept their farm house and sold some of their land to make the move. In Pasadena they became members of the First Congregational Church, and bought a house that is still standing today on the northeast corner of Paloma and Hill Streets. Jeanne inherited much of her adventurous spirit and longevity from her grandfather Lane. An article from a Pasadena newspaper on July 9, 1944, reporting a family picnic in Griffith Park to observe Eldoras' ninety-third birthday, described how he was a "vigorous and active for a man of his years." Three years earlier he "had celebrated his 90th birthday by taking his first airplane ride, a round-trip flight from Union Terminal, Burbank, to San Diego." Jeanne also inherited her passion for reading from her grandfather Lane, who throughout his life was an "ardent reader." She enjoyed her family trips to the Lane's Nebraska farm and to their home in Pasadena, who in turn would occasionally visit St. Louis.

The Lanes had six daughters—Lenore, Aletha, Ida, Lillian, Blanche, and Edith—who played a large role in Jeanne's life. With the exception of Lillian, five of them graduated from the University of Nebraska at Lincoln. While Aunts Blanche and Edith remained in Nebraska, Aunts Lenore, Aletha, and Ida made the move to Pasadena. Aunt Lenore, like her older sister

Profile photograph of Amanda Lillian Lane Helman, c. 1905–10. This was one of Jeanne's favorite photographs of her mother. Courtesy Jeanne Devereaux Perkins Collection.

Lillian, was a pianist and became Superintendent of Music in the Los Angeles school system; Aletha, also a teacher, was a spinster who lived with and cared for her parents. Aunt Ida married and had two daughters. Jeanne was closest to her Aunt Lenore, who travelled to New York to see her dance and is often mentioned in Jeanne and Lillian's personal letters. Jeanne later said that over the decades Lenore and Aletha were engaged in "slow moving battles that women have had to wage to get an even playing field. There still are a lot of gaps."

Jeanne grew up with no siblings nor relatives in St. Louis except for close family friends, like her two sets of godparents—Kate and Jack Leigh and Florence and Dick Houck. Her godparents would often join her family on their camping and canoeing trips, but after she and her mother moved to New York Jeanne rarely saw them. Her godmother Kate Leigh, the Assistant Director of the Missouri Botanical Garden, eventually married the Director, and she moved into a magnificent mansion on the grounds. Until she was fourteen Jeanne lived across from the Missouri Botanical Garden, one of America's oldest botanical institutions founded in 1859 by the botanist and philanthropist Henry Shaw. After work Kate Leigh and many of the senior staff would walk across the street and have supper with the Helmans. "It was a wonderful place to grow up across the street from when you were a kid," Jeanne reminisced. "I can remember as a young child visiting the Garden with my mother and admiring all the gorgeous flowers."

Lillian Lane Helman and William Douglas Helman, ca. 1911–15. Jeanne's talented parents were married on January 28, 1911. Jeanne's mother Lillian was her manager, dresser, and constant companion throughout Jeanne's dancing career until Lillian's death in 1972. Bill, Jeanne's mentally ill father, remained in their hometown, St. Louis, Missouri. Courtesy Jeanne Devereaux Perkins Collection.

In the early 1930s Kate Leigh brought Mr. Pring, the legendary botanist at the Botanical Garden who founded America's orchid industry, and his wife to see Jeanne dance in St. Louis at the Loew's State theatre. When they came backstage Pring, thinking of Jeanne's exquisite pirouettes across the stage and the shimmering folds of her ethereal yellow costume, told Jeanne that he planned to name a yellow orchid after her called *oncidium stipitatum*, which is one of the "The Dancing Girls" orchids with delicate sprays of flowers shaped like skirted dancing girls with tiny waists. He told her he would always think of her when he saw her special flower "the dancing girl orchid." Jeanne was honored to have one of the thousands of species of orchids purportedly named for her.

Jeanne was adamant that she was never resentful about dropping out of eighth grade at age fourteen to work in vaudeville to support her family. She felt that her childhood was different from most children: "I lived one part in childhood with friends and the other with grown-up, mature adults. I didn't go through a childhood like other children. When Dad had his nervous breakdown, I was already in the adult world of theatre, speaking with an adult vocabulary and having adult interests. It seemed normal to me to go to work among adults." As Travis D. Stewart notes in *No Applause—Just Throw Money* in the vaudeville of Jeanne's era "most of the performers had dropped out of school at a young age."[1] Jeanne joined an elite group of performers in the 1920s who had also gone to work as teenagers to support their families. The famous vaudevillian Sophie Tucker helped to support her family throughout her professional career. Other troupers like Milton Berle were the sole support of their mothers who, like Jeanne's mother Lillian, were often companions and managers. The toe dancer Lucile Iverson South wrote in her memoir *On Toes of Gold* how she supported her mother, who chaperoned her when she started dancing professionally at age eleven, until her death. "Everyone knew Mother had been my constant companion," she wrote. "I teased her once. 'We are like a married couple. I earn the money like a husband and you take care of me like a wife.'"[2]

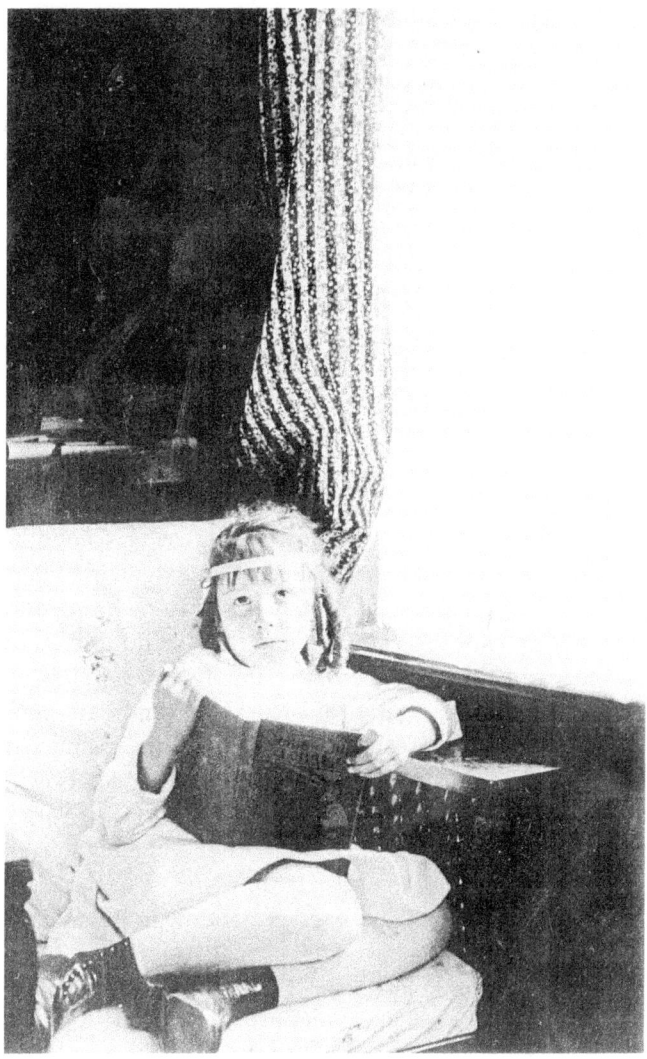

Eight-year-old Jean Helman reading Daniel Defoe's *Robinson Crusoe*, a favorite book. Jeanne had a passion for reading and learning throughout her life. After retiring from her dancing career, she became an admired public lecturer in the Los Angeles area and a researcher and writer at the Huntington Library, San Marino, California. Courtesy Jeanne Devereaux Perkins Collection.

Early in Jeanne's life the family had a penchant for changing their surnames. After World War I Bill thought his name "Helman" sounded too Germanic. In 1924, when Jeanne was twelve, Bill ushered the family into the car, and took them to see the popular silent movie *The Thief of Baghdad*, starring the celebrated actor Douglas Fairbanks, Sr. Bill so admired the swashbuckling Fairbanks that he changed his surname, using his middle name, and was known informally thereafter to his friends as William "Bill" Douglas. This was Jeanne's first time at the movies, and she never forgot the dashing Fairbanks and all the spectacular special effects.

As Jeanne matured she instinctively knew that she needed a stage name. In 1923, at age eleven when performing in the local St. Louis theatres, she changed the spelling of her first name to "Jeanne." That same year she danced on the bill at the Loew's State Theatre along with the famous, beautiful vaudeville and music hall singer Nora Bayes, who had been a headlining star of the early *Ziegfeld Follies*. Nora was known for singing "Shine On Harvest Moon" and introducing George M. Cohen's wartime song "Over There"; in the early decades of the twentieth century she had performed in vaudeville and Broadway shows with her songwriter second husband Jack Norworth, composer of "Take Me Out to the Ballgame." Recognizing that the little ballerina had a big talent, Nora advised Jeanne: "You're going to be going on for a long time in theatre, so you need to choose a family name that would look good on programs." Nora herself had changed her original Jewish name Leonora Goldberg to one with more show biz cache. When Jeanne eagerly told Nora her candidate family names, she choose the French sounding "Devereaux," Jeanne's maternal grandmother's maiden name, which had a long history in France, Ireland, and England dating back to the Middle Ages. Four years later when Lillian accompanied Jeanne to New York she also used the name Devereaux, and within a few years both mother and daughter had their surnames legally changed. Lillian, however, appeared ambivalent about her identity over the many years of her distressed marriage, and later as a widow in Pasadena. She used her various surnames to suit the occasion.

Jeanne told an endearing story of how her mother got the nickname "Bob White," the popular name for a quail since it approximates in English the loud call of the male bird, which will sit and repeat this clear sound for nearly a half an hour. Since her childhood in St. Louis Jeanne and her father often referred to Lillian as "Bob White." Bill Helman could whistle "Bob White," sounding just like a quail, but Jeanne could not whistle, so she called her mother "Bob White" when she wanted her attention. Later in the theatre world Lillian became known as "Bob White," or just "Bob," and was affectionately called "Bob White" by her family and friends the rest of her life. Thereafter when Jeanne wanted to get someone's attention she subtly called "Bob White!" "Since I was thirteen years old and went out on the road for the first time," Jeanne later reflected, "'Bob White' and I were never separated even one day."

When Jeanne left her hometown to pursue her dancing career, she left behind her beloved Scottish collie dog named Laddie that her father had given her on one of the family's touring trips to California and the Northwest when she was nine years old. As a child Jeanne and Laddie were inseparable. Later in life Jeanne described her close connection to Laddie: "Since I had no siblings or young relatives close by, Laddie was my dear friend. He was beautiful, loveable, and absolutely darling." Her love for Laddie created in her a lifelong affinity for animals. Jane Holman, an old family friend of her parents in St. Louis, wrote a tribute to Laddie: "All was well until his little mistress began the study of the dance. More and more, he [Laddie] missed her carresses, but the neighborhood children did their best to supply him with attention. Then the blow fell. His loved mistress Jeanne was leaving for New York to pursue the professional duties of a good toe-dancer. Being an only child her mother accompanied her and the home was broken up." In 1930, when her father moved to the St. Louis YMCA, he reclaimed Laddie at a nearby ranch and brought him home. "His little mistress" was by 1930 "an acknowledged artist and busy in Hollywood and New York," Jane Holman wrote, who will "have a great surprise awaiting her" when she returns home to St. Louis. Jeanne's lovable Laddie always reminded her of home.

2

The Making of a Ballerina

Jeanne Devereaux possessed from an early age the physical talent, personality, discipline, and focus that it takes to excel as a performing artist. When she was dancing in the Detroit Civic Light Opera's production of *Balalaika*, a background story appeared in the *Detroit News*, April 15, 1945, that mentioned her strong character: "'The Story of Miss Devereaux' life sounds just too good to be true. But back of it is hard work, from the time she was 7, and persistence that would daunt many another." At an early age Jeanne made great personal sacrifices for her art, and later reflected that these sacrifices were needed to attain excellence: "'When I was a little girl,' Miss Devereaux said, 'I used to feel cheated when other girls went swimming and riding and to parties. I used to grumble about it, but now I know that it was worthwhile. It gave me a head start.'" From the beginning she understood that dancing was her destiny.

In 1937, a friend of Jeanne's father sent her a letter in which he remembered a "'mite' of a girl ... with a joy in her youthful enthusiasm." When she began taking her first dancing lessons, she had "bounced around like a rubber ball" giving him "an interlude of pleasure," and now he congratulated her on "a good job done well." Beginning her dance training at seven in Adeline Rotty's Ballet School in St. Louis, Jeanne continued her training at the renowned Mrs. Clark's Dancing School. Jeanne was a standout at dancing school and starred in many dance recitals: an advertisement for Miss Rotty's children's dance recital at the Odeon Theatre featured a picture of young "Jean Helman" in a lovely costume and pirouette pose. At these schools Jeanne studied all types of dancing but focused primarily on ballet. Jeanne believed that children should wait until the age of six or seven before beginning this rigorous physical training, for in younger children the knee cartilage is not strong enough to sustain the rigor of ballet; in fact, Russian children were not allowed to begin studying ballet at the Kirov and Bolshoi schools until age nine, and they usually trained for ten years before beginning their professional careers with ballet companies. Although Jeanne danced on toe earlier than some students, she fortunately never damaged her knee cartilage or sustained any serious injuries. She described one of her first dancing lessons:

> I felt the strangeness of a new environment—New rules of behavior—new costume & shoes—new vocabulary & new exact movements to master—Mother sat in the balcony opposite the stage where pianist sat at a grand piano for our exercises. Ballet bars ran along sides of the big hall & mirrors lined the wall below the balcony—We watched the teacher and ourselves in mirrors as we struggled to copy her port de bras, jetes, changement de pied, & arabesques. Special classes in Dalcroixs to beat of tamborine, stepping to rhthms, full notes, half & quarter beats—running—skipping—leaping in pastel chiffon greek tunics all designed to teach us to "feel" the differences in

Jean Helman, later Jeanne Devereaux, age eight, in front of her family's apartment at 2338 Tower Grove Avenue, St. Louis, Missouri, 1920. Jeanne had begun taking ballet classes at Miss Adeline Rotty's dancing school the year before, and soon moved on to Mrs. Clark's dancing school where she starred in many dance recitals. Mrs. Clark's dancing school produced famous New York dancers like William Dollar and Russell Markert's "Sixteen Missouri Rockets," who became the Roxy Theatre's Roxyettes and finally the Radio City Rockettes. Courtesy Jeanne Devereaux Perkins Collection.

> Music—We were introduced to "impressions of" ethnic dance from Spanish-Egyptian-Morris Dances-and tarantella to Vienese Waltzes—The Barre Work required us to master the strange new five turned out foot positions as we learned the plies, petite & grand battements, the rond de Jambs on the floor & in the air, passe & developes—We learned arabesques & attitudes and a variety of combinations.

Every student began with barre work and the five ballet positions, and some were able to point their toes precisely from the outset. If one were alert when practicing in front of the mirrors, he or she could improve himself or herself quickly, not having to wait for the teacher to explain how to complete every step. Even as a beginner Jeanne had the natural vigor, energy, and muscular power to do these things to perfection: most importantly, she worked harder than most of the others and was always cast in the best roles in the dance recitals, such as *Peter Pan*.

At seven Jeanne sat on another famous artist's lap. She had joined a family to attend one of the legendary Russian ballerina Pavlova's brilliant performances in a commercial theatre in St. Louis, and went with them backstage after the performance to glimpse the exquisite Pavlova as she exited her dressing room. The crowd was pushing and shoving—it was mayhem—and Jeanne got separated from her friends. When Pavlova made her awaited exit from her dressing room door, one of the stagehands placed a bouquet of brilliant red roses in her arms while she surveyed the adoring fans crowding around her. The crowd surged, and Jeanne was pushed in front of Pavlova, whose eyes fell on the small, excited girl. Sitting down in a nearby chair and motioning for Jeanne to sit on her lap, Pavlova asked her if she studied ballet, and if so, who was her ballet teacher. Jeanne answered, "Adeline Rotty," and Pavlova asked if Miss Rotty were present. When Miss Rotty appeared out of the crowd, she and Pavlova talked at length about her ballet school. Pavlova then asked Jeanne if she loved to dance—a soft and sensitive question that made a lasting impression. In that moment Pavlova became Jeanne's lifelong inspiration.

A prima ballerina with the Russian Imperial Ballet and then with Sergei Diaghilev's original Ballets Russes, Pavlova had quickly formed her own company and toured the world, performing more times outside Russia than at home. Inspiring thousands of young dancers around the world, she was considered the first dancer to popularize ballet in America by touring with her company in many small American communities.[1] In 1905 the great ballet dancer and teacher Michel Fokine had choreographed *The Dying Swan* short ballet to the music of Camille Saint-Saën's "Carnival of the Animals" especially for Pavlova, and it became her signature dance. During her career she performed it nearly 4,000 times, and it later influenced modern interpretations of Tchaikovsky's *Swan Lake*. Pavlova apparently was not a temperamental ballet dancer and had a sense of humor: Buster Keaton describes in his autobiography *My Wonderful World of Slapstick* that when he played on a vaudeville bill with her, "the world's greatest ballerina," and "imitated her doing her classic, 'The Dying Swan.' … Anna Pavlova loved it."[2] Later in 1930 the talented vaudevillian Fanny Brice headlined at the Palace Theatre with her parody called the "Dying Swan Ballet." When Pavlova died in January 1931, the night following her death at The Hague in Holland when the curtain rose in the theatre where she had been performing her signature ballet, the stage was poignantly bare.

Jean Helman, age ten, performing the role of "Harlequin" in Mrs. Clark's dance recital, St. Louis, Missouri, 1922. A year later while dancing in the St. Louis vaudeville theatres and movie presentation houses, Jean changed the spelling of her first name to "Jeanne"; that same year when performing on a vaudeville bill at the Loew's State Theatre in St. Louis, at the suggestion of the headlining star Norma Bayes, she changed her surname to Devereaux, her maternal grandmother's maiden name. Photograph by Todd Studios of St. Louis. Wilson Todd was a well-known vaudeville and celebrity photographer whose studio was located in St. Louis' thriving theatre district. Courtesy Jeanne Devereaux Perkins Collection.

When Adeline Rotty closed her dancing school, most of her students transferred to Mrs. Clark's ballet school, which offered ballet, toe, tap, adagio, and acrobatic classes, typically comprised of fifty students. Mrs. Clark's was famous for training many talented young professional dancers who later had successful New York careers. Doug Coudy, who came from Mrs. Clark's school, as did the first "Radio City Rockettes," became the dance director for the Copacabana nightclub in New York. Also, William Dollar, a close friend of Jeanne's and fellow student at Mrs. Clark's, became a primary dancer with Balanchine's American Ballet as well as choreographer for its immediate successor the Ballet Caravan, both precursors to today's New York City Ballet. Dollar was a gifted dancer and choreographer with numerous American ballet companies for more than thirty years until his death in 1986. While a student at Mrs. Clark's school at the age of eleven, Jeanne was noted for her talent in adagio, which involved moving slowly and executing difficult lifts with a male partner. To dance an effective adagio, a ballerina needed a strong partner, one who could lift her body weight over his head as well as contain the velocity of having a ballerina run and jump into his arms before the lift. Jeanne's partner Bill Winkler was twenty-one years old, and he later went to New York from St. Louis and had a successful international professional dance career.

Jeanne's early dancing career in St. Louis was a family affair requiring sacrifice and money. As her marriage became troubled by Bill's mental illness and financial problems, Lillian increasingly devoted her energy and passion to Jeanne's budding career. After returning home from a month-long trip east, Lillian wrote to her parents on November 23, 1923, that Jeanne had immediately resumed her dancing lessons, and since she had missed four classes each of toe and ballet, she "had to make them up by attending other classes too, as no money is refunded." Lillian had home schooled her during the trip so she started school in the fifth grade "A Class," and had grown almost three inches and gained twenty pounds. In a letter written to her parents, dated May 22, 1925, Lillian described the rigorous routine to prepare for a recital at Jeanne's dancing school: she was exhausted from having sewn Jeanne's costumes until midnight and then arising at 5:00 a.m. to start the day. "We would get to rehearsal at 4:30PM & get out at 7PM. I would run home & have supper on the table in a jiffy but it takes the pep out of me to keep it up." Lillian wrote. But her sacrifice was worth it, for at the recital "Jean was the featured dancer of the evening & got a big name for herself among St. Louis dancing schools."

Lillian proudly wrote how Jeanne was chosen in 1925 among hundreds of contestants from all the St. Louis dancing schools to perform in the ballet for the new outdoor Garden Theatre, to be completed by the end of June. Since she had to entertain Bill's boss that night, Lillian did not attend the competition where the judges narrowed the field down to nineteen of the best dancers in town, including those who had studied for nine or ten years in St. Louis dancing schools and every summer with some important teachers in New York and Chicago. Lillian attended the final tryout where they narrowed the field down to the final sixteen. Jeanne "was challenged about her size the first minute but I measured her up with one of the older girls who was small & she was the same height. I told this right out so they had to let her 'try out.' Their eyes were as big as knobs when she went thro the combinations for she was easily best in the whole bunch." The judges sent her a letter informing Jeanne that she had been selected and that she would receive free instruction and dance for five weeks during July and August for $35.00 a week. The Garden Theatre was scheduled to open with a weeklong run of a Greek play, *Electra*, beginning July 6, followed by the opera *Hansel and Gretel* and then three weeks of the "Fashion Show." Jeanne danced a lead role as the gingerbread boy in *Hansel and Gretel*. When people who knew Jeanne and Lillian saw the announcement of the winners in the local paper, they telephoned on the hour to congratulate them.

Jeanne remembered that during a rehearsal for *Hansel and Gretel* when she was performing grand *jetés*, sometimes called flying splits, she landed on a leaf, and broke her wrist in five places. The next day she was scheduled to practice at the Chase Hotel with a famous ballet teacher visiting St. Louis, and Lillian encouraged her to take the classes regardless of having a broken wrist. So Jeanne diligently attended the class, dancing on the hotel's slippery ballroom floor, with a bandaged arm. Jeanne was learning that a professional dancer must be mentally tough and perform despite injury and pain.

Jeanne's professional career dictated the family's priorities and calendar. In a letter to her parents on September 19, 1925, Lillian wrote that she was overjoyed that they were coming soon by train from Nebraska to visit in St. Louis. In addition to attending school, Jeanne "has just finished a weeks engagement at the 'Missouri,' a large presentation moving picture house here & made $30.00. She got paid for all but one week at the Garden Theatre at $35.00 even after she broke her arm so she is doing pretty well and I am glad someone in this family can earn some money. Jean seems to have struck something by which she can earn a good living in the future if given a chance." In anticipation of her parents' visit Lillian cancelled a "weeks engagement at Springfield Mo. Big movie house for the 5th to 12th of Oct., so don't dissapoint us & not come after all." To celebrate her birthday on Halloween, Jeanne's wish was for her maternal grandparents to bring one of her Nebraska cousins with them and stay until Christmas.

Jeanne is among the illustrious alumni who performed in St. Louis at the famous Metropolitan Opera Theatre, called the Muny, the nation's oldest and largest outdoor theatre. In a commemorative program celebrating the Muny's 1943 silver anniversary season Jeanne was pictured dancing with her large balloon. In 1926, at twelve, Jeanne made her Muny debut as a ballerina in a production of the operetta *Spring Maid*. An article in the *St. Louis Star-Times*, July 10, 1940, recalled the ingénue Jeanne in "Spring Maid" as "the sensational and wildly applauded 'premier ballerina.'" Located in Forest Park, the open-air Muny theatre was constructed in 1917 on a grassy area between two large oak trees and premiered its first professional production of light opera two years later. The vast theatre between the great trees on either side could hold almost 10,000 people and the orchestra pit up to 200 musicians. Over her long career Jeanne had many repeat performances at the Muny during the summer operetta season, starring in operettas like *The Chocolate Soldier, Good News*, and *Sons O' Guns*.

By the summer of 1926, the family dynamic and finances were in shambles and a break-up was inevitable. Lillian was actively looking for bookings so Jeanne could work and supplant Bill's lack of income. The fact that Jeanne was underage and could easily be exploited never crossed her mind given her dire circumstances and the prevalence of child labor in the 1920s. Thirteen-year-old Jeanne knew that her father "was getting a little funny," she said in a later interview, but with her busy daily schedule—school, streetcar to dancing school, picked up by Mom and taken home, and homework—she had little time to pay attention to his increasing erratic behavior. Jeanne danced most of the summer of 1926 at the Garden Theatre and the Muny in St. Louis, so the family did not take their annual summer vacation. In the fall Jeanne was selected by a producer searching for a talented dancer to perform adagio with a dance team to go on a vaudeville tour on Marcus Loew's Orpheum circuit in the Midwest. Chaperoned by her mother, she performed in Milwaukee, Chicago, Cleveland, Indianapolis, and dozens of other cities and towns. It was on this first vaudeville tour that she met the talented dancer Jimmy Givens, who remained a lifelong friend.

While on this tour Jeanne quickly learned that performing could be hazardous. She remembered a night in Galesburg, Illinois, when a thunderstorm flooded the town, the water came in the stage door and flowed up to the edge of the stage. The stagehands frantically kept the water from flooding the stage. Jeanne was dancing an adagio with her partner, and while upside down in a pose over her partner's head, she caught a glimpse of the approaching water. Astonished, frightened, and relieved when the water abated, she and her partner completed their performance and took their bows.

Realizing that his wife and daughter's decision to go on the road despite his opposition presaged a family break-up, Bill wrote to Jeanne's grandparents in Pasadena on September 23, 1926:

> Lill has been wanting to go on the road for a long while with Jean and so they left Sept 1st. as Jean got a job on the Orpheum Circuit and Lill went along to take care of Jean. I heard from them about two weeks ago and they seem to be getting along very nicely. Personally I am very much opposed to them going out, but they simply overruled me and left. I don't know how long they will be gone as they probably signed up for a year or more, and I'm hoping that they'll get their tummy full of theatrical life by that time and come home.

If they failed to return home after a year Bill would give up the apartment "as its altogether too lonesome living in a place all my ones self." He planned to give up housekeeping, store the furniture, and go to boarding, concluding "that's almost as bad as batching it and cooking your own meals."

As Jeanne continued to get bookings and earn money, Lillian knew that she now had an alternative source of income and could leave home. Having returned to St. Louis in December, she wrote to her parents on Christmas day, 1926, asking them for advice—"tell me what to do," she implored—since Bill was acting erratically and not working. She was desperate for money and realized that Jeanne had the potential to support the family during this crisis: "Oh Folks, on this Xmas Day my thots have been with you all day. We are well but not happy. Constant trouble with Bill for more than a year and always trying, trying to make a 'go' of things keeps me almost insane with worry. Last August Jean got a chance to go out on the road at $55.00 a week and my railroad expenses, so as he was making nothing month after month and it was an act with six people in it of good reputation we took the chance so Jean could get the experience necessary to get good jobs."

Acting as Jeanne's chaperone on the vaudeville tour, Lillian had also washed, mended, and pressed her daughter's clothes. She had been eager to leave home because Bill's mood swings, hostile behavior, and unemployment terrified her: "Bill told me to get out & stay out so many times that I was glad of a chance to show him Jean was getting pretty nearly far enough along in her line to support us. And she did because we had no money from him while we were out for the 3½ months," she wrote. When they returned home and promised Bill that they would remain in St. Louis for the remainder of the year, he started to work but reverted back to his old ways. Jeanne had paid for her own dancing lessons with the money she had earned over the past two years dancing at the Garden and Muny Theatres, the local vaudeville theatres and movie presentation houses, and recently on the Orpheum circuit, where everywhere they "played the managers would bring their wives & families back to meet the toe dancer and they told us often that whole dancing schools were out to see that wonderful dancer & would stay thro show after show to get pointers."

Although she had resumed attending school fulltime, Jeanne continued to work throughout December in the St. Louis' vaudeville theatres and movie presentation houses to earn money for the family and her dancing lessons. "This year we are hard up because although Jean has done the solo twice since she is home at 'Loews State' she had to pay it out for her dancing lessons, street carfare, etc.," wrote Lillian. "She has the promise of doing 'adagio' work at the 'Ambassador' in the next two weeks and that will help pay for her next months lessons. Her work is lovely & she is the showcard at Mrs. Clarks Dancing School, but must keep up with her toe technic every day, so she is ready when a job comes our way." Lillian knew that Jeanne needed opportunities for more exposure to earn a big salary, but she could not get those opportunities in St. Louis. As Jeanne later said in an interview in the *Pasadena Star-News*, January 20, 1994, she was a "big frog in the little puddle of St. Louis Mo."

If Bill could earn some money, Jeanne could finish her spring school semester and then pursue serious theatrical jobs. However, Bill continued to ask Lillian to leave, nagging her and complaining about Jeanne's dancing career, since he knew that she was "'my salvation,'" Lillian wrote to her parents, and "that some day I will not be under his thumb." He was "mad as a hatter over things he should be so proud of." Lillian bitterly complained to them that Bill was not working and was on a perpetual vacation eating his lunches out and going down to the river to swim or pitch horse shoes; he had even squandered all the inheritance that he recently received from his Uncle Henry. "Jean's just got to do something sooner or later under those conditions," Lillian desperately wrote.

In the midst of the family strife Jeanne's passion for dance overcame any anxiety about her parents' deteriorating relationship and their financial crisis. Ballet was the perfect art form for Jeanne, for it combined her natural talent for inner discipline, controlled physical movement, innovative choreography, rhythmic music, and clever costume design. From the beginning she excelled in the ballet fundamentals designed to teach the body control and balance in shifting the weight smoothly and rhythmically from one position to another and for achieving the euphoric state of pure balance. Jeanne animatedly described the basic positions of the arms and feet:

> As a child you learn your basic positions both for the arms and the feet, followed by the French words for the positions like *Pas de Chat, Tour Jeté, Changement de Pied*, and many others. You practice in every class these basic positions, repeating them in different ways as you strive to have your feet in the proper positions when you land a jump and the toes pointed and turned out the moment you are off the ground. Ballet beginners had to learn to balance on one leg, tense muscles, flatten kneecaps, and much more.

Later, as a dance teacher, Jeanne wrote: "Children stand out when they follow all the ballet rules. They can't be sloppy—their toes must always be pointed and turned out. The children who caught on immediately were given the principal roles in local dance events."

In classical ballet language a pirouette is a spin requiring perfect balance of the toes of the supporting foot, the opening and incoming arm, and the rotating head; a fouetté is a whirling spin turn involving the whipping around of the front leg while the supporting foot elevates *en pointe*, meaning on the toes; and the three forms of arabesque emphasized one leg extended behind the body and the arms held in harmonious positions to create a long line from fingertips to toes. The fouetté was the most physically demanding of all the ballet moves. Jeanne would later set the world record at that time for doing sixteen triple fouettés. Jeanne noted that "normally a ballerina does only a single and occasionally a double." In her diary she mentions the few special occasions when she challenged herself almost beyond her limits and did four. Later in the 1994 interview in the *Pasadena Star-News*, she described how she could accomplish this technical feat of multiple fouettés "on balance and not finish with a wobble."

Since the days of Russia's Imperial Ballet School the fouetté was daring, acrobatic, and suspenseful. Although earlier ballerinas had done spectacular single fouettés, no one before Jeanne ever did triple ones. In her memoir *Theatre Street* the Russian ballerina Tamara Karsavina remembered the virtuoso Italian ballerina Pierina Legnani dancing in a 1896 revival by Marius Petipa and Lev Ivanov of Tchaikovsky's *Swan Lake* in St. Petersburg's Mariinsky Theatre her dazzling thirty-two single fouettés, the most ever performed at that time: "Legnani walked to the middle of the stage and took an undisguised preparation. The conductor, his baton raised, waited. Then a whole string of vertiginous pirouettes, marvelous in their precision and brilliant as diamond facets, worked the whole audience into ecstasies."[3] In his book *Ballet Is Magic* Walter Ware describes how the popular American prima ballerina Patricia Bowman, to thrill the audience, performed sixteen single traveling fouettés followed by an additional sixteen in one spot during her first appearance at the Roxy Theatre in New York in 1927: "At that time such a feat was ostensibly impossible."[4] Later, Patricia McBride, a dancer with George Balanchine's New York City Ballet Company, remembered the "fouetté contests" she had "with her friends at Miss Vernon's school," her first dancing school in New Jersey, "to see who could last the longest."[5]

Jeanne also claimed to be the first ballerina to do a split arabesque. "With the arabesque, no lady lifts her leg higher than her hip, but mother said to stand in a doorway and do a split vertically and then do it on toe," she said. "I was the only ballerina who did this—a split arabesque. It was considered not a thing to do in those days—a Victorian hangover. Today most dancers do the split arabesque." Jeanne knew that to dance successfully in the immense presentation houses she had to be unique. A "Billing Sheet" for the "Jeanne Devereaux Revue" claimed that Jeanne was "the first dancer in America to adapt her work to the super large picture houses, thereby creating a new style of classic dancing which is visible and interesting to the spectators in the last rows of the theatre."

At an early age Jeanne realized that it took hard work and complete discipline to achieve excellence.[6] In describing the discipline of dance and performing Jeanne emphasized that

Jeanne Devereaux, formerly Jean Helman, performing her whirling spin turn called a fouetté, ca. early 1930s. To have a sensational vaudeville act, Jeanne practiced long hours to perfect this difficult turn involving whipping the leg around and elevating the foot on the toe for velocity. Jeanne said that during her professional dancing career she held the world record of sixteen triple fouettés. In her publicity and show reviews she was often referred to as a "spinning top." Courtesy Jeanne Devereaux Perkins Collection.

mistakes were not allowed in the theatre. On cue was just that "Always Ready" at the rise of the curtain or the conductor's down beat of his baton. The self-discipline was total and extended into all phases of performers' lives. In Ballet class the students strive for the ideal. Perfect turnouts, balance and arm movements, leaps, tour jetés, and pirouettes. On stage the dancer must concentrate on performing each movement perfectly while maintaining a pleasant appearance. No dour looks nor indications that one is suffering aches or pains.

Over her career Jeanne meticulously cared for her feet and sustained many painful injuries. When she was dancing in a show she would often wear out a pair of toe shoes every week. Alida Cervera, who attended Jeanne's ballet school in the late 1950s and early 1960s, remembered that Jeanne's students "loved to hear her tell of how she danced no matter what—with pneumonia, bleeding feet (toe shoes are loveliest to the ballet spectator but brutal on one's feet) and on stages in various states of disrepair." As ballet students, Jeanne taught them "the difference between a 'good' hurt and a bad one."

Toe dancers in popular entertainment were usually responsible for every aspect of their performance. Jeanne was not just a dancer, but usually selected her music, choreographed her dances, and designed and made her own costumes except for those Ida Belle made for her in New York and Vera Murray when she danced in England. She estimated that during her career she choreographed over 200 dances. She needed to be constantly creative, for when she was touring in vaudeville from city to city she could repeat the same dances, but when she was performing multiple shows in the presentation houses after the movie changed for a long run, she had to choreograph many different dances. Even when she performed in Europe and later was the prima ballerina for Radio City Music Hall and Florence Rogge, the ballet mistress and wife of the producer, was choreographer for the corps de ballet, Jeanne choreographed her own dances. She insisted, "Always, my whole life. It was unusual but nobody choreographed for me. I was booked because people liked me and my dances."

Her creative process for designing a dance for performance began with the music. In an interview she said, "I either had a pianist play the music for me or I listened to a phonograph record. As I would hear the high notes—the crescendos—I began mentally to visualize what I was going to do. Then I would imagine the themes and begin to work it out physically." For Jeanne, choreography was like writing: one worked with the themes and topics until one had a finished artistic composition. "It was work of every kind. I had to think up a new theme for a dance, choose the correct music, choreograph it, and then arrange for a suitable costume. Nowadays that work is divided up in ballet companies among different people all in charge of individual tasks. I did the whole bloody thing!" she said. Although Jeanne emphasized that doing "the whole bloody thing" gave her more creative control over her performances than ballerinas who danced in companies, it also involved physical and emotional hard work week after week.

Among the spectacular dances that she choreographed during her career the "balloon dance," also called by the press the "bubble dance," which she introduced in the early 1930s, was one of her most popular. It was technically demanding and depended upon availability of rubber during wartime, requiring her carefully to guard and store her balloons. Using a bellows, Lillian could inflate one of these five feet in diameter balloons in thirty to forty minutes; when one of them burst, it sounded like a bomb explosion. Her signature balloon dance, usually bathed in blue lights and performed to the music of Debussy's "Claire de Lune," was in great demand by theatrical producers. During her professional career Jeanne revived this special dance many times.

Later, after her retirement, she continued to choreograph for her ballet school's festivals, using her natural talent for sketching to make notations and stick-like drawings of the dance steps in her notebooks. For instance, she wrote down her choreography for a dance sequence, with stick-like drawings, in a letter to her mother on May 26, 1948, where she described her practice session in New York with her partner Ken Spaulding, who was a successful dancer in vaudeville, Broadway shows, and later in television in 1950 with his partner Diane Sinclair on "Kay Kyser's College of Musical Knowledge." Jeanne described her dance with Ken in a coded language familiar to Lillian:

> Well we did "Lydia" several times & in that place where he does his tour jete & then always un supported my arabesque promenade we tried his tourjete & that low arabesque turn he did and I followed with a high I & a good old outward pirouette—It'll probably exhaust me more but ... Ive got to do something! So were trying it anyway & if something better comes along well revise that place again—In Clair de Lune Yasvinsky raved over the last step, that lift that switches into the other & then comes down into the old fish—We got started a different way yesterday I tossed the B. [Balloon] ran & caught it & ran & tossed it again then did the pull back step you like just once alone as he entered he was right there as I came around. Well we worked hard & perspiration just poured.

For more than two decades the challenging creative space of the choreographer was Jeanne's only home.[7]

3

New York and the Circuits

In early 1927 Bill Helman tried to commit suicide by jumping off a bridge over the Mississippi River, but his old friend Bert Loewnstein fortunately saw him, ran over and grabbed him, and dragged him off the bridge. Bill then spent time in a St. Louis sanitarium until he was well enough to be released; a doctor suggested that his family be tested for syphilis, considered at this time a common cause of mental illness, and the results were negative. This disturbing incident caused Lillian to make a decision that would change her life and Jeanne's. With only $300 in her pocket, Lillian took her fourteen-year-old daughter and left home, traveling by train to New York to look for work in the competitive professional dance world. For the next twenty-two years her father was rarely physically present in Jeanne and Lillian's life, and they related emotionally as a family primarily through personal letters.

Jeanne then spent her teenage years on vaudeville and Broadway stages, in dressing rooms, on trains, and in hotels, performing, choreographing, designing costumes, choosing music, reading books, and writing letters—often with the wolf at the door. Most days if she had a booking she stood in the theatre wings in heavy stage make-up and glamorous costumes awaiting her musical cues before making her grand entrances. If she were fortunate enough to have a day or afternoon off from work, she and her mother would sightsee. During these years Jeanne and her mother crisscrossed America many times.

Jeanne was among a highly talented group of dancers from Mrs. Clark's ballet school in St. Louis who went to New York to experience the best artistic venue that America had to offer. They also, like Jeanne, needed to work. Although Lillian was college educated, after Bill's mental and emotional collapse she felt unemployable. She was desperate, and needed a sustainable income for the family. Years later in an article in New York's *Daily Times Herald*, August 1943, Jeanne was quoted as saying, "'We were a couple of green apples as far as knowing the ropes of show business.'" Once the $300 for dancing lessons with New York's famous émigré ballet masters had been spent, Jeanne and her mother knew that she needed to get work soon or return home. They were so poor that Lillian could not afford to have her worn out shoes resoled, and her feet were raw from walking. They were now in the highly competitive world of the famous Florenz Ziegfeld and his *Follies*, George White and his *Scandals*, Earl Carroll and his *Vanities*, and other star impresarios who developed vaudeville presentations and expensive Broadway musical comedies and revues. Featuring vaudevillians, a minimal plot or theme, elaborate sets, and a bevy of glamorous showgirls, the Broadway revues that flourished during the first half of the twentieth century ranged from Ziegfeld's lavish spectacles to Carroll's often sleazy variety shows.

When they arrived in New York they immediately contacted fellow St. Louis dancers William Dollar and Doug Coudy, who had already rented a reasonable apartment in a building up on Broadway for $10 a week; Jeanne and Lillian quickly moved in and Bill and Doug lived above them. Over the next months Jeanne exercised and practiced at various ballet studios in New York and worked on and off in some revues and vaudeville presentations in small theatres. To celebrate being in New York, they prepared what they called a belated "Christmas dinner" with the long string of hot dogs, commonly known as "weenies," that Lillian had purchased at a local market. When they left in the morning for Jeanne's daily practice session, Lillian left the windows open to ventilate the room; when they returned they saw a cat jump out the window trailing behind it their long string of weenies. They always laughed together about this first holiday dinner in New York when a "cat ate the dogs."

Jeanne's big breakthrough in show business was getting hired to perform on Broadway in New York's famous movie presentation house called the Roxy, located at 153 West 50th Street and 7th Avenue, which along with the later Radio City Music Hall, offered symphony orchestras, spectacular stage shows, elaborate dance numbers, and the finest talking pictures. When it opened on March 11, 1927, it was the largest theatre in the world devoted to the presentation of stage and screen attractions. Later popularized in the song "What's Playing at the Roxy?" from the Broadway musical *Guys and Dolls*, the Roxy Theatre was the brainchild of the impresario Samuel Lionel "Roxy" Rothafel, who had spent his career reviving struggling theatres across America by combining elaborate stage presentations followed by a movie. The Roxy Theatre was adjacent to the Manger Hotel (renamed the Taft, Grand Bay, Parc Fifty-One, and now the Michelangelo) that had opened in 1926, which had over 2,000 rooms making it the largest hotel in Times Square at that time. The Roxy theatre was finally demolished in 1960 to make room for an expansion of the hotel and construction of a new office building.

A well-placed, illustrated advertisement in *Variety* for March 9, 1927, featured the innovative Roxy Theatre, built on a site of former old car barns, as the "Cathedral of the Motion Picture"—Roxy's dream house. It could seat over 6,200 people in a space with state-of-the-art acoustics, projection, ventilation, elevators, lighting, seating, box offices, and precision service. It had a magnificent proscenium arch and an orchestra dais for the 110 musicians in the Roxy Symphony Orchestra, at that time the largest in existence. It also had a colossal pipe organ played by three organists, a Cathedral chime of twenty-one bells, a choral group, a ballet corps, and later precision dancers called the Roxyettes, who followed Rothafel from the Roxy to Radio City Music Hall in 1932 and became the famous Rockettes.

Sometime before the Roxy Theatre's gala opening Jeanne auditioned for the corps de ballet and was hired. According to a review in *Variety* on March 13, 1927, the Roxy Theatre's gala opening on March 11th played to a packed house and presented "a big show, that was too much show, if anything." The bill opened with a majestic organ concert on the three Kimballs, Stephen Wright's hyperbolic invocation, and the orchestral overture. Then the chorus sang the National Anthem on a patriotic set consisting of a

British warship with the American flag in the background, followed by the ballet. Irving Berlin's "A Russian Lullaby," sung by Gladys Rice and Douglas Stanbury, followed a short pictorial review showing the development of the Roxy Theatre; a Vitaphone film of *Carmen* was introduced by a prelude of orchestral selections from the opera conducted by Ernö Rapée. Finally, a brief prologue of live acts introduced the movie *The Love of Sunya*, starring Gloria Swanson. President Calvin Coolidge and Governor Alfred Smith and other luminaries attended the gala opening. On June 13, 1927, Jeanne could barely make her way to the Roxy's stage door because of the ticker-tape parade for Charles Lindbergh celebrating his solo transatlantic flight. After Jeanne's initial engagement at the Roxy, the choreographer Florence Rogge, along with various agents, helped book Jeanne and other dancers in some smaller vaudeville theatres and movie presentation houses in New York, Philadelphia, and Newark, New Jersey. Every day Jeanne practiced for long hours to prepare for these performances.

During her first engagement at the Roxy Jeanne met the accomplished classical dancer Patricia (Patsy) Bowman, who was four years older than Jeanne and was the prima ballerina at the Roxy from 1927 to 1931. Like Jeanne, Patricia had begun her professional career when there were no major ballet companies in America and had primarily danced in vaudeville and movie presentation houses during the 1920s and 30s; unlike Jeanne, however, Patsy had the financial luxury of occasionally touring as a guest artist with the short-lived classical Michel Fokine Ballet and the Mikhail Mordkin Ballet. After its opening in 1932 she was a prima ballerina at Radio City Music Hall until the early 1950s, appeared in the Ziegfeld Follies in 1934, performed on Broadway and nationwide with opera companies, danced in Europe in the mid–1930s, and was a founding member of the American Ballet Theatre. Throughout Jeanne's career she and Patsy had a healthy rivalry and respectful friendship. In 1994, just five years before Patsy's death in Las Vegas, after a delightful telephone call to reminisce about their performing days, Patsy sent Jeanne her annual Christmas card complete with fanciful ink drawings of ballerinas.

Booking agents were essential for a professional dancer. In New York the agents would come to the big theatres like the Roxy, the Palace, and the Loew's State to see the performers, and decide whether or not they wanted to represent them. The top New York agents were the William Morris Agency, Mark Leddy, Hal Sands, and Harry Krivit; when Jeanne performed in London she was represented by the Harry Foster Agency, which was considered the best at that time. "With a set of professional photographs to show producers the agents would arrange for a producer to catch your performance if he hadn't already seen you before," said Jeanne.

Performing on Broadway in George White's new musical comedy *Manhattan Mary* beginning in August 1927 was Jeanne's next big breakthrough. While she was dancing at the Roxy, someone at her ballet school suggested to Lillian that Jeanne should audition for George White. One night after the performance at the Roxy they visited White at the box office where he was counting the money, and he gave Jeanne a postcard to fill out, saying that when he was ready to have auditions for *Manhattan Mary* he would send her the card. George White had been a featured dancer in the *Ziegfeld Follies* and now was the successful producer of a string of sophisticated Broadway revues and several movies called the *George White's Scandals* that ran from 1919 to 1939 and were

Left: Fourteen-year-old Jeanne Devereaux in a promotional headshot for the Broadway musical *Manhattan Mary*, New York, 1927. The show opened on September 26, 1927, and closed on May 12, 1928. Jeanne was hired by the famous impresario dancer George White to be in the cast with popular vaudevillians Ed Wynn and Lou Holtz. Photograph by Le Barron Studios, New York, 1927. *Below:* Jeanne Devereaux, age fourteen, in a promotional photograph for the Broadway musical *Manhattan Mary*, New York, 1927. Photograph by Le Barron Studios, New York, 1927. Both photographs courtesy Jeanne Devereaux Perkins Collection.

modeled on the *Ziegfeld Follies*. Many famous stars like Eleanor Powell, Ann Miller, Ethel Merman, and Patricia Bowman had appeared in his *Scandals*. Based on her audition, George White hired Jeanne to dance in the corps de ballet in *Manhattan Mary*, starring Ed Wynn, the famous vaudeville comedian, actor, and star of the *Ziegfeld Follies* beginning in 1914. In the playbill the corps de ballet was listed as the "George White Ballet."

Days after being hired to dance in *Manhattan Mary*, Jeanne was appointed the ballet mistress for the chorus of nearly a hundred boys and girls, many of whom were almost twice her age. At this early stage in her career getting auditions, but more importantly getting hired, was a competitive proposition. Jeanne vividly recalled the story of being hired by George White when he lined everybody up behind him at the footlights and had them follow his tap choreography:

> He had one hundred and fifty dancers and showgirls applying for "Manhattan Mary." ... George White was a good dancer and choreographer as well as a producer. At the audition he lined everyone up and did a step and then turned around and evaluated the dancers. He looked over at me in the front row and said, "Don't you ever make a mistake?" I was chosen and again was in the corps de ballet. We were rehearsing the show while his famous "Scandals" was in Chicago, and when a couple of the girls came back from Chicago to be in the New York show, they came over to me, and I said, "I'm not the ballet mistress." But they said that Mr. White had told them to go to the little girl in the black bathing suit with the ribbon in her hair sitting on a trunk and ask her to teach them the dances. So I taught them the steps. When the show was trying out in Pittsburgh, Mr. White called me over and told me that I was the new ballet mistress. The show finally opened in New York and was a smashing success: at the age of fourteen going on fifteen I was in charge of nearly one hundred people in that show!

Always the sophisticated dancer, George White, now also the producer, played himself in the show, introducing a new dance called the "Five Step" on the heels of his popular "Black Bottom" the year before in his *Scandals*. Along with Ed Wynn and the George White Ballet dancers, other performers in the show were tap dancer Harland Dixon, the famous comedian Lou Holtz, the singer and actor Paul Frawley, the teenage dancers and singers known as the Williams sisters, the Twenty-Four Hudson Dusters, and the One Hundred White Beauties. The gorgeous costumes by Max Weldy were based on designs by the famous Parisian artist Roman de Tirtoff-Erté. The book was by George White and William K. Wells, music by Ray Henderson and Lew Brown, and lyrics by Buddy DeSylva. Given its popularity, the musical score was recorded in July 1928 by the popular Paul Whiteman orchestra.

Prior to the Broadway opening the show toured different cities for tryouts "to break it in." On August 24, 1927, *Variety* reviewed the tryout at the Apollo Theatre in Atlantic City, New Jersey, calling it a "feast for the eyes." Although it was officially billed as a musical comedy, according to the reviewer the show "bordered more upon a revue, and at times one became oblivious of the fact that there was such a thing as a plot. The book is rather thin, but suffices to maintain continuity." The storyline involved a love affair between an aspiring actress named Mary Brennan and an aspiring nightclub orchestra leader named Jimmy Moore, who overcame obstacles in reaching their goals with the assistance of Crickets, played by Ed Wynn, the leader of a New York gang called the Hudson Dusters. The reviewer had high praise for the beautiful settings, costumes, and the leading performers; with some cutting, increased tempo, and additional rehearsing the reviewer predicted that the show would be a success on Broadway.

On August 29th the show was performed for one week at the Sam S. Shubert Theatre in Philadelphia at 250 South Broad Street, now called the Merriam theatre, which today is Philadelphia's number one Broadway roadhouse and home to the Philadelphia Ballet. An article in the *New York Times*, September 6, 1927, noted that the original opening date for its Broadway premiere was September 19th, but the date had been delayed since after a tryout at the Nixon Theatre in Pittsburgh, Elizabeth Hines, one of the star singers in the show, withdrew from the cast and was replaced by Ona Munson, a talented singer, dancer, and actress who appeared in vaudeville and on the Broadway musical stage, later becoming famous for her role as Belle Watling in the movie classic *Gone with the Wind*.

Manhattan Mary officially opened in New York on September 26, 1927, in the Apollo Theatre at 223 West 42nd Street across from the Ziegfeld Theatre, running for nearly nine months, eventually closing on May 12, 1928, after 264 performances. The playbills advertised the show as "A New Musical Comedy 'Clean from Beginning to End.'" *Time* magazine for January 2, 1928, included *Manhattan Mary*—along with *A Connecticut Yankee*, *The Mikado*, *Good News*, *Hit the Deck*, and *Funny Face*—as one of the most important musicals of the season. Jeanne claimed that one night the cast of *Manhattan Mary* peered through the curtain to catch a glimpse of William Randolph Hearst with his beautiful mistress the movie star Marion Davies sitting on his left in the front row. Another night one of the performers in the cast started his run across the stage at the same time that Ed Wynn made his entrance leading a horse through two swinging doors at the back of the stage; unfortunately the horse defecated just as the swinging door was closing and the running performer slipped and skidded on the manure. The cast laughed about this incident throughout the run of the show. Jeanne left the show when it closed on Broadway and did not go out on tour.

To circumvent the child employment laws of the times when she was dancing in *Manhattan Mary*, Jeanne pretended to be seventeen years old. The New York Society for the Prevention of Cruelty to Children, founded in 1875 by Elbridge Thomas Gerry and Henry Bergh and commonly known as The Gerry Society, was the first child protective agency in the world. To prevent children younger than sixteen from working in the theatre, the Gerry Society would send their representatives to the various commercial theatres to question the dancers and singers about their age. If anyone said they were sixteen, the Gerry Society would demand a birth certificate to prove it or they were released from the show. Ironically, the Society harassed many child vaudevillians. In her memoir *Thelma Who?* Thelma White recounts how as a child performer in the middle of her first rehearsal at the Palace Theatre in New York a representative from the Gerry Society prevented her from appearing in the stage show. She was forced to team up with two other performers who were taking a show to the army camps.[1] Fortunately, for the young performers the Gerry Society usually targeted well-known theatres in major cities and towns, so underage boys and girls on the vaudeville tours in small towns were undetected.

The sole support of her family, Jeanne was terrified when the representatives would visit the theatres looking for underage children. When the representatives came backstage during Jeanne's run in *Manhattan Mary* and interrogated the dancers about their ages, almost sixteen girls had to leave the show for being underage. When it was Jeanne's turn to be asked her age and she claimed to be seventeen, the representatives replied, "Well, you certainly don't look it." They gave up their inquiry when Jeanne confidently answered that "she was the ballet mistress and in charge of all these dancers so why would you doubt that I am seventeen." In an interview in the *Pasadena Star-News*, January 20, 1994, Jeanne explained that "'I had to lie like a dog,'" since "'we had to eat! ... *I ran between the raindrops* [emphasis added], and we didn't starve.'"

During the run of *Manhattan Mary* Ed Wynn gave Jeanne a promotional picture signed "from 'Crickets,'" the character that Wynn had played in the original production. Jeanne remembered playing backstage with Ed's son Keenan Wynn, who became a famous theatre and film actor. Lou Holtz, the vaudevillian and comic actor who had played Sam Platz, a bond salesman, also gave Jeanne a photograph signed "To Jeanne, 'Charge DAFFAIRS' of The White Ballet." Holtz had become a star in the *Ziegfeld Follies of 1919* and performed in both vaudeville shows and musical comedies, eventually becoming in the 1920s one of the highest paid stars on Broadway; he later hosted his own radio show called "The Lou Holtz Laugh Club" and appeared on many television talks shows until his death in 1980. At the height of his career Lou Holtz was as famous as his contemporary comedians Jack Benny, George Burns, Milton Berle, and George Jessel.[2]

Bill Helman arrived in New York the week before Christmas in 1927 during the run of *Manhattan Mary* with the dog Laddie to join Lillian and Jeanne in their apartment. Since he wanted to live with his family, Bill's company had arranged for him to sell his advertising products from a small office in New York, and Lillian was determined to help him launch his new business smoothly. Writing to her parents on January 7, 1928, Lillian explained that she would not be able to travel to Pasadena for their golden wedding anniversary since she needed to be in New York for Bill and Jeanne. Although Jeanne said "she and Pop can take care of themselves for a couple weeks," wrote Lillian, "I just can't trust it for I have done all the managing of Jean and I'm afraid to leave it to her in this case." Now that Bill would be working again, he and Jeanne were planning to split expenses such as rent, food, and other necessities. Except for the $100 that Bill had given them during the six weeks rehearsal period of *Manhattan Mary* Jeanne supported the entire family from the day she had arrived in New York. "She took the entire supporting of me off his hands," Lillian wrote, so Bill would have an easier time "to make a go of it." Subsequent letters, however, suggest that Bill was unable to hold up his financial end, and he soon returned home to St. Louis.

After *Manhattan Mary* closed on Broadway, Florenz Ziegfeld hired Jeanne to dance in his next musical production, *Nell Gwyn*, based on the famous Restoration actress who rose from an orange seller to a famous stage actress to a favorite mistress of the King Charles II and the mother of his illegitimate sons. In the 1920s Nell had already inspired a Broadway musical and a silent movie starring Dorothy Gish; in the 1930s a revival with sound featured Anna Neagle. Ziegfeld's 1928 musical was to star the stunning actress and singer Ina Clare, who began her career in vaudeville as a child and later became a member of the exclusive Algonquin Hotel Round Table along with Helen Hayes, Lynn Fontaine, and Tallulah Bankhead. Ina went to England to do extensive research on Nell Gwyn, but when she returned to New York the stock market had crashed, forcing the financial backers to cancel the show. One can only imagine the spectacular ballets and dances at the court of King Charles II that would have showcased Jeanne's extraordinary talent.

Most likely in late 1928 Jeanne and Lillian moved to the second floor of a brownstone located on West 70th Street, owned by the Bennett family who lived on the first floor. They maintained contact with the Bennetts for many years including the grandchildren who lived in California. Jeanne referred to the Bennett family as "our first real friends in New York." Mrs. Bennett loved show business and the arts, and she enjoyed renting rooms in her home to theatre people; on the verge of the Great Depression, she also needed the rental income to cover her living expenses. Kay Bennett Paul, six years old at the time she met Jeanne, remembered that "she was always practicing—it was very impressive." She remembered Jeanne's big brown eyes and beautiful white skin and that she wore her hair back in a ponytail when she practiced. Jeanne was always watching her weight, and even though she loved to cook, she was disciplined and ate "rabbit food"; she was attractive, charming, and charismatic. Kay recalled that Lillian, a beautiful woman with crystal blue eyes and flawless skin, was a lovely person with a forceful personality and a great sense of humor. Jeanne and Lillian loved children and spent a lot of time with Kay during those early years. Bill Helman periodically came to visit them from St. Louis, and Kay thought Jeanne physically resembled her father more than her mother.

Inspired by Jeanne, Kay started taking ballet lessons at age seven at a local dance studio on West 72nd Street. Lillian made Kay's first costume by hand. She remembered Jeanne and Lillian being generous and curious people who loved reading and learning, and they would take her to the nearby Museum of Natural History and the Art Museum. During the Depression years no one had enough money, so Kay's mother and Lillian helped each other when they could and became fast friends. Kay remembered how Lillian home schooled Jeanne while deftly managing her dancing career; Jeanne had the extraordinary talent and passion for dancing and Lillian had the business acumen and professional ambition to make her daughter an international star. Although Kay, influenced by Jeanne, performed briefly as a dancer and singer in show business, she disliked the nomadic lifestyle of a trouper, particularly the nightclub work. One night while seated in the audience at a benefit cabaret performance for American military in St. Louis, she was called to the stage to sing, and then encouraged to mingle with the soldiers in the audience, where she met a handsome, young Air Force officer. Although at the time Kay was dating the actor Vincent Price, who was also performing at the St. Louis Muny, she and the officer fell in love and were married two weeks later. Ironically, she ended up traveling the world to his various assignments.

Times were financially tough for show business performers during the Great Depression, and Jeanne and Lillian were desperate for money. Bill's attempt to work in New York had failed, and he had returned to St. Louis. Although he could not offer them any financial security, he resented the break-up of his family, which he selfishly attributed only to Lillian's ambition for Jeanne's professional dancing career. In a letter from Bill at this time, written from his bed at Barnes Hospital in St. Louis while he was awaiting surgery, he pleaded with Lillian to ask her father for a loan since he himself was close to bankruptcy, with not even enough money to pay his doctor's expenses. With a touch of guilt and resentment, he wrote, "I think I have tried my best to do the right by you both in the past and it is no small matter to have everything sacrificed for a career." Lonely and scared, Bill told Lillian that as her husband he could demand that she return to his side in St. Louis, but he knew that Lillian wanted Jeanne to succeed, that she needed "that chance if I can give it to you, though I hate it and with reason but if nothing comes of it you should give it up and we can then live like ordinary people. I think the price is too high for what she [Jeanne] will get out of it maybe a few short years of stardom and then marriage."

Jeanne claimed that she was so focused on her work and earning a living that she never thought much about her father's financial irresponsibility. Bill promised Lillian that as soon as he left the hospital he would try to sell some of his stamp collection to generate some cash or a loan, although he added sarcastically, "You never suggested getting a loan on your Piano did you?" He promised to send them some money when he could. Lillian and Jeanne, however, did not have the luxury of returning home to St. Louis to a secure home or to consider any of Bill's other options, for they needed to focus on getting booked again as quickly as possible.

Jeanne's fortunes changed when her agent Harry Krivit asked her to team up with the "Sixteen Russell Markert Dancers" for a touring vaudeville show. A precision dance troupe founded by Markert in St. Louis, "The Sixteen Missouri Rockets" came to New York and were soon known as "The Sixteen American Rockets," then "The Roxy Theatre Roxyettes," and finally the famous "Radio City Rockettes."[3] A former chorus boy dancer, Markert had danced in 1923 on Broadway in that year's *Earl Carroll's Vanities*, and two years later in 1925, encouraged by Spyros Skouras who later became the head of Twentieth Century–Fox, started a dance troupe of sixteen girls in St. Louis that he called the "The Sixteen Missouri Rockets," who performed at Skouras' St. Louis movie presentation house. Trained at Mrs. Clark's ballet school along with Jeanne and dancing at the theatres in St. Louis, these girls were exceptionally good dancers who had mastered the art of high kicks in unison all the same height while dancing in a line. Having seen the popular British precision dancing group called the John Tiller girls in the *Ziegfeld Follies of 1922*, Markert conceived of an American version that could surpass the Tiller girls with more complicated tap routines and kicks higher than the waist.

In 1927, Markert, acting as a responsible chaperone, took the girls to New York to find work first in the revue known as the *Greenwich Village Follies* and then at the Roxy. An advertisement in *Variety*, November 16, 1927, promoted Russell Markert's dancing troupe "SIXTEEN AMERICAN ROCKETS" as being a "SENSATIONAL, OUTSTANDING HIT" at the Roxy with an indefinite engagement as the newly named "Roxy Theatre Roxyettes." Wanting to create multiple troupes of his precision dancers, Markert placed an advertisement in the November 23, 1927, issue of *Variety* for dancing girls who must be able to toe dance, buck, and kick. When the stock market crashed in 1929, show biz work in New York was scarce, so Markert sought to book his troupes on vaudeville tours. The first agent he called to book a tour was Harry Krivit, Jeanne's long-time agent, who designed a Radio Keith Orpheum (RKO) national vaudeville tour for Jeanne Devereaux and two male dancers and a troupe of "Sixteen Russell Markert Dancers" that toured America for the next two years. Promotional pictures of Jeanne from *Man-*

hattan Mary in gorgeous ballet poses were hung in the theatre lobbies to advertise the stage presentation.

The vaudeville show first played at the RKO theatres all over the East Coast, with the usual format of a symphony orchestra, an organ recessional, Fox Movietone News, a short musical, a stage presentation, and a feature movie. The program for Brooklyn's E. F. Albee Theatre for the week commencing January 13, 1929, featured the Grand Organ, the E. F. Albee Salon Ensemble, the Strolling Troubadours Mario and Lazarin, "16 Russell Markert Dancers" with "Jean Deveraux [*sic*]" and two male dancers, Slim Timblin and others in "a black-faced skit," and the singing comedian Georgie Price, Joe Smith, Chas. Dale and their Avon Comedy Four; the movie was *The Circus Kid* starring Frankie Darro, Joe E. Brown, and Helene Costello. The show played at New York's Keith-Albee Coliseum Theatre from January 20th through January 23rd and the movie was *Wings* with Clara Bow, Charles (Buddy) Rogers, Richard Arlen, and Gary Cooper—one of the first feature films and the only silent one to win an Academy Award for Best Picture. The same bill ran from January 24th through January 26th at B. F. Keith's Eighty-First Street Theatre on Broadway.

The program for Boston's B. F. Keith Memorial Theatre for the week of January 28th featured the "Sixteen Russell Markert Dancers" with "Jean Devereaux." An advertisement in the program for Markert's fledging dancing troupe claimed that "Russell Markert assembles groups of dancing girls into units, and after giving these units the benefit of his skill as a director, they are placed wherever dancing is a part of amusement. The Russell Markert Girls are tripping the light fantastic with musical comedies, revues and in vaudeville throughout the world. At least a dozen of the foremost American productions feature one of his groups; and they are to be found in France, England, Germany and Australia." In the midst of their first national vaudeville tour this pretentious publicity claim was designed to convince audiences of their international celebrity to help sell the show.

For the week of February 17th, Jeanne and the Markert Dancers were the third act at the New Palace Theatre in Chicago on a program featuring the recording musicians Ray Miller and his Brunswick Orchestra, comedians Block and Sully, and singer Leatrice Joy. The final act was the Three Whirlwinds, who were amazing acrobats on roller skates. A Chicago newspaper review for February 23rd praised the dancers for their talent, youth, and flashy costumes:

> A couple of snappy dances and two numbers of the cute type were sandwiched in and held the audience. The Sixteen Russell Markert Girls, with Jean Devereaux and Bill and Ray Morosco, have a dance entry that is hard to beat. The sixteen girls entered doing a routine and they worked as one person. It was a sight for sore eyes to see so much talent and youthful pep. The costumes were pretty. Jean Devereaux followed with a toe routine that was a pippin. The double spins she did on her toes caught the fans' attention, as did her gracefulness. The Morosco boys came next with an eccentric [tap] dance routine that was good. The girls next appeared in flashy jazz costumes and showed another perfect rhythm routine. After a routine by Jean, and a drunk dance by the boys, the girls again appeared in spangled costumes for their best efforts. A great dance entry.

A program for a five-act vaudeville show at Buffalo's Shea's Hippodrome, beginning on March 3rd, featured "Sixteen Russell Markert Girls" with Jeanne Devereaux and Bill and Ray Morosco; the film was *The Shady Lady* starring Phyllis Haver. A review in the *Buffalo Courier Express* praised the entertaining film and "a group of stellar vaudeville acts.... The Sixteen Russell Market Girls, an act that also includes Jean Devereaux and Bill and Ray Morosco, claims the spotlight on the bill and evokes rounds and rounds of applause. Jean Devereaux is a toe dancer of particular talent, and is called back for encores."

A program for May 2nd through May 4th for the Lincoln Theatre in Trenton, New Jersey, listed the first act in the "Stage Presentation" as "Russell Markert Girls—16" with "Late Feature 'Rain or Shine' with Jean Devereaux and Bill & Ray Morosco"; the talking movie was *Sonny Boy* starring Davey Lee. When the show traveled to Syracuse, New York, the *Syracuse Journal* review noted how the "Sixteen Rockets" all "click together.... It is long since we have seen such perfection in dancing rhythm. Likewise, it is good to look at. Why, when Miss Deveraux, the solo dancer, came on, it was like a Degas picture, it was so exquisite." In another issue of the same local newspaper the act was considered "of headline caliber," with the Markert dancers bringing "a little bit of Broadway to Syracuse, with their gorgeous costumes and their faultless rhythm. Miss Deveraux, the solo dancer, is dainty and graceful, and it's a treat to see her backward kick."

To maintain her physical fitness and dancing skills throughout her career, Jeanne practiced several hours daily in addition to her demanding performance schedule, and instead of practicing alone, whenever possible she would attend a ballet class.[4] Attending classes and renting rehearsal space was expensive. Jeanne remembered the several studios in New York on 59th Street where she trained and took ballet classes with other successful professional ballet dancers like Patricia Bowman in between engagements during the late 1920s and 1930s with famous Russian and Italian émigré ballet teachers, such as Louis Harvey Chalif, Constantin Kobeleff, Michel Fokine, Mikhail Mordkin, Ivan Tarasov, and Luigi Albertieri. In the 1940s she occasionally studied with the ballet master Eddie Caton in his studio in Carnegie Hall when she was in the city. After her retirement, Caton remembered her and sent his regards. She singled out Kobeleff from among her famous teachers as an especially nice man and good teacher—"Kobbie was such a darling!"—who would occasionally come to Jeanne's home for dinner when she had a respectable apartment. She also remembered with a devilish twinkle in her eye a particular class in New York when she impressed her peers with her high speed pirouettes. The young legendary dancer and choreographer Agnes de Mille was also attending this class, and when trying to emulate Jeanne's amazing technical feat, she fell off balance and started staggering around. Realizing that some of the other ballerinas were twittering behind her back, the prominent Agnes became upset and embarrassed by being upstaged by a vaudeville toe dancer.

While touring across America Jeanne also took ballet classes with famous teachers. When performing in Chicago she studied with Muriel Abbott, and during the early 1930s when in Hollywood, she studied with Adolph Bolm, a former dancer with Diaghilev's Ballets Russes. She also practiced in ballet studios in the Hollywood area with young dancers like Cyd Charisse and later during the postwar period with Leslie Caron. In 1938, while performing one show a night at the classy Bal Tabarin nightclub in Paris, she practiced during the day with Lubov Egorova and the renowned Olga Preobrajenska.

While in New York Jeanne also continued the tap dancing lessons that she had begun back in St. Louis at Mrs. Clark's dancing school. The dance instructor, theatre

Jeanne Devereaux in practice clothes demonstrating her artistic athleticism in a neighborhood rehearsal hall, New York, c. early 1930s. Jeanne's intense performance schedule required hours of practice each day in rented, rundown rehearsal spaces wherever she was living. Courtesy Jeanne Devereaux Perkins Collection.

director, and producer John Murray Anderson, who had started the popular Broadway revue *The Greenwich Village Follies* that played on Broadway from 1919 to 1928, had opened an art academy on the east side near the famous Rubens restaurant. On the first floor was a dance studio overseen by the revered teachers Michio Ito, Ruth Saint Denis, and Harland Dixon; drama classes were offered on the second floor. Jeanne's tap dancing teacher, Harland Dixon, was one of the featured performers with Jeanne on Broadway in *Manhattan Mary*.

Until the summer of 1935 Jeanne toured America's palatial movie presentation houses coast to coast with the major vaudeville tours. The Fox tour was booked for thirty weeks; a Paramount tour lasted forty-eight weeks; the RKO Orpheum tour was contracted for sixty weeks, and the MGM Loew's tour was twenty-four weeks. Although show business was an exhilarating experience for Jeanne as an artist, her personal letters and postcards beginning in 1929 reveal that the constant touring was exhausting but necessitated by her unending financial demands. On August 10, 1929, from the Victoria Hotel in Des Moines, Iowa, frustrated by the responsibility for supporting the family, Jeanne wrote Aunt Aletha in Pasadena that "Dad is out of the sanitarium now and ok though not very strong yet. And a new man all he wants to do is work and Mother said it won't be Lazy Bill anymore. So that will be nice and if I work steady for a couple of years we will have a house out there near you [Aunt Aletha] yet. It will just be grand if we get to see you this year and that is what we are planning." With her earnings that year Jeanne had purchased for $650 a new Dodge touring car for the family. She sent a postcard to her Grandmother Lane to inform her that she and her mother would spend three more weeks in San Antonio at the Texas theatre, followed by a week in Houston at the Metropolitan and another in Dallas at the Palace Theatre before they closed in New Orleans and could drive to Pasadena for a visit.

Jeanne's initial plan was that her mother and father would join her in Dallas and then the three of them would travel by car to New Orleans, arriving on September 13th. Lillian, however, drove Bill directly to New Orleans, and since Jeanne still had another week to work, her parents drove on by themselves in the Dodge to California. Jeanne followed a week later by train to meet them at her grandparents' home. Bill lived with the family in Pasadena, until he become ill again, going on strange buying sprees. He decided to return to St. Louis, but en route in Wyoming his mental health broke down so much that he was put in a sanitarium until he was well enough to travel again. Jeanne described her father's precarious condition at this time as a mental roller coaster: "He would be perfectly fine," she said, "and then all of a sudden he was off his rocker."

4.

Hollywood, a Fanchon and Marco Tour and Pasadena

During the Great Depression years of the early 1930s jobs in show business—live stage shows and movies—were scarce. By economic necessity Jeanne and her mother were forced to remain with Lillian's parents in Pasadena, California, for months. In 1930–31, while Jeanne was living in the Hollywood area, she made two motion pictures. The first one was an early talkie musical comedy *Are You There?*. It was directed by Hamilton MacFadden and starred the famous English music hall comedienne and vaudevillian Beatrice Lillie—known as "The Funniest Woman in the World"—as the girl detective Shirley Travis with John Garrick, Olga Baclanova, and George Grossmith. Fox Studios released the movie in November 1930. Jeanne's second film, *Kiss Me Again*, one of Hollywood's first all-Technicolor talking pictures, was based on the popular operetta *Mademoiselle Modiste* by Victor Herbert and Henry Martyn Blossom. Directed by William Seiter and starring Bernice Claire, Edward Everett Horton, and Walter Pidgeon, *Kiss Me Again* was released by Warner Bros. in early 1931.

Jeanne's film *Are You There?*, one of Beatrice Lillie's few movies, is a rarity in film history.[1] Since Fox believed in late 1930 that the popularity of musical films had tapered off, only five of the original seven musical numbers made the final cut, with Jeanne's spectacular dance number lost on the cutting room floor. The movie set for Jeanne's omitted dance number consisted of a lovely mansion with a terrace covered with roses down to the stage level and another mansion with a long circular staircase with a balalaika orchestra performing in front on a lovely patterned floor. Surrounded by the corps de ballet girls lying in a radiant circle on the floor, Jeanne was in the middle of the circle performing pirouettes wearing Russian boots. She tells the story about warning the girls not to lift their heads or they might get hurt, but one girl ignored her warning, raising up her head only to be smacked by Jeanne's twirling boots.

Jeanne and Bert Prival, a well-known vaudeville and movie performer, both wore Dutch bob black wigs in the scene. Jeanne cleverly secured her wig with a skin toned piece of elastic that went around her head and under her jaw like a chinstrap, but Bert failed to secure his wig. During the filming when the director of the film crouched down below the set's terrace, Bert danced a double pirouette and his wig flew off and hit the director in the mouth. The director exploded, pointing to Jeanne, telling Bert, "She has done many more pirouettes and her wig didn't fly off." After Jeanne explained what she had done, the director ordered his assistant to "get wardrobe over and fix his wig like hers."

Jeanne Devereaux, age nineteen, on the movie set of *Kiss Me Again*, Warner Bros. Burbank Studios, Burbank, California, 1931. One of the first Technicolor talking movies, *Kiss Me Again* starred Bernice Claire, Edward Everett Horton, and Walter Pidgeon, and included a spectacular dance scene featuring Jeanne toward the end. It was released in movie presentation houses in New York on January 7, 1931. Photograph by M N Pubx. Courtesy Jeanne Devereaux Perkins Collection.

Her second film *Kiss Me Again* included a highly praised signature solo dance.[2] The reviewer in the *New York Times*, January 8, 1931, claimed that the costumes, the dancing, and the attractive Bernice Claire's singing made this Technicolor film most entertaining. At the end of *Kiss Me Again* is a dance sequence featuring Jeanne dressed in white in front of a corps de ballet performing her high-speed pirouettes, with her arms folded against her chest to increase her velocity. Jeanne emphasized that the scene was shot in only two takes. On the back of one of her promotional pictures for the film is a quote from the famous fan magazine writer and occasional dance reviewer Gladys Hall from *The Dance* magazine praising Jeanne's solo dance: "It would be a good idea, if visiting this picture, to come in at the end so as to catch the solo dance by Jeanne Devereaux."[3]

During Jeanne's dancing career she never saw either of her films. Soon after completing them, when she was performing in St. Louis during a seven-and-a-half month Fox vaudeville tour across the nation, one of her films was playing across the street from the theatre, but her demanding performing schedule prevented her from seeing it. On May 24, 1931, Jeanne asked her father if he recognized her in the one of her films when he saw it: "Say Dad," she wrote, "will you tell me before I burst, if you could tell it was me in that picture? We havent seen it yet and it looks as if we wont get to as I think it has played the east." If Bill had seen her in the film, he never mentioned it in any of his letters. When the Great Depression hit the film industry hard in the 1930s, Jeanne continued dancing in vaudeville and musical presentations, and eventually danced in Europe until war was declared at the end of the decade. During the wartime 1940s, she continued to audition for films, even though expensive, spectacular scenes that would showcase her dancing talent were scarce. She even wrote a few screenplays.

In March 1931 Jeanne, now a headliner, performed in a forty-minute unit "Idea" stage show called "Love Letters" created by the famous West Coast producers Fanchon and Marco. Fanchon Simon and Marco Wolff, former vaudeville dancers and now musical revue producers, were proclaimed in *Variety*'s January 29, 1930, issue as "the world's most famous brother and sister producing team" of touring live stage shows for theatres. Beginning their creative "Idea" shows in 1923 in San Francisco, the Fanchon and Marco Company expanded into Southern California, the Pacific Northwest, and nationwide. The "Ideas" were acts loosely connected by a unified theme, performed by a troupe with an orchestra leader and master of ceremonies, and packaged to sell to the movie presentation theatre managers as spectacular stage show "prologues" before the motion picture. Like classic vaudeville, the "Idea" shows included dancers, singers, comedians, musicians, acrobats, and other specialty acts. The Idea themes were derived from Broadway musicals, holidays, animals, foods, nursery rhymes, and many others, and they usually changed every week or two when a new movie began. Fanchon and Marco's first "Idea" show named *Love Tales* opened in October 1923 at the Warfield Theatre in San Francisco, and by 1929 the show *Gobs [Sailors] of Joy* toured the national theatre circuits of RKO, Paramount, and Fox. Plans were underway to produce two Ideas a week, but the Great Depression had forced many theatres to close, diminishing the market; also the demands of the emerging union of stage personnel made the spectacular stage show units too expensive to produce.[4]

Jeanne performed a five-a-day grueling schedule of live performances of "Love Let-

Jeanne Devereaux and George Ward in Fanchon and Marco's "Idea" show *Love Letters*, March–Fall 1931. Jeanne and George are dancing a tap specialty with the Sixteen Sunkist Beauties. The "Idea" shows were thematic units that were booked on the vaudeville circuits across the country. The opening song and dance novelty act featured Jeanne and George carrying a large envelope addressed to Jeanne Devereaux. This is one of a few known shows that featured Jeanne's superior tap dancing talent. Photograph by Curt Fox LA. Courtesy Huntington Library, San Marino, California.

Jeanne Devereaux and George Ward in Fanchon and Marco's "Idea" show *Love Letters* with the Sixteen Sunkist Beauties, March–Fall 1931. Photograph by Curt Fox LA. Courtesy Huntington Library, San Marino, California.

ters" in large movie presentation houses across America.[5] These bookings were advertised under the "Fanchon & Marco" heading in a section of *Variety* that printed the week's "Variety Bills," with Jeanne's name prominently displayed. In larger ads her name was highlighted in large, bold black letters. Jeanne was also featured in the company's publicity newsletter "The Idea" for the stage show "Love Letters" that was sent to theatre managers and drama critics nationwide. Staged by the noted choreographer Gae Foster, the show was a tribute to the United States mail system and was organized around the theme of mail service from Colonial times to the pony express era to the current day's air mail service. Jeanne, known as "The Dancing Sweetheart," followed the other headliners on the bill: the comedian and singing guitar player Will Aubrey and the dancing and singing comedians Billy Nelson and Irene Knight. Other cast members were songwriter and song and dance man George Ward, who danced several numbers with Jeanne and wrote the principal song "I'm Looking for a Mail Box" for the opening act; Jim French's Aeroplane Girls, who performed their unique aerial trapeze act in the grand finale where they were suspended from revolving miniature aeroplanes, flying at thirty miles per hour; the Fanchon and Marco Sunkist Beauties, sixteen talented dancing chorus girls under the direction of Gae Foster who performed throughout the show and on roller skates in the grand finale; and the singing and dancing beauties Eugenia Reynolds and Mildred Stencel, who performed a singing duet in the opening Colonial scene and later in the show with the Sunkist Beauties.

The Fanchon and Marco newsletter contained biographies of all the performers and highlights for editors to use as publicity fillers. Jeanne's entry included her main credits and emphasized her exceptional dancing: "An unusually talented Premiere Danseuse featuring a sensational routine of toe ballet work. Receives a tremendous ovation for her whirlwind triple turns on one toe. She is the only performer on the stage who is able to accomplish this difficult feat. Works in several spots during this presentation ... two solo specialties and twice with George Ward. Also scores a hit with her clever eccentric [tap] dance."[6] Other publicity stories for newspaper space mentioned Jeanne and George Ward in their opening act as "two talented principal performers during one of their most entertaining song and dance contributions."[7]

The Fanchon and Marco newsletter was one of the few public records that provided detailed information about the staging of the show and Jeanne's tap dancing ability. "Love Letters" opened with Jeanne and George Ward in front of a full stage drop decorated with love letters, "while George comes on carrying a huge cardboard letter addressed to Jeanne Devereaux. This letter, upon being delivered to Jeanne, who makes her entrance from a tiny prop 'house,' is carried by the two during a clever song and dance novelty."[8] At the conclusion the letter is reversed revealing a verse introduction to the ensuing Colonial episode, recited in unison by Jeanne and George. In the Colonial scene, set in a black and white garden with the beautifully costumed Sunkist beauties posing in the background, Jeanne was "featured in a dainty toe specialty that borders on the sensational. Her remarkable ability in performing whirlwind triple turns on one toe adds the big punch to this lavish spectacle."[9] Completing the scene were the beautiful harmonies of the sopranos Eugenia Reynolds and Mildred Stencel.

In the second scene, "one of the highlight episodes" depicting a Post Office building and United States mail car in the background, Jeanne, George Ward, and the Sunkist beauties, who were attired in natty blue mail carrier uniforms, performed jazzy tap routines, including one by the Sunkist beauties who clicked wooden letters carried in their hands for a special effect. Immediately following this routine was "a clever eccentric tap dance, offered by Jeanne Devereaux, which scores a big hit."[10] A "unique telephone scene" with Jeanne and George talking to each other from opposite sides of the stage introduced the sensational finale featuring Jim French's aerialists and the Sunkists performing a roller skating routine while wearing white costumes and aviator helmets with small propellers attached on the top. They performed "difficult march formations, splits, high kicks and pivot turns on their skates with as much ease as though they had on ballet slippers."[11]

Jeanne remembered an accident during the "Love Letters" run at the Pantages theatre in Hollywood when the dancers on roller skates performed on a stage sprinkled with pumice powder to prevent slipping. As the girls were skating in a circle holding hands, one girl's skate broke and she fell, causing the circle to "crack the whip," resulting in several girls falling into the footlights and others falling into the orchestra pit. The pumice powder burned the skaters who fell on the stage. The company manager ignored the situation, locking himself in his dressing room, so Lillian used the house first aid kit to treat the girls' cuts and scrapes. She then went to a nearby drugstore at Hollywood and Vine to purchase adhesive tape, bandages, and salves for further treatment. Will Aubrey, one of the headliners, escorted the girls who had fallen into the pit onstage in front of the curtain to reassure the horrified audience that they were not seriously injured. "Between shows my dressing room was a backstage clinic that day," said Jeanne. "Luckily none of the chorus suffered any lingering injuries."

Since Jeanne was a headliner in "Love Letters" she made a decent wage during the run of the show in a Depression year. The chorus girls' weekly salary of $35 was an adequate living wage in 1931, but their many expenses caused financial hardship. The girls had to pay for their train tickets, hotel rooms, taxis, tips, and restaurant meals, and many sent money home to their struggling families. Making matters worse was the company policy of charging a $2 fine for any swear word uttered in the chorus girls' dressing room, reported by one of the stage manager's many spies.

The frequent family letters began during the run of "Love Letters," when Bill was living permanently in St. Louis, had recovered from a serious illness, and was now able to put pen to paper on a weekly basis. While Jeanne was earning accolades for her virtuosity as a dancer in "Love Letters," she was also dealing with her father's physical and mental illnesses, which threatened the ideal of a normal family that she inscribed in her letters. Attempting to cheer him up during his bouts of illness and depression, Jeanne and Lillian knew that he was their closest connection to family, and they were not ready to give him up. While Jeanne was performing in San Francisco, on March 6, 1931, Lillian wrote to Bill, who was recovering from malaria in a St. Louis hospital and suffering from depression, that she wanted her letter "to comfort and help you to look toward the future with hope instead of hopelessness. In the first place, dear, you have allowed yourself to become frightened over getting to the end of your money and not being able to make more," she wrote. "This fright is bad for anyone & is doubly bad for you. I only wish I had been able to send money more quickly to you, before you had begun to worry." While he was recovering, Lillian advised him to "read, draw or anything you are let do," she wrote, "but keep your spirits up and banish all worry." They would send him an optimistic magazine article that Jeanne found about recovering from malaria "to bring hope to you, and that is all you need." Lillian signed her letter, "From your old wife & pal."

With Jeanne curled up asleep in her dressing room in her mother's old fur coat, Lillian wrote her "Old Pal" Bill on March 24, 1931, while she and Jeanne were in Portland, Oregon, having "a series of train jumps, midnite shows in addition to the regular 4 a day we do." When Jeanne recently had played in Oakland in the San Francisco area her name had been up in lights out on the marquee in front of the theatre. "Boy did it give us a thrill! Plenty," Lillian wrote. When they had taken the train from San Francisco to Portland, Lillian was reminded of the family's touring trip years ago along this same route and she wrote, "I firmly resolved then that when you are recovered permanently we will take this trip again." Lillian heard from Bill's good friend O'Malley that he was "allowed to write letters so we are looking forward to one from you. He says you are better again, but you must have some treatments he thinks. My darling you are all Jean & I have and we surely hope you will not despair as we feel you can be cured. Have always felt so." Once again, exchanging gifts had to substitute for close proximity, so

Lillian asked Bill if he would like any books or a sweater, since "we like to know things like that as we love to send you something."

Since mention of Jeanne's admirers usually upset Bill, making him feel neglected and jealous, Lillian assured him not to worry about the comedian in the show who thought that Jeanne was great and was bringing her magazines, verses, and apples for all the sixteen girls. She described him as too old at thirty-nine years old and with "a big tummy." Four days later Lillian wrote from cold, rainy Seattle, affectionately reminding him to write them a letter and that they would be back in St. Louis in a few weeks: "Dearest old man you are all we have, and you mean a lot to us," she wrote. "We are looking forward to seeing you so much it is all we can think of or talk about."

An undated review in Jeanne's scrapbook of "Love Letters" in the *Seattle Star* featured a picture of Jeanne in full arabesque in the stage show attraction at the Seattle Paramount Theatre. The film was *Tailor Made Man*, starring William Haines, Dorothy Jordan, Marjorie Rambeau, and Joe Cawthorne. The reviewer specifically praised Jeanne's balletic virtuosity, writing: "She features triple turns on one toe, an unusually difficult part of toe routine." In another undated review in the *Tacoma Daily Ledger*, her eccentric tap dance was deemed a star turn: "Before a background of lavishly beautiful sets on the stage this week we have Jeanne Devereaux, a dancer of unusual grace and charm, featured in Fanchon & Marco's 'Love Letters' idea. Miss Devereaux's numbers are outstanding for the rhythm and beauty which she puts into them and if you don't like her I hope you have to listen to tap dancers for the rest of your life."

Bill's serious illness had been upsetting for Jeanne and Lillian, making them nostalgic for their early life in St. Louis and fearful of losing their family connection. Jeanne's commitment to her dancing career and the necessity to support the family financially, however, coupled with Lillian's devotion to Jeanne's career made it impossible for them to visit him in St. Louis. Nearly a month later on April 26th Lillian wrote her "Dearest Old Man" from bitter cold Milwaukee, Wisconsin, while listening to some music on the radio in Jeanne's dressing room, thanking him for his recent nostalgic letter, which made her "feel good.... And I, too, have lived over and over every minute we had together in St. Louis. And I firmly believe we can make every dream of ours come true." Their next destinations were Detroit and then Niagara Falls. Jeanne was tired because she went out dancing with the cast last night, and had to perform five shows the next day. In between shows she took naps on the fur coat spread out on the floor. Lillian was relieved that Bill was allowed to go outside and get some fresh air, and she encouraged him to get some exercise. "Dear me but I was glad to hear from you," she wrote. "Write every chance you get, for your letters do us as much good as ours do you." She signed her letter, "Love in large doses to my only sweetheart."

Despite their concern for Bill and the endearing words in their letters, a month elapsed before either Jeanne or Lillian corresponded again with him. On May 24th Jeanne wrote her last letter to him during the run of "Love Letters" in Springfield, Massachusetts. The letter, addressed to her "Darling Daddy-kins," informed him that the New England "prudes" were in action, so that she and George Ward would have Sunday off since they were dancers: "God bless old 'Daddie Blue Law.'" The rest of the show's cast, however, had to work, since "talking and singing isn't immoral on Sunday, and they even let the skating get by (but not with out tights) but my flitting around on a pair of toe shoes might be a bad example to the younger generation." Last week in Utica, New York, the cast had to perform only three shows daily, allowing them to catch up on their sleep. After one of the last shows of the evening they performed at nearby Little Falls for the Shriners and actually got paid for a benefit performance.

The run of "Love Letters" was over in the fall of 1931. Jeanne subsequently signed a contract for a vaudeville tour on the Loew's circuit called "Dive In," starring the comedian Jack Pepper, Madeline Berlo as a diving mermaid, the movie star Johnny Weissmuller, and Mack, Harold, and Bobby in a comic act called "Kids Kiddin." *Variety* for June 14 and 21, 1932, advertised the show at the St. Louis' Loew's theatre and later on June 28th at the Oriental in Chicago and on July 5th at Loew's theatre in Detroit. In all of these advertisements the headliner "Jack Pepper" was featured in large letters with "Jeanne Devereaux, Premier Dancer" in bold at the bottom. Jeanne described how she entered through the gold doors of an elaborate jewel box dressed like Mata Hari in a yellow chiffon skirt and elaborate head dress, performed her dance, and then disappeared back into the box. A large, glass swimming tank was erected on the stage and the mermaids would dive into the pool, their gorgeous bodies visible to the audience through the glass siding. She remembered not ranking Johnny Weissmuller as among the most intelligent performers she had met, saying that he had "water for brains."

In 1933, at the height of the Great Depression, Bill recovered from his malaria, the run of "Dive In" was over, and Jeanne and Lillian headed west. Work was scarce in the entertainment industry, so they again lived with Jeanne's maternal grandparents in Pasadena, taking care of her grandmother who had a broken leg. Over the next couple of years they were forced to borrow money from Lillian's parents and her sister Lenore. Bill visited them briefly in June 1933. While performing in the Los Angeles area, Jeanne was also privately indulging her passion for world affairs by being one of the organizers that year of the Junior Town Meeting of Pasadena. Her maternal grandparents were members of Pasadena's Senior Town Meeting elders, who decided to create a Junior Town Meeting where they could lecture and guide Pasadena's youth away from becoming radicalized socialists or communists. It was at one of these Junior Town Meetings that Jeanne met some attractive young men with whom she corresponded over the years. She met the handsome young engineer Thomas Perkins, who walked her home after the meetings and sat with her on her grandparents' front porch steps to discuss the evening's lecture. She was attracted by his intelligence, and when they discovered they shared the same political views, they became friends. A year later she wrote in her diary on February 1, 1934: "His brain satisfies me. He's so terribly logical—Mathematical calculations for emotions." Tom, however, definitely had an emotional response when meeting Jeanne. The first time he laid eyes on her, Tom later said, "I looked across the room at these big, brown eyes. She was very charming."

In November Jeanne worked at the Pasadena Community Playhouse, a popular regional theatre where many famous actors performed in the 1930s hoping to be seen by casting directors to get hired. The call from the Pasadena Community Playhouse, although not prestigious or lucrative for a star like Jeanne, was extremely welcome during hard times. Jeanne remembered that the young actor Lee J. Cobb performed there during the 1933–34 season to open new doors for his talent. Impressed by Jeanne, a talented dancer with a vivacious personality, Cobb encouraged her to attend the open auditions at the playhouse for speaking roles. Jeanne also met the Texas-born aspiring actor Horton Foote, who was studying acting at the Playhouse. Foote eventually left acting behind and became a Pulitzer Prize–winning dramatist and Oscar winning screenwriter who adapted Harper Lee's *To Kill a Mockingbird* for the screen.

During this same season at the Pasadena Community Playhouse Jeanne starred as the premiere danseuse in *The Master Thief*, a romantic opera based on an old German poem by Arthur Fitger that featured a cast of a hundred singers, dancers, musicians, and actors. According to the program, Jeanne performed as a gypsy dancer and choreographed and directed the dances for the opera, with Guy Williams composing the music and conducting the orchestra. The program note for "Dance Lovers" praised Jeanne's innovative choreography: "The dances created by Jeanne Devereaux for 'The Master Thief' are distinctly different since they help depict the story of the opera and give the ballet girls a chance to pantomime. Three of the ensemble's dances that add color and life to the opera are an intricate dance depicting the weaving of tapestries in the medieval centuries, a wild gypsy dance, and symbolic of flame; whirling requiring perfect lines and rhythm." An unidentified review of *The Master Thief* in her scrapbook states that Jeanne "did splendid work as premiere danseuse."

While living and performing in Pasadena, Jeanne had a welcome opportunity to return to her roots as a classically trained ballerina. In late December 1933 Jeanne starred at the Pasadena Civic Auditorium in the second annual Tournament of Roses coronation symphonic pageant called "The Quest," produced and directed by the legendary Gilmore Brown, founder of the Pasadena Community Playhouse. With a cast of 180 performers, the production was held for the benefit of the local women's relief fund. Jeanne danced two solos, one being her favorite classic ballet *The Firebird*, originally choreographed for the Ballets Russes by Michel Fokine with music by Stravinsky, surrounded by chorus girls, delighting the audiences with her astounding pirouettes and extraordinary grace. The other was also her favorite, *Swan Lake*—a thrilling return to her classical training and lifelong inspiration from Anna Pavlova, featuring thirty-two sensational fouettés. An original playbill promoted her as "Premiere Danseuse"; the ballet master was George Fortunato of the Russian School of Dancing. An article in the *Los Angeles Times*, December 23, 1933, entitled "Rose Coronation Fete to Have 'Living Curtain,'" described how the Rose Queen and her six ladies-in-waiting along with other beautiful girls "will appear suspended on the stage curtain as it descends"; the program will also feature a performance by "Fortunato's ballet dancers, and solo dances by Miss Jeanne Devereaux of the St. Louis Opera Company." An undated review contained a picture "of a girl in a bird costume putting a crown on the Queen's head." The writer identified this young girl as "Jeanne Devereaux Nationally known Premier Ballerina and native daughter of St. Louis, who was starred in the Fire Bird Pageant before the parade"; another reviewer wrote, "After seeing Jeanne Devereaux give the most inspiring interpretation since Pavlova's Swan Dance—I was moved to write poetry."

In early January 1934 after "The Quest" was over Jeanne frantically spent time trying to get a booking at the movie presentation house called the Pantages in Hollywood and had received permission to use her Rose Pageant costumes at this prestigious theatre. She was also in rehearsal for the musical *Camille at Roaring Camp* at the Pasadena Community Playhouse for which she had choreographed all the dances, including a crowd-pleasing energetic can-can. On January 23rd after seeing a performance of the show, she proudly wrote in her new diary that the "girls got the biggest hand of the evening." That same month she also choreographed a dance for *Shakuntala* and played a leading speaking role in the second scene. After a rehearsal of *Shakuntala* on February 12th, Jeanne wrote in her diary, with obvious relief, that her mother, her inspiration and her most rigorous critic, had "approved of the way I am playing my part—I was told that I had very fine diction." Over the next few months with the encouragement of Lee J. Cobb Jeanne read for various speaking parts for Gilmore Brown in the open workshop readings at the Playhouse. She claimed that she had lost the part in *Salome* because her interpretation of the lead character was too innocent and romantic. Although everyone thought she was the best when she had read for the part of Meg in *Little Women*, eventually the female leads were cast with three blonde movie stars.

While rehearsing *Camille at Roaring Camp* Jeanne usually wore a pair of informal practice slacks with a blouse tucked in reminiscent of Katherine Hepburn's favored fashion statement. One afternoon when taking a break during rehearsals, she left the playhouse and went across the street to Colorado Boulevard to buy a coke at a drugstore. She encountered a large middle-aged woman, dressed in a baggy dress and hat and carrying a large bag, who looked at her disapprovingly and said, "Young lady, you should go home immediately and take off those wicket [*sic*], iniquitous pants!"

At age twenty-two Jeanne reflected in her diary that it was time for her to grow up and become a real adult. When not dancing, she devoted her time to reading books and plays from the Pasadena library, cooking for the family, listening to the radio, dreaming about far away places, and dating almost every night attractive young men she had met either at the Playhouse or the Junior Town Meeting. On March 9th she wrote that she must stop and set a few new goals: "But somehow I'm interested in so many things it's hard to devote my time to one." Ten days later she wrote that she couldn't remain "a child toward responsibility any longer. Bob White [Lillian] can't face the reality always."

She also wrote about the hardship of living with her maternal grandparents in Pasadena and how she yearned to escape this environment that drained away her spirit and creativity. Living with her grandparents, who barely earned a subsistence living during the Great Depression years, was unbearable for Jeanne and Lillian. To conserve food and utilities, they would eat only a few vegetables and some bread and butter from a brown paper bag and at night go to bed without bathing. Lillian wrote Bill on March 24th that it had always been impossible to live with her parents and "now its just 'plain Hell.'" They were not eligible for the government's public relief since they had living relatives who ostensibly were able to care for them; her folks, however, were too proud to admit, "they are not able to keep us." So while they were living in Pasadena, they were forced to borrow money from Jeanne's aunts just to survive. Jeanne did not want to leave Pasadena before having her nose, injured in that childhood sledding accident, fixed. When she saw a Dr. Ginsbérg about having it straightened, he informed her that she would be restricted from practicing at least a full week after the surgery, a luxury she could never afford since she had to be ready to respond to future bookings at a moment's notice. It was many years before she had the time and money to have cosmetic surgery.

During their stay in Pasadena work in the film industry was scarce. During February Jeanne had a couple of auditions at the MGM studio for a short film but nothing materialized. On March 24th Lillian described in a letter to Bill how she had tried to sell Jeanne's idea for a Walt Disney picture, but "they said that they had a corps of artists on their pay-roll, which had to be kept busy, so they never buy any outside ideas." When Jeanne and Lillian showed some ideas for short films "to the fellow in charge of the shorts at R.K.O. studios in Hollywood," he told them that "the ideas [were] dandy and said he wished he could do something like them, but he was so cramped for money he had not bought a new 'shorts' idea in over a year." Since Jeanne was unable to get hired by the film studios, she and Lillian began negotiations with Fanchon and Marco to secure a booking as a soloist at the Roxy in New York City for eight to ten weeks, as well as at some movie presentation houses en route in San Francisco, Salt Lake City, Denver, and St. Louis.

5

The Roxy and the Circuits

Jeanne and Lillian's negotiations with Fanchon and Marco paid off, and on March 28, 1934, Jeanne signed a contract with them to perform at the Paramount theatre in Los Angeles from April 5th to 12th and then in a theatre in San Francisco two days later, with a possible booking at the Roxy in New York. That day Jeanne wrote in her diary that she was "so happy to get away [she] burst out singing all day," followed the next day by the entry "We simply cant come back—Rather starve." After many tiring rehearsals and costume fittings from morning to early evening, Jeanne opened at the Paramount before an appreciative audience that included her mother, Aunt Lenore, and two performers from the cast of "Love Letters." After the short run of four shows a day in San Francisco, they returned to Pasadena, where they happily learned on April 23rd that Fanchon and Marco had successfully booked Jeanne in a show in Denver en route to an engagement as "Premiere Ballerina" at the Roxy, an honor which Jeanne later described in her May 2nd letter to her father as "a life long dream come true. So I'll have to be good."

After saying farewell to her friends at the Playhouse and the Junior Town Meeting, in late April and early May, after three-and-a-half-days of driving loaded with suitcases, they arrived in Denver for Jeanne's eight-night engagement at the Orpheum theatre. Since the mile-high altitude made it difficult to catch a breath, Jeanne was constantly tired while dancing in Denver. Performing four shows a day, Jeanne was featured on the bill with the famous vaudevillian Blossom Seeley, whom she described in her diary on May 4th as "just a middle aged woman." She also performed at the famous Brown Palace Club in Denver, since Marco was an investor in the property. Planning to leave Denver en route to New York on May 10th, Jeanne wrote her father: "When we leave here [Denver], I figured it would take eight days of hard driving, with no stoppages, because I'll need every minute I can get, to get in practice again, after jouncing over the plentiful miles of America." They arrived in New York exactly eight days later, had eggs and toast at Mrs. Bennett's, and rented a room at 51 West 69th Street.

Jeanne was billed "second in Newspaper ads at Roxy—Great," she wrote in her diary on May 24th. A review in the *New York Times*, May 26, 1934, described the bill for the Roxy. The feature motion picture was *Now I'll Tell*, starring Spencer Tracy, Helen Twelvetrees, and Alice Faye, and other films included Walt Disney's "Silly Symphony" called "Funny Little Bunnies," as well as a short film entitled "Sealing Wax." The five-act stage show offered the applauding audiences a Fanchon and Marco production called "The Fleet's In," featuring Jeanne Devereaux, Jack Pepper with his four stooges, the comedians Pettet and Douglas, the high wire Gretonas, musician Don Ford, singer, band leader, and emcee Wesley Eddy, and the Gae Foster dancers. The *Roxy Review* revealed the increased interest in motion pictures at this time and listed Jeanne in the program as "The Dancing Sweetheart." The reviewer in *Variety*, May 29, 1934, praised the Navy theme of the scenery and costumes for the Gae Foster dancers, including the battleship set "and all the trimmings," with a reception committee to welcome all the sailors. Headliner Jack Pepper's "high powered vaudeville" act was his "best ... to date." Jeanne made her entrance as emcee Wesley Eddy announced, "They say a sailor has a sweetheart in every port. But that's only a dream. Which reminds me of a very popular song, 'Why Do I Dream Those Dreams?'" Jeanne then performed "a toe dance very nicely, with Wesley Eddy singing the accompaniment." The audience didn't seem to mind "the double talk."

During the New York run at the Roxy Jeanne was invited by Wesley Eddy to take a Sunday afternoon ride with him in his new Packard motoring car. On May 17th she revealed in her diary that when she told him that she "didn't pet, smoke or drink— ... he didn't repeat his invitation." It was also during the run of "The Fleet's In" when Jeanne reunited with the vaudevillian ice skater Bob Lamb, whom she had met at age eleven when she was on the same bill with him and his ice skating parents. She experienced for the first time the thrill of falling in love. Jeanne and Bob met on May 16th after her last show of the night, and he came home with her to dine and visit until three o'clock in the morning. After he had left, Jeanne wrote in her diary that he was the "sweetest handsomest boy I've ever seen." Over the next few weeks he appeared backstage sometimes after the first show, or in between shows, or after the last show, and they would talk, or go to a restaurant, or just tour the historic sites of New York. Finally on June 6th Jeanne confessed in her diary that she might be in love: "Am I, the analytical, till now undaunted, in love? Bob is too good to be true—and as loveable as a young kitten or puppy. Bob White is crazy about him—he's just Irish enough for her. Well if I am, it's the first time."

Over the next two months Jeanne and Bob dated while she was in New York and developed an affectionate relationship despite his annoying smoking habit. They went to the free dances in Central Park, saw the shows at Radio City, and visited his family home on Long Island. Always "the analytical," Jeanne admitted in her diary on June 15th that although Bob was extremely handsome and has a "quick mind—worth developing," it is always a slow process of intellectual development "when people don't read." She was also concerned about linking her fate to someone in show business like Bob who lacked financial stability.

After the run at the Roxy while Jeanne had a weeklong booking in hot, steamy Philadelphia, Lillian wrote Bill on June 19th, reflecting on her recent cross-country drive: "It is not as difficult as I imagined to drive to and fro across the country, and aside from making 450 to 485 miles every day, I got to see the country-side all over again at the spring time. Fruit trees and Lilacs in bloom and in the Allegheny Mts. Of Penn, we found pansies and violets, so I let Jeanne out and she picked them for an HOUR. But with such a mileage record we didnt do much late rising, for it takes many hours every day to get that average." As Jeanne's companion and business manager, Lillian was always protective of the talent, who also happened to be her sole source of financial support, so it was her decision to "let Jeanne out" of the car. Picking the flowers that day was a special treat for Jeanne, since she had always noticed the natural landscape passing by—the beautiful flower blossoms and how the trees were bent and shaped and moved by the wind. Lillian ended her letter by saying that it "takes 'dough' to keep a car," so most vaudeville performers were taking the trains.

Always planning for the future, Lillian wrote: "We hope for some good booking here in New York before forming a vaudeville act to do Loews." Since returning to New York from Pasadena they had met many old friends from their show biz days, and they had both enjoyed "getting back to work again in earnest." However, they were in financial straits and needed to secure a booking right away. Mrs. Bennett generously arranged a credit for them at a nearby grocery store so they wouldn't starve. When Jeanne's agent Hal Sands decided to build an act around her, Jeanne was elated and signed a contract on the spot. She immediately set a strut dance to the music "Sweet Georgia Brown," and had the music arranged; Lillian rented a daring black lace costume from the Roxy, which she later purchased. For the rest of the year and half of 1935 Jeanne toured with a successful vaudeville act billed as "Jeanne Devereaux and Company," featuring Jeanne in a smart "flash" act—a high energy production number usually with multiple performers and scenery—with an adagio trio of two women and a man named Bob Foy and the solo boy tap dancer Jack Seymour—which toured the RKO circuit of movie presentation houses. The act ran sixteen minutes, so Jeanne had time between shows to catch her breath; she also eliminated singing from her "Sweet Georgia Brown" strut. After a tryout at the Gates theatre in Poughkeepsie, New York, the act opened at the Orpheum theatre in New York on August 3rd,

Jeanne Devereaux in a promotional photograph in a white feathery dress for a vaudeville tour, August 3, 1934–35. Jeanne toured with her successful act, including an adagio dance trio and solo boy tap dancer, billed as "Jeanne Devereaux and Company." In April 1935 the famous Mexican actress and comedian Lupe Vélez joined the tour as a headliner and befriended Jeanne. At Lupe's suggestion Jeanne wore fashionable bangs during most of the tour. Photograph by Bloom Chicago. Courtesy Jeanne Devereaux Perkins Collection.

and Jeanne was thrilled to see her name in lights on the theatre marquee once again. Bob Lamb and his parents saw the show and liked it immensely.

On August 11, 1934, Jeanne sent a postcard to her Grandmother Lane from Toronto, Canada, where she was dancing for a week at Shea's Hippodrome. This was the first time she had ever played in Canada and she wrote: "Act going great. The office is more than satisfied & my manager said we could work a year or two with it—Got a lovely write up in 'Variety.' So we are more than happy over it—Are thankful we don't have to bother with [pound sign] & shillings up here—But I do have to change the whole payroll into American money the last day—So back to N.Y.C. from here and play around there till the 31st when we open for Loew's tour."

When she returned to New York, Jeanne was so sick she could hardly breathe, but nevertheless performed five shows a day in a dirty and dreary theatre called the Tivoli in Brooklyn that she knew had affected her performance. On August 24th she opened at the Academy of Music in Brooklyn in five shows a day until midnight, lamenting in her diary the "strain" of "always working as if your life depended on it, and never knowing what show the bookers are out there." So despite the theatre's old composition stage floor and wanting to impress the bookers, she attempted her four fouettés with success, figuring that she could repeat this spectacular technical feat again if she gave her best effort and was successful. Jeanne confided in her diary two days later her emotional need for praise and affection from her stoic mother for having achieved this technical feat: "If Bob White would only kiss me or pet me at a time like that—just as recognition of a step up my private ladder." Amazingly Jeanne did "fours" again at the last show the following night.

After taking time to see Michel Fokine's touring ballet company at the Capitol theatre in New York, which Jeanne thought was unexceptional, she drove to one of the New York piers to perform at the Grand Hotel. Suffering from a bad cold, Jeanne gave five shows a day with only twenty minutes in between and was allowed by her agent Hal Sands to spend the nights recuperating at the hotel instead of commuting back to the city. During this engagement she saw Mae West for the first time. Jeanne and Lillian then drove to Scranton, Pennsylvania, where she was on a bill for three shows a day with the Mills Brothers while sweating away her miserable cold with hot baths, steaming lemonade, and quinine. When the act next played at Trenton, New Jersey, Jeanne wrote in her diary on September 14th how fun it was to play on a bill "with a pidgeon act." After returning to New York after the last show, she then danced in five shows a day at the Chester theatre, noting in her diary on September 15th how she'd "got 'em all going with that black dress." Now dating two new men, shopping, and again seeing the Fokine ballet at the Capitol theatre with her friend William Dollar in the cast, she commuted to Newark, New Jersey, for her booking, where she was thrilled to see her name again in lights. The act received a poor review from one of the local newspapers. Jeanne, having slipped on the floor during one of the second shows, on September 25th, after a prominent booker had come to see the show, wrote in her diary how she and her mother "battled" over the quality of her performance that day, with her mother saying it was "lousey just to be mean." Jeanne's next booking was back in New York at the Saint George theatre for two shows a day. During one of her performances the strap on her new white feather dress came undone and she executed a "whole dance holding it up."

She wrote in her diary on October 6th about having another battle with her mother over the incident: "She can be nastier about nothing than anyone living—I did a good show but she had to complain when she hadn't even seen it."

In New York and dating Bob, Jeanne was perplexed about how she felt about Bob and about their possible future together. While admiring his sweet disposition, cleanliness, honesty, and common sense, she could not determine how she felt about him, but knew that she wanted to help him "get a set of values & an appreciation of Books, Music, Art & Drama"—those aspects of her own life that defined her—concluding in her diary on October 7th that he was still "too young & flighty to really love." She attempted to end her romantic relationship with Bob and just be friends, but he refused. Keeping her suitors separate from one another, she was also dating a fellow trouper named Van, who a few days later proposed marriage to her, offering to pay off all her family debts and move her to his large stock farm in Nashville, Tennessee. At the same time she was fending off the romantic advances of her friend Will Fox. When Bob and his ice skating partner left for an engagement at the Wintergarden in St. Louis, Jeanne was pleased for him and also relieved. During the rest of her tour she enjoyed the letters she received from Bob, Will, and sometimes her Pasadena friend Tom Perkins.

After days of rehearsal, Jeanne and Lillian packed up their car with the scenery for the act in the rumble seat and left for Hershey, Pennsylvania. There in an attractive theatre she wrote in her diary on October 30th that she performed "marvelous shows— Real turns of all kinds." On her birthday the following day the kids in the act gave her a book of poems. Jeanne and Lillian drove all night back to New York, eagerly anticipating Jeanne's engagement at the Loew's State: "Lowe's State next week Whee! Whee!" Jeanne wrote in her diary on October 2nd. Before Lowe's, however, she played at the Paradise theatre, where she had almost perfect performances. Learning that the impresario George White was creating a new show in New York, Jeanne especially wanted him to see her at Lowe's State, since she was currently doing her "best work [and] finished finale [at the Paradise] with 12 pirouettes & continuous fours for Pullins," she wrote in her diary on November 3rd.

For her engagement at Loew's State Jeanne worked on new dances and a new orchestration for her strut. In an advertisement in *Loew's Weekly* for the week starting November 6th the vaudeville bill featured Jeanne Devereaux and Company in "On with the Dance" at the Loew's State Theatre at Broadway and 45th Street; the movie was *British Agent*, starring Kay Francis and Leslie Howard. Jeanne wrote in her diary on November 9th that opening night had been a "madhouse." The writer of a detailed column about special stage costumes in "Among the Women" in *Variety*, November 13, 1934, singled out Jeanne for her recent performance at Loew's State: "Jeanne Devereaux for her first solo number was daringly dressed in a black lace with no lining. Then she donned a feathery gown of white." Despite later protestations that she never wore provocative clothing, Jeanne dazzled her audiences with gorgeous but sometimes suggestive costumes. This particular daring sheer dress was often mentioned in subsequent reviews of the show.

Loew's State was followed by a three-day layoff in New York, a fortuitous hiatus since Jeanne and Lillian had received a telegram from Bill that he was in the city on a business trip. They enjoyed a rare family reunion, shopping, seeing a show at Radio

City, and touring the city before Jeanne and Lillian left for her booking in Philadelphia and Bill went to his company's factory in Jamestown and home to St. Louis. With no future bookings Jeanne was forced to draw on future earnings since the kids in the act were broke, in order to put some money in everyone's pocket for the Christmas holidays. For the next week they saw plays, shows, and films and hoped to go on a vaudeville tour to Africa that would allow them to pay off their family debts. Jeanne only had a booking for a low salary in a barn-like theatre in Richmond Hill. To her chagrin the kids were continuously threatening to quit and move on to other shows. When she returned to New York she had a showdown with her agent Hal Sands over whether or not the kids in the act were leaving for Europe.

With no bookings on the horizon, little money, and cold weather, New York was not a hospitable home during the holidays; however, as Jeanne wrote in her diary on December 15th, she would rather be poor in New York than dependent on her grandparents in Pasadena. She had enough money to practice at a studio and buy a few Christmas presents for the kids in the act; in return they gave Jeanne and Lillian some coveted books and drawing pencils. On December 20th they drove to Washington, D.C., for her booking at the Capitol theatre, arriving for the early rehearsal call the following morning. Jeanne wrote in her diary on December 21st how she almost passed out after the first show that afternoon and how "hungry and overtaxed" she had been performing in four shows a day for almost a year. On Christmas day after the first show at 3:30 p.m. the theatre management invited the entire cast to dinner at the historic Willard Hotel. They slept off the festive drink and food in between the next shows.

Touring with her vaudeville act in 1934 had been a hard year of travel and multiple daily performances that continued into the early months of 1935. "Headlining all over the place," wrote Jeanne in her diary on December 31st. As the act left for a one-night stand in Pottsville, Pennsylvania, there was snow everywhere, and they were flat broke. Pottsville was followed by Shenandoah on New Year's eve and finally Hazelton, where after the first show their fate was in the hands of the local people who called the manager to tell him what acts they had liked: "We got the votes—Hurrah," wrote Jeanne in her diary on January 1, 1935. From Hazelton they drove in bad winter weather for more one night stands in Philadelphia and at the Stanley theatre in Camden, New Jersey, followed by a short layoff in New York, where she shopped and straightened out the act's salary troubles with her agent Hal Sands. Jeanne left by car for Boston on January 10th, and attended an early rehearsal the next morning where the manager, who had known her at the Warfield theatre in San Francisco, complimented her on her lovely act. Her muscles exhausted from the rigorous performance schedule, Jeanne was elated that as a dancer she was not allowed to perform in Boston on Sunday; the kids, however, were not considered dancers but acrobats and had to perform an adagio.

After Boston they drove in the snowy evening to Providence, Rhode Island, for a weeklong engagement at $450 a week. Again rebelling against her mother's authoritarian demeanor, Jeanne reflected in her diary on January 22nd how harsh her mother could be when it came to the quality of her dancing: "Bitter Battle with Bob White. I don't know why we hate each other so—A few moments of gay comedies, enjoyment while talking Philosophy or Politics, and hatred during my work." Her livelihood totally dependent on Jeanne's earnings, Lillian had assumed the role of mentor, critic, and motivator to ensure that Jeanne's dancing was of the high quality demanded by the bookers. Four days later, with her mother still in mind, Jeanne wrote for the first time in her diary that she and her mother needed a vacation from one another every few months, since "nothing is so tiresome or ruinous to ones disposition as continuous association with a person for years without end." They were continuously in each other's company and rarely spent a day apart.

The snow was so deep that roads were closed to New York, so the cast took a train to Jamaica in Queens for their weeklong booking and then on to Bridgeport, Connecticut, and back to New York. Driving at night on roads like frozen glass to Detroit, Michigan, they opened for five shows a day in a presentation stage show before a wonderful audience, with a magician, some ice skaters, and a boxer on the bill. Exhausted, Jeanne's leg muscles ached: "A massure rubbed my legs until they felt like they belonged to me," wrote Jeanne in her diary on February 8th. Irritated by her mother's controlling hand, Jeanne confessed in her diary on February 13th that they needed to "keep out of each others way for a few days," for she was going "crazy having to tell Bob White where I'm going if I just step into the hall—I hate being ruled every minute all day long." She was also irritated again by the petulant youngsters in the act: "With the kids threatening to leave the act it again leaves us with nothing to do this spring & will only have about $325.00 saved out of a hard year!" Jeanne wrote in her diary on February 19th.

From Detroit the act went to a theatre in Peoria, Illinois, that had a terrible stage and tiny, unattractive dressing rooms. A week later when they arrived in Chicago for their four shows a day booking, Bill surprised them after rehearsal, and the family reunited for two days until Jeanne and Lillian left for a one night stand in nearly Joliet. They returned to Chicago for another engagement of four weekday shows and five grind ones on Saturday, followed by a quick train jump to Saverans Cabaret in Buffalo, New York. Back in Chicago in early March Jeanne was on the bill again with her good friends The Three Swifts. She had occasional suitors when on the road, but when window shopping alone on Chicago's fashionable boulevards, Jeanne missed having friends, especially boyfriends, with whom she could share her itinerant life. "I'm so lonely with never any one to enthuse over things with," she lamented in her diary on March 19th. Her loneliness was mitigated by the thrill of stopping the show with her artistry: she wrote on March 24th that she had "stopped it cold" at her last show in Chicago that week.

Her next engagement was in Minneapolis–St. Paul, Minnesota, where she performed on a bill with the famous actress and comedian Lupe Vélez, later known as the "Mexican Spitfire," for a series of movies of the same name that she made from 1939 to 1943. Already a theatre star in Mexico, Lupe—petite, beautiful, charismatic, temperamental, and sexually liberated—arrived in Hollywood from Mexico in 1925 at age seventeen and took Hollywood by storm. She became famous for her singing, dancing, and acting talent, as well as for her affair with the handsome actor Gary Cooper and her tempestuous marriage and divorce in the 1930s to Olympic swimmer and star of the *Tarzan* movies Johnny Weissmuller. Jeanne had worked with Weissmuller in the show "Dive In" on a Loew's vaudeville tour in 1931, and was surprised to learn that Weissmuller had married the "Mexican Spitfire" Lupe Vélez. Throughout her famed career Lupe never forgot her roots in theatre and continued to perform in stage shows and went on vaudeville tours. Film historian Michelle Vogel in her definitive biography *Lupe*

Vélez: The Life and Career of Hollywood's "Mexican Spitfire" describes Lupe's big heart and generosity to her fellow troupers from the headlining stars to the lowest chorus girls: "Whether it was a stranger on the street, her servants or her cast and crew, rich or poor, Lupe treated everyone as equals," wrote Vogel. "One crew member said, 'She had a gift for making people feel free, themselves, and that she was one of them. There never was that 'queen' atmosphere about her.'"[1] Lupe, however, was also prone to manic depression and Catholic guilt and committed suicide in December 1944.

A reviewer of the show at the Orpheum Theatre in St. Paul, Minnesota, in *Variety*, April 10, 1935, effusively praised the headliner Lupe Vélez, saying, "Hollywood's Hot Tamale ... has plenty on the ball here," and was ecstatic about "Jeanne Devereaux and Company," who performed as a headliner in the top spot on the bill next to closing: "A class dance turn of three gals and two boys," wrote the reviewer. "One of the latter, working with two girls, does some unusual trick stuff, while Miss Devereaux does a few outstanding solo turns. In one of which she's clothed in a sheer net costume. Then came Lupe for a sock windup." Only a few lines at the end of the review were devoted to the film. In her scrapbook Jeanne posted a 1935 review of the show at RKO's Orpheum theatre in New York praising Lupe's impersonations and the dancers: "The next ranking act on the bill is the Jeanne Devereaux company, a group of five dancers. Miss Devereaux is an excellent toe dancer and three of her colleagues do adagio dancing, one tap dancing. The lad who does the tap routine is fine. In the adagio unit there are two girls to be hurled about, only one man to do the catching. This is a new note for adagio followers." Another untitled newspaper review praised Jeanne's classy company, her innovative choreography, and her ability to please the audience: "Jeanne Devereaux, whose name heads the act, is a toe dancer of special merit. She does two numbers, one as a hotcha gal to the melody of 'Sweet Georgia Brown,' sung by one of her supporting dancers. In this one she wears a very daring net costume. Other number leading up to the finale features a lot of clever spiraling on the toes."

During the run in Minneapolis–St. Paul Jeanne and Lupe developed a close friendship, with manic Lupe assuming the role of Jeanne's big sister. Since Jeanne was performing next to closing with Lupe last on the bill, she often announced Lupe's act. Lupe advised Jeanne to return to Pasadena to have her nose fixed by Dr. Ginsberg, and she was willing to pay for it. She insisted that Jeanne wear fashionable bangs, which Jeanne did for most of the run. Lupe also told Jeanne to add to her repertoire by choreographing a Mexican hat toe dance. Lupe would even sing her favorite Andalusian songs for her new friend. On Sundays and evenings after the last show they would eat chop suey and ice cream together and laugh hilariously; during the day they watched movies. Jeanne believed that her friendship with Lupe positively affected the quality of her performances. "I've really enjoyed knowing Lupe—she's so confident that if one hangs on long enough & works hard the breaks will come—She has taught me many things I'm grateful for and her poise on stage is superb—I've been doing swell shows," wrote Jeanne in her diary on April 4th. When they were riding together on the train to Chicago and sat up all night talking, Jeanne learned the true story of Lupe and Johnny Weissmuller's fiery romance and marriage. "What a life she has had and what an actress," wrote Jeanne on April 7th. "I almost cried when she told of her mother and herself almost starving" after the Mexican Revolution when her family had lost their fortune.

When Jeanne and Lillian arrived in Chicago for a ten-day layoff, they ran into Bob Lamb and his parents, who were performing in an Ice Carnival at a nearby stadium. "Poor Bobby, when will he find himself—He's so unhappy and unaware of it," Jeanne wrote in her diary on April 10th. They were unable to see Bob's performance at the ice stadium, but attended a party in his room the next day. Jeanne was in angst over Bob, deliberating whether to end their romantic relationship or to wait until he had a stable job; her angst disappeared when Bob and his parents soon left Chicago for New York without saying farewell: "It hurt me deeply besides being terribly rude," wrote Jeanne in her diary on April 15th. After a one-night stand of four shows in nearby Waukegan, Illinois, to earn some money during the layoff, they returned late at night to Chicago in a fierce windstorm. Their next booking over the Easter weekend was in Cleveland with the best band that Jeanne had ever performed with on stage. The kids in the act were still threatening to quit after the last show in Cleveland, with the trio even refusing to perform after the intermission. Lupe was furious with the unprofessional behavior of the two women in Jeanne's act, and went "on a rampage over the brats—wants to have them trailed by detectives & caught with men," wrote Jeanne in her diary on April 20th. "She's a hornets nest when she gets it in for someone & she certainly hates Maurine & Vera."

When Jeanne and Lupe visited the astrologers on the bill to get their forecasts, Lupe was told that she had a big decision to make. Later that afternoon Lupe received a telegram from London offering her a role in the musical *Anything Goes*, a revival of the Broadway show the year before with madcap antics and lyrics by Cole Porter, at £350 a week. On their last day together before Lupe left for London they ate chop suey, frog legs, and fried rice and said their sad farewells. Jeanne and Lillian then drove all night to their next booking, missing the first show because one of the kids had failed to get their trunk on the last train out. A few days later Jeanne reflected in her diary on the many things that Lupe had taught her over the past months, and how much she hoped to see her special friend again that year.

In early May Jeanne and Lillian drove all night in pounding rain and over terrible roads for Jeanne's booking in Philadelphia. Jeanne was so exhausted by lack of sleep and the intense summer heat that she could barely make it through her four shows. A week later they arrived in New York for her engagement at the famous Palace Theatre on Broadway at the end of the vaudeville season, and within days they had seen everyone they knew in New York. Jeanne's thrill of playing at the Palace was lessened by her exhaustion and the slanting raked stage that was difficult for toe dancers. New York's Palace Theatre had switched to a film only format in November 1932, but reverted back to a combination of film with a few vaudeville acts between April 1933 and September 1935. Agents, bookers, and impresarios attended the shows to assess the talent. Jeanne said that when George Black, the legendary British theatre manager and impresario who owned and managed the London Palladium, saw her perform on the famous Palace stage in May 1935, he said, "I'm going to have that girl in my next show." Bob Lamb and his parents had also seen her dazzling show at the Palace. Jeanne forgave his earlier rudeness, and was happy when he visited her in her dressing room between shows until it closed on May 23rd.

Jeanne's next booking was on New York's big stage at the Albee theatre, its last show for the season. She was still with the kids in the act, but contemplating working solo with only a pianist on stage after their inevitable departure. Again Bob visited her between shows, and Jeanne wrote in her diary on May 25th that he was "his old self again charming and fun—I can't make him out—Except he cant stand not having any money—But then who can." Later that year she mentioned that money was a big factor in their relationship, for Bob was definitely not ready for marriage until he had a steady income. After the Albee theatre closed for the summer, Jeanne and Lillian drove back to Boston hot and tired, with Jeanne attending to her aching feet that soon must endure breaking in new toe shoes.

George Black most likely had seen Jeanne perform at the Palace theatre, and impressed by her amazing talent, offered her a contract to perform at his London Palladium in England. She mentioned in her diary on May 22nd that she had given the contract for London to her agent Hal Sands "to look over." Jeanne remembered that when she had been on the bill with Lupe Vélez the year before and had confided in her famous friend that she might have an offer to perform in Europe, Lupe advised her to "do it. You'll have a wonderful time and get to visit interesting places and see historic sites." While in Boston she received a call from Dick Henry, George Black's assistant, saying that he must have her signed contract in hand by June 7th when he was scheduled to sail on the *Normandie* to England. Within days they drove all night to New York through a thick fog to the pier just in time to sign the contract and have it delivered to Henry before he embarked, and then dash to Jeanne's rehearsal at the Orpheum theatre. "Excitement—Tingling with it—I signed the contracts & they were rushed to the 'Normandie' to Dick Henry—I was late for rehearsal but after very nonchalantly signing the papers nothing else seemed quite real," wrote Jeanne in her diary on June 7th. From this moment on Jeanne was focused on preparing her dances, costumes, and music for the London engagement, as well as obtaining their passports, earning enough money to purchase their steamship tickets, and managing all the other logistics for her first transatlantic trip. Most importantly, she still needed bookings to pay for the trip.

After her engagement at the Orpheum theatre, where she endured the continued bad behavior of the kids in her act, Jeanne performed at the smaller Boulevard theatre, with the last show of the night at 12:50 a.m. She was dating Bob as well as other pursuing suitors, but was unsatisfied: "I want companionship & company—but everyone wants to make love to me," wrote Jeanne on June 16th. She was still not ready for love even though sometimes she thought she was in love with Bob despite his immaturity, lack of intellectual curiosity, and constant worry about money. When Jeanne learned that she had the option to pay for the steamship tickets to London on an installment plan, she quickly asked her agent Hal Sands to sign the plan for them. She was also working in the rehearsal hall on two new dances for the London engagement—"The Lady in Red" rumba with its tricky rhythms and the "Acceleration Waltz" to the music of Strauss—but she still had no costumes. Desperately needing to earn money for the steamship tickets, she performed at the Fox theatre in Brooklyn, where she was assigned a hot, stifling dressing room and a mistaken billing that infuriated her. On July 3rd she wrote that it "is getting to be a nightmare" trying to earn enough money to purchase the steamship tickets, rehearse the new dances, get the costumes made, and washing and pack their clothes. Jeanne and Lillian were also working on obtaining a loan with

Jeanne Devereaux in a promotional photograph in an arabesque pose holding a bouquet of roses, New York, July 1935. A similar photograph taken at the same time was used in the Souvenir Program for Jeanne's Royal Command performance at the London Palladium in 1935, published as a supplement in various trade journals. Photograph by Murray Korman, a famous New York "glamour" photographer of beautiful women celebrities. Courtesy Jeanne Devereaux Perkins Collection.

Hal Sands' help to purchase the steamship tickets outright. In the midst of all the travel preparations, they left for Jeanne's two-day booking in Poughkeepsie, New York, where during a performance her toe shoe split open causing her to suffer through six shows.

Back in New York Jeanne and Lillian made the final preparations for their departure. Jeanne received the musical arrangements for her two new dances and had fittings for the exotic red velvet gown with matching hat for "The Lady in Red" made by Ida Belle, a talented New York seamstress. They also continued negotiating for the loan to purchase the steamship tickets. Jeanne practiced diligently every morning, hoping to "get inspiration for a real knock out routine" with the rumba number, she wrote in her diary on July 12th. She dated her favorite young men, and then said farewell to her New York friends. Her father arrived in New York a week before their departure, and accompanied her to Murray Korman's studio where she had some promotional photographs taken before leaving for London. When Korman photographed her in her new red dress, "Dad took offence at Murray … calling me Darling—it was really amusing to see him bristle," wrote Jeanne on July 20th. They went as a family to the Bennetts for what Jeanne considered their last Sunday dinner in America. When she received the proofs of herself in the red dress from Korman, she was unable to decide which ones were her favorites, for they had all turned out so well. Since Bob Lamb had a booking at an ice rink in St. Louis, he was planning to ride there with Bill in Jeanne and Lillian's Chevy. Jeanne was not devastated by her imminent separation from Bob, reflecting in her diary on July 24th that although she probably loved him, she "could never be happy with him." After having toured her vaudeville act with the kids for almost a year, she was relieved and excited to take her solo act across the Atlantic and perform before thousands on the big stage at the London Palladium.

6

The London Palladium

The London Palladium was the flagship of British music halls that offered variety entertainment. Unlike the Americans, the British had not embraced the French term "vaudeville," but used the original term "variety" to describe live stage shows. Many vaudevillians compared playing at the London Palladium to playing at the Palace Theatre in New York—the absolute top. With American vaudeville in decline and only the Loews State and Radio City Hall in New York offering live stage shows along with their films, Jeanne's decision to perform in England was fortuitous. Lillian later wrote Bill from London on September 26, 1935, that one of Jeanne's agents Hal Sands had promised upon her return to America that he would book her in South America and "from there we can go to Australia and keep ourselves from starving to death if vaudeville is still 'On the Fritz' in U.S. as he says it is, right now. He says he is thankful we are over here, and working, as he has never known it to be so bad in U.S." As Jeanne's business manager, Lillian wanted Jeanne to perform in Europe long enough so they could pay back the loans from her parents and her sisters that they had been forced to take while living in Pasadena, and then save a few thousand dollars for security. "Then I'll be happy," she wrote Bill. "After that we can rest in our minds and relax a little."

Because scantily clothed and nude showgirls were more prominent in the European variety houses, Jeanne made certain that the Foster Agency in London included in her original contract with Black's General Theatre Corporation, Ltd., that she would not be required to do any nude dancing. Also the management was to furnish her with all her costumes except for the two to be used in her specialty dances. Her contract was for a six-week engagement for the sum of fifty pounds per week, of which she would pay the Foster Agency 10 percent. In addition, she would appear throughout the run as required by management and would attend rehearsals at 11:00 a.m. without pay every day of the week prior to opening as required during the engagement, as well as agree that comedians and singers in the program could make appearances in her act. Management would also have the option to the engagement indefinitely upon the same terms and conditions. The show had a long run, closing on March 7, 1936. During her run at the Palladium Jeanne also performed in London benefits for many worthy causes.[1]

Living in the age of luxurious, transatlantic ocean liners, Jeanne and her mother sailed on the RMS *Berengaria* for London on July 26, 1935. She hoped to follow in the footsteps of the American vaudeville star Josephine Baker, who exactly ten years earlier had sailed on this same ship for Paris, where she became an overnight sensation. Like other luxury ocean liners, the *Berengaria* included hotel quality staterooms, multiple dining rooms, a Ritz Carlton restaurant, a grill room, tea garden, veranda café, a palm garden, a ballroom, and a gymnasium with baths. To maintain her fitness, Jeanne practiced every day in the gym and swam in the luxuriant pool. As with other entertainers, she was often asked to give benefit performances on board the ships.

The day Jeanne and Lillian embarked for England was also a happy family reunion. Both Bill and their good friends the Bennetts came to the dock to see them off, and they were all allowed to go on board the immense *Berengaria.* According to Kay Bennett Paul, Jeanne looked very beautiful that day, dressed fashionably in a white skirt, brown jacket, and brown felt hat, and everyone was excited. On July 14, 1935, Bill had humorously written that "responsibilities" in St. Louis—such as "paying Mr. YMCA"—might prevent his traveling to "your burg." He admitted that there was nothing he would rather do, however, than "'kiss you on the dock,'" and that is apparently what he was able to do, leaving a few days later via Greyhound bus for New York. Her father stood on the pier saying good-by and waving a white handkerchief as the *Berengaria* put out to sea. Jeanne later wrote on August 2nd that she and her mother "hated to see the beloved top of your head disappear as the ship passed the end of the pier, but we kept sight of your handkerchief waving in your own inimitable manner till the last minute."

Hard pressed for money, Bill had sacrificed to come to New York to bid his darlings "Bon Voyage," and Jeanne later wrote from London that she hoped he was well and the trip to New York had not been too expensive for him. They left their old Chevrolet touring car with Bill. When Lillian wrote from London on September 26th, she mentioned how glad she was that Bill had the Chevy: "I can just see it all

Jeanne Devereaux on the steamship *Berengaria* in New York harbor embarking for London on July 26, 1935. Her father along with her first New York friends the Bennett family bade Jeanne and her mother farewell aboard the ship. Mrs. Bennett's granddaughter, Ginger Paul, remembered in an interview her mother saying how attractive and fashionably dressed Jeanne was that day. Courtesy Jeanne Devereaux Perkins Collection.

shined up in my minds eye. Its like having charge of a baby or a young child, something to do for it all the time. I hope you are getting in some nice outings on Sundays with it, and I know just how pretty the hills of Missouri can be in the fall."

Jeanne's first transatlantic voyage took six days on this fast ship, losing an hour and becoming colder each day. Jeanne waited until the boat docked in Southampton at mid-night on August 1st to write her father about the trip: "Most people have been writing their friends and relatives all day long in the writing rooms and haven't had the time to dance, swim, play ping-pong or look at the ocean," she wrote. "Therefore they might as well [have] stayed home. However I thought it wiser to wait until the trip was over, so that I could make a complete report." On board Jeanne and Lillian met some old acquaintances and new people, including famous industrialists and actors traveling in first class, such as financier Andrew Mellon and actor Leslie Howard and his family.

She spent her days and nights enjoying the ship's amenities, writing how she "went in the pool two mornings, danced at night, and walked miles on the deck with the usual ship board acquaintances." "Suave Englishmen" flirted with her, inviting her to events in first class and afterwards for drinks in the Captain's quarters, which she later returned to after her benefit concert for the sailors' charitable fund. "Lemonade for me," abstemious Jeanne wrote. Except for the first night, the "sea has been as calm as a lake, all the way across." She told her father that her agent, Hal Sands, had "sent a grand box of fruit, candy and nuts, jam, and preserves, or rather a steamer basket, that was

Jeanne Devereaux and her father Bill Helman on the steamship *Berengaria* in New York harbor embarking for London on July 26, 1935. She did not see her father again for two years. Courtesy Jeanne Devereaux Perkins Collection.

a work-of-art"; Aunt Lenore and the Bennetts had also sent gift boxes to the ship that made the glamour of the trip complete. Jeanne had forgotten her coat in New York at the Century Hotel, and asked her father to write them to confirm that he had had the Hotel send it to the Foster Agency in London; in a later letter she thanked him for sending the coat.

Jeanne's appearance as a prima ballerina in London propelled her dancing career to new heights. The London Palladium on Little Argyll Street, designed by the noted architect Frank Matcham and built in 1910 on the site of Hengler's circus, was the venue chosen by George Black for his variety show "Round About Regent Street," the most lavish show ever staged at a music hall at that time. It was created, directed, and produced by George Black with the assistance of Charles Henry and with choreography by the famous British ballet dancer Frederick Ashton. George Balanchine and Ashton were the two great classical choreographers of the twentieth century. In 1935 Ashton joined Ninette de Valois' Vic-Wells Ballet Company, which became The Sadler's Wells Ballet, and eventually in 1946 The Royal Ballet Company, where he stayed for thirty-five years, becoming the Artistic Director from 1963 until his retirement in 1970. Ashton, in a 1973 interview with his biographer David Vaughan, said it was a "marvelous" experience to work with George Black, an impresario who "knew exactly what he wanted" and never deviated from his "initial plan."[2]

Born into a show business family, George Black had managed and sold two cinema show house companies before 1929, when he decided to revive live variety entertainment in Great Britain by restoring the run-down music halls, which were then only showing films, back to their palatial splendor and popularity. As the head of Moss Empires Ltd., George Black produced not only spectacular variety shows at the London Palladium, but also those in the suburban Hippodrome and Empire theatre chains. At this time Black's mission was to rescue the variety palaces from the dominance of the film industry by producing spectacular shows with large casts and elaborate scenery, blending the acts with thematic consistency and ending with a crowd-pleasing finale featuring the entire cast filling the vast stage. While his productions

Jeanne Devereaux, promotional headshot for the variety show "Round About Regent Street" at the London Palladium, 1935. The show ran from August 27, 1935, until its closing on May 7, 1936. The British impresario George Black had seen Jeanne perform at the flagship Palace Theatre on Broadway in May 1935, and then hired her to perform at the London Palladium. Photograph by Landseer of Regent Street, London. Courtesy Jeanne Devereaux Perkins Collection.

shared many characteristics with the revue, they were more like old-time variety or big-time vaudeville shows with a theme organizing the specialty acts.

During the 1930s, the London Palladium was the home of "The Crazy Gang," a popular group of British comedians and singers including Bud Flanagan and Chesney Allen, Jimmy Nervo and Teddy Knox, and Charlie Naughton and Jimmy Gold, all of whom performed with Jeanne in "Round About Regent Street." When George Black died in 1945, Black's show "Happy and Glorious," starring Tommy Tinder, was still playing, and had the longest run ever at the London Palladium. Despite Black's legendary efforts, as well as the work of his successor Val Parnell who had been the booking agent in the late 1930s when Jeanne was there, music hall variety entertainment was eventually subsumed by film and television.

In an article in *The Performer*, October 31, 1935, titled "Mr. George Black Explains: Importation of American Acts," Black described how he had been forced to hire American vaudeville stars like Jeanne because the "British market cannot answer the demand"; without American stars "it would be impossible to carry on Variety on its present scale in this country." Instead of putting British performers out of work, as some critics have argued, "the presence of these stars from abroad creates employment for native talent. They enable Variety to be presented at houses which otherwise would be forced, because of the lack of 'top-of-the-bill' novelties, to become cinematic." Nevertheless, British resentment persisted: Jeanne kept a newspaper picture of "Round About Regent Street" with the names of many of the American cast members, including Jeanne's, left out of the caption.

The day after Jeanne had arrived in London she encountered George Black in his office at the Palladium, and excitedly told him about the two dances she had recently choreographed—"The Lady in Red" and "Acceleration," the former based on a song with the same title that had been featured in the 1935 movie *In Caliente*, starring Dolores Del Rio and Edward Everett Horton, that had popularized a new American dance craze called the rumba. She had brought with her the phonograph record of the music and a full orchestra arrangement for sixty-five musicians; she had also brought her stunning costume, which consisted of a long, clinging dress of red silk velvet lined with cloth of gold, flesh colored net from her wrist to her elbow with one-inch bands of sequins in different colors designed to look like bracelets, a matching red hat, and red satin toe shoes. Jeanne remembered exactly how she had choreographed this special dance: "That year mother and I were in our room at the Belvedere Hotel in New York listening to the radio one morning when we heard 'The Lady in Red' rumba," she said. "We looked at each other and I said, 'Wouldn't that be a great number!' And I immediately proceeded to plan the music, the choreography, and the costume." Black informed her that he had already chosen her solo dance for his show, called "The Moth and the Flame," in which he had already invested more than a thousand dollars in obtaining the rights to the act from the American producer Michael Todd, as well as providing a spectacular set and expensive costumes. The act had been performed in America and was a great crowd pleaser. "Ye Gods! Everything we had set is out—What a headache," Jeanne wrote in her diary on August 3rd.

"Round About Regent Street" was in preview during a two-week run performed twice nightly beginning on August 12, 1935, at Brighton's Hippodrome, where Jeanne danced in Part One "A Flower Market" and "Buy My Cherries," in Part Two her daring "The Moth and the Flame dance," and in the grand finale. Residing at Harrison's hotel on King's Road in Brighton for the run, Jeanne and Lillian were looking forward to moving into their apartment in London at the Mount Royal (now the Thistle Marble Arch), the first hotel in London with rooms with private baths, where they had a kitchenette, modern plumbing for a proper bath, and an iron to press their clothes in their own space. On opening night Jeanne received a congratulatory cable from her agent Hal Sands, and wrote to her father two days later on August 14th that she "felt yours by mental telepathy. Righto?" and that the "show is beautiful and is going beautifully." Recalling Bill's offbeat sense of humor, Jeanne wrote on April 19th: "There is a scene in the show I know you would like ... —Prehistoric Regent St. All Cave Men and women, and the pay-off is a dinosaur race over the high cliff in the background. Then they bring in the winner ridden by a dwarf in Baboon suit, its very funny."

The popular seaside resort of Brighton charmed Jeanne and Lillian, who ate more fish there than during the rest of their lives. On Sunday, their one day off, Jeanne wrote her father that they "walked miles along the ocean and little twisted streets," and Lillian bravely sampled the local jellied eels. Despite Jeanne's disclaimer that the moth dance was safe and her tendency to downplay any injuries, she admitted to her father, "I got burned rather painfully once on my leg below the calf. When one of the wings dropped against it while on fire. The moth is a number when the properties work right," she wrote. Earlier she had written in her diary how during rehearsals in London she had the hair singed off her legs, and in Brighton the asbestos flame costume still was not working properly. She had been slightly burned during the second show of the second night. On August 15th she wrote in her diary that "every inch of me is cut—burned—battered." However, for the rest of the tryout in Brighton the wings burned beautifully, and she was performing great shows for appreciative audiences. In an interview with his biographer the only fact that Frederick Ashton remembered about "The Moth and the Flame"—what he called a "terrible" dance because it was so dangerous—is that Jeanne "used to get burnt when performing."[3]

Three members of the London City Council's (LCC) Fire Committee had attended one of the afternoon tryout performances at Brighton, and then reported back to the LCC's Entertainment Committee, who recommended that the LCC ban Jeanne's act. Apparently the LCC had not been censoring music hall variety performances for a long time, so the banning of Jeanne's dance was sensational news. Although the members who saw Jeanne perform agreed that she had exceptional skill and grace and her dance was thrilling, the LCC deemed that the dance was physically dangerous and possibly apt to incite crowd panic. The extensive publicity throughout England about the show's cancellation fired imaginations, causing a media uproar that was printed in newspapers all over Europe and America.

When Jeanne had danced this daring number in Brighton's Hippodrome without any major problems, it had been approved by the Brighton Fire Committee and had been a smash hit every night. The stunning set consisted of a large, open book with the corps de ballet dressed as colorful butterflies lounging on the pages. Costumed in a tan asbestos leotard, Jeanne entered an open window behind the book, danced down its spine, and then spied the flaming candle. According to an article entitled "The Banned

Dance: L.C.C. and Palladium's New Production" in *The Performer*, August 29, 1935, the dance was creative and daring:

> In the "banned" ballet, Jeanne Devereaux, dressed as a moth, comes in through an open window and flutters around a giant lighted candle; as she gets closer and closer to the flame her wings [made of magician's flash paper] catch fire and are burned off. She is clothed in an asbestos tunic and helmet which protect her completely. There is a momentary black-out, during which she strips off the asbestos clothing and emerges in skin tight fleshings. The dance is then brought to a finish with her posturings as a dying moth.

"I remembered Anna Pavlova's 'dying swan' in the production I saw in St. Louis when I was seven," Jeanne later said, "and I choreographed my little moth to die like Pavlova's elegant swan." When the dance was finished, she put on a robe negligee over her fleshlings and fitted leotard to take her stage bow. Jeanne's act was obviously a big success, for a review in *Variety* for August 29, 1935, praised the dance's artistic qualities: "The dying moth may impart to the beholder some such exalting sense of pity as was imparted

Jeanne Devereaux in an asbestos costume performing the daring and dangerous "The Moth and the Flame" dance for the tryout of the variety show "Round About Regent Street" at the Hippodrome Theatre, Brighton, England, August 1935. George Black, the impresario of the London Palladium, had purchased the rights to this sensational dance from the New York producer Michael Todd. The dance was later banned by the London City Council's Entertainment Committee for potentially inciting crowd panic, and replaced with Jeanne's "The Lady in Red" rumba dance. Courtesy Jeanne Devereaux Perkins Collection.

by Pavlova's dying swan of immortal memory. Condolences, therefore, to Miss Jeanne Devereaux. The London public would appear to have missed a treat."

In a letter to Jeanne dated August 26, 1935, a fan made a suggestion regarding her recently banned "Moth and Flame" dance: "Would it not be possible to have a red 'devil' inside the candle, representing the flame? The Moth would flutter about the candle, while the Fire-devil leaned out snatching at the wings—finally, as the Moth ventures too close, ripping them triumphantly off. Naturally it would not be nearly so spectacular, but it could be made quite effective." In her scrapbook Jeanne had a rare copy of the advance program for "Round About Regent Street" with an advertisement including pictures for "The Moth and the Flame" dance. In a handwritten note on the page featuring the famous African American dance team called the Four Flash Devils, Chas Gill, one of the devils, wrote on September 11, 1935: "To Jeanne—America sent you as her representative and you really upheld her. A wonderful little Moth who lost her flame."

George Black considered the censorship unjustified and unfair, especially since the LCC's Entertainment Committee had made their decision only three days before the London premiere. He was despondent, for he had invested a large sum of money and his own enormous passion in this popular dance number. He immediately sent Jeanne and her mother to their London apartment to fetch the phonograph machine, the record, musical arrangement, and costume for the "Lady in Red" rumba, and during tea-time when the cast was on a break, he auditioned Jeanne and hired her new act. After informing Jeanne that he and his wife had seen the rumba on a trip to Havana, Cuba the previous summer, he quickly commissioned new "Havana" style sets for the London premiere. During rehearsals in Brighton Jeanne insisted that no comedians or singers would appear in her rumba scene, which featured her famous pirouettes and fouettés. The rehearsals were exhausting. When she returned to London and needed to continue rehearsing the new act on the Palladium's slanting raked stage, the ceiling of this renowned, old theatre crashed down the day before opening night, forcing George Black to work his magic to keep the newspaper media from seeing the wreckage.

"Round About Regent Street" successfully opened in London on August 27th to rave reviews. The elaborate show consisted of nineteen acts referred to in many newspapers as a "revue-vaudeville show." *Variety News* for August 29th reported an enthusiastic opening night audience with celebrities of stage and screen. Smiling sweetly throughout her routines, avoiding any painful grimaces, Jeanne danced a solo in the opening "Flower Market" act; in the "Olde London Towne" act she danced as a fetching cherry maid in "Buy My Cherries." In the back of the stage were cherry trees and in the front were cherry pickers and big wicker baskets three feet high loaded with artificial cherries; when the scene opened, she descended a high ladder in toe shoes in front of one of the trees and danced "Cherry Ripe," so called after one of the old London street cries. In the sixteenth act Jeanne appeared as "The Lady in Red" in the Cuban rumba dance, which captivated British audiences, most of whom had not yet seen a rumba, with its enticing rhythmic movements and music. She also appeared in the finale with the entire company.

During the run of the show Jeanne wore out three pairs of toe shoes per week, since all of her dances were *en pointe*; she completely demolished her white lace and

Jeanne Devereaux in a promotional photograph for "The Lady in Red" rumba dance for George Black's variety show "Round About Regent Street" at the London Palladium, 1935–36. Photograph by Murray Korman in his New York studio shortly before she sailed to London on July 26, 1935. When Jeanne's conservative father had watched the photograph session, he became upset when Korman called her "Darling." Courtesy Jeanne Devereaux Perkins Collection.

Jeanne Devereaux in a promotional photograph for the dance "Cherry Ripe" in "Round About Regent Street" at the London Palladium, 1935–36. Jeanne choreographed all her solo dances, but "Cherry Ripe" was created for her by the famous British dancer and choreographer Frederick Ashton. Photograph taken in her dressing room. Courtesy Jeanne Devereaux Perkins Collection.

tulle costume for "Cherry Ripe" every five weeks and needed to replace it; and she required two red velvet costumes with hat and gloves for "The Lady in Red." The reviewers praised Jeanne's dancing with language like "beautiful artistry," "rare grace and style," "graceful movements," and "brilliant dancing"; the newspaper clippings were so numerous that Jeanne was forced to purchase a large, leather scrapbook on August 28th to hold them. In her diary for November 15th Jeanne included a quote from the "old spotlight man" who loved her dancing: "You know Miss Devereaux, Me mate & myself don't pay much attention to the show, but we never miss really watching you dance it's a great treat—In the Lady in Red I put on 10 extra amps. Of light to make you stand out—but we take it off the minute you're thru' the rest of the show can get along without it." In a letter from a fellow cast member written to Jeanne many years later on February 3, 1948, Marian Harvy reflected that she could "always see you Picking the Cherries ... & also 'The Lady in Red,'" obviously two of Jeanne's iconic dance routines.

The stage show featured 200 variety and vaudeville performers, including the Palladium's Crazy Gang, the singing cyclist Joe Jackson, the dance team Harrison and Fisher, and the African American dance team Four Flash Devils, who performed in the coveted vaudeville spot next to closing and whose exhilarating eccentric tap dancing was in contrast to Jeanne's graceful specialty ballet act. The show's star singer was Hannah Watts, who sang the opening number "Round About Regent Street" in Jeanne's "Flower Market" act, as well as many other songs throughout the program. The first half of the show ended with the spectacular set of "Vauxhall Gardens, 1750," based on a print by the artist Thomas Rowlandson, featuring elaborate eighteenth-century costumes, with the whole auditorium illuminated with multi-colored lights; another highlight was an elaborate burlesque of the famous waltz "The Merry Widow," choreographed by Frederick Ashton, starring a couple of the Crazy Gang comedians.

In *London's New Chronicle*, December 3, 1935, a reviewer noted Jeanne's determination and technical virtuosity in "Round About Regent Street," as well as the challenge of such a demanding performance schedule:

Suddenly your eye is caught by a twirling sculptured figure dancing madly against the background of drab canvas and ropes. It is Jeanne Devereaux, the American toe dancer, practicing. She is spinning and pirouetting and striking poses with enormous determination. Stagehands walk by taking no notice, the gaudily-painted chorus girls and comedians gave her a glance—no more. "Always dancing, that gel," somebody says.

She comes and stands resting near me, breathing as one who has raced.

Shortly she will dance for the public for four minutes; she has just practiced for twenty. But that is nothing—she puts in two hours apart from that.

She finds the "rake" (the slant) of the stage, trying. The "rake" is half an inch to the foot, but in New York every stage except one, the Palace, is flat. The "rake" alters her balance, she explains, prevents her throwing her foot so high, and the rubber surface of the stage slows down her spin.

"You see all those little white marks on the floor—all over—they say they're my signature. Yes, it tires me—you have to give them everything in those four minutes. It's more self-hypnosis than anything."

As she talks she is tying chiffon bows on to her bare arms; bit cherries are on her shoulder; her eyelashes are blobbed at the end with eye-black.

Throughout her dancing career Jeanne was plagued by this thick eye make-up that she was forced to wear while performing on stage. The "eye-black" usually made her eyes red, itchy, and sometimes swollen. After visiting various doctors, she realized that her only recourse was to use diligently the correct products when removing the make-up and to make her best effort to keep the make-up out of her eyes.

During its long run the show was performed twice nightly at 6:20 p.m. and 9:00 p.m. Jeanne made four appearances in the first two-and-a-half hour show, followed by a seven-minute intermission to clear the house, and then repeated her performances over again. On matinee days on Wednesday and Thursday with an additional show at 2:30 p.m. she performed this rigorous routine three times a day. Her schedule was "like a non-stop flight," Jeanne wrote in her diary on August 28th. There was "no end to the shows once they start," and matinee days were just as hard as any five-show a day schedule she had had in America. On September 26th, a month after opening night, writing to Bill in Jeanne's backstage dressing room at the Palladium where she could "hear the finish of our second show tonight," Lillian commented on this London schedule: "As one has to get here early to practice and 'makeup' it means we are here 12 hours continually on Wed. and Thurs, the two matinee days each week," she wrote. "So all week we don't have any more time than we did doing four shows each day at home, only, WE DO GET <u>Sundays free</u>, and so we are doing all our sightseeing on that day."

The stress of this schedule was mitigated for Jeanne by the loud audience applause for her elegant dancing, the prestige of playing at the London Palladium, and her pride in having many celebrities attend the London performances. In addition to the royals who attended the shows during the London run, other celebrities included the actor and musician Larry Adler, Douglas Fairbanks, Jr., the featured American movie actor Eugene Pallet, and Gracie Fields, one of Britain's favorite variety, film, and television stars. When the famous actor Frederick March saw the show, he was introduced to the audience and received a rousing ovation. Charles Laughton, Elsa Lanchester, and Maurice Chevalier were also introduced as special guests when they were in the audience. When the Oxford and Cambridge football teams were out front, they were "terrible rowdys even if they were in Formal attire," Jeanne wrote in her diary on December 10th.

Jeanne was thrilled to peek out the curtain and see these famous men and women in the audience who appreciated her artistry and made her feel like a star.

Jeanne had now earned enough money to purchase a special item that she and her mother had admired daily in a nearby shopkeeper's window: "Life isn't so bad—Dear me! After only eight years of work we finally got the little yellow Tea Set," she wrote in her diary on September 9th. However, despite her dazzling performances, the thrill of applauding audiences, new friends and suitors, improved finances, and the charming tea set, Jeanne still felt the loneliness of the itinerant vaudevillian lifestyle: after another round of incessant window shopping she wrote in her diary on September 10th how she was "so tired of never knowing anyone, going anywhere or seeing anything—Always looking at clothes to buy but never any where to wear them." Although she and her mother were a team, her loneliness was also exacerbated by Lillian's perfectionism and lack of affection. On September 18th after Lillian had seen "Round About Regent Street" in London for the first time out front in the audience, Jeanne wrote in her diary that to her "surprise she [Lillian] was delighted with everything about me—the first time in history, my make up, dance & lights were all right." Later on October 10th Jeanne explicitly expressed in her diary her desire "to write a book—[more of] a saga of our family than a novel—Id call it Lonesome Child after G. Grandpa Devereaux, Grandma, Mom & Me."

Since Jeanne had finished her formal education in the middle of the eighth grade, Lillian made certain that her daughter's informal education occurred daily. Their London apartment less than a block away from Hyde Park, Jeanne and Lillian spent many Sundays walking over there to join the crowds gathered to hear the political speakers, including socialists, Muslims, and Communists. On free afternoons they toured the historic sites and went to plays and movies. When they attended serious dramas they enjoyed the pleasurable British custom of having tea and cake or a scone served on a tray at your seat during the intermission. Jeanne later said that during matinees while performing in England she would look "down at a tea drinking audience." Some Sundays when it was chilly and raining they just relaxed at their London apartment and rested.

With her spectacular "Lady in Red" dance number, Jeanne had saved "Round About Regent Street" for George Black, and he was forever grateful; he generously befriended Jeanne and her mother, inviting them for many a holiday to his lavish homes in London and Angmering in the county of West Sussex. The Black family's magnificent London flat was located on the corner of Hyde Park and Oxford Street next to the Marble Arch just across the street from the Mount Royal Hotel where Jeanne and Lillian were staying. The Black's marvelous manor house forty miles southwest of London on the coast in Angmering near Worthing contained an antique staircase from Oliver Cromwell's house that Black had purchased at an auction. Many legendary star entertainers had lovely houses in Angmering, including Gracie Fields. Jeanne and Lillian were often invited to Angmering for elegant Sunday night dinners, and were picked up at their hotel and then driven back to London on Monday morning in George Black's Rolls Royce.

Jeanne had fond memories of George Black and his lovely wife and their three children—Alfie, George, and Pauline. On their first Christmas in London Jeanne wrote in her diary how they were "so lonely" that they had walked "four miles in the cold"; much to their delight when returning to their apartment they discovered an invitation to the

Blacks' London flat for a traditional English dinner. When everyone was seated, their host looked down the table at Jeanne and asked, "Jeanne, tell us how can you live in a country without a King?" Jeanne answered pertly, "Well, I think we've been doing alright so far!" When Jeanne did not have a matinee performance, she would take nine-year-old Pauline to the ballet matinees at the recently opened Sadler's Wells; she and Pauline would continue a correspondence well into the 1940s. Alfie and George, young men in their early twenties, both had crushes on Jeanne. George would often come to Jeanne's late night show at the Palladium, and then take her out in a taxi for a bite to eat at the Trocadero on Piccadilly Circus. When he occasionally was late or failed to show up for a date, Jeanne was disappointed and distressed.

Jeanne also remembered going with Alfie and George in their Rolls Royce to the race track at Epsom Downs; when it was empty they ran around and around the track like exuberant thoroughbreds. Sometimes they would go together to the famous Miter restaurant in Oxford. Lillian wrote Bill from London on December 8, 1936, that she and Jeanne would probably just go to a movie that night: "George Black Jr. has asked Jean for some dates, but he will probably be in Liverpool, so it will be a case of a picture-show we haven't seen, probably. Jeanne had many admirers who would become steady beaus, if she would let them, but she preferred," Lillian wrote, to be "foot-loose," giving each a date now and then. Lillian lamented that Jeanne did not "have time enough off to have many evenings for fun."

Given her uncertain booking schedule and incessant travel, Jeanne's relationship with friends like the Black family was transient and later sustained only by letter writing. Jeanne continued to correspond with the Black family after she returned to America—even after George Black, Sr.'s death in 1945. Writing to Bill from New York on January 21, 1940, Lillian related, "Mr. Black's little girl in England, wrote Jeanne a letter in which she envied Jeanne for being over here, out of trouble and war, and blackouts. They have that Million dollar home, but are living in a flat, instead, as the Govt only allows 10 Gals [gallons] a month, and most other things are rationed also, such as coal." As late as 1992 Jeanne received a letter from Alfie in which he brought her up-to-date about the youngest generation of the glamorous Black family.

Jeanne's scrapbook contains three manila envelopes filled with letters from 1935 by fans who had seen her dance in "Round About Regent Street." These fans recognized Jeanne's artistry and celebrity and requested autographed pictures of their star. One fan wrote to Jeanne requesting an autographed picture, saying, "I do so wish to express my very great and sincere appreciation of your most brilliant performance which I have had the very great pleasure of witnessing on two recent occasions at the Palladium in 'Round about Regent St.' Your beautiful dancing is quite the loveliest thing in this magnificent show—I am a great lover of really good dancing and I find in you an ideal and perfect exponent of this art." Other fan letters, however, were idiosyncratic, such as that written by a collector of ladies' kid gloves, requesting that Jeanne send him "a pair of kid gloves that has been on your lovely hands," and the letters by a London surveyor who, captivated by Jeanne, requested to meet her backstage after the show. Lillian, however, replied immediately to this London surveyor, noting how inappropriate she considered his letters were to her well-mannered daughter. Protecting her talented daughter's reputation so she would be able to work in any theatre had always been a priority for Lillian.

Two letters in particular, pasted on two facing pages, must have amused Jeanne and her mother enough to single them out. Written in a flowery prose praising her feminine attributes, an admirer waxed effusively on September 12, 1935, about Jeanne's beauty and extraordinary grace, requesting an autographed portrait "of your exquisitely beautiful and adorable self." Two weeks later, having received an autographed picture from Jeanne's agent, her admirer wrote a thank-you letter comparing Jeanne to sylvan fauns, Aphrodite, and a Damascus blade, among other classical images. He passionately wrote that he was even more moved than before by her beauty, youth, eyes, skin, and hair "to worship at the 'Shrine' of ... [her] adorable loveliness."

When Jeanne remembered Frederick Ashton, who had choreographed all the dances for the show except for her solo dances and those of the dance team Harrison and Fisher, she became strident. According to Jeanne, Ashton was furious that she was allowed to choreograph her own solo numbers, convinced that he had lost income and status as the show's official choreographer. During one of the rehearsals he sat in the front row next to Lillian, and she noticed him peering at the pair of Jeanne's toe shoes in her lap. In his biography of Ashton, David Vaughan included a quote from a review in *The Tatler*, September 11, 1935—that Jeanne was "'a sort of human top'" whose amazing pirouette speed resulted from ball bearings that she had in the ends of her toe shoes and that Ashton had choreographed "'several numbers'" for her.[4] In retrospect, Lillian realized that during that rehearsal he was looking for evidence of ball bearings in the toe shoes in her lap. Perhaps Ashton, associated primarily with elite ballet companies, felt that a variety toe dancer like Jeanne was more of a tricky technician than a true artist.

Although Jeanne considered Ashton's accusation an affront to her artistic ability and dancing talent, some of her contemporary toe dancers had resorted to toe tapping, which involved dancing *en pointe* with taps attached to the tip of the toe shoe. Since the early twentieth century, particularly in vaudeville and nightclubs, popular dancers like Harriet Hoctor, Marilyn Miller, Helen Brown, Ethel Norris, Gloria Gilbert and others performed toe tapping routines on the popular stages of the time to amaze their audiences with their virtuosity. Gloria Gilbert's father had invented ball bearings that fit in the end of her toe shoes along with a little spike on the tip of the toe. Billed as the human top, she would turn her leg inward and jab the spike into the stage and then rotate, often spinning while performing a backbend. Not a classical soloist like Jeanne, Gloria danced primarily in nightclubs, and when she danced at the Silver Slipper Casino in Nevada, the stage floor was pocked with holes caused by the spike in her toe shoe. According to Jeanne, because of the ball bearings and spike in her toe shoes, Gloria was subsequently banned from many engagements thereafter.

Jeanne wrote to her father during his time how homesick she was and how difficult it was for performers to be hired in America during the Great Depression years: Europe was her best chance. Lillian was constantly concerned with finances, for they were on an extremely tight budget and money was scarce. Out of financial necessity Jeanne was forced to work primarily in Europe for three more years.

7

A Royal Command Performance and a European and North African Tour

Jeanne had the distinction of appearing in seven performances before royalty: at the London Palladium before King George V and Queen Mary and King Edward VIII, before the King and Queen of Siam on their state visit to London, and before Queen Maud of Norway when she attended George V's funeral; at the Chateau Bagatelle in the Bois de Boulogne in Paris before King George VI and Queen Elizabeth; at the Bal Tabarin nightclub in Paris before King Gustav of Sweden and his companion Marlene Dietrich; and in Monte Carlo before King Alphonse of Spain. Jeanne claimed that during her professional career she most likely danced before more crowned heads than any other American theatrical performer. "When you did royal command performances and the queens and kings of Europe and nobles and the audiences were applauding you, crying out 'bravo' and smiling," she later noted, "it didn't dawn on you that this was something unique and rare that the average person would never experience."

She specifically remembered her Royal Command performance at the London Palladium when the tall, handsome Duke of Kent rose up in the royal box as the performers were taking their bows. He looked at Jeanne, winked and grinned broadly while saying "bravo," clapped loudly, and turned up his thumb in approval. As Jeanne often explained, "I think the managements considered ballet as something of quality for the royals and they were delighted that I could do spectacular ballet. My routines were more dramatic than most soloists in general." She also remembered that when the cast stood at the footlights after the end of the first London performance of "Round About Regent Street" singing "God Save the King," she had never heard the song before and did not know the words, so she quickly "fastened" her "gaze on a large lady in the front row who sang loudly" and then "silently mimicked her mouth and lip movements." Later, when she told George Black how embarrassed she had been, he sympathetically gave her a typescript of the lyrics to memorize before her first London Royal Command performance.

When Jeanne had sat in Anna Pavlova's lap in St. Louis at the age of seven, she could not imagine that she would succeed Pavlova's stunning inaugural Royal Command performance in London in 1912. No other ballerina had presented a Royal Command performance in Britain until Jeanne's on October 29, 1935, at the London Palladium, the sixth consecutive year at that prestigious venue. Created as a fundraiser for the Variety

Artistes' Benevolent Fund for old-time variety performers, London Royal Command performances began on July 1, 1912, at the Palace Theatre on Shaftesbury Avenue before King George V and Queen Mary, and subsequently were held fifteen times at different theatres. As was customary, members of the royal family attended variety shows at the Palladium, and then made their recommendations to the Lord Chamberlain. Jeanne was dancing in George Black's "Round About Regent Street" when she was seen by the royals, and then selected for the 1935 Royal Command performance before King George V and Queen Mary during their Silver Jubilee year when excitement was greater than ever and tickets were purchased by people worldwide. King George V had been a great supporter of variety in Britain, and this was his last royal variety performance; he would die in January of the following year.

Five years later when being interviewed by the *St. Louis Star*, July 10, 1940, Jeanne described how proud she was to have been chosen for her first Royal Command performance:

> To be asked to appear on the program is probably the biggest honor in the entertainment business—I have heard of famous American acts trying to buy their way into the Palladium bill so they'll have a chance at this distinction.... You can imagine how I felt when my name was announced! The whole theatre, you know, is reserved for royalty and members of the nobility. Duchesses act as ushers, and only those of royal blood sit in boxes near the King and Queen. The streets are roped off and the whole of London turns out to see the spectacle of arrival and leave taking. And here I was, the second ballerina ever to appear by royal command—Pavlova appeared in 1912—and the first American ballerina ever to be so honored! Who knows but what I will be the only one, considering the way things are going in Europe?

Later, in an article in the *San Francisco Chronicle*, November 27, 1943, she noted that "the most difficult thing to remember is that performers must bow to the King and Queen first, and they must never turn their backs upon the Royal box. It was frightening because it is natural to play to an audience in front, not to someone up in a box."

The ornate leather souvenir program of her 1935 Royal Command performance is embossed in gold with the royal coat of arms and bound with a purple ribbon. Organized and managed by George Black and Harry Marlowe, the performance was attended by 3,000 people and featured six American artists, including Jeanne, the Diamond brothers, the singing cyclist Joe Jackson, the dance team Harrison and Fisher, and the comedian Will Mahoney, along with twenty-one British performers and one Austrian. The British performers included some members from the cast of "Round About Regent Street," such as the singer Hannah Watts, the Austrian acrobats The Six Lias, and The Crazy Gang comedians, as well as other popular variety stars like Stanley Holloway, J. Sherman Fisher's Palladium Girls, Harry Roy and His Band, and the British ballet star and choreographer Anton Dolin. The show had fifteen acts, the first being "A Flower Market 'Round About Regent Street,'" with Hannah Watts and Jeanne Devereaux. In Act Seven, "Old London Town," also from "Round About Regent Street," Jeanne danced as a Cherry Maid in her star turn "Buy My Cherries" and then in the grand finale. A few days later Jeanne's agent placed the following advertisement in *The Performer*, October 31, 1935:

> Jeanne Devereaux/ America's Most Sensational Premier Ballerina/ Wishes to thank Messrs. GEORGE BLACK and HARRY MARLOW, and All Concerned for the Great Honor Bestowed Upon Her by Being Chosen to Appear Before THEIR MAJESTIES THE KING AND QUEEN at

7 • A Royal Command Performance and a European and North African Tour

Souvenir Program for the Royal Command performance at the London Palladium, October 29, 1935, printed as a Supplement to the trade journal *The Performer*, October 31, 1935. Jeanne Devereaux is second from left in the second row. Jeanne was the next ballerina and the only American one to follow Anna Pavlova's Royal Command performance in London at the inaugural event in 1912. Courtesy Jeanne Devereaux Perkins Collection.

the ROYAL PERFORMANCE, LONDON PALLADIUM, OCT. 29, 1935/ 12th Consecutive and Successful week in GEORGE BLACK'S "ROUND ABOUT REGENT STREET," DIRECTION: FOSTERS AGENCY.

The British press provided extensive coverage of this noble pageantry in the years leading up to World War II. In her diary Jeanne described the extensive publicity that appeared in almost every British publication. Pictures of King George, Queen Mary, and the Duchess of York filled the front pages for weeks after the performance, and all the newspaper reviewers praised Jeanne's dancing and artistry, often singling her out as the star of the show. An article in *The Performer*, October 31, 1935, titled "Another Brilliant Success. An Outstanding Royal Variety Performance," praised the benefit and beauty of variety entertainment:

> Success upon success. Such is the record of successive Royal Variety Performances. For that which was presented before their Majesties on Tuesday night at the London Palladium certainly attained a high level of achievement. Indeed, as one commentator remarks, the performance was given before "the most brilliant and crowded audiences yet gathered even within those many memoried walls." Not only that, but the performance, which went with a swing, was itself a brilliant affair, glorifying Variety and testifying to the fact that music-hall entertainment is not only dear to the hearts of sovereignty and people, but is a truly joyous and satisfying affair.

The finale with the entire cast onstage was, according to the article, a "piece of stagecraft and grouping that the house has never before staged nor is it likely to do so again for a long time to come."

Jeanne wrote in her diary on October 29th that soon after she had arrived at the London Palladium at 10:00 a.m. George Black invited her to sit in the royal box. When recollecting this Royal Command performance for the *St. Louis Times* five years later, Jeanne recalled the special moment when Black knocked on her dressing room door before the performance and invited her to visit the royal box with him: "The performance itself was wonderful, but I really think I got more kick out of something that happened before the show when I, wearing curlers in my hair and an old pair of practice pajamas, was taken by Mr. Black to the royal box much to my strong protestation. At his insistence I sat on the King's chair and then on the Queen's chair, and all this despite the horrified protests of an English stagehand who took one look at my apparel and cried, 'But you can't go out that way!'" Later, Jeanne described how the royal box was decorated with delicate maidenhair ferns and the gold throne chairs were covered with needlepoint tapestry. George Black always placed a five-pound box of chocolates in the royal box for the Queen, but she tactfully never touched it. Usually after the show he took the box of chocolates home to his wife, telling Jeanne that "when you and your Mother come to dinner on Sunday, you can each have a piece of the 'Queen's chocolates.'"

Jeanne also wrote in that October 29th diary entry that when her "big moment came" she danced before the King and Queen "almost stopping the show." A few days later on November 5th Lillian wrote to her sister Lenore how proud she was that Jeanne had been selected for the Royal Command performance, which was "the greatest honor 'tis said, that can come to any one in this profession. The producer says her number and Will Mahoney's were the 'tops' of the show and that the Queen and King especially enjoyed her number." Lillian took credit for having made the beautiful new white costume for the "Cherry Ripe" number, humorously calling herself "Dressmaker to the Queen." In an uncharacteristic burst of pride Lillian described how exhilarating it had been to witness Jeanne's triumph on the Palladium stage before royalty: "She came so near to stopping the show that night, and the applause was so spontaneous and thunderous I really almost cryed when she was called again & again and was curtsying to the King & Queen of Great Britain. The moment was so tremendous that I am almost crying again while I write about it to you. I don't suppose I will ever experience anything like it again in this world as the 'Acts' were picked from all over the world as 'tops' in their line of comedy, singing or dancing." As Lillian had always been her harshest critic, it was a significant triumph for Jeanne that her mother was reduced almost to tears with her magnificent performance.

Jeanne's Royal Command performance put her in a unique category with headlining stars who had also received this special honor. The year before Jeanne's royal performance the American singer Sophie Tucker had also experienced the excitement and pride of being chosen to perform before King George V and Queen Mary, which she vividly described in her *Autobiography*.[1] Like Jeanne, Sophie cherished her memories of this exceptionally proud night the rest of her life.

Jeanne's triumph, however, was short lived as the very next day she had to perform an exhausting matinee and evening performance of "Round About Regent Street" at the London Palladium; five days later she wrote in her diary that she was "still tired from the Command Performance." After a successful run of almost six months "Round About Regent Street" closed on March 7, 1936. On closing night Pauline Black had sent Jeanne beautiful roses and tiger lilies and the stagehands cheered, "as we bowed the last time—I got the most—almost cried," Jeanne wrote in her diary. Life had been strenuous before the closing at the Palladium: they had had to prepare their clothes for future touring in the spring and summer, look for bookings in London or on the Continent, break up their apartment, and get Jeanne's two new dances with costumes ready for performance. Unfortunately, Harry Foster turned out to be a bullying, arrogant agent who attempted to force Jeanne to take bookings at salaries lower than her former engagements and who argued with her about her billing. When she refused to sign a contract to perform at the British Blackpool resort at only forty pounds a week, Foster became livid, but continued to introduce her to European theatre directors who might hire her when the Palladium contract was finished. Jeanne dealt directly with agents from the Continent and followed every lead she had for future bookings. On March 19th Jeanne went with the Black family to see the new show at the London Palladium—"Couldn't compare with our show," she wrote in her diary—and then to dinner afterwards. Most importantly Jeanne signed a contract that day to perform in Paris for two weeks at the famous Parisian music hall called the Alhambra.

Flush with her successes in America and England, Jeanne began thrilling Parisian audiences with her intricate toe work, twirling pirouettes, and spinning fouettés. After packing up their trunks and suitcases, on March 25th Jeanne and her mother took their first airplane ride across the English Channel to Paris in a four engine plane that held forty-three passengers, which Jeanne said in her diary was one of "the biggest thrills of their lives." Jeanne performed for two weeks in a big variety show at the Alhambra on a rough, barn-like stage floor that tore her toe shoes so that they had to be replaced after four shows. A translation of the French caption under her publicity picture in the official Alhambra program for March 27th praised "her grace, her lightness, her admirable technique"; *The World's Fair* for April 11th described her Parisian debut at the Alhambra as a "clever, classy act," and her "spins and twirls are superbly graceful and rapid."

Jeanne played at the Alhambra with the American performer Larry Adler, the best-known harmonica player in the world. Adler was a friend of the stars, including Charlie Chaplin, and later had well-publicized romances with film goddesses Greta Garbo and Ingrid Bergman. Like many other entertainers of the time, in the 1950s he was suspected of participating in American Communist Party activities, and was eventually included in the Hollywood blacklist of suspected Communists, prohibited from performing in American theatres, and settled in London for the rest of his life. Jeanne and Larry began dating during the run at the Alhambra: "I've certainly been seeing Paris with Larry. He's a complete dear," Jeanne wrote in her diary on April 4th. Later she remembered one day between the matinee and night show at the Alhambra when Larry asked her to walk with him along the Champs Élysées, where they went into a café for coffee. A roving musician playing a violin egregiously off key approached their table with his hand holding his hat out for money. "It was so incredible," recalled Jeanne. "Here was one of the greatest musicians in the world being asked to pay to hear another musician who couldn't even hit one right note."

Since bookings were scarce after the Alhambra engagement, Jeanne accepted an offer for a week at Cannes in the French Riviera despite the low salary of 400 francs per day. At least they would have an opportunity to see the south of France and feast their eyes on enormous yachts in the harbor. In between shows Jeanne and Lillian walked all over Cannes in the unseasonable cold and rain. In her diary for April 11th Jeanne wrote Larry Adler, who was performing in nearby Monte Carlo, that the "Casino is a madhouse, no one trying to help or understand"; she had rehearsed and then "went over big both shows." When Larry was preparing to give a royal performance before King Alphonse of Spain, he called Jeanne and asked her to take a taxi to his Monte Carlo theatre to dance in the show, reminding her that she would have to arrange for the taxi driver to wait so he could get her back to Cannes in time to do her own show. Jeanne later referred to this arrangement as "tour hopping on the Mediterranean."

After her engagement in Cannes Jeanne had an offer to perform in sunny Lugano, Switzerland, northeast of Milan. After riding all day on the train from Cannes through Italy to Lugano, Jeanne danced two afternoon and two evening shows in the fancy Compaine Lake Casino across the lake from her hotel, frequented by a very wealthy clientele of diners and gamblers. She loved the clean fresh air in Lugano and its idyllic setting. Lillian, fighting to overcome her homesickness, wrote to Bill from Lugano on April 23rd that "there is so little work at home, and we want to see Europe while over here, so we will stick to our guns and see as much as possible while working for a living, but it is a strenuous life we lead, to do this," She told him that after Lugano they might go to St. Moritz or Zurich—or Tripoli or Milan or Rome or Naples or London or Paris—wherever there was lucrative work: "It has been such a worry and strain to try to communicate in French and Italian that I would be glad to be in London again," she wrote.

While performing in Lugano Jeanne received a telegram from an agent about dancing in Tripoli, Libya. She was at first skeptical about going to such a remote place, but when her fellow performers persuaded her that she would have a thrilling time visiting Italy and Sicily en route to Tripoli, she decided to pursue the agent's offer. With the assistance of fellow troupers, Jeanne and Lillian negotiated a salary of 500 liras per day for ten days with two round trip fares by boat. They would travel by train via Milan, Rome, Naples, the Straits of Messina, crossing over to Sicily past the great volcano Etna, then on to Syracuse and across the Mediterranean to the North African shore. In a postcard from Lugano to her Grandmother Lane in Pasadena on April 26th Jeanne wrote that she would be performing in Tripoli for ten days: "do a tea show at about 5 P.M. & then a dinner show at about 11P.M. so we wont have to work very hard.... We don't get to see much while we are working but may later."

In 1935 Africa entered into World War II when Italy invaded Ethiopia and the League of Nations imposed mild economic sanctions against Italy. As a result, America avoided trading arms with either Italy or Ethiopia. By May 1936 the Ethiopian emperor Haile Selassie was forced into exile, and Italy annexed Ethiopia, which was then occupied by Italian troops, who used poison gas to defeat the Ethiopian military. With the economic sanctions in place Italians were not allowed to take any money in or out of their country. In her April 23rd letter Lillian had advised Bill that if he sends any letters to them in Italy "do not write anything joking or otherwise that might be misconstrued, as they are opening all letters or mail coming in or going out of Italy, for any Lira that might be smuggled out of the country, or anything derogatory to the cause of Italy." Mussolini built a lavish casino in the Italian-occupied Uaddam Hotel and Casino in Tripoli, where wealthy Italians could gamble and see spectacular stage shows. Since Tripoli had only a few run-down hotels at that time, most of the Italian millionaires anchored their luxury liners in the Tripoli harbor and used their boats as floating hotels, coming ashore to gamble. Jeanne had signed a contract to dance in Mussolini's lavish hotel and casino.

While waiting in Syracuse for the ship to take them to Tripoli, Jeanne and Lillian visited an ancient Roman, open-air, marble amphitheater on the outskirts of town looking out over the Mediterranean. They were alone except for a few sleepy lizards on the marble seats. Sitting there and reflecting on the ancient Greek plays and performers, Jeanne said to her mother, "I've got to dance on this stage." So she got up and went down onstage. Remembering the poses and postures of Greek performers painted and etched on old Greek and Roman pottery, she improvised some dance steps, emulating these classical performers. "While dancing on this empty stage, I had a tremendous sense of ancient history," remembered Jeanne. She often included dancing in this ancient Roman amphitheater in her list of royal command performances, undoubtedly imagining the day when she danced for the gods. Jeanne humorously recalled that when they had returned to town they met an old Sicilian man selling lemons, who immediately recognized them as Americans and said, "I sold peanuts in Yonkie Stadium." Then he started to cry because his greedy Syracusian relatives thought that everyone who worked in America was rich, had spent all his money when he had returned home, and now he had "no money to go back to New York," he bemoaned.

Conditions were primitive in Libya when Jeanne and her mother disembarked in Tripoli. Although they had stayed at one of the run-down hotels, in her reports home

Jeanne emphasized the thrill of being in a strange land. When they shopped in the bazaars, Jeanne remembered buying a silver powder box from an artisan sitting and working on a dirt floor in his shop. She recalled how women in the nearby town of Gadamous were stationed on the roofs of their houses, and when they spied a camel or caravan across the desert sands, they would cry out to other women from one roof to another, spreading the news. On May 1st she reported to her father that they had taken a long horse and buggy ride in the countryside, seeing interesting sights such as "Goats & donkeys, Camels—Palms, Flowers & Arabs. The streets are all paved & smooth as silk & the buildings are all new & very beautiful.... The famous auto races are due on the 10th and people are coming from all over to see them—The Casino is grand & the food is wonderful." In her diary for the same day she noted that the Mediterranean was beautiful and enchanting and that Governor General Balboa had been a guest at the casino and had seen her perform.

A few days later she sent her father a postcard telling him about a terrible sandstorm in the desert that covered them "with a fine dust in just a few minutes." They were also awakened by a 100-gun salute to the new Emperor of Ethiopia, and were surrounded by the thousands of people who had arrived for the auto races, sleeping in bath houses and on the big ocean liners docked in the harbor. To celebrate the establishment of the Italian empire, the director of the casino had taken them to tea, and then much to her amazement, the director proposed marriage to Jeanne. The "Sisters G" were also performing in Tripoli: "Remember they were in the movies with me," she wrote. Jeanne was referring to the stylish vaudeville dancers and actresses Eleanor and Karla Gutchrlein, known as the "Sisters G," who in 1930 had performed with Jeanne in the movie *Kiss Me Again*.

After Jeanne's successful engagement in Tripoli she and her mother returned to Syracuse, and then took the boat train to Naples, hoping for a rare, short vacation in the south and to visit world landmarks. On May 15th Jeanne wrote her father from her room overlooking the Bay of Naples that her mother had been "terribly sick last night in Tripoli and the long trip had to be broken or it would have been just too bad—We are very tired but she is better & will go to Milano day after tomorrow" perhaps with a short stop in Rome along the way. Since they were not permitted to take Italian lira out of the country, they went on a shopping spree, with Lillian purchasing a coat and Jeanne buying a beautiful, cowhide leather suitcase and red leather calfskin purse. They toured Rome and then took a train to Milan, where they met a French agent who introduced them to Leoni, the Italian owner of all the big movie presentation houses in Milan, who booked Jeanne in a small theatre for a two-day run so he could see her work, with the promise of a longer booking in Rome's large Odeon theatre. Although Jeanne suspected that Leoni was a skunk who just wanted someone to play in his damp, dirty, and freezing small theatre, she needed the 700 liras so accepted his offer. After her show Leoni disappeared and never paid the money. "I had a good cry I was so terribly miserable," Jeanne wrote in her diary on May 24th. Jeanne subsequently was offered a contract to perform in Madrid, but before they were scheduled to leave for Spain, the Republican coalition, called the Popular Front, won the Spanish 1936 elections. In July the right-wing Spanish military revolted, and civil war ensued. Jeanne and Lillian's friends who had just visited Spain warned them not to go there, for they had barely escaped with their lives when gunshots were fired into their Madrid hotel room, forcing them to duck and crawl on the floor.

In early June 1936 Jeanne and Lillian were at the Hotel Daniel at 18, Rue Caulaincourt in Paris relaxing while looking for new bookings despite the strikes by Parisien workers that often brought the city to a standstill and had closed the big French summer resorts. Jeanne was spending two hours daily in a rented rehearsal hall, they were sewing new costumes to be ready when bookings opened up again, and they window shopped for hours while touring the city. On June 7th Lillian wrote Bill of her constant fears and frustrations mitigated only by Jeanne's international stardom: "As you know by now, the show business is the most difficult racket in the world, and the most exacting, and nerve wracking so a little relaxation will not harm us. Well, at least it keeps us, and we are a few good steps ahead of the Wolf. We have several tentative things to consider as well as some offers to sign on the dotted line, as your dudder is now an International Dancer and is sought, where before in the olds days it was us that were seeking."

In this same letter Lillian complained about the cold, rainy weather in Paris, about the fact that she and Jeanne both had to have some teeth pulled, and how tired they were from the constant traveling. The next day Jeanne wrote to her father that the tooth extraction had left a big hole in her jaw, which she fills with chewing gum that she had bought in a Parisian drug store. On July 14th—Bastille Day—when the workers celebrated winning a forty-hour week with a paid vacation and the Sorbonne students sang "Le Marseillaise," Jeanne, given her sympathy for socialism, wrote in her diary how "chills & thrills" ran down her spine. Jeanne was hoping that her agent Hal Sands could book her for six months in South America at her premium salary of $250 to $300 weekly: they could take this booking and then return to Paris when the strikes had ended.

Though they were homesick, Jeanne and Lillian knew that their fortunes in Europe at that time were still better than in depressed America, "since there isnt one weeks work in America at my present salary, and not more than ten weeks work at a small salary," wrote Jeanne. Within days Lillian was the victim of an aggressive pickpocket at the market in Montmartre, losing all their money, their passports, and their tickets back to America.[2] Jeanne and Lillian were devastated by this disastrous turn of events in their lives, and blamed themselves for not being more vigilant. "Shorn lambs, penniless in Paris—what a future—The work of a year gone without hope of regaining it," Jeanne desperately wrote in her diary on June 16th. Continuing her remorseful tirade on the next day, she wrote that "all we can do is moan & cry to ourselves over our stupidity the first time in our lives we were independent and able to be free of the worry of what we would be doing the next week—We certainly prized it lightly to let it go so easy." With only $250 to her name, Jeanne felt like a prisoner stranded in a foreign country. Jeanne was adamant that her unstable father should never know that at the moment they did not even possess enough money to purchase tickets home.

Since the robbery in Montmartre, getting bookings took on a new urgency. Lillian even sent a telegram to George Black in London asking for his assistance during this crisis; he made an enquiry to Scotland Yard but with no results. They invited more agents to watch Jeanne practice, hoping to get a contract for a long run at the Parisian *Folies Bergère*, and contacted more bookers for shows in neighboring countries. Jeanne was finally hired to perform in a one-night gala for 500 francs at the famous Longchamp Racecourse, immortalized in paintings by Manet and Degas, located next to the Seine in the Bois de Boulogne: "It's the swankiest affair of the season so should be something to see," Jeanne wrote her father on July 2nd. The Longchamp gala was also a spectacular fashion show where the rich women paraded around in designer gowns that dragged in the dirt. After the rehearsal at the Lido Club in Paris Jeanne joined ten orchestras with all their instruments and almost forty foreign acts with all their costumes to take the buses from Place Pigalle at 7:00 p.m. to the racetrack. There were no dressing rooms: the girls dressed in the hospital at the track and the boys dressed outdoors. Beginning at midnight, most of the cast performed on stages placed around the racetrack; Jeanne danced in the big restaurant and had problems with her music, lights, and dance floor. We waited "hours for buses homeward; in bed exhausted at 5:00 AM," Jeanne wrote in her diary on July 4th.

Eager to return to her beloved London, Jeanne was thrilled when two days later she received a contract for a two-week engagement in late August at the Mayfair and Dorchester hotels in London, immediately applying for her British labor permit and setting two routines with new costumes for her signature balloon dance. "Darling we have had enough of Europe for awhile so we are tickled to death to go back to our little apartment in the Mount Royal, and have a little herring for breakfast once more," Jeanne wrote her father on July 6th. Also, with the political battles in France and news of the recent troubles in Spain, they would feel safer in England. Practicing long hours every day for her London engagement and working on her balloon costume, Jeanne wrote to her father on July 20th that her constant practicing had caused her feet to be "so hot after dancing on them two hours, B.W. [Lillian] took the bellows for my balloons and blew on them to cool them off. It was very funny & will write again from England."

8

Touring the British Provinces with George Ahoy!

When Jeanne and Lillian returned to the Mount Royal in London in the fall of 1936, they began the exhausting process of contacting agents and bookers, especially the powerful Harry Foster and also Val Parnell at the Palladium. Jeanne eagerly called her friend Lupe Vélez at London's swanky Claridges hotel to enlist assistance with bookers, but even Lupe was unable to help her friend get work. Jeanne resumed her practice sessions in a local rehearsal studio to prepare for her luxury hotel bookings. She was elated when her picture appeared in one of London's premier newspapers before her opening at the Mayfair hotel, where she was a great success despite her perfectionist mother's fears that her dance number would be a flop.

As Jeanne was rehearsing for her weeklong engagement at the Dorchester hotel, Lillian was so exhausted from sewing costumes, Jeanne wrote in her diary August 3rd, "she watched me practice from under her down coverlet like a doll." After the first show at the Dorchester, Jeanne had visited Lupe Vélez in her Claridges hotel room, and after the final show that night, Jeanne went with some of the performers to London's trendy 400 Club Ltd., where she again saw Lupe: I "danced & listened to injured male vanity until 4:30 AM," she wrote in her diary on August 8th. Lupe planned to see Jeanne perform in the late show at the Dorchester the following evening.

Jeanne wrote her father on August 11th about their first free day spent window shopping and "amusing ourselves at just doing nothing. That 'doing nothing' line is funny, because to be able to resist buying things is 'doing plenty.'" They hoped to get into a touring variety show and see more of the British countryside. They enjoyed their visits to nearby Hyde Park to hear the public speakers, where Jeanne was amazed at the number of Communists there and the discussions about the recent Spanish Civil War. Many of the speakers appealed to her socialist leanings. Jeanne claimed to have received most of her education about politics at these gatherings, and wished that America would allow these free outdoor meetings for the education of the masses. She also feared that the troubles in Spain, dividing major powers like Russia and Germany, would lead to world war.

Years of financial struggle and hard work took a toll on Jeanne's interdependent relationship with her loyal but controlling mother: "Because I wanted to wear a certain hat we had a fight that lasted into the morning," Jeanne wrote in her diary on August 15th. "B.W. [Lillian] started to walk out—and the whole damn affair made me ill—Years of strain are telling." When they traveled to Brighton to see the tryout of the new Palladium revue, starring the American ballerina Patricia Bowman, they met the Blacks before the show, and Jeanne informed Mrs. Black about their difficult financial status. As for Patricia Bowman's performance, in a presumably impartial assessment of her rival, Jeanne wrote in her diary for August 18th that she hoped George Black and the Crazy Gang "are royally disappointed in Patricia Bowman—If it's the sensational they want"; writing again on August 27th after having seen the tryout Jeanne concluded that Bowman "didn't stop any show." Although her famous boyfriend Larry Adler was back in London, Jeanne was so upset about not having sufficient funds that she hoped she would not see him until her situation was improved.

By September George Black, perhaps with Mrs. Black's intervention, came to the rescue of his distressed ladies by recommending Jeanne for his eight-month musical comedy *George Ahoy!*, which toured the British provinces three times. Finally Val Parnell from the London Palladium called Jeanne with an offer to perform in *George Ahoy!*, staged by Tom Arnold and starring the popular stage and screen comedian George Clarke. *George Ahoy!*, a big-time variety show performed twice nightly six times a week with Saturday matinees and Sunday travel days, was scheduled to tour for week-long runs in old theatres in British towns with no modern amenities. In this successful show, featured as the American dancing star from the London Palladium, Jeanne showcased her versatile solo dancing, including her famous "Lady in Red" rumba number, as well as played a dramatic speaking role. Although Jeanne was offered a salary less than her standard and would have to use her own worn out costumes, she was grateful for the opportunity to replace one of the performers in the show and especially to have some spoken lines in all five scenes. Each night the show ran from 6:30 p.m. until midnight; in addition to her required three costume changes for her speaking role, she performed two dances, each with different costumes, and then changed into an evening gown for the finale. Jeanne was listed in the program as the character Kitty, one of the nieces of Mrs. Didcott-Didcott, played by the famous Norah Dwyer. Jeanne would laugh when she remembered how Norah, normally a very well-mannered, circumspect lady, reacted when anything went wrong during the show: she would storm into the dressing room, stamp her foot, and say, "Hell, Damn, Spit!"

Having had only four days' notice of her booking in *George Ahoy!*, Jeanne rushed to begin rehearsals and costume fittings before the show opened in Northampton. Since she was now in England only as a visitor, in order to tour professionally Jeanne had to re-enter England on a worker's visa, forcing her to fly to Paris, obtain the visa from the British Passport Office, and fly back to London. The next day Jeanne and Lillian took the train to Northampton and settled in their chilly rooming house called "digs," the British troupers' name for lodgings while performing on the road that included a home cooked meal and guaranteed hot water often in a rundown, cracked bathtub and only if ordered hours in advance. When the performers returned at midnight to their digs, they had to climb flights of narrow, creaking stairs in the dark to reach their rooms.

On opening night in Northampton Jeanne danced in two shows and, unlike other cast members, remembered all her lines. The three Saturday performances were always a drag. Jeanne kept up an exhausting schedule during the run in Northampton, including long rehearsals with the orchestra, line run-throughs with the cast, refinements and changes, and daily practice sessions to maintain her fitness, with no time for books or letters. On September 11th Jeanne noted in her diary that the performers would sometimes miss their entrances, the drummer would move his set-up traps causing her costumes to catch and shred, and she and her mother would participate in social gatherings after the last show when they would "sit up with the dancers till all hours dishing dirt—Drinking tea."

After the opening in Northampton, the show traveled to the Portsmouth Hippodrome via London for the week of September 14th, where they spent most of the first dreary day looking for digs. In Portsmouth Jeanne was forced to dance on a painted stage that slowed down her fouettés; the backstage area was closed during the afternoon, limiting practice but allowing time for touring this well-known seaport town. Although the stage floor the following week at the Birmingham Hippodrome was "a dancers dream," Jeanne wrote in her diary on September 21st the town was drab, and their digs were far from the theatre. Once again the theatre was closed for the afternoons. On Septem-

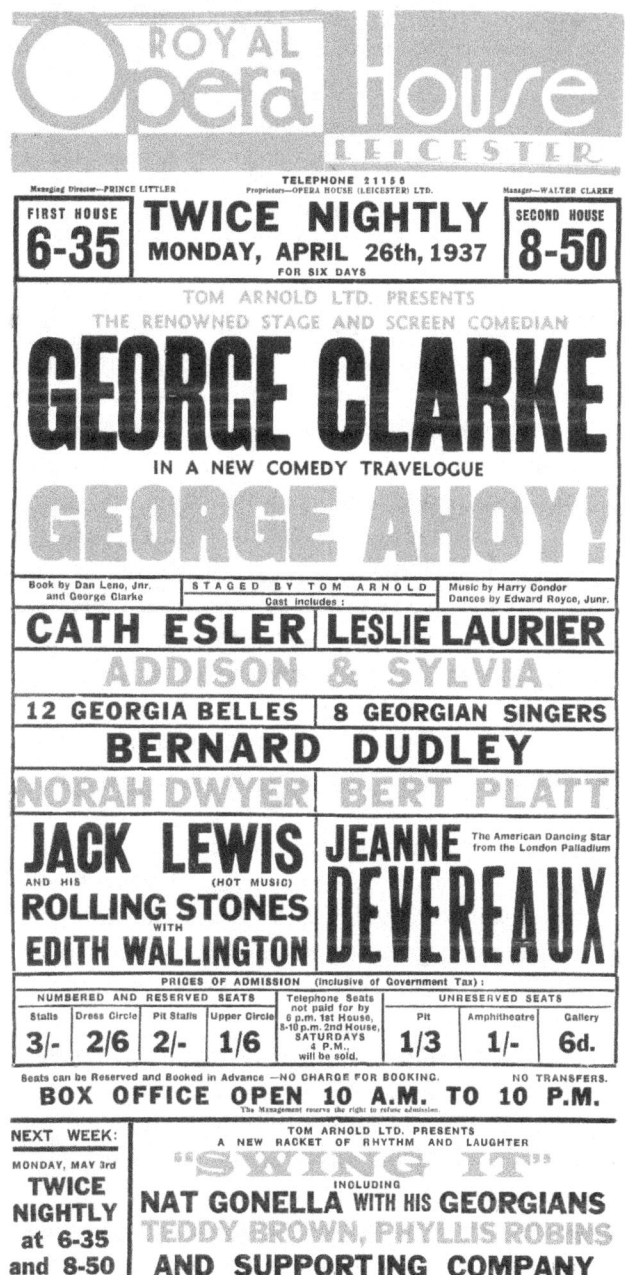

Playbill for Tom Arnold's touring variety show *George Ahoy!* at the Royal Opera House in Leicester, England, for a six-day run performed two times nightly during its third tour in the British provinces, beginning on April 26, 1937. The main headliner was the famous British stage and screen comedian George Clarke. Jeanne Devereaux, "The American Dancing Star from the London Palladium," is advertised in large, black bold lettering in the lower right hand column. *George Ahoy!* premiered in London in September 1936, and toured the British provinces three times until closing on May 22, 1937. Courtesy Jeanne Devereaux Perkins Collection.

ber 26th Jeanne wrote her father to describe her schedule, the show, and last night's raucous British audience in the Birmingham theatre:

> Last night the house was full of colledge boys who liked my "Rumba on Toe" so much they yelled at the end of it. It's a paradox that the stolid, solid, torpid, and calm English who school themselves never to show any emotion, let themselves to [sic] completely in the theatre and Boo what pleaseth them noteth, and cheer that which giveth them pleasure. You remember seeing that beautiful red velvet dress I had my picture taken in, don't you? It's a complete wreck now, but still looks like a million from the front.

Also, the last night in Birmingham two East Indians in the audience howled with laughter at the scene where Jeanne's character and her cousin were taken prisoner in a harem—"a ridiculous take-off of their homeland." The show traveled to the Liverpool Empire for the week of September 28th, where they found comfortable digs located far from the theatre that had a room with a fireplace with plenty of coal. On the morning of the required cast pictures, Jeanne was so "tired I went to sleep on suitcases," she wrote in her diary on September 30th.

On Sunday they traveled by train, enjoying the pleasant but polluted English countryside, to their next booking at the Nottingham Empire the week of October 5th. Arriving the day before opening, Jeanne described in her diary the unique sight of "all the actors barging along the same street in Nottingham trying to get fixed in digs": principals like Jeanne were able to take a taxi to town and settle in the best digs, while the chorus boys and girls had to walk. To her dismay the small Nottingham Empire had a new slanting raked stage that adversely affected her performance: just give her "big flat stages! Small theatres with crowded stages & cramped dressing rooms makes for poor shows," Jeanne wrote in her diary on October 5th. While performing in Nottingham Jeanne wrote a long letter to her father on October 9th in which she described their sightseeing excursions around Nottingham's historic sites. Mesmerized by the history and beauty of the old castle's museum exhibits, particularly that of the local lace, and the large art galleries, Jeanne felt transported through time and invulnerable to the petty troubles of everyday life. While touring these sites, however, she became bothered by a bad cold.

George Ahoy! opened in London on October 12th in a small suburban theatre called the Finsbury Park Empire. Jeanne wrote in her diary that night in her apartment at the Mount Royal that she had performed two shows before a "tough audience," with "terrible lights, floor full of holes"; her red dress had been torn to ribbons and her cold was even worse. The costumier hired by the producer Tom Arnold fitted her for a new bodice for the red dress. Jeanne and Lillian blamed their recurring chest colds and sniffles on the English lack of central heating, particularly in the theatres: "I got my charming case of sniffles from these draughty stages. No heating of any kind in a theatre, doors all open, with a 60 mile gale per hour, blowing through, and then I have to buck it after dancing until I'm quite overheated," Jeanne wrote to Bill on October 14th. Finsbury Park Empire was followed by a weeklong booking in Wolverhampton near Birmingham in a theatre with a tiny stage. On her last day in Wolverhampton Jeanne rehearsed with the rest of the cast for line cuts where three new scenes had been added before returning on Sunday to London for the booking at the Holborn Empire, the second most prestigious theatre in London next to the Palladium. Jeanne, again remembered for her star turn at the Palladium, received glowing reviews in the London newspapers for her sensational spins and turns at the Holborn Empire, executed with such grace and style. Despite Jeanne's continual triumphs on stage, Lillian continued to push her daughter to network more to maintain her competitive edge, and Jeanne, wanting to focus on her artistry, naturally rebelled: "We fought over me not playing up to people who can help me—All we do is fight now days—I'm sick of it!" she wrote in her diary on November 1st.

After the final week in London *George Ahoy!* traveled to the British provinces for a second tour—Hull, Newcastle on Tyne, and Sunderland—and then on to Scotland, returning to Sheffield in England. Frantically preparing to be on the road for five-to-six weeks, Jeanne wrote her father on November 1st to thank him for her birthday gift, explaining that after her final costume fitting for a new top on the "Lady in Red" velvet gown they had to catch the train for Hull, the first stop on their new tour; the dress alteration, however, was delayed. Writing from Newcastle on November 6th, Jeanne graphically described the hectic schedule of a trouper scrambling to make the show's opening in another town:

> After missing one train after another, I finally had to take all the luggage and Tear for the last train that would get me to Hull in time for the show. B.W. [Lillian] stayed waiting for the dress. She caught a train by the skin of her teeth, had to change trains at some junction, and finally got there "As the curtain rose."
>
> When I got there I couldnt get a porter for ages, and only had an hour before the show started, no make-up on or clothes unpacked.—I asked for a taxi,—Porter put my things on a pushcart, and went out of the station into the street with me running after, insisting on a Taxi. He stolidly kept on pushing my baggage thru traffic, while I kept up with him, almost crying in my exasperation at his refusal to get me a cab.
>
> I didnt know where the theatre was, and time was precious to be walking, on and on we went, after three blocks I was mad as hops and while panting and running to keep up with the Blighter—I called out "You make me sick. I asked for a Taxi, I'm liable to miss a show while you walk me all over town.—When I ask for a cab, haven't I anything to say in the matter. How dare you take matters into your own hands."
>
> I was practically crying by this time, and afterwards B.W. and I had a good laugh over it. After it was all over.

Although their digs in Hull were dirty, they were elated that they had now earned $630, sufficient for them to purchase two steamship tickets home. Returning home, however, was not the best option, since jobs in American show business were still scarce. Jeanne's labor permit was renewed in late December, and she was allowed to continue touring with the show.

In Newcastle-on-Tyne Jeanne added another week to her string of perfect shows. To their surprise and delight, good friends of the Bennett family visited them backstage, and they had reminisced about New York and home. The following week in Sunderland their nest egg had grown to $700. On Sunday they traveled by train to Edinburgh, Scotland, and settled in cold but attractive digs. Jeanne wrote in her diary on November 24th that despite a sore throat she "stopped the show cold [in Edinburgh] for five minutes"; even the singer in her act "couldn't be heard as he tried to carry on with that big voice of his—but all to no avail. On and on they cheered—Its a great thrill when it's a dead certain stop." Although the rain and foggy weather prevented much sightseeing, Jeanne and Lillian managed to tour the Edinburgh Castle and other sites. Later, on

December 17th Jeanne wrote her father to emphasize how significant her sightseeing was to her general education, since "in the future all of our reading will be colored by memories of what we saw."

On Sunday when they traveled to Glasgow, Larry Adler met Jeanne at the train, and they drove in his fancy Packard car to the ocean at Turnbury, a famous golfing resort, where they had tea and dinner. They passed through Ayre, the home of the Scottish poet Robert Burns. When Larry Adler returned to visit Jeanne in Glasgow two days before she left for Sheffield, it rained and snowed so all they could do was go to the movies. Larry Adler proposed marriage to Jeanne, but she insisted that she was not ready then to tie the matrimonial knot with Larry or anyone else, given her financial responsibilities and her round-the-clock professional schedule.

Jeanne and Lillian allowed themselves a rare splurge with their replenished funds, buying a silver tea set and a tea cozy with a matching cloth for the tabletop for Christmas and having it delivered to London. "Do we feel swank," Jeanne wrote in her diary on December 1st, envisioning the wonderful gatherings for tea and cakes in their apartment at the Mount Royal with fascinating people and stimulating conversation. On Sunday they took a train to Sheffield, where the weather was so cold and their digs so uncomfortable that they both felt miserable and longed for their London apartment. Lillian, on her knee in front of a fire in the grate of in their cold room in Sheffield on December 8th, wrote Bill her annual Christmas letter, which was filled with a brief account of their previous two weeks in Edinburgh and Glasgow. When they return to London George Black, Jr., has asked Jeanne for a few dates, but since he will most likely be in Liverpool, she and Jeanne will probably just see some movies as usual.

Their two-week layoff in London from December 13 to 26 for the Christmas holidays was a nostalgic vacation, marking a full year since they had left American shores. They were thrilled to return to their warm, comfortable Mount Royal apartment. "First time I've ever had such a wholly carefree vacation—Yipee!!!" Jeanne wrote in her diary on December 22nd. Jeanne had diligently mailed her father his Christmas present early—a special wool sweater she had had knitted for him. She wrote her father on December 21st, thanking him for the "swell picture of my pappy" that he had recently sent, which will be stuffed in her suitcase and taken on tour, where it will be "sitting in a ladies dressing room from now on, watching the make-up and quick changes." She had had a few dates with Larry Adler, who was performing in London, and saw the show starring her friend the ballerina Patricia Bowman at the Palladium that she had earlier seen at the tryout in Brighton. On December 21st she wrote in her diary again with a hint of rivalry that the "rowdy noisy audience laughed & called all thru the 'Don Juan' scene. Bowman acted as if nothing had happened and bowed to no applause whatsoever—Same thing happened in Brighton." On Christmas Eve, despite having the stomach flu, Jeanne had enjoyed Christmas dinner at the Black family's luxurious London apartment, where she wore her new cherry velvet evening gown and George Jr., romantically fawned over her. Then she and Lillian packed all night long to be ready to leave on their third tour of the British provinces the next morning.

While Jeanne and Lillian were on tour with *George Ahoy!* in the fall of 1936 the world had been riveted by the scandal surrounding the American divorcee Mrs. Wallis Simpson and King Edward VIII of England.[1] When commenting in her December 8,

1936, Christmas letter on the scandal involving the King and Mrs. Simpson that year, Lillian was sympathetic to the King's dilemma: "I feel quite sorry for him in having to decide whether to be a Cad and King, or Abdicate." After his abdication, Jeanne wrote her father on December 21st that the loyal English were hurling insults and innuendoes about Mrs. Simpson: "Well, anyway it caused a new Christmas carol to be sung by the children, 'Hark, the Herald Angels sing, Mrs. Simpson pinched our King.'"

During the fall of 1936 Jeanne and the cast of *George Ahoy!* also paid close attention to the news coming out of Spain. They devoured daily newspapers and listened to reports of the ongoing Spanish Civil War on the French and German radio stations. Lillian devoted a large part of her October 10, 1936, letter to Bill to the pivotal role played by France, England, and Russia in the war in Spain. Four days later Jeanne wrote her father about English hubris and nationalism, commenting that local people "speaking of the trouble in Spain and strikes in France, say, 'Oh, that can never happen here, This country has the greatest government in the world.' However the Fascist party created terrible riots in the East End [of London], and did appallingly cruel and destructive things to the Jews in that section." In her November 6th letter Jeanne described how they had been listening to the radio stations and reading newspapers all Sunday afternoon about the surrender of Madrid. They continued following the progress of the Spanish Civil War until it ended in April 1939 with Franco's fascist victory just months before the beginning of world war.

In December after their year touring in England, Jeanne and Lillian realized their good fortune during the years of the Great Depression of being booked in a secure touring show. They had escaped the fate of their friends and fellow vaudeville performers the Three Swifts, who arrived in London with their families in September 1936 but had to return to America since there were no bookings. Conditions for troupers on this British tour were in some ways superior to those for vaudevillians in America: "We carry our own musical director, stage manager, carpenter, electrician, and wardrobe woman, and everyone goes in a private car by train, and not over the treacherous ice covered roads in bitter winter weather, which is all American acts can afford to do now-a-days," Jeanne wrote her father on December 31st. When they read *Variety* they were even more aware of the benefits of living abroad where Jeanne could work without long layoffs until they had sufficient funds to return home again. "Are you listening Franklin D? Everyone would give their right eye to get 20 solid weeks over here, so wont look horse's gifts in the face," wrote Jeanne.

At the end of December 1936 Jeanne began her third tour in the provinces with *George Ahoy!*, leaving audiences loudly applauding until the final show in Wales in the spring of 1937. Jeanne was once again giving the audiences a treat with her beautiful, high-speed pirouettes and fouettés, and local newspaper reviews were glowing. Having not practiced during her two-week vacation in London and having the stomach flu when she arrived in Nottingham on December 26th, her muscles ached "like a toothache," Jeanne wrote in her diary on December 29th, and she was grateful that she could perform her pirouettes without getting dizzy. When she attended a pantomime performance in Nottingham, she ran into her mercurial suitor George Black, Jr., who promised to come backstage after her show but avoided her when he did. Jeanne and Lillian toasted the New Year at their Nottingham digs with their landlady.

The following week, despite having written ahead for digs in crowded Birmingham, Jeanne and Lillian were forced to search on foot for two hours until they found some available digs that only had gas lights and a broken wash stand. The highlight of their stay in Birmingham was when the wife of the star George Clarke took Jeanne to her furrier, where Jeanne purchased two fur coats with such elation that at night she performed "a sensational show for joy," she wrote in her diary on January 8, 1937. Three days later she wrote her father about a dangerous incident in Birmingham when before the show's finale a mob appeared at the stage door:

> A crowd of race-track tours, hoodlums and ruffians, ganged up on the door-man in an effort to get into the theatre to see the chorus girls. They knocked him down a long flight of stone stairs, after kicking him viciously in the stomach. Some of the stage-hands rushed to his assistance, and one had his eye almost gouged out, and another is now minus three teeth. Thirty policemen were called out, and the riot raged for almost a half hr.
>
> Our little call-boy although 17 years old, is a wiry little mick about 4 foot six, and in and out of the melee, tripping the rowdys and darting in and out like a wasp. Our stage manager had one of the prop pistols loaded with blanks, ready to fire in case they tried to break into the stage. It made a terrible stir, as it was "Pack-up" night, and we weren't allowed to leave the theatre till all was clear.

The police were called to deal with the mob and order was restored. The next day on Sunday they traveled by train as usual to their next booking.

In Leeds they quickly found decent digs despite the cold temperature. They spent most of their spare time in the small town seeing the free trade show movies and reading the stateside magazines and newspapers that Bill faithfully sent them; they had their trusty ten-year-old clock repaired.[2] At their next booking in a nondescript town Jeanne performed in another cold theatre with a terrible stage. In these provincial towns "the cue [sic] ask the first house people what the show is like. If they say 'Not so good' the cue just disappears," Jeanne wrote in her diary on January 18th. "[Our] Show considered the best in years—what fools we are! If we're too good they'll offer us a return week—God forbid!" Overjoyed to have nearly $1,000 in their nest egg, enough to pay Jeanne's income taxes and purchase two steamship tickets home, Jeanne and Lillian were finally able to relax.

They traveled to Chatham on Sunday. As customary Jeanne had written ahead to the addresses of various digs, but this time she did not wait for a wire back from a landlady who had a vacant room, assuming her letter would be the confirmation: when they arrived in Chatham the landlady claimed that she had not expected them, forcing them to walk for miles in the rain before they found a room in a 300-year-old hotel. Since the star George Clarke was sick, Jeanne had filled in time in the harem scene with her "Blue Danube" dance. Returning to London from Chatham for a few days, they rented a room in Charing Cross, where Lillian finally washed Jeanne's white dress costume, they had the red rumba dress cleaned, and Jeanne had an electrotherapy treatment. When they went to see Mrs. Black and Pauline for lunch, George Jr. and Alfie were there since they were not working, and Lillian was convinced that George Jr. was in love with Jeanne and would ask her for a date. Lillian was disappointed when he failed to call, but Jeanne realistically confessed in her diary on February 5th that she was not hurt by his arrogant, mercurial English personality since she was not in love with him: all she wanted was "to have someone to go about with," she wrote.

On Sunday they dashed to Waterloo station to catch the train to rainy Plymouth, where their digs had no bath, an outdoor privy, and the beds as hard as granite. Having brought along specialty items they had purchased in London's Selfridges food store, they amazed their landlady and the other natives by using some of these items to spice up the bland English food. Although the tiny theatre in Plymouth had barely enough room for her dancing, Jeanne managed to perform outstanding shows. In their free time they toured the countryside with a fellow cast member. They also were relieved to learn that Jeanne's work permit had been extended through April.

On February 7th Jeanne told her father he made them laugh when he recently wrote about his obsessive habit of shopping, wanting to purchase things of any size and shape for them, and how when they would read his letters over they hesitated at key words and phrases, fondly remembering happy family events and his basically "nice personality" despite his mental illness. "We are always saying 'Dad's such a darling!' Or 'Dad has such a sense of humor,' or 'He's so darn clever,'" she wrote. "So really the company thinks you're a paragon of all virtues and talents." Their idealization of Bill in the family letters was always an emotional lifeline and a hedge against their deep rooted feelings of isolation, loneliness, and fear of being destitute.

A train wreck delayed their trip to Brighton on Sunday, so they were forced to take a bus to another station and change trains twice. It had been in this charming seaside town where two years ago "Round About Regent Street" had tried out before its London premiere at the Palladium. Now much to Jeanne's delight she gave another great performance in Brighton the night when George Black was in the audience during this weeklong run. Once again Jeanne and her mother nostalgically took their lovely night walks along the ocean after the final show; during the day they walked along the bridge by the amusement pier. Jeanne reflected in her diary on February 15th that even though the stage floor in Brighton was "marvelous" so she could "dance for joy," the audiences were "lousy for applause." Audiences were always the losers when they failed to appreciate the beauty of her performances: "A dance is such an ephemeral thing, when the loveliest pose in the world is over, it's gone without leaving a tangible record except in the mind," she wrote. They were grateful to be working in a steady show with future bookings and had slowly grown their nest egg to $1,225. Jeanne ended her final letter to her father from Brighton on February 18th with the exciting news that airmail service across the Atlantic was scheduled for the spring: "Can you imagine me writing you on sunday and you getting it on Wednesday morn."

Next week in Portsmouth, despite the brilliance of her dancing, Jeanne continued to perform before lackluster provincial audiences. "Our best efforts bring no response so we sulkily work Cross Word Puzzles in the dressing room," she wrote in her diary on February 24th. Continuing to reflect on these "heartbreaking audiences," she wrote how the cast's "emotions over their [the audiences'] apathetic receptions vary from disgust to livid anger." In a letter to her father from Portsmouth on February 26th she considered how her unique family dynamic, based on the idealization of her father stripped of his mental illness inscribed in the family letters, was superior to families who actually lived together. This idealistic distance relationship sustained her emotionally while constantly on the road: "You know sometimes I feel sorry for these people around me for not having a pap like you. In spite of the fact that their families are together they never have known the real companionship we all feel for each other," she wrote. "This way, we see only the best, Virtues and Talents, and it idealizes our relationship. We cant annoy each other yet because we are all busy. We can share our pleasures and fun without any reservations because of a quarrel at breakfast, or a chip on the shoulder."

Back in London on February 28th for a two-week run in two small theatres in the suburbs followed by a week at the prestigious Holborn Empire, Jeanne and Lillian were happy to be settled again in an apartment at the comfortable Mount Royal and spent their free time cooking, shopping, working on Jeanne's income tax due April 1st, and calling agents and bookers. Jeanne performed in cold suburban theatres in East Hampton and New Cross with barn-like pocked stage floors that were an hour outside of London. Lillian had eight teeth extracted, and they continued enjoying the American magazines and newspapers sent by Bill. While performing at the Holborn Empire, Jeanne had a run of swell shows with perfect spins for the week. In her diary for March 10th she recorded that the Holborn Empire's stage manager claimed to have heard gossip from someone at the Palladium about the implications of her always living with her mother and predicting her marital state. Someone had told him that she "was married or going to be soon— ... these stories!"

While in London Jeanne and Lillian attended a production of *On Your Toes* at the Palace theatre in Cambridge Circus; that night after Jeanne's last show at the Holborn Empire they dressed up in their formal finery and went out together on the town for the first time in their lives, joining friends at the swank London Casino for dinner, dancing, and the floor show. Lillian had purchased a new black chiffon evening dress, and Jeanne wore her favorite cherry velvet gown that she had previously worn for Christmas dinner with the Black family. Jeanne believed that these dinner theatres like the London Casino were different from nightclubs and represented the new popular trend in show business.

On March 22nd they left the comforts of cosmopolitan London for chilly Newcastle-on-Tyne and performed in a theatre with a terrible raked stage. Although one night everything "went wrong," Jeanne wrote in her diary two days later, there were "swell hands & cheering for my numbers." A review in the *North Mall, Newcastle,* March 23, 1937, praised Jeanne's acting and dancing skills: "Leading feminine roles are convincingly taken by Cath Esler and Jeanne Devereaux, whose 'Lady in Red' dance is one of the highlights." On Sunday they traveled to Sheffield, where they found acceptable digs but a freezing theatre. They learned that the show would be booked for two weeks in May in Belfast and Dublin in Ireland, major cities in a country they had always wanted to visit, so they would be celebrating the coronation of the new King George VI in Dublin with the feisty Irish. The tour would most likely end in Swansea, Wales, by the end of May.

Exhausted from touring, Lillian wrote Bill on March 26th, the day they had arrived in Sheffield, that people who only live in one place like her family and himself are not able to understand a profession that requires constant traveling. "Most of them couldn't do half what Jeanne and I get done and yet they call us to task over not writing, as if we were just leisurely living over here. This, of course gets under our skin," she wrote. If Bill could experience work "of this sort for a few months," he would "go back and be the world's greatest and keenest advertising man, and I dont mean to hurt your feelings either, but by comparison you would just find out how leisurely you had been before." In Sheffield the star George Clarke "clowned thru second houses so much he completely broke me up in Haram," Jeanne wrote in her diary on March 30th.

After returning to their apartment at the Mount Royal in London, Jeanne performed at the Finsbury Empire Park theatre and then had a week layoff since George Clarke went on vacation. After the last show at Finsbury Park George Black, Jr., unexpectedly came backstage and took Jeanne to the Trocadero restaurant for a late dinner; the next day on Sunday they went to the London zoo and then saw an excellent film. During her week layoff Jeanne window shopped, went to see the show at the Palladium, worked on her contracts for her two-week booking at the Savoy hotel, bought a new hat and dress, and read the American magazines and newspapers that Bill had sent from home. On April 19th they took the train to Bradford, known for its woolen mills, where Jeanne performed with a bad cold—"So sick with cold I could only do Rumba and breath," she wrote in her diary—and Lillian treated her with hot lemonade, whisky, and aspirin. Fortunately, her pay was not docked for the two dances she could not perform. On Sunday they traveled to Leicester for a week-long booking beginning August 26th at the Royal Opera House, where they anxiously awaited the contracts from the Savoy supper club. While performing in Leicester they heard the rumors that the coronation would be cancelled because the King is suffering from violent fits and is confined at Windsor. In her diary for April 27th Jeanne complained that the British troupers were so anti–American that they would be happy if her booking at the Savoy fell through. "Everyone is so jealous and since they cant get it on me for my work, or that I drink or smoke they take it out in petty digs—about when we get up and terrible Americans & Mrs. Simpson—," she wrote. She was euphoric when the Savoy contracts arrived in Leicester three days later, but was realistic enough to know that when she performed in hotel dinner theatres applause was at a minimum and fine dining and being seen was the audience's priority.

After a day of sightseeing in the countryside around Leicester, they traveled by boat to Belfast. "Last night I stood up on deck in the lovely breeze watching the star-laden sky as the shore of England slipped out of view," Jeanne wrote her father on May 3rd. Basking in the bright summer weather and pristine air, they bought Irish linen handkerchiefs for everyone in the family and mailed them off by post, visited the historic Belfast sites, and took a side trip to Bangor on the coast. Belfast's *Irish News*, May 4, 1937, praised her "expert dancing. Jeanne Devereaux must be without a rival in the matter of twists and twirls—she spins as easily, and more gracefully, than any top"; on May 8th Jeanne wrote in her diary that she "did two swell shows—Fours in Pullins—Have about $1,600 in checks." On Sunday they traveled by train to Dublin and toured the town in the rain, admiring the attractive Irish people. Although the theatre had a terrible stage, Jeanne managed to give "swell" performances in front of appreciative Dublin audiences.[3] King George VI's coronation in rain soaked London occurred on May 12th: "Didn't hear the Coronation but heard the Kings painfully spoken message to the Empire at night," Jeanne wrote in her diary. Later when Jeanne and Lillian saw the color coronation film, they thought the theatrical values of the pageantry superficial.

On May 15th they caught the boat to Liverpool and then traveled by train to their final booking in Swansea, Wales. Once again the theatre was closed during the afternoon, and the stage was littered with scenery that had to be cleared. In her diary on May 18th Jeanne reflected that these afternoon theatre closings limiting practice and rehearsal time for the performers was the main reason that "English acts never have anything new to offer." However, in Swansea the theatre manager managed to open the theatre for afternoon rehearsals, and Jeanne practiced with her biggest balloon, which burst during her final performance of the run. The cast had been together on the road for many months, but on closing night they did not celebrate with the usual "fun and sparkle & sadness," Jeanne wrote in her diary on May 22nd. They just felt the "gloom" when something really special ends: "Did 'Lady in Red' for the last time in this show," she emotionally reflected. With the end of the *George Ahoy!* tour in Swansea, Jeanne completed one of the longest show runs of her professional career, earning enough money to rebuild her nest egg after the disaster in Montmartre and to purchase two steamship tickets back home to America.

9

International Casino and a Royal Performance in Paris

Traveling back to London on Sunday, Jeanne was shocked to learn that George Black, Jr., had left for New York in mid–May for a year's employment at the Morris Creative Agency. In addition to shopping and enjoying movies and theatre, she was immersed in the preparations for her upcoming engagement at the Savoy supper club. For the first time Lillian was not involved in selecting the costumes, which "are going to be beautiful," Jeanne wrote in her diary on May 28th. "White Lamé I designed myself and will allow me to bend easily." After the wild rush to get costumes and music ready, opening night at the Savoy on May 31st was a great success. The Savoy booking was marred only by the incessant popping of the large balloons she had used in her signature dance, most likely due to age or the weather. According to a review of her performance at the Savoy in the *World's Fair, Oldham*, June 5, 1937, "Miss Devereaux is a consummate artiste and her dancing is enhanced by a winning personality."

Jeanne recalled an embarrassing moment one evening when she was performing at the Savoy: "The dance team on the bill came offstage and instantly got into a very loud fight the instant the curtain closed. It continued through the Masters of Ceremonies introduction of the next act, which was me. The loud fight stopped just as the curtain reopened with me in a ballet pose—One waiter said people thought it was me rageing because of the cutoff & curtain timing." Jeanne later was excited to be reunited one night backstage with her friend and former adagio partner from St. Louis—Bill Winkler.

Since the British Minister of Labor refused to authorize any more work permits for Jeanne, she and Lillian purchased tickets home to New York on the *Queen Mary* leaving Southampton on June 16th. Jeanne had written her father on June 8th that they were finally coming home, and after securing her future bookings, planned to head to St. Louis for that family holiday in the Ozarks. She advised him not to take the bus to New York to meet them at the boat, but to save his money for the vacation. She wanted the family to have "a real carefree holiday [where] we don't have to feel we are spending too much after Mr. Grayhound has his 'Up and Back' slice," Jeanne wryly wrote. They would take a train to St. Louis with their trunks and baggage on their way to the West Coast, where they hoped Jeanne would perform in films. They needed also to visit the elderly Lanes, whose health had declined.

Jeanne performed her last show at the Savoy on June 13th with her last balloon, and three days later they bade farewell to their good friend Cath Esler, who had performed with Jeanne in *George Ahoy!*, at Waterloo station in London, and that night boarded the *Queen Mary* at Southampton bound for New York. Impressed by the size and grandeur of the boat, Jeanne wrote her father that it was the "finest of vessels afloat since the world began." With telegrams wishing them *"Bon Voyage"* and dozens of flowers sent by friends that scented their room, their departure from England was a "glamourous thing to remember always." On board Jeanne enjoyed fine dining and movies, played tennis, practiced in the gym, and danced at night with her usual entourage of admirers. When she received a cable from her suitor Bob Lamb informing her that he planned to meet the boat in New York, she wrote in her diary on June 18th that seeing Bob again is "going to be swell with Geo. [Black, Jr.] there too perhaps." Although she was eating two meals a day, she was relieved not to be obviously gaining weight.

When Jeanne and Lillian disembarked from the *Queen Mary* on June 21st, their close friends the Bennetts and Bob Lamb were at the dock to meet them. Jeanne wrote in her diary that Bob looked "like a god." After taking the Bennetts to dinner, Bob, now gainfully employed and owning a car, took Jeanne for a drive and then to the New Yorker where he was performing in an ice show; then they danced. The next day after completing his show Bob proposed marriage: "Rather sweet of him—I wish we were in a position to marry—Saw his show at New Yorker—It gave me a terrific thrill to see him zooming around as slim and straight and swift as Mercury—He's so beautiful it hurts—," she wrote in her diary on June 22nd. Kay Bennett Paul, who was also at the dock to meet Jeanne, later remembered that a handsome boyfriend was there also, and she often thought that Jeanne would marry this fine young man. For the rest of the year Jeanne dated both Bob Lamb and George Black, Jr., whom she still found unreliable but more relaxed living in New York rather than London. She still suspected that George would eventually propose marriage. Lillian wrote Bill on June 30th that Jeanne has many suitors "to take her around some, and altogether I have a hard time keeping her various beaus out of each others way." Jeanne, however, emphasized in a later interview that she was too busy with her career in 1937 to think about love or marriage with anyone; besides, she was still the sole economic support of herself and her mother.

Upon their return to New York Jeanne and Lillian resided at the Century Hotel at 111 West 46th Street. In addition to surviving the summer heat and spending time with Bob and George, Jeanne saw movies with her mother, went to the legitimate theatre and Radio City, visited museums, practiced daily, and attended Kobie's master dance classes, where other dancers would often applaud her incredible pirouettes. When she participated in these master classes and met the other talented and dedicated dancers, Jeanne predicted that ballet in America was experiencing a renaissance. She also visited Hal Sands, Dick Henry, and George White's press agent, as well as other bookers and agents to arrange some engagements for her. Ironically, Jeanne felt that the stress of frantically looking for bookings was essential for her general well-being, for in New York "you have to be on the go every minute or you feel lonely," she wrote in her diary on July 13th. Finally one of the agents booked Jeanne into the Michigan theatre in Detroit the week of July 23rd for $200 plus two train fares, to be followed by an engagement in Chicago. Once again she would experience the grind of performing four shows a day instead of the two shows nightly in Europe.

After a one-night performance in Buffalo, New York, and an audition for the new International Casino scheduled to open in August, Jeanne and Lillian left for her booking in Detroit, where she introduced a new dance with a huge balloon that fortunately only broke one time during the weeklong run. She shared the bill with Betty Boop, Popeye, the Rio Brothers, and some acrobats. While in Detroit she received news first from Hal Sands about her booking into the Metropolitan theatre in Boston for $250 a week beginning August 12th and then from the Morris Creative Agency about an exciting booking for four weeks at the lavish International Casino located in the heart of Times Square in New York for $200 a week. Writing in her diary on July 27th that she had "confirmed both dates so play time is over for us," Jeanne was eager to return to New York to find a comfortable apartment with an adequate kitchen for cooking since the International Casino engagement could possibly have a long run. She also began rehearsals for her dances at the International Casino. When she and Lillian visited the official costumier to review sketches for the costumes, they felt the sketches were not up to their usual standard, so they immediately had duplicate ones made by their own dressmaker Ida Belle that they were certain would function on stage. For the moment the family reunion planned for St. Louis would have to happen in the apartment in New York.

On August 11th Jeanne and Lillian took the train to Boston, where she was relieved to be performing only one show nightly at the Metropolitan theatre in a lovely scene with excellent production values. When Lillian saw the show from out front, she said, "it was gorgeously lit for my dress," Jeanne wrote in her diary on August 12th. Although Boston still abided by the blue laws prohibiting dancing on Sundays, Jeanne performed as a ballerina during the week and as an acrobat on Sunday. Shortly after she returned to New York, Bob Lamb woke her up early, told her to get dressed and come downstairs, and then proposed that they elope. "Finally went up to talk it over with BW," Jeanne wrote in her diary on August 20th. "He was so sweet but I didn't know how serious to take him because of the Tom Collins. I do love Bob but we haven't talked it over enough to dash of [sic] so precipitately." Bob was leaving for Chicago soon, and was obviously frustrated about his relationship with Jeanne: "He neednt worry he started this marriage business not me—," she wrote in her diary on August 22nd.

After apartment hunting they finally signed a lease for one in a newly renovated hotel with a kitchenette, dinette, bedroom and bath, and attractive living room at 57 West 45th Street—big enough for the anticipated family reunion and close enough to the new International Casino so that Jeanne could walk home for tea and cakes with fellow troupers during hours between shows. Most of Jeanne's time was consumed by rehearsals, costume fittings, photography sessions, and master classes to re-set her balloon dance in preparation for the opening at the International Casino. She had her first rehearsal in the casino space with scenery on September 4th and then the opening was delayed again so the stage could be redone. Finally the Morris Creative Agency was able to get half salary for the cast members to cover rehearsals and the many delays. When she was exempt from rehearsals, Jeanne continued to take Kobie's master ballet classes.

The extravagant International Casino show was a musical revue called "Bravo," which included 125 performers from ten countries before an audience potential of 2,500 people. Advertised as a "revue-restaurant" and taking more than a year to build, the International Casino was an entirely new performance space in New York that combined large-scale vaudeville entertainment with dining and dancing. It was designed to compete with impresario Clifford C. Fisher's successful nightclub called the French Casino Follies, which had been deemed by *Variety*, January 16, 1937, "the No. 1 nitery entertainment of the town." Lillian wrote Bill on October 13th that the audiences at the International Casino have been packed "to the dome, most of the time": she had also heard that the French Casino, "which formerly held full sway," was practically empty. Pierre Sandrini, head of the famous Bal Tabarin in Paris, and Jacques Charles, associated with the Casino de Parée and the Moulin Rouge, were brought over from Paris to stage the big show, since its French counterparts inspired the International Casino. When these important French producers sailed home on the *Normandie* for Paris at the beginning of October, nearly the entire cast went to the dock to wish them "*Bon Voyage.*"

Jeanne danced in the premiere on September 17th, which was such a "curtailed show with no production scenes," Jeanne wrote in her diary, that the audience was "invited back free."[1] It took a few weeks before the show was up to par and began its official run: the reviewer for *Variety*, September 22, 1937, announced that he would be deferring his official review of the show "until the proceedings are smoother." At the premiere Jeanne received congratulatory telegrams from George Black, Jr., Jimmy Givens, Patricia Bowman, Ida Belle, and many others. Between the afternoon rehearsal and opening night someone had "waxed the floor like glass" making it slick and dangerous, and she also had to replace a big bonnet she had worn in one of her solos with a lighter pink tulle turban. At the premiere there was a dinner show at 8:30 p.m., followed by a late show at 10:30 p.m.; at subsequent shows the dinner show was at 7:45 p.m., followed by a supper show at midnight. Once the afternoon rehearsals were over and the show began its official run, Jeanne's typical schedule was to return to her apartment by 10:30 p.m., enjoy tea and cakes and spirited conversation with invited cast members and other friends, return to the theatre by 11:30 p.m., and then home again around 3:30 a.m. for a snack, bath, and hair in curlers before bed. Going home between shows broke the monotony of her schedule, giving her some relief from the overcrowded backstage area. To keep up her glamorous appearance and high energy, most days she would sleep until 2:00 p.m.

The program featured the headlining acts, which included Jeanne's two solos, along with the Show Girls, the Chester Hale Dancers, the Ballet, and the Gertrude Hoffmann Girls. The "Bravo" revue was in two parts: in the second part after the intermission Jeanne danced as the "Preterit" along with Vera Troizky in "Conjugations," where she wore her own pink costume, and then performed her amazing balloon dance as "The First Sun-Rays" with the International Ballet in "Sun's Glory." She also danced with the entire cast in the finale. Dressed in an exotic, harem-like costume that she had designed and performing to Debussy's "Claire de Lune," Jeanne was costumed in a turquoise pleated chiffon skirt with a matching bodice studded with sequins, while blue lights bathed the five-foot diameter balloon she spun with her hands. Jeanne laughed when she recalled how in one of the promotional pictures her skirt yoke slipped, revealing her "tummy button"; of course, the photographer airbrushed it out. In what she later called today's "belly button culture," this revealing photograph would have been accept-

Jeanne Devereaux in a promotional photograph for her signature balloon dance at the International Casino, New York, September 11, 1937–November 11, 1937. Her tummy button has been air brushed out. Her balloon dance was her most sensational, and she performed it many times during her dancing career. Photograph by celebrity photographer Maurice Seymour in his New York studio. Seymour photographed the most famous ballet dancers of his time. Courtesy Jeanne Devereaux Perkins Collection.

able. Jeanne emphasized how "difficult it was to control this massive balloon: it wanted to have its own way, reacting to every breeze from the wings, but I had to control it while dancing effortlessly." In her diary she described the many nights when the balloon dance went beautifully. However, one night during the run of "Bravo" the balloon burst at the end of Jeanne's dance, astonishing both Jeanne and the audience; being a seasoned professional, she was able to complete the dance. Lillian later wrote about the mishap to Bill on October 13th, noting that Jeanne had "finished up as good without it, which caused an ovation from the packed audience."

During the run of "Bravo" on September 22nd Lillian accidentally slipped on the Casino steps, breaking her ankle in three places, and spent two weeks at City Hospital, followed by weeks of recovery on crutches with plaster cast changes. Not wanting to worry Bill, Jeanne and Lillian waited for a week to tell him about the accident. Jeanne, however, hinted in her letters that he might consider visiting them right now, or later at Christmas, in their wonderful New York apartment, but only if he had adequate funds. Though he responded that he needed to wait until his fall orders were closed before coming to New York, Jeanne continued to encourage him to visit them. Having finally told him about the accident, on October 1st Jeanne wrote her father that Lillian was home and life was easier now, since she would not have to travel back and forth to visit her mother in the hospital. While recuperating in the apartment, Lillian would nervously wait up every night until Jeanne returned safely home around 3:30 a.m., relieved that no harm had come to her on the dark streets often lined with unsavory characters.

On closing night November 11th Lillian, still in a plaster cast but now managing without crutches, saw the show from out front for the first time. The cashier at the International Casino withheld Jeanne's final check since she refused to sign a release for back salary; later when she told the Morris Creative Agency and the American Federation of Artists (A.F.A.) about the devious situations they assured her that they would resolve the issue. Wanting to stay in America longer, Jeanne had turned down an offer from Sandrini to perform in Paris, and was once again unemployed, spending her days in Kobie's master classes and her free evenings seeing movies and stage shows at Radio City. She treated herself to a night at the American Ballet, where she reunited with cast member Bill Dollar, her good friend from her early days in St. Louis, and invited him to dinner. Jeanne wrote her father on November 15th that they would soon be leaving for a booking beginning the week of December 10th at the lavish Chicago Theatre in that windy city, so if he wanted to visit them in their wonderful New York apartment he had better get on a bus within the week; otherwise they could have their family reunion in Chicago. One of the first baroque movie presentation palaces in the country, the Chicago Theatre had opened in 1921 and featured some of the best stage shows combined with movies until it discontinued stage shows in the 1950s.

Since Lillian learned that her ankle and foot had healed except for one place, probably requiring surgery when she returned to New York, she was attempting to arrange a legal settlement from the International Casino owners before she was to leave for Chicago. Jeanne, needing to stay trim and fit so that she was ready to work at a moment's notice, had been strenuously rehearsing and practicing every day in addition to attending master classes. They visited Jeanne's costumier for fittings for two new costumes to use in Chicago. In her letter to Bill on November 24th Lillian reflected that the Great Depression had taken a great toll on American's entertainment industry: no movie is shown in the theatres for more than two weeks, and theatres, once filled to capacity, are now almost empty.

On November 25th Jeanne and Lillian celebrated their first Thanksgiving dinner in two years with a fried chicken dinner with close friends in their New York apartment.

The next day Lillian attended Jeanne's master class at Kobie's for the first time since her accident. They enjoyed hosting tea in their spacious apartment with friends and colleagues until their departure for Chicago on December 5th. On the bill with Jeanne for the booking from December 10th to 17th at the Chicago Theatre were the musical Continental Varieties Revue and the singing cyclist Joe Jackson. The movie was *I'll Take Romance*, starring the opera singer Grace Moore and Melvyn Douglas. Once again, Jeanne was thrilled to see her headlining name in bright lights on the Chicago Theatre's landmark marquee. Although there is no documentation providing details of the family reunion at the Sherman Hotel in Chicago, Jeanne confirmed in her diary that Bill had joined them in Chicago, where he took an iconic photograph of the Chicago Theatre's marquee. They then accompanied him on the bus home to St. Louis and continued en

Jeanne Devereaux as a headliner with star billing for stage revue on the Chicago Theatre's landmark State Street marquee, Chicago, Illinois, December 10–17, 1937. The revue cast also included the musical Continental Varieties Revue and the popular singing cyclist Joe Jackson. The movie *I'll Take Romance*, starring the opera singer Grace Moore and Melvyn Douglas, had been released in America by Columbia Pictures on November 17, 1937. The iconic Chicago Theatre, one of the first opulent baroque movie presentation houses in the country seating over 3,000 people, opened on October 26, 1921, discontinued stage shows in the 1950s, closed in 1985, and re-opened after an extensive restoration the following year. Photograph by Jeanne's father Bill Helman. Courtesy Jeanne Devereaux Perkins Collection.

route to a brief Lane family reunion in Pasadena. Jeanne and Lillian left St. Louis on a modern train with large windows and few passengers on Christmas Eve, spending a relaxing Christmas day on the train in New Mexico and Arizona. They were surprised when the entire Lane family met them early in the morning at the station in Los Angeles. On December 29th Jeanne had her first surgery on her nose at the City of Angeles Hospital. She wrote in her diary the following day that she was all "bandaged with two cute swollen bright red eyes—Family took me home—I'm the prettiest spotted pup in the family—Feeling queer." Jeanne ended 1937 with this final entry in her diary, and she never wrote another word in her treasured tome.

This three-week family reunion with Lillian's family was one of the first times that Jeanne and Lillian had visited Pasadena when they were not destitute and in need of shelter. When the bandages on Jeanne's nose were removed in early January 1938, she was eager to introduce her new nose to society. They left Pasadena and returned to their apartment in New York, where Jeanne signed a contract to perform for three months in Paris at the Bal Tabarin nightclub. Jeanne's nose and now Lillian's new dentures and doctor expenses for her broken ankle had taken a toll on their finances, so Jeanne needed to resume work immediately. They sorted through their belongings, deciding what to take to Europe and what to send to Lillian's sisters in California and Nebraska. They ended up traveling with twelve suitcases and two trunks, not wanting to purchase many household items while abroad. Before they left they hoped Hal Sands could arrange a booking with George Black for Jeanne to dance at the resort in Blackpool, England, after Paris, and then in a unit in South America in June, as well as a booking for her to perform at the World's Fair in New York in 1939. Although the steamship tickets for Paris were included in Jeanne's contract, other expenses such as fees for passports and visas, tips on the boat, and railroad fare from Le Havre to Paris, and a deposit on their apartment were not covered, so Lillian asked Bill for a loan of $100, which she promised to repay after their first paycheck in France.

Although their departure for Paris was noted in *Variety*, February 2, 1938, Jeanne unexpectedly heard from her manager the Music Corporation of America that the French producer Sandrini had postponed the opening of his show for two weeks, compounding their shortage of funds and forcing them to pay two weeks additional living expenses in New York that were unbudgeted. Since all their frantic efforts at securing work for the week before their departure were unsuccessful, Lillian was forced again to ask Bill to send them another $100 to be repaid by the second paycheck in France. She and Jeanne now "must bend our noses to the grind stone again," Lillian wrote Bill on February 18th, thanking him for sending a check for $200 to tide them over. They were concerned about crossing the stormy Atlantic in the early spring, but were "off in quest of Gold." They were also concerned about war in Europe, hoping that Germany would focus on absorbing Austria while they were there and not launch any new attacks on their neighbors. They were confident, however, that if war were to break out, their French producers would immediately arrange for their passage home.

On March 2, 1938, Jeanne and Lillian embarked on the *Normandie* bound for the Continent. Bill had sent them a *"Bon Voyage"* telegram, and they had received the customary steamer basket of fruit and flower bouquets from friends. During the crossing they encountered a huge storm, forcing many passengers to remain in their cabins or hold on to doors, walls, and railings. Despite the bad weather, Jeanne managed to see movies, play ping pong, eat fine food, and dance in the evenings. By March 8th the passengers bound for England disembarked at Southampton while the others continued on to Le Havre to catch the boat train to Paris, where it was chilly enough for them to wear their fur coats.

Having settled into their apartment in the Terrass Hotel at 14 Rue de Maistre overlooking the famous tree lined Pére La Chaise cemetery where famous celebrities like Sarah Bernhard and Chopin were buried, Jeanne and Lillian frantically worked to prepare two sensational dances with new musical arrangements for the show's premiere. Since the ones Jeanne had already prepared for her two scenes at the Bal Tabarin were not approved by the producers, she choreographed a balloon dance to fit the new music, as well as a modern waltz instead of her standard "Blue Danube." A few weeks later she had to create an extra number for the show, requiring new choreography, a costume, and hours of rehearsal—all negotiated in difficult conversational French, which Jeanne was now diligently studying three times a week just to conduct daily living. On Sundays they toured the main historic sites like the Louvre, the Luxembourg Palace and Gardens, and Versailles.

On March 29th Jeanne finally opened at the Bal Tabarin, home of the original Cancan dance, starring in a spectacular revue called *Les Heures Sont Belles*, where she

Jeanne Devereaux performing her signature balloon dance on the spacious dance floor surrounded by the dining audience at the Bal Tabarin nightclub revue in Paris, France, April 1938. This was a benefit performance for the Yacht-Motor Club of France. Her booking at the Bal Tabarin began on March 29, 1938, and ended on June 29, 1938. Photograph by J. Clair-Guyot as an illustration in an unidentified publication dated 9 April 1938. Courtesy Jeanne Devereaux Perkins Collection.

danced in the "Coeur sentimental" act as "L'Amoureuse" and in "La Publicité" as "La Loterie Nationale." The performers at the Bal Tabarin rarely used the small stage, but moved out onto the spectacular, narrow glass floor lighted from underneath, closely surrounded by the audience. As "L'Amoureuse" Jeanne performed her new balloon dance in front of sold-out audiences, and newspaper reviewers praised her specialty dancing as the hit of the floor show, especially her amazing toe dancing and pirouettes. The show also included the nightclub's renowned Le Corps de Ballet de Tabarin and Le Celebre French Cancan de Tabarin, with many of the beautiful dancers appearing semi-nude. Among the packed crowds who attended the show night after night were celebrities like the actress Mary Pickford, the Woolworth heiress Barbara Hutton, the King of Sweden, and Britain's Minister of War; during the intermission the small dance floor was always overcrowded. Since Jeanne's show began each night at midnight and on Saturdays there were two shows, when they returned to their chilly apartment they rarely went to bed before 4:30 a.m. and usually slept until 2:00 p.m. the following day. Jeanne was to be paid in dollars and not francs, making her more expensive than the European performers given the current exchange rate, so her first two paychecks were late. They were relieved when they could finally send Bill an American Express check for his $200 in late April, honoring their promise to repay his loan.

Jeanne was rarely seriously ill or injured, and she expected to fulfill her contract to perform in the Bal Tabarin show until its closing on June 29th. However, after performing for two nights with a terrible sore throat and other flu-like symptoms, around June 14th Lillian rushed her to the American Hospital of Paris in Neuilly-Sur-Seine, where Jeanne was diagnosed with diphtheria, requiring powerful serum injections and throat paintings with silver nitrate. She remained in the hospital for a month until her throat cultures were negative, losing a month's salary and the ability to practice to keep fit—both crushing blows to a solo toe dancer on a tight budget. On June 22nd Jeanne sent her Aunt Lenore and Uncle Roy the witty verses she had composed while recuperating (see Appendix One).

Trapped in her hospital bed, Jeanne was thrilled when booking agents in England signed her up for the finest London cabarets and variety music halls. Her French contract for the Bal Tabarin engagement had stipulated that the cost of two steamship tickets home to America would only be included if Jeanne and her mother sailed from Europe one week after closing. If they were to go home right now, however, they would most likely not work all summer, so they decided to forfeit the paid tickets for a solid eight-week booking in England with the possibility of an extended stay. Jeanne wrote her father on July 4th that the "Music Corp of America (London) has gotten Leeds, Coventrey, and two weeks at Grosvenor House, London, for me and perhaps can fill in the entire fall, so we shall be once more delighted to retreat from the French front, into the embrace of an English speaking country."

As she remained in the hospital being treated for diphtheria, Jeanne's extraordinary talent and artistry recently exhibited at the Bal Tabarin were rewarded by her being chosen for a special performance before British royalty to be held on July 20, 1938, in Paris at the Chateau Bagatelle in the Bois de Boulogne before King George VI and Queen Elizabeth. Jeanne thought that the objective of this state visit was to demonstrate to Hitler that England and France were strong allies. French security forces were on high alert when the British king and queen arrived in Paris. Their royal barge, protected by a bullet proof screen and escorted by naval launches, sailed down the Seine river to the Hotel de Ville, where the Parisian Municipal Government was headquartered.

Still recovering and only released from the hospital nine days before her performance, Jeanne danced two solos before royalty at the Chateau Bagatelle on a floating stage in the middle of a lake surrounded by lilies in a program called "Fantaisie"—one with her lunar-like balloon, bathed with blue light, to the music by Debussy and the other a fast ballet to Gershwin, both featuring her famous, world-class pirouetting. President and Madame Lebrun and the Paris Municipal Council hosted this open-air garden party for King George VI and Queen Elizabeth, who were seated on golden chairs and surrounded by 200 privileged guests. Called in the *Daily Mirror* for July 21st "The King at a Cabaret," the program consisted of girls from the current Bal Tabarin revue, and the main feature was Jeanne's balloon ballet. Many of the local newspapers mentioned that since the King and Queen could not attend the cabarets and music halls of Paris, particularly the nightclubs of Montmartre, the Parisians staged Montmartre in the sunshine of a public garden.

Dressed in white tulle edged with roses, Jeanne danced with her large balloon on the floating stage in the center of the lake, surrounded by sky and clouds, seeing her reflection in the water as she twirled and spun, which she later described as quite disorienting. The *New York Herald Tribune* for July 23rd published a lead article titled "American Was Entertainment Star of Garden Party for King, Queen," where Jeanne was quoted as saying, "'I was really thrilled to be asked to dance two solos for the King and Queen. When I first came out, I kept watching out of the corner of my eye, just to see what their [the King and Queen's] reaction would be to my numbers.... Every artist doesn't know what to expect. But when it was over, and I had bowed to them, and then to the audience, I found them applauding with the rest of them.'" Jeanne felt that British royalty truly admired foreign variety artists like herself and that the Queen was more interested in ballet than the King: "One of the nicest things about the present English court is the sympathetic interest they have in foreign artists," she said. "It is really a pleasure to work in an atmosphere like that."

For all of Jeanne's previous performances Lillian had been her dresser, but having failed to obtain an official pass to the garden party, she was replaced for this special occasion. According to the newspaper article, Jeanne's young maid was so "interested in watching the royal couple from behind a clump of bushes, Miss Devereaux, with three-and-a-half minutes to change between numbers, nearly missed her second entrance cue." In a later interview Jeanne elaborated on this humorous episode with her costume maid that night at the Bois de Boulogne: "After taking my bow, I rushed up the tree and shrub covered hillside at the back of the floating stage to the costume tent, out of sight of the guests," but the costume maid was nowhere in sight. Since she needed to make a quick change, she struggled into her next costume, which had a long zipper in the back that was difficult to reach. "At the last moment before I had to run down the path to the stage again for my second number," said Jeanne, "she [her costume maid] arrived in a panic and pulled on the zipper so hard that she tore the silk bridal veil tulle skirt down the back—luckily the tulle floated with every movement and the damage wasn't noticeable." When Jeanne asked the costume maid where she had been,

Jeanne Devereaux in a royal performance before King George VI and Queen Elizabeth on a floating lake in the Chateaux Bagatelle in the Bois de Boulogne, Paris, France, July 20, 1938. Jeanne had been performing her signature balloon dance in Paris at Montmartre's Bal Tabarin nightclub. She was chosen from among all the entertainers in Paris to perform before the British royals who were making their first state visit abroad since King George VI's coronation. Courtesy Jeanne Devereaux Perkins Collection.

she replied, "she was crouched down in the shrubbery to catch a view of the king and queen."

Having achieved stardom for her royal garden party performance in Paris, which had generated extensive publicity, Jeanne wrote her father from London on August 1, 1938, that "I've gotten some grand publicity over this King and Queen affair and shall try to keep the 'ball rolling' as publicity is the life blood of my business." The International Press Service had assured her that news of the royal performance with color pictures had also been sent to American newspapers. She soon discovered that her former celebrity in England had also not been forgotten. When they had docked at Southampton, a "customs man passed us, then his fellow worker came over and watched my things being passed," Jeanne wrote. "I heard him say 'That's Jeanne Devereaux, I saw her dance the 'Moth and Flame' in a crazy show.'" The same man had also seen her perform in Portsmouth in *George Ahoy!*

Relieved to be back in London, Jeanne was soon a smash hit at the luxury hotels—Grosvenor House, the Mayfair, the Dorchester, and the Savoy—as well as at famous theatres like the Holborn Empire and the Stratford Empire. Sharing the "vaud" billing with her for a variety show in August 1938 at the Stratford Empire were the Del Rios, Freddie Bamberger, Jack Leonard, Fats Waller, Douglas Leonard, Marie Burke, Bobby Wright and Marion, and the singing cyclist Joe Jackson. In a weeklong show at the Holborn Empire beginning on August 15th she was on the bill with the aerialists Les Storks, the comedians Murray & Mooney, the street singer Arthur Tracy, the Sparkes Brothers, and Freddy Zay the juggler on a high unicycle, performing with the Six Dancing Dudes the same two dances she had recently presented in Paris to the King and Queen in the Bagatelle. In September she was dancing in a cabaret show at the Royal Bath hotel in "Stars on Parade" with other famous vaudeville performers: the *Daily Echo*, September 13, 1938, claimed that "for sheer artistry in movement, Jeanne Devereaux ... has an act of incomparable beauty."

In September Jeanne made her first television appearance just two years after the British Broadcasting Company (BBC) had debuted the world's first high-definition television service with three hours of daily programming from its London studio in Alexandra Palace to the 2,000 television sets in Britain. Having spent another wonderful week with the Black family at their palatial country house, returning to London in their Rolls Royce, she wrote her father on September 5th that she "had to come back to town because of a television Broadcast in the middle of the week, so went down again after it was over. Another television on Sept 10th, but since it only transmits 50 miles at most, I doubt if you can see it." Having been selected as one of the premier performers in Britain that year, she reprised her spectacular balloon dance to the music of "Claire de Lune" on British television at London's last pre-war Radio Exhibition at Olympia, called Radiolympia, where in 1938 television sets and demonstrations were the main attraction. When Jeanne danced live in front of a large screen in the BBC's television studio at Radiolympia, she was reminded of the royal performance in Paris dancing on the floating lake and seeing her image reflected in the surrounding water. She was later recognized as one of the outstanding performers on television that year, and was honored at the annual award ceremony held at Alexandra Palace, part of which had been leased since 1935 by the BBC for its public television transmissions until the early 1950s.

"Had a lovely week" performing in Bournemouth, wrote Jeanne to her father on September 19th, "there sunny and warm. The ocean view was georgeous, and we spent most of the day out in the air." Now back in London Jeanne's throat no longer hurt, and Lillian's ankle, still not completely healed, was as strong as possible. In a few days they were scheduled to sail on the *Normandie* to New York, so she included a laundry list of items to be accomplished before departure:

> CALL 12 PEOPLE. LABEL ALL BAGGAGE. BUY WOOL FOR KNITTING. BUY RUBBER FOR BALLET SHOES. RETURN BOOKS TO PEOPLE. THANK MR. BLACK FOR A WEEK END. TRY TO BUY SILVER TEA POT USED BY HOTELS.—O.K. STEAMSHIP TICKETS. GATHER PASSPORT AND WOOD BLOCKS AT MANAGERS. CASH TELEVISION CHECKS. PAY COMMISSIONS. GET INCOME TAX PAID. AND A FEW EXTRA THINGS.

Always ending her letters on a positive note, she said, "I'm worn out just thinking about it, but it will be swell to be home again."

When they encountered a huge hurricane halfway across the Atlantic aboard the *Normandie*, Jeanne and Lillian were terrified and gripped tightly the large, chrome handles securely fastened on the walls of their cabin. When the huge ship had started to sway and vibrate from the violent winds and huge waves, bobbing around in the turbulent waters like a child's toy, they were fearful that it might capsize and sink. They were experiencing the Great New England Hurricane of September 1938 that had travelled up the Eastern seaboard and killed over 500 people and destroyed thousands of vessels in New England. In her letter on September 27th after docking in New York and moving into their temporary lodgings at the Schuyler Apartments at 57 West 45th Street, Jeanne recounted for Bill the terrifying hurricane that had made them so seasick they only wanted "to die and get it over with." It took them weeks to recover from their seasickness. Jeanne soon resumed her master classes and practiced daily until she tore a ligament in her toe when her shoe broke in half *en pointe*, resulting in a long layoff from performing. For the first time in her letters to her father Jeanne mentions her entourage of suitors: "I have a 'court' of sorts, and they all want to take me to dinner and shows, so it's been hectic," she wrote on October 18th. Their return to America occurred at a dangerous but opportune time. Jeanne and Lillian later learned from a German friend who had performed with Jeanne in Paris at the Bal Tabarin that a German submarine had followed the *Normandie* across the Atlantic and would have sunk it with a torpedo if war had been declared. Before departing Jeanne had known that the ship's crew was apprehensive about the crossing, but at the time she never knew the extent of the risk they were taking by sailing on that ship. Her German friend also had informed her that when the other performers at the Bal Tabarin were suddenly ordered home by their consulates before war was officially declared, the French producer Sandrini had refused to buy their steamship tickets as contracted. She also heard that the impresario George Black was in critical condition in a London hospital most likely caused by the stress of impending war and the threat of losing his personal fortune. The other stories Jeanne and Lillian heard from friends and acquaintances only made them feel even more grateful for having made it home to New York safely.

10

Radio City, Brazil and Lean Times

In the fall of 1938 while Jeanne nursed her injured foot she constantly looked for jobs in a depressed entertainment market. Except for the presentation movie houses, American vaudeville was on a steep decline, and jobs were scarce. Predictions were afloat, however, that with the 1939 World's Fair in Flushing Meadows, New York, scheduled to open on April 30th and close on October 31st, show business in New York would revive: the next year would be one of the best in ten years. Jeanne hoped to get a booking in one of the revues or musical comedies being cast at the end of 1938, anticipating a good run during 1939 when tourists would fill the theatres.

When they returned to New York from England, Jeanne and Lillian were exhausted by the hectic pace of having rushed all over the world looking for work. Jeanne's diphtheria and their stay in London cut short due to threat of war also had reduced their hard-earned nest egg to the bare necessities, and now Jeanne's foot injury had forced a layoff. On November 2nd Lillian wrote Bill that they were "both in need of letting a couple of months elapse before working again," but would not have this luxury since they always have to worry about expenses. Although Jeanne had received an offer to return to Paris, Lillian wanted her to have "a chance at a big show, and 'Fame' in her own country." Lillian predicted that in a few weeks their negotiations with Radio City Music Hall would result in Jeanne's first engagement in years at a New York theatre that was "such a wonderful spot to be seen in." Jeanne, confident in her talent and artistry from her successful tour in Europe, passionately wanted to perform at Radio City Music Hall, the world's largest presentation house, where vaudeville lived on longer than at any other theatre across America.[1] Since her arrival in New York with her mother eleven years ago, Jeanne had taken every opportunity to see the spectacular vaudeville revue shows at Radio City, often starring the popular prima ballerina Patricia Bowman. Jeanne had idolized Radio City since its opening in 1932, and just walking through the buildings had always thrilled her and inspired her to achieve stardom. Recalling her vaudeville tour with the "Sixteen Russell Markert Dancers" in 1929–30, the precursors of the Radio City Rockettes, she dreamed of sharing the stage once again with one of these famous precision dance troupes.

Although Jeanne continued to take her master class every day, she protected her injured foot, anxious about it being healed in time for her possible booking at Radio City. An x-ray had revealed no broken bones, but she needed to refrain from toe work for fear of permanently injuring her arch. Lillian had figured that if all else failed and Jeanne were unable to perform, to keep from starving they could always get jobs with Uncle Sam in one of the armaments factories making munitions in anticipation of war. George Black, having recovered from his recent serious illness, and his son Alfie, were in New York for a week scouting the shows for talent. Jeanne and Lillian invited them to their apartment for an American home cooked dinner. A couple of weeks later they encountered Jeanne's godmother Aunt Kate Leigh from St. Louis while walking up Fifth Avenue and took her to Radio City Music Hall that night.

Jeanne and Lillian made a tentative proposal to Bill for a quick family reunion over Christmas in their comfortable New York apartment. Jeanne hoped to have a solid booking at Radio City so they could be assured of being in town over the holidays, but she could not guarantee her father anything. Previously booked based on her stellar professional reputation, Jeanne was now forced to show up for auditions with one pianist accompanist instead of an orchestra, with unflattering lighting that made her face look pale and her eyes sunken: "Well, it makes no difference how many wonderful performances you've given in the past, what public acclaim you've earned," she wrote her father on December 7th. At auditions "the lords that be sit amidst clouds of cigar smoke and judge you under those uncomplimentary conditions. I hate auditions like poison—But I guess I have to take my poison." Moreover, the theatre owners "pay only a pittance for cheap acts these days, and even if you play in both good and bad American theatres, your route can only be stretched to thirteen weeks, whereas in England there are enough theatres and repeat bookings in those theatres for a route lasting three years." In a letter on December 31st Lillian revealed that the family reunion at Christmas never happened, since Jeanne had been hired to perform at Radio City and started rehearsals immediately.

When Bill learned that the Christmas reunion was cancelled, he wrote Lillian about his lack of business this year, requesting that in lieu of Christmas gifts from now on he preferred at his advancing age for them to open a savings account for him. Lillian could understand his increasing need for a sense of financial security, but canceling Christmas was unacceptable: as hard as Jeanne worked to support the family, she deserved time off with some holiday cheer and festivities. "It is not so easy for Jeanne to forego holidaying and gifts and all the colorful trimmings of life besides the work and worry of making a living which takes up her time and energies till she cant even have a moment for having fun or going with the young people on pleasure bent," she wrote Bill on December 31st. "Young men want her to go here and there but she always has something she has to do in connection with her work, so its nearly impossible for her to have dates with them. She is always on the outside, looking in, at other people's Xmas festivities, parties, etc. so its natural for her to want a little Xmas too," she wrote. To manage her loneliness, Jeanne needed to maintain her fiction of a loving, nuclear family especially during the holidays even if it meant celebrating only through the mail; Jeanne later wrote to her father on January 1, 1939, "giving presents to people we love is as old as the world itself." Lillian encouraged Bill to improve his wardrobe, since she and Jeanne had learned early on that they needed to "dress up to kill" in order to be successful.

When her foot was finally healed, Jeanne resumed dancing with her first appearance on the spacious stage at Radio City, premiering on December 29, 1938, in the revue

"Dawn of a New Day," the World's Fair's slogan connoting an optimistic vision of the future based on the world's impressive technological innovation. "When I say that I danced at Radio City," Jeanne later mused, "people usually assume that I was a Rockette," although she was always featured in the cast as a soloist performing a star turn in front of the Music Hall Corps de Ballet. Like most of the early stage revues at Radio City, Jeanne's show was produced by Leon Leonidoff with sets designed by Bruno Maine, featuring the famous Rockettes; Vincente Minnelli was often the stage manager. In her début performance Jeanne danced in "Drum Roll" with Jane Sproule and the Music Hall Corps de Ballet, as well as in the grand finale; the movie was *Topper Takes a Trip*, starring Constance Bennett and Roland Young. The show having closed after a weeklong run, Lillian wrote Bill on February 5, 1939, that the "STAGE SHOW" had been "the best one Radio City Music Hall had [presented] all year ... netting them $120.000 in one week, next largest intake since the Music Hall first opened. But the picture ... was such a weak picture they could not hold it over." Lillian was pleased that Jeanne had been told by the booking agent for Radio City that they would definitely use her again soon, "as they liked her so much": she would be guaranteed to play at least three times a year, but the dates would be flexible. Since they would not be able to live on promises of "three times a year," Jeanne and Lillian looked for other engagements.

They also needed to find a more affordable apartment, with a longer lease than the one they presently had at the Schuyler Hotel, where the monthly rents were increasing by $20 because of the influx of tourists attending the World's Fair. They eventually moved to a furnished apartment at 56 West 65th Street. It had been twelve years since they had a place to call home where they could leave their few belongings and treasures safely and travel with just one suitcase. Lillian asked Bill to send them some of their table linens, blankets, sheets, and towels in his possession, as well as one of their Indian rugs that he was not using; he eventually sent them only one blanket. Jeanne hoped that her father would come visit them in their new apartment during this special year of the World's Fair, especially if she were performing again at Radio City: "If I work there again soon I do hope you can come, because its a great honor and reflects on the moral stamina of the family," she wrote him on January 15th.

Following the advice of her agent Hal Sands to be ready for all contingencies in a shifting show biz market, Jeanne auditioned a few talented dance teams and then selected the best one to join her in a new "act." Producers for the shows coinciding with the World's Fair were moving slowly to provide employment for the entire summer, so she needed to explore all her options. Jeanne and her dance team frantically rehearsed and prepared music and costumes. Since they had not yet recovered financially from the layoff caused primarily by Jeanne's foot injury, Lillian reluctantly asked Bill to send them $200 right away, which they would repay in a few weeks as soon as the "act" was booked or Jeanne was hired again at Radio City. She knew, of course, that they would have to pay both a monetary and emotional price for asking Bill for a loan, as they had in the past, but she had no other option. In her letter to Bill on February 5th Lillian, frustrated by their lack of finances, itemized in detail all their expenses for the move and the "act"; they had been forced to take a more expensive furnished apartment for the moment and could not afford to install a telephone, a dangerous situation for a performer dependent on receiving calls daily from bookers and agents.

A few days later on February 8th Lillian wrote Bill to thank him for the loan, which she wanted him to consider a wise investment in his wonderful daughter who had become a world-class dancer in show business, a pinnacle of success that Jeanne had reached with much sacrifice, hard work, and no financial security from anyone but herself. "It would do your heart good if you could be around with us when we contact other performers, or producers, or just lay folks, and find that she is known by name or by performance by practically everyone," she wrote. "You, yourself dont even know that your daughter has a great name, and has had the choice spots in Europe and America to dance in.... How proud you ought to be! ... What a thrill it gives me when I can quit worrying long enough to realize it," she wrote.

The producers were still waiting to cast their shows until just before the World's Fair festivities opening on April 30th, to ensure having sufficient audiences and financial returns. As a result, all the unemployed vaudeville acts were rushing around New York competing for the bookings for the World's Fair. On February 22nd Lillian wrote that the current dismal state of live show business was the result of the movie studios having purchased all the good theatres throughout the country and then eliminating the stage shows. Also, by avoiding dealing with the musicians and stagehands' unions, it made it cheaper to run only movies, forcing the vaudeville acts around the country to flock to New York and to compete for the few available jobs. The bookers considered ballroom dance teams more appropriate for nightclubs and hotel floor shows than theatres, so Jeanne had to add more dancers to her "act," making it more expensive to book. She could offer her dancers no more than $150 weekly, because when added to her own standard salary plus the expenses of transportation and booking fees, the "act" would be too expensive. When one of her engagements was cancelled, Jeanne hired a new dance team with a musical comedy style, including high kicks, in anticipation of performing in Philadelphia.

Insecure about his finances, especially the recent loan of $200 and pressure from the YMCA to pay his storage fees for the family heirlooms, Bill sent a bitter letter to Jeanne and Lillian filled with angry accusations and resentment for having had to pay a significant sum of money over the years for storage. Over the years he had repeatedly assured Lillian that his storage at the Y was rent free and always refused to send them any of the heirlooms. In reality, after Jeanne and Lillian left St. Louis for New York in early 1927, Bill had paid his storage bill by selling the family furniture, and now he was obligated to pay the YMCA for what remained. As for his recent loan, Lillian reminded him in her March 3rd letter that she had considered herself self-supporting since she left St. Louis with Jeanne: "I always have kept myself from whining about your limitations, and never asked much of anything of you, assuming all the burden myself, but just as soon as I ask a coup of hundred from you, I find it scares and embitters you to the place where I despair that I have asked you at all."

Jeanne added to Lillian's letter her own reflections on the problem of the storage fees and her unstable father's unhealthy resentment. She reminded him of his good fortune over many years of being unburdened by normal family responsibilities and still being loved: "A family who loves you—and thinks you're a great guy, and yet—none of the worries of other men who have the same kind of families," she reassuringly wrote. "You dont have to buy their clothes, food, pay rent, stand the expenses of any average man, dental, doctor bills, medicines, you dont have to worry what will happen to your family if you don't make so much each month, like millions of other men." He had been fortunate during these Great Depression years to have only the responsibility of taking care of himself and the luxury of some loyal friends. Urging him to stay calm and healthy, Jeanne advised her father to be philosophical about life's adversities and not dwell on his insecurities.

During the month before the World's Fair opened when work was scarce Jeanne was relieved and thrilled to be hired again at Radio City Music Hall to perform in the sixth spectacular Easter pageant—a two-part program called the "Glory of Easter," opening on March 30, 1939. Jeanne and Lillian had already spent the $200 loaned to them by Bill, and were now living on eighty cents a day until Jeanne's next paycheck. While rehearsing she was told that the excellent movie would most likely extend the run to three weeks, since management expected long lines at the box office; then after that show closed she would be hired to perform her balloon dance for an additional week. For the Easter pageant Jeanne was included in the cast of the stage presentation "In Quaint Williamsburg," dancing as prima ballerina in an act called "Dame Fashion" with the Corps de Ballet. The movie was *The Story of Vernon and Irene Castle*—the famous vaudeville dance team in the early twentieth century—with Fred Astaire and Ginger Rogers. According to *Variety*, April 5, 1939, the "Glory of Easter" spectacle served as an "hors d'ouvre to the major stage presentation" and the atmosphere is "super-Roxy." The second part of the program set in Williamsburg, Virginia, was the creation of Leon Leonidoff, who had "produced a beautiful flash, harking back to pre–Revolutionary holiday festivities." The fashion parade was introduced by Jeanne Devereaux and the Corps de Ballet, followed by George Meyer as the Town Crier, singers Marion Raber, Robert Landrum, and the male choir, the Three Swifts, and a patriotic finale by the "ever-socko" Rockettes; the set and lighting enhanced "the presentation considerably."

On April 9th Jeanne wrote her father about a thrilling event that had happened one night when she was practicing on the spacious Radio City stage. The "producer Leonidoff brought Walt Disney (Creator of 'Micky Mouse' and 'Silly Symphonies' cartoons) down on stage for a tour of the theatre," she wrote. When Leonidoff called her over to introduce her to Walt Disney, she "was so thrilled, because he is a genius of first water. I told him I'd seen 'Micky Mouse' in Italian and French in Europe and that people loved it the world over." Disney then told Jeanne that he was creating a new "Silly Symphony," which was "a takeoff on a Ballet Company with the Ballerinas all ostriches." Jeanne reassured him that his creation would not hurt any feelings among the dance community: "I said I had always noticed a great similarity between animals & people so I was sure even dancers would have to laugh at the take-off."

During the Easter pageant run Jeanne and Lillian had to deal with many visitors backstage at Radio City between shows. Jeanne remembered how fascinating it was for people to watch the show backstage and be closer to the performers. The Rockefeller brothers—John, David, Laurence, and later Nelson—enjoyed watching the shows from the wings, often mingling with the performers, even though they had a large, private box at the back of the theatre. Kay Bennett Paul, her young friend and protégé from her New York boarding house days, loved to watch Jeanne perform from the wings, recalling all the hustle and bustle backstage of the stagehands and performers. When

Kay visited Jeanne in her dressing room, she felt like she was in a luxurious hotel. The backstage community included a restaurant, library, tailor shop, carpenter shop, clubrooms, rehearsal halls, studios, dressing rooms, and miniature models of the stage sets in the art director's office. Above Radio City's huge main stage on the second floor was a rehearsal hall of the same large dimensions and a costume department where women sat in rows at sewing machines making the hundreds of costumes required for the performances. The orchestra members and performers would go to the little theatre upstairs to preview newly released free films every day except the weekend with the cast and the staff, including all the Music Hall ushers, technicians, and elevator boys, and then recommend their favorites to management.

"The long drag is over," Jeanne wrote her father on April 26th after the Easter pageant ended. She learned that her next Radio City engagement the "Perfume" show, where she would showcase her sensational balloon dance, had been postponed in hopes of drawing the usual New York audiences as well as the large crowds who would be attending the World's Fair. Her agent Hal Sands wanted Jeanne and Lillian to sail for Brazil in early June, where Jeanne could make some good money to sustain them during their layoffs in the depressed American market. "We get the plums of work everywhere, and with the competition, it shows we are 'Tops' in the World's Markets—yet there isn't enough work to get even a meager living out of, in this country," Jeanne lamented in her letter. In 1939 very few vaudevillians could afford to live in America: their friends who were jugglers, singers, acrobats, and dance teams were literally starving. Working abroad would enable them to save enough money to live at home.

Jeanne was content that she would not be performing at the World's Fair at Flushing Meadow. It opened with much fanfare on April 30th, but the shows scheduled for the fairgrounds had not begun, and because the price of the concessions were so high, the fair officials were unable to pay their performers an adequate salary. Since the weather was cold and rainy and the traffic more congested than usual, Jeanne and Lillian had decided not to attend the opening ceremonies. They did manage, however, to listen on their radio in their apartment to President Roosevelt's impressive speech at the opening ceremonies, as well as those by Secretary of Labor Frances Perkins and Mayor La Guardia. Weeks later when they visited the fairgrounds they were thrilled by the exhibitions, convinced that the marble Russian pavilion was the most beautiful of all with its life-sized replica of the new marble subway stations and other technological wonders that promoted the accomplishments of a socialist country. Even though Jeanne had grown up with radio and movies, both of which offered vicarious experiences, she was in awe of the progress of accomplishment made by mankind exhibited at the fair.

Since the next show for Jeanne at Radio City would not be for a couple of months or more, their day was focused on getting work to fill in this time lag. Although Earl Carroll offered her a job at his large Hollywood restaurant, he had refused to pay their round-trip fare to California or guarantee a run for more than four weeks; moreover, she would be required to train the chorus girls for free and the hot summer weather would undoubtedly affect audience attendance. Her best option was to take a solid booking in South America in Rio de Janeiro, Brazil in a fancy casino with an eight-week guarantee with a possible extension, hoping to live frugally and save enough money to support them for six to eight months after they returned to New York. For the booking in Rio Jeanne needed to create at least twelve new dances, because the audiences in Rio tended to be permanent residents who usually came to see the show two or three times a week instead of tourists and other transients who would see it once. Having to change her dances every week required new choreography, costumes, and orchestrations—more dances for a single booking than any other of her previous jobs.

With hopes to stay in Rio for a couple of months, followed by engagements in other South American cities and then in Australia, Jeanne and Lillian once again packed up their belongings in the apartment for storage. Since her bout with diphtheria Jeanne had not been able to wear her usual thick black eye mascara that now made her eyes swell nearly half-shut, so she needed to purchase enough false eyelashes for the trip so she would be able to perform. To have curly hair in the hot South American climate, Jeanne had a permanent wave at the local beauty parlor. Leaving on June 1, 1939, Jeanne and Lillian sailed for fifteen days aboard the SS *Uruguay* for the guaranteed two-month booking at the Casino de Urca, located near the Copacabana Beach in Rio de Janeiro. They paid full fare for Lillian's round-trip ticket and a discounted fare for Jeanne's, since she was required by the Rio management to perform four shows on the boat on her way to Rio. Since the Radio City booking was delayed, they had been forced to use the money Bill had loaned them to pay their travel expenses for Rio, and now desperately had to ask Bill, despite his insecurities, for another small loan so they could pay their rent and purchase one week's food in Rio before Jeanne received her first paycheck from the casino. Bill, pleading his helplessness, refused to loan them additional money. With only $12 to their name, having reached the equator, Jeanne wrote her father on June 12th that they were en route "to earn more blood money, and this is the last trip to foreign parts Bob White wants any part of. She is fed up."

On the day of their departure Jeanne had an afternoon rehearsal aboard the ship for a press show that night before they sailed out of New York harbor. With rough seas battering the boat on the second day, they were confined to their cabins, unable to either eat or lift their heads from their pillows. By the third day out to sea Jeanne had performed twice on board the ship in a floor show starring the Arthur Murray Dancers, Vicki Manners, Eddie Baron, Herbert Wood, and Lydia and Joresco. Still seasick from the rough ocean, Jeanne performed on the third night in first class, where two-thirds of the passengers were booked, and then another show on deck for tourist class. "However toe work on a swaying boat is a risk, and my easiest dance, the Balloon number is not practical out doors, where the wind can carry it away. So another crisis has arisen," she wrote her father on June 4th. When they docked for the day in Barbados, they spent some of their precious $12 to enjoy this beautiful tropical island. All the passengers had been rowed to shore in colorful little boats; they then walked miles along the wharves watching the rum and molasses laden freighters and wandered the market streets in the town; and after lunch a native driver took them to tour a sugar plantation.

Bill had visited Brazil as a young man many years ago, and though he had taken some photographs, his memories had faded. Writing on June 15th, Bill revealed to Jeanne that he "used to have a sweetheart" in Rio "long before Ma and I hooked up, but I've lost track of her, and don't even remember her last name but her first name was Suzette." He also remembered that she had dark brown eyes and a mole on her chin. Having emotionally turned sixty years old on June 12th, entering a new decade of his life, and with his connection to Brazil as a young man and now as an aging father and husband, Bill reminded them that that he didn't "have to tell you folks that <u>PART OF ME</u> is down there with you."

Performing in Rio at the Casino de Urca was challenging. Jeanne shared top billing with an all-star cast including the famous French performer Mistinguett and the celebrated expatriate American dancer Josephine Baker, whom she called Josie. Interestingly, although Josie now spoke with a Parisian accent, she, like Jeanne, had been born in St. Louis, Missouri. The casino owner was a coarse man, addicted to gambling and liquor, who had made his fortune in mining, moved to Rio, and bought the fancy casino. Since they spoke no Portuguese, in order to communicate with him, they had to rely on Hal Sands' representative in Rio, who spoke only broken English and was so intimidated by the casino owner that he could not effectively negotiate adequate music, lighting, and other show business necessities for the American acts. Although the casino was lavishly appointed for the audience, performers, in order to get to the stage door, had to leap over a polluted ditch.

At the first rehearsal Josie appeared in an elegant Chanel gown and sang a beautiful French song, but threatening to fire her, the owner demanded that she appear in less clothing. Outraged and insulted, Josie told Jeanne that with her stellar international reputation she could not afford any bad publicity resulting from being fired. So she designed a new jungle set replete with a black jaguar sprawled on a tree limb and a cellophane waterfall, where she appeared semi-nude and sang a Brazilian song called "Itta Quari." Jeanne laughingly recalled how the nonchalant Brazilian stagehands cranked the cellophane waterfall strips to go up instead of down as originally designed. Jeanne fared better than Josie, for although the casino owner previewed Jeanne's famous balloon dance and balked, he settled for opening night on one of her Strauss waltz dances. She had wisely included in her casino contract her standard clause about not performing nude. The Brazilian audiences loudly applauded Jeanne's creative dances and costumes, and she was thrilled when one night President Getulio Argas of Barbados and his wife were in the audience.

While in Rio, Jeanne and Lillian stayed at the Luxor hotel, where every room had a little balcony overlooking the beach, so they could hear the ocean waves lapping the shoreline all night long. The Luxor was located on a distant island requiring a half-hour ferry trip across the bay and then a taxi ride to the casino. The first night they made the trip officials at the dock searched their costume bags for Fascist and Nazi propaganda. After the last show around one or two o'clock in the morning, they were afraid of taking the wrong ferry back to the hotel and being marooned on a strange island. Their first night at the hotel the beautiful amenities were overshadowed by the tragic death of a little boy who fell down the elevator shaft and died. When Jeanne and Lillian walked down the stairs, they saw the boy's blood-stained body on the floor at the bottom with his father shielding the body. Jeanne was so upset by this tragedy that she could barely finish her performance at the casino that night.

Jeanne and Lillian were astonished by the rich ladies walking their dogs along the boardwalk and famous Copacabana beach, whose canine hair was dyed exotic colors like purple, green, and magenta. The streets of Rio were paved with marble mosaics and the homes had many windows and doors to let the air in all year long. They also experienced a different type of poverty than they had ever seen anywhere in the world. When they visited the slums in the black communities along mountain goat paths, they realized that the people were so poor that the children ran around naked until their washed clothes were dry and had distended stomachs from eating dirt and rotten food. "Yesterday we returned to give them some of the photographs they posed for," Jeanne wrote her father on July 11th, "and would you believe it, in the middle of the afternoon the Jungle-drums were echoing over the hills, beating out rhythms as if they are in darkest Africa. We were up there a half hour. It Never Let Up."

Before Jeanne and Lillian had made the decision to travel abroad again, they were concerned about the threat of world war. In Rio they watched the newspaper headlines, often only understanding the Portuguese word "Guerra" in the headlines, which was cause for panic because at that time there were no international highways or air routes back to the United States. Relieved to be in South America and not Europe, Lillian predicted that war was probably only a few months away. When Jeanne's contract ended in mid–August, she and Lillian embarked the following day on the American Republic's *Argentine* ship sailing to New York for a tense voyage home across the Atlantic. With the threat of war looming large, American security was tightened at all ports of entry. Getting through customs was a long, tedious, and even threatening process: some of their belongings were held for hours before being returned. Lillian's prediction came true, for on September 1st Germany invaded Poland, and on September 3rd Britain and France declared war on Germany. World War II in Europe had officially begun. Bill was extremely relieved when he learned that his family was out of danger and once again back on American soil.

Upon returning to New York Jeanne and Lillian were caught up again in the whirlwind of finding an apartment at the height of the World's Fair, finally obtaining a discounted lease in a familiar building where they had lived before. Since they had financially just broken even in Rio, they were unable to pay Bill back his recent loan until late September, when Jeanne had a new booking at Radio City Music Hall. They again invited Bill to visit them before Jeanne was immersed in rehearsals at Radio City and see the World's Fair, but he declined, saying that right now he needed to tend to his business. Resuming her career at Radio City in the stage show called "Piquant Perfume," commencing the week of September 13th, Jeanne was featured in a stellar cast including the ballroom dance team Harrison and Fisher, the exquisite Danish ballet dancer Paul Haakon, soprano Viola Philo, and ballet dancer Nicholas Vasilieff along with the Music Hall Rockettes, the Corps de Ballet, the Glee Club, and the Symphony Orchestra. Jeanne danced with Paul Haakon and another ballerina Rabona Hasburg in "Sous Le Vent"; the movie was *Golden Boy*, starring William Holden and Barbara Stanwyck. Like Jeanne, Paul Haakon had been the Russian ballet master Michel Fokine's student in New York, and when Paul needed money, he danced in popular operettas in New York and at the St. Louis' Muny, as well as in vaudeville, revues, and nightclubs. Also inspired by Anna Pavlova at an early age, Paul had been a member of her touring company during the last year of her life in 1930. According to the *New York Journal and American*, September 6, 1939, the six dance-filled musical scenes, produced by the renowned Russell Markert, featured Jeanne Devereaux, "holder of the record for the fastest pirouette turns," and had something for everybody: "With the ballet, the Rockettes, the glee club, and orchestra, and special performers, no one could honestly say that he didn't find at least one act exactly to his taste."

Variety for September 13, 1939, noted that the stage show had been "nicely staged, designed, and lighted." Each scene was named after a different perfume, and dancers who appeared in "Sous Le Vent" carried sheets of silk to give the illusion of wind against the background of moving clouds. Paul Haakon along with two prima ballerinas performed with the theatre's regular ballet corps: Jeanne Devereaux was mentioned as the "one in a very pretty dance with a large bubble." The tap finale was a "climactic sock delivered by the Rockettes." According to the *Daily Mirror*, September 13, 1939, the show was loaded with talent: "The balance of the stage show presents so much delightful talent we just don't know what to mention next. But, wait. Do you like toe dancing—truly marvelously executed? Then the twirling feet of Jeanne Devereaux are her best recommendation. Her dancing has an ease, grace, and speed that make you want more and more. It's a rare treat!" In the same newspaper celebrity entertainment reviewer Walter Winchell mentioned "The Music Hall's stage show this week includes a balloon dancer—fully clothed!"

During this engagement at Radio City war was constantly on Jeanne's mind. On September 8th, after apologizing to her father for not writing more often, she exclaimed incredulously, "Just think, War in France and England." While performing in Rio, she had had an offer to return to Paris for an engagement with the *Folies Bergère*, but thought "it was foolish to put ones life in danger, going to Europe, when everyone knew the 'showdown' was bound to come." In an admittedly hurried explanation of her feelings about the war she said, "Its sad to think of my friends in the war, perhaps killed, and I wish someone would take a crack at Hitler and Goering and Goebles [sic], and then I'm sure the fanatical rule of Germany would be over, and peace could reign once more." Jeanne hated war and was worried about her friends in Europe: she occasionally dreamed of escaping to a remote farm in the country where she could grow her own food and remain impervious to the increasing threat of Hitler to the world order.

Lonely and emotionally isolated, Bill asked Jeanne and Lillian to send him more informative letters. Even though he was unable to loan them more money, Bill sincerely hoped that everything would work out for his family in the coming year, and all their needs would be fulfilled. He continued to send them their favorite newspapers and magazines, printed labels for the backs of Jeanne's promotional photographs, and a variety of knickknacks. In response to their complaints about the precarious lifestyle of show business, he sent them his customary reply about his own frustrations in the advertising business. In Bill's self-centered mind his trials and tribulations at the Y were on par with their constant struggle to avoid starvation. Bill's escape into the epistolary mode, shopping sprees, and visits with old friends were his primary means of survival. A compulsive record keeper, he was pleasantly relieved when Jeanne and Lillian returned the carbon copies of the lost original letters that he had sent them, and immediately put them back in his file cabinet so he could often re-read them in the solitude of his room at the Y and feel connected to his loved ones.

Bill was irritated that Jeanne and Lillian had failed to show any sympathy for his precarious professional predicament. On November 22nd he began a heated written diatribe that lasted until the end of the year about his declining personal finances and their desperate requests for loans. Claiming to just barely making a living, he stridently wrote that he was in no position to finance his wife and only daughter: "That is supposed to be done out of your earnings, not mine. That's a part of your end of the business." As usual, he followed his venting with a money wire of $75 with the hint of more coming later. Jeanne conveyed how hurt they had been by his accusations, and Bill replied on December 5th, noting how hurt he had been by their apparent indifference to his misfortunes. Fashioning himself the diplomat in the family, he wrote: "So, lets sort of forget our 'touchy feelings,'" ending his letter with "Suppose we all three 'Kiss and Make Up.'" Three days later Bill wrote that they should retract some of their negative accusations, especially the one where Lillian wrote "For I've decided you're a family man as long as no one asks any help from you." Continuing to act erratically, on December 10th Bill conceded that he was willing to help them out financially, and they should advise him of their needs.

As the demand for live stage shows in America declined and there were no European bookings because of the war, looking for work was time-consuming, frustrating, and often futile. Recovering from pains in her side that forced her to layoff performing, Jeanne worked hard to get a booking at the Muny in St. Louis for the coming summer. Lillian was resolving her lawsuit over her broken ankle; and Bill finally managed to get some business from his most trusted clients. Jeanne signed a contract to perform at the Loew's Capitol theatre in Washington, D.C., and was busy with practices and rehearsals. On December 18th Bill sent Jeanne his best wishes for a successful engagement in the nation's capital, as well as a nostalgic picture of the whole family—the three of them—taken in New York in 1928 that he had retrieved from his cherished "'Jeanne's treasure' box of pictures." Feeling the spirit of the Yuletide season at the Y, on December 23rd he wrote that he had received his customary Christmas cards addressed to the Helman family, and had sent them an extra $100 in response to Jeanne's recent personal appeal for a loan before she received her paycheck in Washington, D.C.

On December 23, 1939, Jeanne opened in a weeklong Christmas stage show at the Loew's Capitol theatre in Washington, D.C. The reviewer for *Variety*, December 27, 1939, described the live acts as a "clever adjunct" to the holiday Sonja Henie ice skating film. The live stage show opened with the Gauchos, a "teeterboard outfit" whose daring routines required two boards, a tall tower, and a chair. Dancers Jack Lenny and the Statler Twins performed tap and jitterbug routines, and comedian Don Cummings executed a rope trick like Will Rogers. On a fantasy toy shop set complete with a shopkeeper and chorus line dressed like toy wooden soldiers and assorted dolls, Valya Valentinoff and Jeanne Devereaux—"he in period full dress and gal in long net skirt"—pose as customers and awakened the chorus girls for some specialty dancing: "Valentinoff does spectacular conventional ballet solo, and Miss Devereaux scores with spin-filled toe solo," wrote the reviewer. The scene ended with the shopkeeper returning and the toy shop resuming its normal routine. In the finale "Arctic Fantasy" the "toe dancer" Jeanne Devereaux, costumed in white pompoms, spun against "the elaborate snow scene," which cleverly complemented the Sonja Henie film. The two featured ballet dancers in the show—Jeanne Devereaux and Valya Valentinoff—were also praised in the *Evening Star*, December 23, 1939: they "are capable people and it is a genuine pleasure to watch them, especially when Miss Devereaux gets spinning like a top, a very lovely top at that." Years later in 1951 when Jeanne and her mother passed Valya, now a movie star known as Paul Valentine, in New York, he dashed across the street when he saw them. On September 10th Jeanne wrote, "He is a gorgeous lad now, and like old wine, improves with age."

For the first half of 1940 Jeanne and Lillian continued pounding the pavement in New York looking for bookings. Writing to Bill on January 21, 1940, at midnight, after walking home on her stiff, sore foot on a cold Sunday night from Jeanne's rehearsal hall in the run down Roseland building on Times Square, Lillian described the precarious state of the professional artist in New York. Jeanne had had only one week's work for the past four weeks, money was extremely tight, and spirits were low; her only two bookings were scheduled for February—a return date at the Loew's Capital in Washington, D.C., followed by the Paramount theatre in Chicago. She was scheduled to have played the Chicago theatre in early January, but cancellations and delays were common. Lillian complained, "All of the artists are in the same pickle. Just arent any places to dance. Music Hall has just given Jeanne a tumble again, by calling up and saying they can use her some time in March. Every date pushed back even after getting them!!" The pressing issue was how to support themselves "in the interim"; fortunately their rent was paid until mid–February.

Their days during these cold winter months were taken up with calling on agents, keeping in touch with the bookers of the Loew's, the RKO's, and Warner's few theatres still including stage shows, which now are requiring an "Act" with multiple performers rather than Jeanne's customary specialty solo presentation, calling Radio City Music Hall, staying in touch with the bookers of the best nightclubs like New York's Rainbow Room, and constantly calling agents for musicals and revues. Also, Jeanne practiced and rehearsed daily for three hours in a rented room. Lillian resolved to stay the course for Jeanne's sake, writing, "Its not easy, and I am pretty tired of outwitting skunks [agents and bookers], but then, I'll last awhile longer, I hope, for I can't let Jeanne down, and it takes two heads to figure it all out, and two to run it, and a few dates in Feby as assets."

As a hedge against unemployment and poverty Jeanne was now rehearsing her new act with two talented male dancers, and the three were anxiously awaiting bookings. "The big booker of all R.K.O.s houses told Jeanne he remembered her former 'Act' and if this 'Act' was as good, he would be glad to promise her all six R.K.O. theatres," wrote Lillian. "We'll have a good act, for all three [dancers] are wonderful, and anxious to be in an 'act', hoping to pick up the dates they cannot get alone. All three are in the same boat, so lets hope for some luck now." Jeanne would continue performing solo in Washington, D.C., in February and in any subsequent Radio City shows; always the astute manager, Lillian calculated that the new act would provide Jeanne a small salary after deducting expenses. Jeanne planned to show the RKO booker her high caliber act by the end of February.

During this perilous time, Jeanne and Lillian were again forced to ask Bill for a loan, an event that precipitated another contentious exchange of letters and a transparent deterioration of the family relationship. Over the years Bill had grown increasingly paranoid about any threat to his financial security and acrimonious whenever money was mentioned. Lillian's January 21st letter was filled with complaints, frustrations, and requests that Bill have faith in them and "send along some more dollar bills, till we can swim out": she warned him not to "let our depression get you down too, as we've been hard up before and came out on top again. Its been so prolonged this time, with only that week in Washington, and no dates so far, for January, unless we get something this week." If they only had a home where Jeanne could practice instead of having to use a commercial rehearsal studio, it would "be a big help" with expenses.

Lillian maintained a positive perspective on Jeanne's career, and told Bill how proud she was of Jeanne's professional success at age twenty-eight: "Jeanne is getting to be more of a person every day. She creates dances or poetry with equal facility, and is really talented beyond anything we had a right to hope for," she wrote. "Her dances are so perfect and sensational, it just sets her apart from them all." Their good friends the Three Swifts, however, an "old and established 'act'" that they had known in England and France, had been unemployed for more than two months. Waiting around with their wives and children and worrying about their next paycheck "made them so nervous, that one of them who is an artist took one of Jeanne's pictures, and made a pastel in color of her. An exact reproduction, and so beautiful that its hard to believe anyone would take that much time for a friend. His wife and little girl brought it over this week, with a request to frame it in a light colored frame," wrote Lillian. They eventually had the pastel portrait framed in a beautiful gold frame. Together with her professional headshots this pastel portrait captured Jeanne's beauty, grace, talent, and celebrity as she began the final decade of her dancing career.

In the past when Lillian asked Bill for a personal loan during the lean times, he would reluctantly agree, even leaving it up to their discretion when to pay him back, but only after much vacillating protestation and incrimination. He would then complain about his finances in subsequent letters until he was repaid. On January 26th Bill wrote that he was "still barely making a living" by selling gift items to companies and was in no position to help them with their expenses. He reminded them that he had already sent them $175.00—"which is approximately half of what I made last year"—an amount he was able to loan them since he did not have to pay his rent in advance. With an incriminating tone, Bill ended his letter questioning why they found themselves "broke" despite Jeanne having earned $300 from her Washington, D.C., engagement during Christmas week; however, on the following day he sent Jeanne a telegram saying, "Folks I'm Wrong," followed by another on January 30th informing them he had mailed them $100. He reported in a short letter the next day—short because he was "pretty much unstrung"—that he was willing to "once more help out, with another tremendous sacrifice—To me. To help Jeanne land her jobs. Here's 'Hoping' Kiddo." As with his prior loans, he emphasized that they did not need to repay him until they were on better financial footing.

In February Jeanne was successful in obtaining a short booking at Fays in Providence, Rhode Island, where she broke in her new act with "Jack & Arthur from Radio City Music Hall." Formerly the Union Theatre, Fays had opened in 1916 as a movie house, but a year later added the vaudeville acts that garnered its fame for decades. On the bill with Jeanne was Harry Rose, "Broadway's Favorite Jester," who was a popular master of ceremonies in big-time vaudeville and the movie presentation houses, as well as a popular songwriter and star of Broadway shows in the teens and twenties, known for singing the risqué song "Frankfurter Sandwiches." The dancing Variety Gambols provided fantastic entertainment along with circus performers Joe and Hannah Gibson, who performed a daring knife throwing act. Music was provided by the well-known instrumentalists called the Romano Brothers. The movie was *Oh, Johnny, Oh, How You Can Love*, starring Tom Brown and Peggy Moran.

The Fays booking was followed by Jeanne's return engagement in February at the Loew's Capitol theatre in Washington, D.C., in a stage show complementing the film *The Light That Failed*, starring Ronald Colman, Walter Huston, and Ida Lupino. Bill wrote her on February 16th, "It's a big relief to me to hear that you are finally getting some lucrative employment, and are booked for Washington again until the end of the month…. It's a BIG RELIEFE for me to know it, as I have been under a nervous strain also, primarily for 'Your Welfare.'" Despite his aggravation about the loan, he continued sending her old photographs, route sheets, and reviews of her performances, to be used for publicity. In fact, she repeatedly requested that he not send them any more since they had no place in their small hotel apartment to store them. When Lillian finally settled her lawsuit with Radio City over her broken ankle, she was able to send Bill some money orders for repayment of his loans; on February 22nd Bill promptly deposited the money orders back into his savings account.

On March 3rd Lillian wrote to her mother in Pasadena that the weeklong engagement at the Loew's Capitol in Washington, D.C., where Jeanne had headlined in front of the "Rhythm Rockets" chorus line, had been a great success, and the manager told Jeanne that he wanted her to return again in a few months. "As you remember, we were there Xmas time. It is very unusual to repeat any one in less than 6 mo. or 1 year," she wrote. The following morning after the show had closed they toured the White House grounds; by mid-afternoon they boarded a train back to New York. The next few days they focused on securing a booking with Earl Carroll's Hollywood restaurant-theatre, which would mount a new show that spring. If they were successful in getting the Carroll booking, they would cancel the already booked three-week engagement at the Muny for the summer. Within days Lillian became seriously ill with an abscessed tooth and other bodily aches and learned that her sister Aletha, who had cared for her parents, had passed away suddenly in Pasadena. No Easter greetings were exchanged by the family this year.

11

Aunt Lenore's Dream House and Performing at the St. Louis Muny

By the end of March 1940 with no bookings, Jeanne and Lillian decided they would buy a car, pack it up with their belongings, and head to Lillian's family in Pasadena, California. Although they had worked hard to sign a contract with Earl Carroll, their agent had received a wire from Carroll negotiating down Jeanne's salary, which was already at a reduced price, and having lowered her price even more, they had still not heard any word from Carroll. Their living and professional expenses, including the rental of a rehearsal studio, would be significantly cheaper in Pasadena, and they also needed to take care of Grandma Lane who was recovering from a stroke. Bill was surprised at first to learn that they were heading west, but on reflection he thought it was a wise move given the lack of jobs on the East Coast and their dire financial situation. He was excited that they would be coming through St. Louis in the summer when he hoped Jeanne would be playing at the Muny—a rare family reunion—and on March 30th wrote that this visit "will give us a chance to tell each other lots of things that have been overlooked via the air-route, and mail route."

Writing to her parents on April 1st, Lillian expressed her shock and sadness about her sister Aletha's recent sudden death, suggesting that a family trip to Doniphan, Nebraska, that summer might be comforting, for she nostalgically envisioned them all working together to make the farms there productive and beautiful. The following day she wrote her sister Blanche in Nebraska to confirm that Jeanne would be playing the Muny in St. Louis for two weeks that summer for a salary of $250 per week plus $50 for traveling expenses. She hoped that Jeanne could follow this booking with at least six weeks in Hollywood at Carroll's. Their schedule permitting, Lillian wrote that they could drive her parents from Pasadena to Nebraska, and then continue on to St. Louis for the Muny engagement in July, eventually returning to Doniphan to re-join the family. Since bookings in show business were so scarce throughout the country, Jeanne became serious about opening a dancing school in Pasadena for a steady income, so this time while they were in Pasadena, they would need a car for Jeanne to visit all the little foothill towns surrounding Pasadena "so she can make a go of having a dancing school that will bring in a living. The last time we were so broke we couldn't even try it, but she doesn't want to just sit and not bring in a dollar, this time," Lillian wrote. "She wants to make some income every week also I can stay around my folks and help pay the grocery bills."

In 1940 many out-of-work performers were now eligible for the new unemployment program under the Social Security Act. On April 8th Lillian informed Bill that before leaving New York for California, she needed to buy a used car, get a new driver's license since she had not driven in five years, get new dentures, and have the final fittings of Jeanne's costumes for her appearance at the Muny that summer. Most importantly, Jeanne needed to apply for unemployment insurance:

> Jeanne is allowed $15.00 per week, for 15 weeks, and it can be transferred to her, even in California. Social Security in the theatrical field, allows anyone, who has earned a certain amount during the year (before) and then unemployed, a certain sum each week, proportionate to the amount that the artist has earned each week, while employed. So we have to tend to that, and have it transferred to Calif, so that we can begin to get some of the money she is entitled to each week. Most artists have done that for a year or more, but Jeanne has been in and out of the country too much, and has just become eligible since April 1st 1940. So many good artists would have starved to death between jobs if they hadn't had this help from the U.S. Employment Insurance.... All told, Jeanne is to get 13 weeks, at $15.00 per week, which is the maximum. That makes $195.00 in all, and it has been a life saver to more singers and dancers than you can count.... Don't tell any of your old cronies about Jeanne, as they might look at it as some form of charity, which it isnt, but it might harm her prestige, and she is coming to the Muni Opera this summer at $250.00 per week, plus $50.00 traveling expenses. You see it wouldn't do to say anything about it to anyone.

Jeanne was also entitled to an "Old Age Pension" at sixty-five years of age. Lillian suggested to Bill, who was always an independent contractor, he "ought to drop everything and get on a pay-roll," so that he also would be eligible for this government pension.

Lillian wanted to leave for California quickly, but she still needed to figure out how to finance the trip to Pasadena. On April 5th Lillian wrote her own father that they had not heard back from Carroll, so they would have to look for jobs on the East Coast to earn money for their traveling expenses. Two days later Lillian wrote her mother, urging her to stay healthy so that the family "can keep you and Grandpa with us to comfort us and help us just by being around." After the summer booking in July at the Muny in St. Louis, Lillian's plan was to return to Pasadena so that Jeanne could rent a studio and start the new dancing school. "This time Jeanne is determined to make money," Lillian wrote her mother, and if Jeanne is going to teach, she means to make it "go."

Lillian felt an urgency to be in Pasadena to care for her seriously ill mother and aging father, so once again they reluctantly asked Bill, their only resource, for a personal loan to cover their immediate expenses. He was his usual recalcitrant self. Promising to repay him out of the $550 that Jeanne would earn from her summer engagement at the Muny, from her unemployment checks, and extra money she could earn playing at the Park Plaza Hotel in St. Louis after the Muny, Lillian asked Bill on April 8th for a loan of $300 to cover the car and other expenses, and if he worried about being paid back "it will mean that 'either that you like to worry' or that you DON'T BELIEVE US. One or the other." As he had accused them of trying to make a living in a depressed profession where the overhead negated any profit and being a star dancer was no compensation, she responded that they were being eaten alive by their expenses in the glamorous, competitive, and unpredictable world of show business, assuring him once again that he would be paid back after the Muny engagement. Bill reluctantly sent them on

April 17th a bank draft within the week for the full $300, which represented for him, he wrote, "Approximately 10 months SECURITY."

As Jeanne and Lillian drove across country in late April and into mid–May, Jeanne sent her father numerous postcards describing the fascinating sights along the road as well as their visits with Lillian's family in Nebraska and Colorado. Kay Bennett Paul had accompanied them as far as St. Louis, where Jeanne had arranged for her to sing in the chorus in a show at the Muny. Jeanne wrote her grandparents on May 6th that they had stopped in St. Louis for a few days to sign a contract for a booking at the Plaza Hotel to follow the Muny in July, as well as to check up on her father, and were now on their way to Pasadena. In a handwritten ledger of travel expenses Lillian figured that their trip had cost them $798.67. Their stringent budget now included only a small portion of food and stamps. Since Jeanne still had not received her first unemployment check, she was rehearsing around the furniture in her grandparents' living room.

Jeanne Devereaux performing in the operetta *Good News* at the renowned outdoor Municipal "Muny" Theatre in St. Louis, Missouri, July 15–21, 1940. The "Muny" provided Jeanne with bookings during the hot summer months when the New York theatres, lacking air conditioning, were closed. Jeanne had made her début at age twelve in 1925 at this enormous theatre before an audience of 10,000 people. Courtesy Jeanne Devereaux Perkins Collection.

They looked forward to Jeanne's booking in two operettas at the Muny that summer, planning to return to St. Louis by July 1st for Jeanne's star turn in *The Chocolate Soldier* from July 8th to 14th and *Good News* from July 15th to 21st. In his May 21st and 22nd letters Bill enclosed several publicity articles from the St. Louis newspapers about Jeanne's dancing career and her upcoming Muny engagement—clippings that immediately were pasted in her scrapbook. A promotional piece on Jeanne in the *St. Louis Globe-Democrat* for May 26, 1940, mentioned "on her twelfth birthday she was promoted to premier danseuse of the Municipal Opera and since that time has enjoyed amazing success in the show world." To encourage even more publicity for her Muny booking, Jeanne sent additional photographs to the Muny Opera Association. Having recently read an interview with the famous actor Vincent Price who was playing at the Muny, on June 9th Bill offered Jeanne advice about preparing for an interview, to which she replied the following day that this was a skill she already possessed: "You tickled my funny bone, telling me how to get ready for an interview," she wrote. "Honey, that's as much a part of my trade as price lists are of yours. I know how you meant it, dear, and I'm not laughing at you just chuckling to myself, for no one ever seems to understand the 'other fellow's trade.'"

Living with Jeanne's maternal grandparents in Pasadena kept them fully occupied, for Grandma Lane, helpless and paralyzed on her left side by a stroke, required extensive care: the daily housekeeping and cooking was exhausting. On May 31st Jeanne wrote to Kay Bennett Paul, who was performing at the Muny, about how time-consuming it was to look after a big, old house that had no ice box or vacuum cleaner, a dark cellar for food storage, and a sink out of order, as well as a debilitated grandmother. Jeanne wrote on June 10th that despite her grandparents' primitive living standards, she and her mother were "still kicking and must keep up with things and the world, for we must still cope with it."

Jeanne's daily schedule was exhausting: she practiced two to four hours and then hurried home to fix dinner for the entire family. She described cleaning out the cellar that was filled with years of "Grandma's mania" for saving everything—a hoarding trait ironically perpetuated by Jeanne and Lillian until the end of their lives. Bill sternly reminded them on June 15th that others have had it worse and "would you two ladies rather be in New York without ANY money? And 'nothing coming in' You can answer that one, cant you?" He compulsively queried them about their financial records, especially his recent loans—"I think it will be to your interest to give me the answer," he sternly admonished them.

When Jeanne and Lillian returned to St. Louis a few times to play at the Muny, their professional commitments had to take precedence over visiting with Bill. On June 9th he explicitly asked them to stay at the Warwick Hotel since it was close to the YMCA, giving them all "a chance to be together much more than elsewhere." In a letter on June 18th between strenuous practice sessions, Jeanne informed him that they would need to stay at a hotel closer to her work than his room at the YMCA. So while performing in St. Louis that summer Jeanne and Lillian lived in an apartment at the Commodore Hotel, close to the Muny and where Kay Bennett Paul was currently living. Despite the distance, they were still able to share meals as a family and have some family talks.

For the first time in their letter exchange Jeanne became visibly upset with her father, confronting him in her June 9th letter about his obsessive paranoia over money and his lack of financial support for his family. Using the language of "tough love," she wrote that she was exasperated by his recent request for a financial accounting, with the implication that they would not repay his loans, a sensitive subject they had already discussed:

> Gee, Dad, I completely give up: How do you get along with such a short memory? Heavens above. We explained all your questions in the long talks while we were in St. Louis. The whole long subject was Covered from Cover to Cover, and you said what a long lot of letters your and our problems had covered....
>
> Just read further into your letter, and the more I read, the more I burn. You have been paid back, every time, in full, and you know you will be repaid again, so why in heaven's name do you act as if we were absconding with your security...
>
> So calm your fears, and consider yourself a lucky man, who has a loving family he don't support and hasn't for 12 long years.
>
> So face yourself, and realize you hurt us deeply when you write as if we thought nothing of you, and were so grasping we would take your money and not return it.
>
> I've given it to you straight from the shoulder, because I do love you and feel you needed a little straightening out, like all of us do once in awhile.
>
> Mom and I straighten each other out, but you are alone so much you never come up against any other point of view, in personal matters, than your own. And life is giving the "other fellow" his way once in awhile, and also believing in him, so that he will give in to you occasionally, and believe in you.

The following day Jeanne wrote that since she still had not received her unemployment check for $75, they were struggling to finance their trip to St. Louis for the engagement at the Muny, saying "And not a single check. Mad! I'm boiling!"

At the beginning of July they arrived in St. Louis. A review in *Variety*, July 10, 1940, noted that *The Chocolate Soldier* had been played profitably at the Muny four times before and had returned for a weeklong run "with the most costly galaxy of songbirds and warblets of the current season." The stellar cast included well-known opera singers and ballet soloists Jeanne Devereaux, Miriam Seabold of the Ballet Russe, and Susan Scott, who performed in "colorful ensemble routines" choreographed by Lew Christensen. "Jeanne Devereaux, native-born who was a solo dancer in this al fresco theatre at the age of 12, returns as chief ballerina and clicks." The operetta was set in Bulgaria in 1885 when the country was at war with Serbia, and contained many lively songs and fast-paced folk dances like Hungarian czardas. For one of her dances Jeanne wore a native Hungarian costume with a matching headdress performing a czardas in high black leather boots.

The Muny's next operetta was *Good News*, advertised in the Muny program as a hilarious play about college life in the roaring twenties featuring a "Rootin' Riot of Comedians, Singers and Dancers." The book was by Laurence Schwab and B. G. DeSylva, with lyrics by DeSylva and Lew Brown and music by Ray Henderson; it had premiered on Broadway at the 46th Street Theatre in 1927, the same year as *Manhattan Mary* and the smash hit *Show Boat*, and ran for a record 557 performances. In later years Jeanne remembered that it featured a new dance called "The Varsity Drag."

Suffering from the intense St. Louis summer heat and humidity, Lillian wrote to her sisters in Nebraska: "We found Bill so thin & poor he didn't look natural but have eaten together every supper & some lunches also in our apartment, for we do our own cooking, and he is looking so much better. Face filled out & looking natural again. Says he feels fine & never has an ache or pain, and stands the heat better than Jeanne or I." Later that December 1st when remembering how thin and unhealthy he looked to her during their summer visit and how he improved by eating their home cooking, Lillian wrote to remind him to eat healthy food—lots of nutritious fruits and vegetables—"as I want an old man around the place, and you were elected years ago."

Jeanne now unemployed, they first drove to Grand Island, Nebraska, for Lillian's parents' anniversary picnic, and then after a week started the long trip west to Pasadena. "Gee! we hated to leave you on that curb!" Jeanne wrote her father on August 11th from Nebraska, sending him greetings from the whole family. Enjoying the fresh Nebraska air and leisurely farm life, Jeanne dreamily wished she could stay in Grand Island for months. Writing from Pueblo, Colorado on August 23rd, Jeanne reported having had a nice visit nearby at Aunt Edith's home, and recalling the wonderful motoring trips she had taken with her father as a child, she added, "Have the back seat empty, and wish you were in it." From Springer, New Mexico, she told "Pappy" that this "town brings back memories, eh? Well, after all our travels"—remembering their trip in 1924 outside of Pueblo during a rain storm. Two days later Bill thanked them "for the invitation to sit in the back seat, and share 'pot luck.' Damn nice of you."

Arriving back in Pasadena on August 27th at her grandparents' house, Jeanne was able to practice in the same studio as before since the owner was on vacation. She desperately needed to practice again after two weeks off in St. Louis, the ten days in Nebraska, and the trip to Pasadena: "My feet were soft, so got two gorgeous blisters, which arent so pleasant to dance on, but I use that mole-skin Adhesive, like I put on your [Bill's] feet, and it helps a lot," she wrote on September 5th. They explored their entrepreneurial idea to make filmed dancing lessons for teachers and students. Over the next few months they worked with a professional photographer to film some preliminary dancing lessons. During September Jeanne worked with her father on a small advertising pamphlet for her proposed ballet school. On October 7th she graciously thanked him for his hard work, while suggesting it was unfortunate that he could never find an adequate paying job for his talents: "You're a wonder at uncovering of facts," she wrote, "and you sure would be an excellent-contact man. If there were only an outlet for our best talents, that would pay a salary, what a fine place this world would be."

Jeanne's passion for owning her own home was vicariously fulfilled when in September her Aunt Lenore and Uncle Roy Marsh purchased their Pasadena dream house, which became the family's gathering place and a haven for Jeanne and Lillian when they visited Pasadena, particularly when times were tough. As early as June 2nd Jeanne had described to her father how she and her mother had been accompanying Aunt Lenore in looking at Pasadena houses for sale: "We visited houses for sale, and Pop, if ever I longed to have money, I did then. Houses that had cost their owner $50.000 are now $17.000, and for $5000.00 there are grand little homes. How I wished I had belonged to the generations before the depression, who had Uncle Henrys to leave them $5000.00 [Bill had inherited this amount from his Uncle Henry]. Just to think of these homes that people live in, lovingly look after, and feel secure in, made my mouth water."

11 • Aunt Lenore's Dream House and Peforming at the St. Louis Muny

Later, on June 9th, undoubtedly feeling guilty, insecure, and resentful, Bill commented sarcastically on her house hunting:

> You have been exploring empty houses, and rebuilding interiors, in your mind's eye, which, I'd say was darn good sport on a slack afternoon, and I'll tell you how we can handle that problem easily. You pick out the house that would suit you, and "BE SURE OF IT" and I'll send you a check, to cover the amount, and you can no doubt find SOMEONE to cash it. However, you will have to take care of all the other details such as taxes, repairs, depreciation, upkeep, etc, and earn a nice income so it wont be a burden to you, instead of a pleasure. To keep it going. You know a lot of people have gotten grey hair "trying to keep them up" and then "Lost" them, just like these people who want to get rid of them now. That's why they're a bargain.

Aunt Lenore and Uncle Roy bought a grand Pasadena edifice at the southwest corner of California and Euclid Avenue that remained vivid and majestic in Jeanne's memory. The house, designed by the famous architect Frederick Roehrig and built in 1905 like a horseshoe with a center patio surrounded by all the rooms, was most likely modeled, Jeanne believed, on the aristocratic Moreno family's famous Mexican hacienda estate romanticized in the popular novel *Ramona*, written by Helen Hunt Jackson in 1884. Known in architectural histories as the "Eddy House," after the art collector and critic Arthur Jerome Eddy who was the original owner, Aunt Lenore's house was filled with Eddy's Native American pottery and basketry and Japanese prints and specially-designed, heavy wooden furniture that corresponded to the large rooms.[1]

On September 16th Jeanne wrote her father that although she thought the exterior of the old house not particularly attractive, the interior design and decorations were spectacular:

> The house is old but was built by a man with such a sense of artistry that it's still a gem.... It must have cost at least $25,000 or $30,000 when it was built for all the tiles are handmade on the roof and walks and the floor of one room. The living room and dining room are all in one and measure about 30 × 65 ft. with a stone fireplace at one end. There is a library and three bedrooms and two baths and an entrance hall 20 × 20ft.... Besides a butlers Pantry and kitchen there are two Maids rooms and bath and two cellars with two furnaces that burn gas but give steam heat.

She particularly admired the ceilings that were "foot square redwood beams with hand beaten brass arms," as well as the wrought iron guards over all the windows. Slightly over one acre, the property had been on the market for four years at its original price, but since the owner could no longer afford the taxes, the price had been reduced to $8,000. Jeanne planned to use Aunt Lenore's large living room in her new house for a practice studio. "In the mean time many people drop in [the current rented studio] to watch me," Jeanne later wrote on October 16th, "and in the event of my opening a school, would like to come to me for lessons. So the delay [in moving to Aunt Lenore's house] is, in a way, advertising among another school's pupils."

Since Aunt Lenore purchased most of the house's contents, during her stewardship the interior remained essentially as Arthur Eddy had originally furnished it. Using their aggressive but diplomatic bargaining skills learned in show business, Jeanne and Lillian successfully negotiated with the seller on Lenore's behalf the best prices for the furniture. On October 23rd Jeanne described to her father how reticent and inept Aunt Lenore was in business dealing and how she and her mother had to take over the tough negotiations:

It takes times like that to make one completely realize how much our life out in the world has taught us, and how having to face unpleasant tasks has made us strong. By adroit wording we got things at the price we wanted without casting reflections on the item, or appearing to be driving a bargain. Which our family could no more do than fly. Now the woman is to move Friday, and Sat, Aunt Lenore is to move in, so we are all to help, and are taking a picnic lunch to facilitate staying on the job all day.

Gee, Dad, how I wish you could see that place. Its absolutely my dream of a house (Altho 20 years old) and if I had only $8.000 I could have bought it for a studio and home for life.... Too bad I didnt belong to the generation who inherited little lumps like Grandpa and you did, for I could have had that house and Bob White [Lillian] a home for her old age, with the studio the earning power to run it. Hi Ho, and a long sigh.

When Bill learned about her bargaining success for Aunt Lenore's furniture, he proudly wrote on October 26th that his daughter had "the makings of a DAMN GOOD purchasing Agent; ... you have 'rubbed elbows' with the world, and know what its 'all about' and what makes the 'wheels go round.'" Bill also sarcastically reminded her, "Had you had $8.000 10 years ago, you wouldnt have bought a house in Pasadena with it, now, would you? Not being able to look into the future."

Perhaps her father's acrimonious reaction to her longings made the tone of her remaining letters to him that year increasingly contentious. After having thanked her father for his birthday wishes and gift, in her October 23rd letter she harshly informed him that he had previously given her the same gift. On November 4th Jeanne wrote that she and her mother had decided on another birthday gift that could be from both her parents: Lillian had written to a store in the Grand Canyon to inquire whether or not the turquoise ear rings that Jeanne had admired on their recent trip across country were still for sale: they would go with her favorite "Wampum and Turq bracelet and ring," to complete a proper "Indian outfit." "Oh, you cant know how much I like and appreciate your and Mom's birthday present. For beauty and style they cant be beaten [she included a sketch]," wrote Jeanne on November 15th. "Pop, I cant tell you how successful your handling of my 28th birthday was,—because seeing those earrings is the only way you can understand how worthy of appreciation you and Mom's combined gift was. I'm getting to be a big girl now, huh?"

During Jeanne and Lillian's stay in Pasadena they enjoyed the warm family dinners with the Lane relatives and reunions with old friends from St. Louis. On November 25th Jeanne described for her father the wonderful family Thanksgiving dinner at Aunt Lenore's new house and her renewed sense of family: "There were twelve at the festal board, and a luscious 18 pound Tur-key had place of honor. We enjoyed the huge stone fire place, and all sat around its beneficent circle of warmth. I certainly wished you were 'Withus.'" Remembering their happy time living in St. Louis before the family break-up, Jeanne and Lillian also enjoyed visiting with friends from the "olden days" who lived in nearby Los Angeles. On November 25th Jeanne told Bill that while they were in Hollywood visiting agents they had seen Helen Lewis, their former neighbor in St. Louis and one of Jeanne's childhood friends who had attended the same ballet school, who was now working in the Hollywood real estate business, nostalgically reflecting how Helen had told them later over the phone: "'We were all such close friends in the olden days. I cant help feeling that we'll all be together again sometime.'"

During the first week of November Jeanne and Lillian made a date to visit Jeanne's movie agents in Hollywood to look for work. On November 10th she had told her father that the agents were "on the trail of a picture for me. I hope one materializes, as it means a nice hunk of dough." On November 25th Jeanne related that her Hollywood agents were hoping to get her cast in a new movie at Paramount to be called *Ballerina*, based on a book of the same title: however, it was still uncertain whether the movie would literally follow the book or "play up the personal side of the Ballerina's life, and let the professional side alone—thereby saving thousands on expensive theatre scenes, and dancers. Its in the lap of the Gods." On December 1st while Jeanne and a "local swain" were touring the historic Huntington Library, Art Collections, and Botanical Gardens and then seeing a movie, Lillian, alone in her parents' home for the first time, wrote Bill, repeating how she accompanied Jeanne downtown every afternoon to her practice in a studio and then to visit agents in Beverly Hills and Hollywood for possible bookings in movies, nightclubs, and the downtown Los Angeles Paramount theatre, dressed up in their finery: "Yes, it takes planning, but I am determined to get in some money around these holidays, and after, if possible." As for the dance studio project, "since we have bided our time about getting a studio to teach, we have gotten quite a lot of information about these things here in Pasadena, so we wont be caught napping, if we do go into it, in the spring," Lillian wrote. "Are getting the low-down on many studios, and how they operate."

The family letters in 1940 again took on an acrimonious turn when Dad informed them on November 27th that their remaining valuable belongings stored at the YMCA with him were once more in jeopardy. The YMCA's management had recently informed him that they could no longer handle his storage. The management had kept his storage gratis for about ten years, which would have cost him nearly $600.00. During this Christmas season his constant failure to pay the storage fees struck a burning sensitive nerve with Jeanne and Lillian, resulting in Jeanne's angry letter on December 6th. Jeanne confronted her father about his fearful, inconsistent, and belligerent behavior on this subject dear to her heart: "About the storage problem," she wrote, "I wonder that you have the nerve to write us about it, after the fight about that very subject this summer":

> You promised you would stand up like a man and keep those things for me, since you wouldn't let us take them with free transportation, to put with our other valuables. You insisted you'd pay the storage if it ever came to it. And now, just as we said, you are going weak, and saying, What shall I do.
>
> After the whole thing was gone over, this summer, there should be no doubt that if you must at last start to pay storage, then you must, as I expect you to be a man of your word, and keep all those things for me, as they are the only inheritance I shall ever have, and I WANT to have the heirlooms of your family, to cherish and preserve.

If he now wanted to send them everything by freight, it would cost less than one-year of storage at the YMCA. Ultimately, since the heirlooms were in Dad's possession, it was his decision whether to store them or send them to Pasadena: "You see, dad, you hate to face the unpleasant truths. So you hide your eyes, but it doesn't keep them from happening, for one must deal with them anyway. You wouldnt bring yourself to deal with the problem, or even 'face' it, preferring to pretend it wasnt there." Reminding him again that even if he did not value the family heirlooms, she did—"all the things left are very dear to me"—and if he decided to send them by freight to Pasadena, "it certainly will be in loving and appreciative hands, and you will be free of the responsibilities."

During this year in Pasadena Jeanne reunited with handsome Tom Perkins, the highly intelligent young man she had met seven years earlier who had made such an impression on her that they had exchanged a few letters and Christmas and birthday cards since. When Tom and his mother went this year to see Jeanne dance at the Paramount Theatre on Broadway in downtown Los Angeles, he thought she was exceptionally talented and visited her backstage in her dressing room after the show. He was attracted to this intelligent, glamorous woman with an international dancing career who periodically lived with her aged grandparents in Pasadena.

Jeanne and Lillian continued to enjoy Aunt Lenore's beautiful historic home during the holiday season. Jeanne had made by hand her clever Christmas cards and sent them to her friends and colleagues around the world. In her Christmas card that year Aunt Lenore wrote Jeanne and Lillian that she intended to make her new "home a place for all to assemble happily. That is my ambition.... This house needs many people in it and I intend to make it so."[2] She and Roy planned to have a large fire burning in their spacious fireplace for New Year's day and gather all the family around them.

For now Jeanne and Lillian had a surrogate home in Pasadena where they could relax and enjoy their family, but show business and life on the road was just around the corner. Throughout the year they had been contacting the bookers for Earl Carroll's dinner show in Hollywood, hoping to get hired for his fall production that was scheduled for a long run.

12

Touring with Earl Carroll's Vanities

Jeanne and Lillian's persistent efforts throughout 1940 to negotiate with the bookers for Earl Carroll's dinner theatre finally paid off at the end of the year when the legendary impresario signed her up for his spectacular Hollywood revue. Jeanne began performing in Hollywood in the early months of 1941 in *Earl Carroll's All New Hollywood Revue*, and in June toured nationally with this show. Taking care of her grandparents, practicing, commuting from Pasadena to Hollywood to rehearse for Carroll's show, and then daily performances in Hollywood well into the night was all-consuming. Despite her love of dancing, the glamour of performing, and her need for money, Earl Carroll's egregious exploitation of the performers, the poor working conditions, and the grueling schedule often made the tour a dreadful grind. The family letters alleviated the loneliness and exhaustion from her demanding schedule, and her father continued to send his letters now by airmail on a weekly basis, as well as the little knicknacks and souvenirs that made him feel connected to his family.

Earl Carroll's dinner theatre in Hollywood on Sunset Boulevard was built in 1938 and combined a good restaurant, nightclub environment, and large dance floor. Famous theatrical producer and songwriter Earl Carroll was a contemporary of Florenz Ziegfeld and George White, and his lavish, bawdy revues, called *Earl Carroll Vanities*, always advertised as vaudeville, were popular in New York between 1923 and 1940, featuring the world's most beautiful girls, often nude. Jeanne was sometimes forced by financial necessity to perform in burlesque type vaudeville shows like Carroll's revues, but never nude, which had long runs and became successful touring shows.

Beginning on June 26, 1941, Earl Carroll took his Hollywood nightclub follies, now called *Earl Carroll's Vanities*, out on the road. In order to please audiences in small cities and towns, the touring show was a sanitized version of the original *Vanities*. The cast of sixty performers included Jeanne along with beautiful, scantily clad show girls, the acrobatic dancers the Slate Brothers, comedian Buster Shaver with the little people Olive and George, singer Faye Carroll, dancer Anna Lee, dancer Al Norman, the Bynton Dancers, and the popular comedy team the Wiere Brothers. During the West Coast tour Jeanne and the cast consistently received positive reviews in local newspapers. When the show played at the Golden Gate Theatre, the reviewer for the *San Francisco Chronicle*, July 3, 1941, referred to Jeanne as "a twirling ballerina, ... [who has] established the world's record for consecutive spins." The reviewer in *Variety*, July 9, 1941, considered the booking at Golden Gate a tryout prior to touring. "Basically another Earl Carroll 'hodge-podge,'" the reviewer wrote, but conceded that this "Vanities" was a better version with more novelty than had previously played in San Francisco. The bill opened with a male song and dance line, followed by a parade of eighteen girls, who danced up a staircase after the curtain parted, waving white and red flags. Next came the dancing Slate Brothers and Al Norman with his showgirls performing a fast tap routine and tango. Faye Carroll's vocals were complemented by brightly costumed showgirls and "Jeanne Devereaux in pale green skirt and bra toe-and-bubble dances in front of the line for okay results," wrote the *Variety* reviewer. The dancing little people Olive and George with Buster Shaver received a standing ovation; the Slate Brothers returned with high kicking dancer Anna Lee. After the Slate Brothers' acrobatic dance number, "Miss Devereaux ... returns for a fast toe-spin routine which lands solidly." Other specialty acts included the comedians the Wiere Brothers and the Byton dancers. To conclude, the show "has atmosphere of perspiration rather than inspiration, and general tone of humor," the reviewer concluded, "while okay for Hollywood and probably New York, won't endear Carroll to family audiences or Parent-Teacher groups."

Since Carroll pressured to maximize his box office receipts, the cast performed five shows daily and six on Saturdays that lasted one hour and twenty minutes each: "We have been working untill we are ready to drop," Jeanne had written her father from San Diego in her August 6th postcard. The *Los Angeles Times*, August 19, 1941, announced that "Earl Carroll's 'Vanities' has finished successful bookings in California and has left for the East, where the show will play in many major cities before returning to Hollywood; the cast is 'one of the brightest ever presented by Carroll in a long line of theatrical hits.'" Subsequent reviewers conceded that it was a better show than Carroll's last efforts but questioned its low, burlesque tone and lack of inspiration.

The packed itinerary often changed weekly from the route established at the outset of the tour. To Jeanne's knowledge her itinerary for the East Coast tour was to begin in Denver, followed by Des Moines, Iowa, Chicago, Cleveland, St. Louis, and Dallas until the middle of October. Writing from the Palace Theatre in Cleveland on August 31st, where Jeanne was performing for a week, Lillian expanded the grueling itinerary to include Toledo for three days, Dayton, Cincinnati, and then two weeks in Dallas, with a brief lay-off after the show in Dayton. Unfortunately, the St. Louis performance had been cancelled, for "Carroll wants to make thousands every week, and it seems Fanchon and Marco (Who operate the St. Louis theaters) just wouldnt offer enough to let him make so much." Lillian was exhausted: "And this show, like all big shows, takes a great deal out of one," she wrote Bill, "for these are hard times in the show business, and the dimes have to flow in waves, or we cant get future bookings, so we've made records in dollar grosses at every theatre we've played."

Lillian and Jeanne needed to live frugally, she explained, wearing their old clothes and saving every dime they could, for "Carrol is so erratic we never know what he will do next, and the American Guild of Variety Artists [AGVA] are after him for working this show 5 and 6 shows daily, and paying for extra shows, since he receives thousands extra, for he gats [sic] a guarantee, besides a percentage of the box office."[1] The performers were virtually unprotected from management, and although they remained silent with their grievances, Lillian believed that the truth is "no person can give 5 or

Jeanne Devereaux in an informal photograph with dancer George who was in the cast with Jeanne in the vaudeville/revue *Earl Carroll's Vanities* from its premiere in Hollywood in early 1941 to the opening in June of its touring show to its closing in April 1942. The little people George and Olive starred in the act "Buster Shaver with Olive and George," and during the run of the show Olive and Jeanne became good friends. After she retired, Jeanne continued her friendship with Buster, Olive, and George, who also lived in Los Angeles, California. Courtesy Jeanne Devereaux Perkins Collection.

6 shows daily and hold up long." Later on October 29th Jeanne wrote her father to describe the company meetings that Carroll would call not only to give the performers their notes, but also to raise false hopes about taking the show to New York:

> Earl Carroll arrived today, and after the first show, called his usual CO. meeting, where we all sit around in a stuffy basement, and listen to his voluminous note on what was wrong with the show.
> They are never important points, just silly ones. He keeps harping about the New York show he intends to do, with us later in the year.
> He uses it as bait, or red herring, so he can get away with dirty tricks in the meantime.

In a later interview Jeanne vividly recalled how Carroll, a notorious womanizer, picked a lovely girl from the dancing chorus to accompany him on a quick trip to New York, only to discard her brutally when he returned to Los Angeles.

Carroll was usually able to circumvent the required Sunday prohibition on dancing. Writing from Pittsburgh on December 17, 1941, Jeanne told her father that most of the time they were following Earl Carroll's grueling schedule, even performing without pay on Sunday in a nearby Ohio town since performances on Sunday were prohibited in Pennsylvania: "Life goes on and there is never a dull moment. Sunday shows are prohibited in Pa, so the theatre's management arranges for Greyhound buses to take us to Stubenville, Ohio, about 50 miles away. The busses left at 10:30 and when we got there the first show wasn't until 3:00 with four of them coming thick and fast. The long trip back to Pittsburgh—to the dark theatre, to return our costumes—and to bed at 3 A.M." Carroll would go to great lengths to make a buck with total disregard for the well-being of his performers.

Fortunately, the labor laws protecting performers were stronger in Pennsylvania than in other states. On February 24, 1942, Lillian, having just received Bill's last letter and fatigued from the two day jumps instead of weekly bookings, wrote him from Harrisburg, Pennsylvania, about her own "worries" related to Earl Carroll being forced by the American Guild of Variety Artists (AGVA) to pay for a full week's work as well as extra shows:

> In addition, the Union of American Guild of Variety artists has been holding meetings, trying to force Carroll to pay for an extra Midnight show, in Boston, and an extra day in Philadelphia. He has fought all over the ground, while we played Loew's State in N.Y. and then at Philly, at Easton Pa, and here at Harrisburg. Where I hear Carroll has agreed to settle it for the day extra in Philly.
> The Penn Labor Commissioner is on the job now, and Carroll must, but the Boston extra shows is still "hanging fire." Every card has been played on each side, but it took a labor commissioner and not the A.G.V.A.
> Our union is so weak, it can do nothing but collect dues, which it does...
> The A.G.V.A. man has just poked his nose in the door to say he is calling a compulsory meeting tomorrow at 12 noon again ! ! ! ! ! No rest. Just meetings and so few results. What we need badly is a Federal Theater.... The State of Pennsylvania, however, is so strong on labor protection, (Doe [sic] to the many abuses it had to correct), that we have real labor laws in this state for performers in shows, as well as for the clerks, miners, etc etc. and as 6 days is considered a week in this state, and must have a weeks pay. The state wont allow any shows on Sunday. But Carroll only paid the Company for 6 days, and so he ran afoul of the Penn laws, and its Labor Commissioner. He has been trying to get Carroll to pay up, without closing the show, but has finally attached the Box Office Tomorrow. So things are a-jumping in our show tomorrow.

It took the intervention of the Pennsylvania state labor commissioner to advance the case to make Carroll pay up, with the implication in Lillian's letter that he eventually, although reluctantly, did pay something.

When Jeanne was employed on tour, the family letters diminished in frequency. At the beginning of the Earl Carroll tour Lillian, after not hearing from Bill for a month, asked him in her February 24th letter to write her at Toledo or Dayton "telling me all about yourself, and what goes on. It seems too bad to be neglectful after the faithfulness of us both all these years." Since President Roosevelt was saying that America was close to war: "We just have to get started and earn some money not daring to get down to our last money, before earning some more." Sending his September 3, 1941, letter to the theatre in Toledo, Bill complained that he did not have the route list of the theatres. In her September 29th postcard from Memphis, Tennessee Jeanne elaborated on the tour schedule, telling her father that they will play in the auditorium of the fair grounds at the Texas State Fair from October 4 to the 19th—"I hear we only do two shows a night and 4 matinees a week—so we may get to see prize COWS, and JELLY after all"—and they are hoping to play in St. Louis in November around Thanksgiving.

The two miserably hot weeks in Dallas at the Texas State Fair were a big success. On October 5th the *Times Herald*, the largest newspaper in Dallas, featured a sensational promotional picture of Jeanne "of the EARL CARROLL VANITIES." Jeanne, writing on October 10th, confirmed that her reduced performance schedule gave her ample free time to look "the fair over from stem to stern." Indulging her curiosity and love of nature, she "inspected live stock, and Afghans, poultry, prize jelly, tractors, and the hot dog situation." She included in her letter to her father a direct, vivid description of both the lovely fair grounds and her ardent admirers, showing her love of art, museums, natural beauty, and people:

> The grounds permanently house the Civic Auditorium and Natural History Museum, and Art Museum, so there are gardens, lawns and pools to glorfy the place, and rest the eye.
>
> Fireworks light the sky at night. The moon rides high. Twinkly tunes drift in the window from a near-by Merry Go Round, and great bumptious cloud banks go lumbering by.
>
> Whee! The air is rarified here. I just refused a date with the grandson of J. P. Morgan. Kenneth. He was a trifle worse for Scotch- and wavered as [he] bowed over Bob White's hand.
>
> He pleaded so hard I finally promised to Rumba with him "some" night, just to make him happy.
>
> His friend Mr. Morris- sent me 6 dozen roses, lovely red roses, and we are almost crazy trying to house them.

Bill responds on October 29th that obviously her admirer Kenneth Morgan was "still on the Waiting List."

Their bookings since Cleveland had been exhausting day jumps, which were expensive as porters had to handle their baggage four times and the hotels only offered discounted rates for a full week. Writing from Tulsa on October 25th, where they had a three-day run at a theatre, which is "more like a prison term than an engagement, for there are no lights, horrible music, and worst of all, great grease spots and streaks all over the stage, that are slick as glass," Jeanne explained that the day jumps did have the advantage in that they were able "to drink in the real Americana. Lovely green fields, cattle grazing, laden orchards. Tobacco drying in open barns. Cotton fields. It so nice to see country life again." Revising their Midwest itinerary and canceling shows suddenly, Carroll set a weekly or two-day itinerary beginning at the Tower theatre in Kansas City, followed by the Orpheum in Omaha, the Paramount in Des Moines, the Capitol in Davenport, and the Fox in St. Louis. Perhaps, Jeanne wrote, the family will "get our visit after all, and Thanksgiving at THAT."

A review of the show at the Tower theatre in Kansas City in *Variety*, November 5, 1941, noted that the regular "presentation policy" of the theatre had been interrupted for a week for the *Vanities* booking. The reviewer wrote that the bill was "sufficient to give the turnstiles a whirl and the customers a tasty cut of entertainment." With the comedy dominating, the other specialties on the bill served "as backgrounds or spring boards for the fun biz," and in the inimitable Earl Carroll style "there's a quantity of femme flesh plenteously displayed." Although the *Vanities* was better than most of the "variety bills" playing at the Tower, it still did not surpass one or two other "tab shows routed in here." *Variety*, November 19, 1941, reported that the show opened the season in Des Moines a week later "to excellent business."

Jeanne and Lillian had been looking forward to spending time with Bill during the show's booking in St. Louis over Thanksgiving, but their plans were subject to the vagaries of Earl Carroll's erratic touring schedule. Bill learned from Jeanne's November 13th letter from Omaha, Nebraska, that they would not be coming to St. Louis after all: "We had been looking forward to seeing you, and playing St. Louis, and are naturally so very disappointed at going past" she wrote. "However it will be grand to stop there in the SPRING, as the show troops west, so we've got our fingers crossed." At the company meeting after the first show in Omaha they learned that the maestro Earl Carroll had cancelled the St. Louis booking, since he was unable to reserve two Pullman and two baggage cars, as the railroads were transporting troops. Bill wrote on November 14th that he had "learned all about the shortcomings of our friend Carroll and if I can ever get a chance to put 'Arsenic' in his spinach, you can be assured I will gladly do it."

Back on the road the new *Vanities* itinerary included the Riverside Theatre in Milwaukee, the Orpheum in Madison, an open week, the Palace in Columbus, the Stanley in Pittsburgh, a lay-off in New York for December 19–25, ending the year at the RKO in Boston on December 26th. Beginning in January 1942 the show would play in well-known theatres on the East Coast. In a November 24th letter from the Riverside Theatre in Milwaukee, Jeanne again described the grind of constantly traveling from city to city, usually on buses for short hops when trains were not easily available. The bus ride from Des Moines to Davenport had been "terrible, getting us to our hotel at 5 A.M. with a full days work ahead of us"; the one from Omaha to Des Moines, which they shared with the touring *Hellzapoppin* Company—a lowbrow vaudeville revue created and produced in 1938 by the famous comedy team Ole Olsen and Chic Johnson, which had been a smash hit on Broadway for three years—was "so crowded we couldnt lie down and didnt get in till 5 A.M.," The next day some of the girls were asked to do "publicity stunts at 9 A.M., and between shows," wrote Jeanne, with one of them becoming temporarily blind from exhaustion.

Vaudevillians, however, were like a big, extended family, and their grueling itineraries were lightened while on the road by running into old friends and fellow performers and relatives. During their rare free time around midnight after the last show in Tulsa, Jeanne and Lillian visited with a few old friends living there, such as the adagio team who had been in Jeanne's company in the early 1930s before they went to Europe. After the show in Oklahoma City a man approached them on the street calling Lillian by her first name and introducing himself as her cousin, Ray Devereaux, who had driven fourteen miles with his wife Ida Belle up to the city from Edmond to see the show. "We talked until 4 A.M. and next day they called for us, since we were laying off there, and took us for a ride and sight seeing," Jeanne had written on October 25th, and Ray Devereaux and his wife drove them to their home town where they stopped "in front of Sol Devereaux's store." Jeanne recalled that during the summer of 1940 when they had veered off Route 66 and driven through a small town, they had passed a store with a large sign "DEVEREAUX" on the front, wondering if it were owned by a relative, and "sure enough, it was the one we'd seen last year."

"It's a rather pleasant thing to know so many people from all over the world, that hardly a week goes by that someone I POP UP," Jeanne wrote her father on November 24th. She was thrilled when in Omaha they encountered the *Hellzapoppin* show with the Sterners, who were sexy dancing sisters who had worked with her at the Bal Tabarin in Paris, as well as Grace and Niko from Europe, who had worked once with her at Radio City Music Hall. In Milwaukee they were re-acquainted with the dancer Anito Lou from the Bal Tabarin, as well as the Bernards, with whom she had worked in 1930 in California and later in Paris. Anito was currently dancing in a local burlesque show, and the *Vanities* cast was invited to a midnight show to see her perform. This was the first burlesque show that Jeanne and Lillian had ever seen and they were disgusted:

> Of all the filthy, nauseating, revolting, unspeakable slime, that show was it. I [Jeanne] really felt dazed and ill, to know people actually could descent so low as to see or perform in one.
> Suddenly on the stage came a dancer, Anita, (she of course was fully clothed, and did a nice dance), but for her to even associate with such trash, hurt us both. But I guess she had to eat, and couldn't be choosy.

Jeanne also discovered that she and the manager of the Riverside Theatre in Milwaukee, Mr. Wiesfeld, had worked together many times in Detroit, but had not seen each other in eight years: "He complimented me most highly," Jeanne wrote in her November 24th letter. "He said My dancing had always thrilled him, and still did. Whenever he had wanted a sock production scene, he had asked for me to put it over.'"

Jeanne and Lillians's hotel rooms occasionally offered a comfortable refuge from the dark, drafty, and often overheated theatres. Sometimes a scenic view from her hotel window during the show's run was the only time Jeanne had to sightsee. It snowed heavily the night before they arrived in Milwaukee with the temperature plummeting to eighteen degrees. Jeanne poetically describes the wintry scene out her hotel window to her father in her November 24th letter: "Our theatre was well named, for it is literally on the riverside. If I drop a grape from my dressing room window, it goes slap in the water, straight below. The vistas from the window are grand, and last night two boats went by whistling. The bridges rose to let them pass, and the snow diffused the scene, so that it looked like an old color print. By day, the reflection of the tall office buildings shimmer in the water, and gulls gracefully glide and swoop for bits of floating food." Unlike the stifling heat of the dressing rooms at the theatre in Des Moines located over the boilers, that made the performers extremely fatigued, the large hotel room in Milwaukee was refreshingly warm, had room for her Christmas card painting, and a window that they could open to let in the fresh air.

In her postcard on December 4th Jeanne describes the long and exhausting trip to Columbus, Ohio, for the booking at the Palace theatre:

> Yesterday we arose at 5 A.M. (Got to bed at 2 A.M. after packing) A bus picked Company up at hotel to take us to train track 14 miles away, so when we got there it was dawn. We were miles from nowhere and the train was waiting, so out we plied, and had to carry all our heavy baggage up a wet incline, and a block down the track over wet mud and gravel. Some fun! Then after 1 ½ hours we arrived in Chicago, and had to unload once again, and change trains once more, riding till 6:15 P.M. Were we tired and dirty!

After arriving, they had three days off to sleep late, shop, and see the movie *Life with Father*, which Jeanne highly recommended to her father. After the second show on opening day in Columbus the cast listened to the news of the Japanese bombing of Pearl Harbor, and were numbed by the shock of such a sudden, brutal attack. While performing the next show, Jeanne knew that going forward the real drama of her life would be occurring on the world stage.

Now that America was officially at war their itinerary became even more erratic. Jeanne reported that the show would go from the Stanley Theatre in Pittsburgh to Syracuse for three days and then straight to the RKO in Boston, followed by three days off before it opened there on December 26th. Later that month a review in *Variety*, December 31, 1941, declared the show in Boston "a feast of entertainment that would most likely run through New Year's." Because of the bomb scares, Jeanne and Lillian purchased a bright flashlight to use in case of blackouts while on the East Coast. Carroll's dinner theatre in Hollywood recently had been forced to close a few nights because of blackouts, and the New York booking had been cancelled because of the war. They were not sure of their schedule for 1942, but had heard that Carroll was pursuing as many bookings as possible. Although logistics were chaotic, they were confident that the show would play in Philadelphia, Baltimore, and Washington before the show closed, as well as Detroit, St. Louis, and Indianapolis—cities they had not yet played in—if the show made its way back to the West Coast.

Bill was lonely over the Christmas holiday season, since he had not received a letter from his family since December 17th and had not seen them for over a year. Throughout the tour he had sent Jeanne newspaper clippings and his usual trinkets. Selecting the proper Christmas gifts and sending them on time was a preoccupation in many of the December letters. Jeanne again suggested that her father give her a joint gift with her mother so she could purchase a necklace that she had recently admired in a store. Jeanne had already sent her father his Christmas gifts, including her customary fruitcake, in early December, admonishing him to show some self-discipline and not open it until Christmas day; however, as usual, he opened the package containing the fruitcake soon after its delivery and placed it on a top shelf in his room next to the previous year's that he had never eaten.

On December 21st Bill wrote how he had bought himself a five-pound box of candy and a gallon of wine "to abound with good things for the holiday season." Having just been on a shopping spree, he sent Jeanne the customary newspapers as well as a pen and a little fur tail that he had seen in a shop that she might be able to use in a costume. On December 29th, exasperated from having his letters returned, he wrote that he doubted whether his system of following their route schedule for sending letters was working. Once again the family was not together for another Christmas holiday.

In 1942 Jeanne toured with the *Vanities* until her engagement at Radio City Music Hall that April. Earl Carroll continued exploiting the cast, revising their itinerary from week to week and canceling bookings. The promised New York engagement at Christmas was pushed up to January. On January 6, 1942, from Bridgeport, Connecticut Lillian wrote that they were "in the midst of a 20 day tour thru New England, and what dreadful days we have. Three days in a place. No porters to carry bags. No hotels except at $4.75 double. Food sky high. Stingy." When they finally had their week off in New York Jeanne and Lillian were elated. "We have had a nightmare of work, travel and fatigue for 20 days, all thru New England," Jeanne wrote on January 28th. "I cant begin to describe how hard it was on us, and how happy we were to be back in New York City, even if we were commuting to Patterson, N. Jersey every day." Bill and Lillian had been married since 1911, but had been separated physically for sixteen years while Lillian had been on the road with Jeanne. In this letter Jeanne had to remind her father that today was a joint celebration—their wedding anniversary and Lillian's birthday—which he apparently had forgotten. Jeanne's grandparents in Pasadena had recently celebrated their sixty-fourth wedding anniversary, but any celebration was tempered by the fact that Grandma Lane had suffered another stroke followed by pneumonia. Lillian was "worn out with worry" and with writing letters to manage the situation in Pasadena.

War raids were expected in New York, but in spite of their anxiety about possible bombings, they relished the thought of a week off in New York—"JUST THINK. A WHOLE WEEK OFF WITH NO WORK AND WORRIES ABOUT WORK," Jeanne wrote. Staying again at the Hotel Belvedere at 319 West 48th Street just off of Times Square, Jeanne described the bomb scares: "Officials are expecting a 'token' raid on Manhattan any night now, so it isnt the safest place in the world, yet we must take our chance. We are on the fifth floor and have our instructions to dress warmly, grab a blanket, turn off lights, lock door and go to the 7th floor till all clear signal sounds. All I hope and pray is, it doesnt come, because to destroy the grand buildings of N.Y. would be man's greatest sacrilege." After their weeklong vacation they were scheduled to open at the Loew's State in New York on February 5th for a week and then travel to theatres in Philadelphia, Washington, D.C., Brooklyn, and the Bronx. They planned to stay at the Belvedere for the Brooklyn and Bronx bookings; as for Washington, D.C., "Where we are going to get room in Wash, I don't know, for I've heard they cant be had for love nor money, due to influx of officials and clerks," Jeanne wrote. After the Bronx booking Carroll was sending them back to Texas, followed possibly with six weeks in Mexico City.

Jeanne's voice was wistful when during an interview she talked about *Vanities* cast members Olive and George—two talented little people who performed a specialty ballroom dance. Olive especially had been not only a fellow performer but also a good friend whom Jeanne protected, and while on tour, Olive and George consistently received positive reviews. The reviewer for *Variety*, December 31, 1941, described the performance at the RKO theatre in Boston where Buster Shaver's act was rearranged "so that he and his tiny partners do only a part of their regular routine in one spot. However, George works in and out of the Wiere [Brothers] turn and Olive is featured in a swell Miranda [the much satirized Portuguese-born Brazilian singer, dancer, actress, and film star Carmen Miranda known for her fruit hat outfit] impersonation, backed up by the Wieres and Shaver. Olive and George also have a solo part for their fast-stepping ballroom specialty." During the winter months when they performed together in New York "Olive always wore a luxuriant mink coat," Jeanne said with a laugh. Given her diminutive size, it was difficult for Olive to negotiate the frenetic city traffic, so Jeanne helped her cross the busy streets, arm in arm, on the way to work or after hours for a late bite to eat. Jeanne maintained a long friendship with Buster Shaver and Olive who, after their retirement from performing, also lived in the Los Angeles area.

Bill wrote Jeanne on January 30, 1942, that he was sympathetic about the hardships of touring and pleased that they were finally having a week of rest. He offered Lillian belated birthday and anniversary congratulations, with the caveat, "You know there has been a lot of AQUA has gone over a few DAMNS, since Jan 28th 1911 don't you?" He had copied out their new itinerary on a card to guide him in his mailings, and he was confident they would find satisfactory accommodations in Washington, since he heard that "F.D.R. is going to try to put the Para-sights out." He enclosed a letter he had received from his boss informing all the salesmen that due to government restrictions on brass and steel the company would now edge their rulers with a different option. He had visited the local library and looked for a copy of *Billboard* magazine: an article for January 31st under "Night Clubs Vaudeville" noted that Earl Carroll "is setting up another VANITIES, which will probably take the road, when the first Company finished its schedule, and Bill Miller is rounding out a unit with Harry Rogers. 'Bring on the Women.' Tentatively slated for the femme lead is Imogene Coca." Miles Ingalls is casting "the new Carroll unit" and rehearsals start around February 1st. He wondered if Jeanne were planning to continue with this second touring show.

On February 17th Jeanne wrote her father from Philadelphia that their days "are so rushed with four-one hour and 15 min shows all week, and 5 on Sat and Sunday, that we have less time than on any tour before." They were still exhausted from the steady stream of agents and visitors backstage between shows and at their hotel when they had played at the Loew's State in New York the previous week. Jeanne described an adventure that had recently occurred in New York. They had visited the William Randolph Hearst Collection, offered for sale on the fifth floor of Gimbel's department store, which showcased fabulous "Silver, China, Jewels, Wood Panelled rooms, Stained glass windows, Armour, Rugs, furniture, paintings," and more rarities: "It was an eye-opener, to see what he was able to squander fortunes on, for most of his treasures have never been out of their crates in the ware-houses," she wrote. Despite her lifelong fascination with beautiful material objects, Jeanne was only able to squander her meager "fortunes" on necessities, such as the twenty-five pairs of new toe shoes she needed to buy immediately since material was scarce: she was fortunate the shoemaker had "just enough to get mine made." She also updated her father on their new itinerary after the engagement in the Bronx, which now included Akron and then Youngstown, Ohio, for a "split week," followed by a week in Detroit and Buffalo. "Rumors abound of booking here and there, but we'll never know till a week or so ahead," she wrote.

On February 22nd Bill informed them that he was very concerned that the YMCA's management in the midst of war was trying to make the older residents move out, so they could rent their rooms at a higher price for soldiers and sailors: "They are turning down people everyday," he wrote, "and since all the hotels are crowded, they are making room for all the soldiers and sailors looking for housing in St. Louis." As an excuse for evicting him, management "came to me a few days ago, and complained that I had much more belongings in my room, and a few things on the floor (a couple of sample boxes) and that it was a big 'cleaning problem' and I would have to <u>find other quarters</u>." Bill definitely did not want to move from the only home he had known since 1930; the Y was centrally located, most of his customers knew where he could be reached, and he would not be able to find even a second class hotel for the rate he paid here. "If I were making a good income, I wouldn't care," he wrote, "but I am just making my living, that's about all."

Although Lillian was sympathetic about Bill's fear of being evicted from the Y, she was worried about her own expenses during wartime. On February 24th Lillian wrote Bill about the financial difficulties of Jeanne's income tax filing. Jeanne could claim a $1500-deduction for her mother as a dependent, but since she had no home, that is, no permanent residence, she was prohibited from deducting hotel bills. As for Bill's "worries," about being evicted from the Y, she refused "to worry too much, as I feel the Nation will soon have us all working for defence in some capacity. You are more fortunate than I, in that respect, for you have good eye-sight, without glasses, where I shall be handicapped a lot." So they "don't get lost from one another" she provided a new route schedule that included Washington, D.C., Brooklyn, the Bronx, Akron, and Youngstown for a split week. She ended her letter with "Now dont you worry. Keep your chin up, and put up your snoot."

"My affairs [living quarters]—which I outlined, doesn't seem to interest you—only offering the admonition, 'Dont worry' 'and keep your chin up,'" Bill angrily replied on February 26th. Threatened by having to move, he once again brought up the sensitive topic of the loan to them for $300 two years ago of his "DARNED HARD EARNED SAVINGS." He reminded them that he had not mentioned the loan as long as they were "not on a pay-roll," but they had been on one since last August and still had not reconciled with him. He had forgotten that the topic had previously been discussed both in person and in letters over the past two years, and the agreement was that they would pay him back when he needed it. Now he claimed that he was "just about able to make a living" and take care of his expenses, implying that he now needed the money. "Have a <u>lot more</u> to write about, but lets 'straighten' this out first," he wrote.

Two days later, having calmed down, he was in a more conciliatory mood. He wrote that he had cleaned up his room and was still living at the Y, and since he had been paying his rent in advance, hopefully the situation would be resolved. Acknowledging that Jeanne and Lillian had their hands full with pressing business, he would defer the repayment of their loan for the moment. That week he had picked up the photographs of Jeanne that he had made for her and had enclosed a set for her perusal: he had some friends who had already asked for autographed sets. "While I was having same made, I had one of my 'MUGS' taken also, in the 4x6 size, so can have them made up occasionally. Will enclose one for the tribe." Then he stopped writing letters for almost two months.

13

Radio City and Clifford C. Fisher's Folies Bergère

The prospects for future bookings for *Earl Carroll's Vanities* were not encouraging, so Jeanne left the cast at the end of March 1942 when her contract expired, and was thrilled to be back dancing at Radio City Music Hall during the spring and early summer. After the grueling tour with the *Vanities*, the five shows a day at Radio City were a welcome relief. At the end of March Jeanne appeared in the patriotic revue "To the Colors!" featuring five brilliant scenes of music and dance that were added to the ninth traditional Easter stage show "Glory of Easter." The star-studded cast included Gil Maison and Company, Henry Calvin, Owen McBride, the Rockettes, the Corps de Ballet, the Choral Ensemble, the Symphony Orchestra, and other specialty acts. Jeanne thrilled the Radio City audiences with her spectacular balloon dance and featured spot in a flag-waving routine with the other ballerinas, twirling round and round on her toes.

The movie was Cecil B. DeMille's *Reap the Wild Wind*, featuring Ray Milland, John Wayne, and Paulette Goddard. DeMille had attended the opening night live performance, and according to the reviewer for *Variety*, April 1, 1942, even to DeMille "the stirring music, the beautiful costumes, the tremendous cast, the overwhelming set, the sheer bigness of it all, and the simple solemnity with which it comes off must be something he, perhaps, has found unequalled on the screen." This reviewer praised Francis Scott Key's "Star-Spangled Banner" finale celebrating the national anthem, but he felt that the ballet and prima ballerina Jeanne's energetic flag waving routine suffered as it was too similar to that of the famous Rockettes.

Jeanne now lived with her mother at the Hotel Knickerbocker at 5th Avenue and Broadway in New York and wrote her letters in between shows at Radio City. On April 5th Jeanne wrote her father, whom she had not heard from in "ages, except for the telegram, which I have stuck in the edge of the mirror" in her dressing room. She had been sick with a cold and "staggered" through ten days of rehearsals and costume fittings, reviving only the day before opening. The *Vanities* cast recently had had a six-day layoff, so most of the performers came to New York to see her at Radio City "and were tremendously impressed" with the production. The *Vanities* show was "wobbling on thru a few more weeks of work"—two in Canada and perhaps a Chicago nightclub for two months—she wrote her father, but "there is so much talk about what 'may' happen I'll believe it when I see it."

Although the current show might continue into a fourth week, Jeanne had no guarantee that she would have back-to-back Radio City engagements. Between shows Jeanne devoted her time to looking for new bookings, even contacting her agent about performing in the summer operettas at the Muny Opera. She was also contacting the USO Camp Shows, Inc., where vaudeville was still flourishing, to inquire about touring the Army camps to provide entertainment for the soldiers. Following the progress of Jeanne's Radio City show in the New York newspapers in the library, Bill predicted on April 9th that this popular show would probably run a fourth week. The run exceeded Bill's prediction: "We are on our fifth week at the Radio City Music Hall," wrote Lillian on April 24th. "It has been a very important engagement, and after playing with the 'Vanities,' it has seemed like Heaven to us. Of course one has to keep right up on the toes every second, to make everything go exactly right- show after show-day after day- and week after week." In addition to Jeanne's daily rehearsals, they had to "get some new numbers ready, and tend the many irons in the fire, but outside of that we can relax, what little time there is left in a day." After this run was over they were looking forward to relaxing before the next bookings. She had copied Jeanne's attractive, patriotic costume including the dyed gloves, and had made a large silk flag to be used in future dances.

Shortly after Jeanne and Lillian had returned to New York with the *Vanities* they contacted the booker for the Muny in St. Louis, who informed them that the summer shows were already cast. Later, after Jeanne's engagement at Radio City had ended, they encountered the talented ballet dancers Paul Haakon and Patricia Bowman, whose show had followed Jeanne's at Radio City. Paul and Patricia were booked for the Muny from June 1st to 10th, but feared that if their show at the Music hall were extended by a week, they would be unable to fulfill their contract. Since Jeanne had to have a new dance ready for a future booking in Washington, D.C., she quickly choreographed a patriotic number with the large silk flag and new musical arrangement in case she needed to substitute at the Muny in June. Much to Jeanne's regret, Paul and Patricia were not held over at Radio City, and were able to perform at the Muny that summer. The two weeks spent creating the new dance and preparing the musical arrangement and sewing the costume so quickly after the long grind of the *Vanities* and the five-week run at Radio City was exhausting. Jeanne's new patriotic dance was performed with a problematically heavy six- by eight-foot silk flag that she swung around while doing her difficult toe work, which now included a difficult back bend on toe that usually affected her lower back. The stage carpenters at Radio City volunteered to make Jeanne a replacement flag out of the lighter wood they had used for the corps de ballet's flags in her recent show, but even this lighter flag was difficult to maneuver, since during the dance it needed to resist the wind and be kept mostly in a furling position to avoid wrapping around the stick.

Lillian was concerned about Bill's precarious living arrangements at the YMCA and his financial instability. Not having heard from him since he had mentioned his possible eviction, she assumed in her April 24th letter that "it is a thing of the past by now. It is easier for you to live there, I know, so I do hope no more trouble about staying there, comes up." She suggested that he take some courses to prepare himself for a defense job during wartime. If necessary, she would apply for the job as a typist herself, but she had "never used a typewriter, altho I can spell," while "so few can." During the summer they would like to do the USO Camp Shows that would begin in June, for "Uncle Sam's boys in the camps need entertainment, and so many performers are doing that. It will be hard riding—all day, and giving shows, and then riding all day, and giving another show at another camp, all summer. But I guess we can put up with it, if the other people can," she told him. She feared, however, that most of the Camp shows for the coming summer season were already cast.

In these lean times in the show business world during wartime, Bill's paranoia about money and the threat that he might have to move from the Y once again reached a crisis level, resulting in a contentious letter exchange about the $300 loan he had made to them in April 1940. His letter to Lillian on April 28th consisted of a heated, one-page diatribe devoted to the topic of the 1940 loan, with most of his points emphatically capitalized and underlined. He had understood that it would be re-paid as soon as they were on a payroll again, and since they had been on a payroll since last September, he was confounded why they had never said "a word on THAT SUBJECT. Thought I would hear from you about Xmas. But it seems not." He had mentioned this problem in a previous letter, but received no response, so "let us hear from you on this subject, and we will go on from there. Suppose you read these letters [previous letters he enclosed] over carefully and THINK before answering. When I hear from you on this subject, we will go on from there."

On May 25th Lillian, hurt by the bitterness of Bill's letter, reminded him that the agreed upon verbal terms of the loan was that he would be re-paid when he absolutely needed the money. Jeanne was practicing and rehearsing long hours every day to prepare for her booking at the Capitol Theatre in Washington, D.C., where she hoped to perform her new patriotic flag dance, and they were disappointed that the date for the Capitol booking had been changed from the week of June 18th to that of July 4th. With no other booking or promising prospects on the horizon, they were considering signing up for the USO Camp Shows in the fall. Lillian had been applying to schools that offered instruction in defense work, but they had been rejecting older people, especially women like herself. She still had aspirations to work in the defense business, so she could "bring in some income and get off Jeanne's neck, so that she can get married, or whatever she wishes, within these next years," Lillian wrote. "So far there has been no release for her and 'the nose to the grindstone' must have worn pretty thin many times."

The good news was that New York had not been bombed. Even though it was a major target for German bombs, New York was still more economical for them than other cities, offering affordable rehearsal space, reasonable rent, and transportation on foot almost everywhere they needed to travel. Since they had no kitchen in their room at the Knickerbocker Hotel, they usually ate onions, radishes, and cottage cheese at night in their bedroom, enough nourishment to keep Jeanne's weight at an acceptable level and both of them in good condition. They enjoyed reading the liberal *New York Post* and even more the new, progressive *P.M.* newspaper started by Marshall Field, Sr., that had a socialist bent, advocating labor unions and the common man.

Lillian addressed the sensitive issue of Bill's 1940 loan and the family's agreement for its repayment. Although Jeanne had earned a decent salary in *Earl Carroll's Vanities*, their expenses allowed them to break even and not save a cent. However, Lillian had always kept the $300 he had loaned them "intact" in case he needed it or for other emergencies. She reminded him that their verbal agreement was that he would tell them when he needed it. "You can have it back whenever you need it, but it serves us as a back-log when things dont pan out, and it feels good to have it, 'but I wont spend it.' I always felt that if anything happened to you I would be enabled to get to St. Louis if I had this little 'nest egg' to come," Lillian wrote. "You see there are many times when I wouldnt be able to get enough money together to come at all." Since Jeanne had to support two people on her salary, they had never been able to save much money, so his loan is all the savings they had. Also, this nest egg gave her consolation that she could cope with any bad health she might be forced to face in the future.

Lillian also reminded him of a letter he had later written her saying that if he had the money it was as if it were "in the bank, as it was, and doing nobody any good." Since it was doing them some good as an emergency fund, they "were welcome to its use for security." Lillian realized that Bill had a history of forgetting all verbal family discussions and remembering only what was said in the family letters. Although she wanted to keep this nest egg, if he absolutely needed it now, she was willing to repay it immediately. She ended her letter by reminding him about his good fortune of living in the inexpensive YMCA and having "no one but yourself to feed, clothe and house."

Bill answered Lillian broodingly on June 20th and obsessed on the sensitive subject of their money proposition. In the past when he had loaned them money when they "'were up against it,'" they had paid him back "without" him having to "ASK for it. Thats why you got it, the last time—two years ago." Bill now claimed that if he had known two years ago that they needed to keep this money "as a back-log for the next two years or more, (not interested in how it effects you)" he would not have sent it. "Now if you can get that money back here, we could go over and 'wipe the slate clean,' and get back to our 'old terms' do so," he wrote, but if "for any reason even after playing a no doubt very profitable five weeks engagement at Radio City, you find you cant send same back without crippling yourself, <u>advise me</u>."

On July 1st Jeanne opened in the patriotic "Victory Revue" at the Capitol Theatre in Washington, D.C. Her father sent her a telegram on July 4th wishing her "a happy fourth. Hoping our flag brings down house." The bill opened with an orchestral medley, followed by the singing Murphy sisters, the comedienne Cynda Glen, the acrobatic Lane Brothers, the Sixteen Rhythm Rockets [the Roxyettes], and the Sam Jack Kaufman House Orchestra. *Variety*, July 8, 1942, reported that the show closed "with a terrific ensemble, 'Wave that Flag, America,' with Fague Springman singing the solo and the Roxyettes taking part. All sock showmanship." Since the patriotic scene set had taken up most of the stage, there was no room for Jeanne's flag dance; she had to substitute her gorgeous ballroom number featuring her large balloon that she had fortunately rehearsed for a week before the Washington engagement in case of an emergency. "They lit the large balloon exquisitely. It was breath-taking in beauty, so we came out O.K. except that we didn't do the Flag dance, and had to rent a costume for the balloon dance," Lillian wrote Bill on July 22nd. Being on a tight budget in the nation's capital, a city even more expensive than New York, they "went around hungry" except for the two occasions when Jeanne's beaux took them out to dinner.

When they returned to New York on July 9th the theatres were mostly dark for the summer, except for the nightclubs with their dangerous, slick floors. Jeanne had earned $300 for her weeklong engagement in Washington, D.C., but after expenses she netted $154, not counting the $370 it had cost them to prepare the flag dance. Lillian reminded Bill that although Jeanne had earned $900 for her five weeks at Radio City, after expenses and living costs most of that money had been spent. She now had his $300 loan and an additional $220 to live on until Jeanne's next booking. "This terrific money you think we make! Where is it?" Lillian wrote. Although Bill knew that they were usually laid off during the summer months, he still demanded the loan to be repaid. Lillian gave in: "The agreement was, however, that when you needed it, you could have it back, so I'll live up to the letter," she resignedly wrote.

Although Bill was still upset that Lillian had taken a month to respond to his letter asking for repayment of the loan, he wrote on June 26th he was relieved that she had finally given him a detailed explanation of why she had not repaid the loan. It gave him "a little different slant on the matter, and 'Laying your cards on the table' has helped matters a lot." Although his business was "almost extinct" with one of his long-term clients going out of business and his main supplier, the American Manufacturing Concern, unable to buy enough supplies to make their rulers and yardsticks as well as lacking customers for their advertising line, he was not in dire straits, so they could keep the $300 "to tide you over a little, with my best wishes, and with the understanding that it will be returned later in the fall," he wrote. For now he was willing to forgive them for either forgetting or disregarding his request for three months.

On August 5th Lillian thanked Bill for allowing them to keep the $300 "intact" until the entertainment job market improved in the fall: "It will save a lot of anguish even if we do not have to use any of it, to feel we have it in back of us." Jeanne was spending the hot summer days in a "vicious merry-to-round" of practicing, rehearsing, and dressing up for appointments with producers and agents. Lillian contrasted Jeanne's pressured life with salesmen and businessmen who "dont have to be gotten up beautifully to call on prospects. And no one cares if they have put on one or two pounds more. But weight is noted, and viewed with alarm, in this business," she wrote. After her appointments Jeanne changed her "best glad rags," put on her practice clothes, and then they walked ten or twelve blocks carrying a heavy suitcase to her rehearsal space. Trying "to keep the wolf from the door" was constant hard work, and Lillian again wished that she had been qualified to get a job in the war industry. She encouraged Bill to try to get hired with Uncle Sam as perhaps a filing clerk or photographer, for a government job would undoubtedly be continued even after the war ended.

Writing on August 24th, Bill asked for confirmation that he would be repaid in the fall. "In other words, I would like to have some assurance from you, that you will try to get same back here, as soon as you are in a position to do so," he wrote. Bill never raised the larger issue of his lack of financial support of his family for most of his adult life, and fixated on these occasional small loans to his hardworking wife and daughter who were struggling to make a living in show business. He was obsessed with getting paid back even when Jeanne and Lillian were most destitute.

On October 1st Lillian wrote Bill that they had given up their room at the Knickerbocker Hotel and traveled to Brockton, Massachusetts, for Jeanne's week-long booking at $200 per week at the Brockton Fair. Desperate to earn some money, they had packed all their belongings in their trunks, which were now piled high in the hotel's basement storage room. When they returned to New York from Brockton, they had discovered that the manager at the Knickerbocker had raised the room rents, forcing them to look elsewhere for lodgings in a crowded wartime real estate market. After a long search in the summer heat, they rented a room that had a small pantry with a sink at the Belvedere Hotel, where they had stayed in January. After purchasing a tiny stove for the pantry, they were no longer restricted to eating only cold, raw food in their hotel room, but could cook their own hot meals for less money than eating in restaurants. They were optimistic that Jeanne would eventually get hired, enabling them to build their nest egg. Among their current prospects were Clifford C. Fisher's musical comedy, the Latin Quarter in Boston, some Deluxe Concerts produced by Jerry Cargill, Radio City Music Hall, the USO touring shows, a repeat at the Capitol Theatre in Washington, D.C., the Roxy when it changes its policy in December and adds stage shows, and a theatre in Chicago. This letter was "to certify that we are alive and kicking very hard to get going on lots of new projects," wrote Lillian.

On October 25th Lillian wrote Bill about her failed attempt to sell her old Ford car stored in Pasadena in her parents' garage. She had hoped to get $450 cash for the car and then use $300 of the proceeds to pay back Bill's loan. When a prospective purchaser would only offer a flat $300, she refused his offer, so Bill would have to wait patiently for a while. Though the businesses, theatres, restaurants, and nightclubs were all making large wartime profits, the big corporate employers were paying the performers salaries the "lowest in history," she wrote. Since these employers only hire cheap "nudes, and burlesques etc, or second rate dancers, and 'has been's," most dancers like Jeanne "cannot remain in this business, pay for costumes, and toe shoes, plus living expenses." If all else fails, they have at least been promised the USO Camp Shows tour, although they have heard that hotel accommodations while touring were scarce and that the hotel managers cheat everyone.

For her birthday Bill sent his talented daughter a beautiful scrapbook for her professional clippings and photographs, and on October 31st, the night of her birthday, Jeanne took pen in hand and thanked him for his thoughtful gift. She then reflected on many of her young friends who had joined the armed services. "Perhaps an offer may come through for me—to fly by U.S. Army Bomber to Ireland, England, or Just Bermuda. It probably wont happen—but what a thrill if it did, to entertain the soldiers," she wrote. If German bombs were to fall on New York, they would likely destroy the top seven stories of any high rise, so New York had a partial blackout of all windows over the fifth floors; factories and some affluent private homes, however, continued being brightly lit up as usual. Jeanne started to send her Christmas cards to lonesome soldiers far from home, and they all asked her for professional photographs. In his December 1st letter Bill enclosed his customary roll of St. Louis newspapers, as well as copies of personal letters from mutual St. Louis friends. Jeanne and Lillian both wrote him on December 14th with the sad news of Grandma Lane's death in Pasadena. Jeanne's Aunts Lenore and Ida were to accompany her Grandpa back to Nebraska later this month for the funeral on December 20th; Lillian was devastated that she lacked the funds to join her family in Nebraska for her mother's burial. She had hoped, but to no avail, that Jeanne might have been secured a booking in a nightclub for one show to pay her round-trip ticket despite the danger posed for toe dancers by the nightclub's highly waxed floor.

Since the New York theatres and touring shows were mostly featuring famous orchestras, movie stars on personal appearance tours, and girly shows, Jeanne created a show with original action, dialogue, set and scenery, song lyrics, costumes, casting, and the obligatory bevy of beautiful girls that she marketed to her agent Hal Sands, who was impressed and agreed to produce it in January 1943. Jeanne included in her letter a brief synopsis of her new show:

> As the curtain rises—a troupe of International Artists are at the pier, having just gotten home from a tour around the world. They decide, instead of disbanding, to take the show all over America, to entertain the people who are keeping them rolling. The next scene is just the plain bare unglamourous "back-stage" as it looks before the scenery is hung. The troupe walks into an old theatre that has been "closed" for years. It's a mess, but they fall to getting it ready for the show. Of course they ignore the audience, who feel they "rekey-hole" peeking. There are farcial situations galore, as these actors unpack, Rehearse the music, find the gavotte costumes havent arrived, and wonder whether to do it in their bathing suits and white wigs and buckled shoes. Of course the men look very funny in wigs, bathing trunks, and skinny legs, as they bow and scrape very Gavotte. We tie the songs on by pretending to be testing the Microphone. Everything looks un-rehearsed and natural. Finally, when everything is ready—then the show is supposed to go on. And its Revue style, from then on.

Lillian wrote on the same December day that since Hal Sands had promised to produce Jeanne's original show with a thirty-person unit for bookings in large theatres around the country at the beginning of the new year, Jeanne would be able to continue supporting them by working in the theatre and keep starvation at bay.

On December 20th Bill mentioned that he liked Jeanne's show synopsis, complimenting her on moving forward into a new creative field—"Author, Composer, Playwright, and Other Things"—and predicted that the show "should go over <u>very nicely</u>." He was sending her a box of miscellaneous items for Christmas from Santa, as well as a couple of engravings for Lillian and some cash. He asked Jeanne to sneak out and purchase something for her mother that she would like since he had no clue these days. The contentious issue of the family loan was not mentioned again until a year later.

Writing to her father on January 8, 1943, Jeanne hoped that this year "proves better than its predecessor." Her agent Hal Sands had not been successful in obtaining the financial backing for her new script and dance unit that she had been working on so diligently, so all other options for work right now were of high priority. Given their tight finances and wartime rationing, they had been carefully purchasing the few food items that they could afford, mostly cheese, bread, milk, onions, and soup, and were living from paycheck to paycheck. In addition to eating as healthy as possible and paying for their hotel room, they also needed to rent rehearsal space so that Jeanne could maintain her dancing fitness. Lillian had even applied for extra work at a New York factory that made sparkplugs for the army, but had not received a response. During wartime rationing their hotel room along with schools and churches were cold during the daytime hours; gasoline rationing had reduced the number of cars on the New York streets; and many food items simply disappeared from the shelves in the groceries of middle class and poor neighborhoods. When Bill responded on January 24th, he never offered to send them any money, complaining that he also has not earned a dime since the beginning of the New Year; he encouraged Lillian to take another loan from her sister Lenore, and sternly scolded Jeanne for not thanking him for one of his recent gifts.

Lillian wrote Bill a month later on February 23rd reiterating the disappointing news that the financial backing for Jeanne's new dance unit had never materialized. However, Jeanne continued to audition every day with the Radio City flag dance: one dance director said that she "was like a diamond among pebbles, and the most terrific 'sock' they had ever seen," she wrote. He promised to hire her for a big Broadway show starring the singer Mary Martin, but this prospect never happened. Lillian's sister Ida had written that they could return to Pasadena and keep house for the now widowed Grandpa Lane, but since they owed Bill the $300, Lillian determined their best chance for repaying it was to remain in New York. In Los Angeles Jeanne could earn only $125 a week at the Paramount Theatre downtown, "but there is so little else," she wrote.

Despite living on practically nothing for three months, "Jeanne is at her peak in dancing, and there is no one who can come within a mile of her spins, and turns, on toe," Lillian wrote. "We've got a race horse of marvelous skill in this family, and all we need is faith in her, to back her up, until she can get into something again." Her voice filled with pride and determination, Lillian stated that they had never failed to survive in this precarious world of show business during the lean times, and if they can manage to get through this month, they will "be safe." She had no doubt that given Jeanne's extraordinary talent they would prevail and eventually be able to pay Bill his $300.

He replied unsympathetically on March 2nd that he personally identified with their financial struggles, stressing that they had no monopoly on losing prospects and business. Like everyone else including himself they need to "'grin and bear it,'" he sarcastically wrote. Lillian responded on April 4th that they were desperately looking for jobs for Jeanne in hotel floor shows, despite the floors being heavily waxed and dangerous. Jeanne had recently had a two-week engagement at the Biltmore Hotel in Providence, Rhode Island, that had included a hotel room but no food: they had lived the entire time on bread, cream cheese, raw carrots, and canned sweet corn. All they had lined up right now for future bookings was a contract for one week in St. Louis at the Muny in June during the theatre's silver anniversary year. Lillian again suggested that Bill should apply for a job in or near St. Louis in a defense plant, and despite his complaints about money, he declined: "I don't want to work in a factory, except as a case of 'last resort,'" he replied on April 12th. Inflexible throughout his life, Bill again reiterated that he had worked for the same advertising company for thirty-five years and planned to "stick it out for a few more."

Two months later on June 12th Lillian finally answered Bill, telling him how letter writing became a lesser priority when one was totally focused on making a living, which in their "field is so much more time consuming than yours, that it is not even funny." In fact, if Bill had put as much time and energy in his business as they had done, he probably "would have been rich." They are also obligated to write letters to many others besides him, including relatives and friends in the armed forces. They are still pursuing any leads for performing in both hotel floor shows and any theatres that are hiring, so their workload has been doubled. They are constantly involved in exhausting preparations, such as impressing the bookers with Jeanne's experience and good looks, updating a portfolio of photographs showcasing her looks and lovely costumes, and having dramatic musical arrangements for her dances. The week before last Jeanne had performed at the Terrace room in Newark, New Jersey, traveling back and forth late at night, and now they have a booking for three weeks in Dallas, Texas, following the Muny in June. Since they will arrive in St. Louis for rehearsals a week before the Muny engagement, they will have time for a brief family visit.

At the Muny Jeanne performed in the patriotic *Sons O' Guns* from June 28 to July 4, a Broadway musical that was augmented by vaudeville and spectacle, resulting in a dazzling extravaganza featuring a cast of 250 performers, with specialty acts like Jeanne's being a major part of the show. *Sons O' Guns* had opened originally at New York's Imperial Theatre in November 1929 and closed after nearly 300 performances. The book was a fictionalized version of the American Expeditionary Forces (AEF), under the command of Major General John J. Pershing. The AEF were the American troops sent to Europe in 1917–18 to fight alongside the allies in World War I.[1] According to the *St. Louis Star-Times*, June 28, 1943, the Muny's show was a "musical version of the A.E.F. in France during World War I," and a "crisp routine of precision drilling, executed by 150 highly-trained soldiers from Jefferson Barracks, will bring present-day atmosphere."

Sons o' Guns was Jeanne's last performance at the Muny in her hometown where she had launched her professional career. Later, when she was living in Pasadena in the summer before her marriage, Jeanne's good friend and fellow dancer Harry Woolever wrote on August 2, 1952, that he had just finished rehearsing his scene with the ballerina Patricia Bowman for their upcoming performance in the Muny's operetta *Naughty Marietta*. Harry lamented that Jeanne would not be his partner for this engagement, hoping to persuade her to come out of retirement for one more starring role at the Muny. "I've just been thinking how wonderful it would be if you were here," he wrote. "Miss Bowman is excellent to be sure but I'd like so very much to see you do something here. I've been telling the other members of the dancing chorus about you so when you dance here again they'll be expecting someone completely fantastic. Seriously though, I wish you would come out and show them some 'real dancing' as the saying goes." Years later when he was the head of the Dance Department at Brooklyn's American Musical and Dramatic Academy, Harry wrote Jeanne on December 17, 1992, to let her know that her "fame continues year after year." He always told his students about her "career and incredible artistry," and would be proud to include a film of her dancing, if she had one to send him, in his program at the Academy.

Later in the summer of 1943, coming directly from Radio City Music Hall and the St. Louis Muny, Jeanne danced in three operettas—Noel Coward's *Bitter Sweet*, Jerome Kern's *Roberta*, and *Balalaika*—at the Fair Park Casino in the Dallas State Fair's Starlight operetta season. She performed six dances—two per week—all requiring different costumes: Jeanne and Lillian furnished two costumes and the producers provided the other four. When they arrived in Dallas in the blazing summer heat with their trunks, they settled in at the Jefferson Hotel and then went out to the fairgrounds to investigate the rehearsal schedule and space and meet her piano accompanist. They ate their daily meals, consisting of bread, cheese, onions, and radishes, in their hotel room. Early publicity for the summer season in the local Dallas newspapers praised Jeanne's internationally acclaimed dancing artistry. According to the *Dallas Morning News*, May 26, 1943, she was considered by "balletomanes as the unchallenged champion in the field of spins and whirlwind pirouettes. Her flawless classic ballet has won her followings in

Jeanne Devereaux in a promotional photograph for her signature balloon dance in the premiere of *Bitter Sweet* at the Fair Park Casino at the Dallas State Fair, sponsored by the Starlight Operetta Season, July 19, 1943. The run of *Bitter Sweet* was from July 19th to 25th, 1943. Photograph by Maurice Seymour in his Chicago studio. Courtesy Jeanne Devereaux Perkins Collection.

America, Europe, and South America." The *Dallas Morning News*, June 20, 1943, said that audiences attending performances of *Bitter Sweet*, *Roberta*, and *Balalaika* could see "Miss Devereaux unfold a dancing talent which has brought her acclaim as the unchallenged champion of spins, whirlwind pirouettes and classic ballet." On July 16th the *Dallas Morning News* reported that "Jeanne Devereaux, Premier Danceuse" was the former "dancing star of Geo. White's Scandals, and more recently of 'Radio City Music Hall."

That summer the newspaper reviewers praised Jeanne's performances in the three operettas. When she danced in *Bitter Sweet* from July 19 to 25, which starred the popular singer Martha Errolle, the *Times Herald*, July 18, 1943, ranked her "among the great contemporary dancers ... [whose] art ... has been acclaimed in London, Paris, Cannes, Monte Carlo, Rome, Milano, Tripoli, and Rio de Janeiro." She danced in *Roberta* from July 26 to August 1, showcasing her famous balloon dance as the prima ballerina.

Balalaika, an operetta that originated in London with music by George Posford and Bernard Grun, ran from August 2 to 8 and featured Jeanne as Varvara, the Russian ballet dancer. A lavish nine-scene production, the operetta was set in a Montmartre cabaret called Balalaika in Paris in 1916, where former Russian aristocrats and military men were earning their living; the scene then shifted back to Saint Petersburg in 1914 where a Cossack Colonel had an affair with a ballet dancer, who coincidentally was the daughter of a nihilist who threw bombs in the Czar's opera box. The final scene moved back to the left bank in Paris, where the Russian lovers are now united as refugees. According to a review in the *Dallas Morning News*, August 3, 1943, Jeanne Devereaux's "pas seul to the Swan Lake music was appreciated and her Flag Dance of the last act was received with even more warmth." During the 1940s Jeanne continued to dance in *Balalaika* at various operetta theatres around the country.

Returning to the Belvedere Hotel in New York in mid–August, Jeanne and Lillian were once again living the grind of job hunting in show business. They had reapplied for their ration book, and food in the groceries was still high priced and scarce. On September 17th Jeanne wrote Bill about rescuing three kittens from a fruit store and the severe case of asthma she subsequently developed. When the doctor came to examine her at the Belvedere, he said that her asthma was an allergic reaction not only to kitten fur, but also to her stressful lifestyle filled with worry over finances and bookings. "He said if I were relieved of worry, and could relax mentally," wrote Jeanne, "I would get over it. Otherwise it will crop up with increasing violence all thru life. Interesting????" Jeanne was plagued for the rest of her life with this chronic respiratory disease.

The year 1943 had been a terrific one for Broadway shows with long runs, preventing many touring and new shows from opening since there was a theatre shortage. When the Philadelphia Opera offered Jeanne a seventeen-week tour as ballerina and choreographer, she had to refuse since the salary was too low. Jeanne did later sign a contract to star in the famous impresario Clifford C. Fisher's spectacular vaudeville-revue, *Folies Bergère*, scheduled for six weeks of rehearsals in Hollywood, a grand opening at the Winterland Theatre in San Francisco in the late fall, and a national tour. In 1939 Fischer had decided to resurrect vaudeville on Broadway in New York for the servicemen living there, acquiring the rights from the Parisian Director to use the French name for his American show. Once again Jeanne performed in a famous show that featured semi-nude dancers, although, as usual, she performed fully clad. According to her contract, Jeanne's salary for the first four weeks would be $200 per week, as well as $60 a week during the rehearsal period. He guaranteed her a minimum of eight weeks unless the show closed earlier, and not more than fourteen shows weekly.

On their way to Hollywood from New York, Jeanne sent her father a postcard on September 25th informing him that they were changing trains in Chicago not St. Louis, so there would not be time for a "'between trains' visit." On October 7th she sent another postcard describing the terrible day they had finding an available room for rent in Hollywood. Promising to keep her father informed of their itinerary while on the road, on November 5th Jeanne sent him a postcard with the news that they would soon be leaving for San Francisco for their engagement at Winterland; in another postcard days later she described their hectic trip north from Hollywood to San Francisco and their current dismal lodgings:

Jeanne Devereaux clowning with George Mann in the Green Room while performing in Clifford C. Fischer's *Folies Bergère* at Winterland, San Francisco, California, December–February 1943. George Mann with Dewey Barto was part of a famous vaudeville comedy dance act from the 1920s to the 1940s known as "Barto and Mann." Acrobatic dancers of comic short and tall heights, they performed risqué dances at the Palace Theatre in New York, on the Orpheum Circuit, in the Fanchon and Marco "Idea" unit shows, in *Earl Carroll's Vanities*, in Europe, in Radio City Music Hall's premiere in 1932, in film, in the hit Broadway show *Hellzapoppin*, and in the *Folies Bergère* with Jeanne. Courtesy Jeanne Devereaux Perkins Collection.

> Hi. We're Here. After much toil and travail, we pulled in to San Francisco and got settled in a terrible hotel, at $3.50 per day. Only one suit case handle went bluey.—Hollywood was a terrible town to get out of at 6:30 in the A.M. Couldn't order a taxi in advance, and at that hour, no place to phone from, open. So we took the majority of baggage down to station Sat night. Sun morn we waited ½ hour, in dark, chill, blear for street car to take us to Los Angeles. Then we walked 8 blocks, with laden hands, to station.—Ah! Me. (How would I go about it?) This town is so overcrowded, a room is as scarce as proverbial hen's teeth.—Still the eternal optimists we hope to find an apt, for this hotel is just one step above a "flop house." Whole company here too.

In her November 23rd postcard Jeanne optimistically hoped that the *Folies Bergère* would have a six-month run at the Winterland.

The highly popular Winterland premiere of the *Folies Bergère* occurred on November 30, 1943. Fisher's spectacular show was a two-and-a-half-hour vaudeville-revue including fifteen acts featuring a large cast, eighty of which were beautiful, scantily-clad show girls chosen from a thousand applicants: Jeanne's friends and fellow dancers, Kenneth Spaulding and his two partners Louise and Alice O'Sullivan, known as the "Spaulding Trio," were in the cast. The spacious Winterland theatre had seats for 3,000 spectators, who surrounded the 12,000 square foot stage on three sides. In two parts with forty scenes the show was staged by Jean Le Seyeux of the Parisian *Folies Bergère*, with choreography by Aida Broadbent and costumes by Helen Rose. For his column in the *San Francisco*, December 2, 1943, Marsh Maslin selected his "Crush of the Week: If I had to choose any one bright, particular star out of the glittering Folies Bergère, I'd take that lovely prima ballerina, Jeanne Devereauz [sic]. She's wonderful!"

Jeanne wrote her father on December 5th that the "show is ON and a huge success from start to finish." They had only had twelve hours sleep in ninety-six hours. They had fortunately moved to a better hotel that had a tiny, one burner electrical stove, so they had cooked some pork chops for dinner. After they recuperated from the exhaustion of opening night, they sent Bill some clippings of the favorable newspaper reviews for his files. A review of the premiere in *Variety*, December 8, 1943, described the show as Fisher's "grafting a circus to a revue," noting that "the show was delayed nearly an hour to clear the mob from the front doors clamouring for admittance." Audiences were offered "pageantry at its best, breath-taking costumes, and outstanding vaude acts." Jeanne danced on a bill with comedians, trapeze performers, jugglers, riders of live horses, pantomimists, singers of musical comedy, unicyclists, trampoline artists, and a chorus of beautiful show girls. The cast included the popular trapeze aerialist from the Ringling Brothers' circus Elly Ardelty, who became one of Jeanne's lifelong friends. The reviewer praised "the superb ballet work of Jeanne Devereaux. The ballerina, supported by a line ... stood out as the individual star of the two and a half hour show.... Malcia, Grace Poggi and Jeanne Devereaux contributed the best dancing the town has seen in years."

With a French flavor throughout, the first half of the show opened with splendidly costumed dancers Ladonna Biroc, Kenneth Spaulding, Lil Liandre, and Grace Poggi. The Russian juggler Truzzi performed on the stage set "A Little Farm in Normandy," and "Saucy Malcia" wowed the audience with her dancing, followed by the comic tramps Monroe and Grant, who "stopped the show." The "Roses of France" number with comic dancers Dewey Barto and George Mann and ballerina Jeanne Devereaux were, according to the reviewer, "outstanding." The show's second half featured the Zebra, Can Can and Moon Ray numbers, the thrills of the Cristianis and their horses, the stunning aerialist Elly Ardelty, and comedians Wille West and McGinty.

The playbill for a Sunday matinee on December 26th enticed audiences to come to the show to "watch Jeanne Devereaux, internationally known ballerina, spin on her toes in the brilliant production now playing nightly at Winterland in San Francisco." The sensational dance number called the "Ballet Rose" in Act One featured a pas de deux by Beverly Bozeman and Frank Marasco, a solo by Barto and Mann, and a gorgeous solo by Jeanne surrounded by a chorus of beautiful girls dressed in rose satin, carrying lighted roses, with a final montage of the girls posed against rose satin columns forming a bouquet of gauze. A souvenir program for 1944 praised Jeanne, "the star of this number, ... [who] has an elegance of style which suited the rich coloring and setting. Her technical excellence is phenomenal." In Act Two Jeanne, listed in the program as "The

Sunday Special Matinee Playbill for Clifford C. Fischer's *Folies Bergère*, Winterland, San Francisco, California, December 26, 1943. The show ran from November 1943 until its unexpected closing at Seattle's Civic Auditorium in March 1944. Soloist Jeanne Devereaux, the featured headliner in the caption under the picture, is in the center surrounded by showgirls. Courtesy Jeanne Devereaux Perkins Collection.

Ray" surrounded by "The Stars," performed her balloon dance in the "Claire de Lune" ballet with a chorus of eighty girls holding luminous pearls that refracted vari-colored lights. She also danced in the "Specialties" and in the finale with the entire company. To perform at this high level night after night, noted a reviewer in San Francisco's *The News*, February 25, 1944, these gorgeous dancers "spend many hours each day in practice and exercise" to "keep their figures trim for their nightly appearances."

Jeanne and Lillian were exhausted by the grueling rehearsal and performance schedule and stress of their constant financial troubles. On January 21, 1944, Lillian wrote to Bill during the show in a tiny dressing room that Jeanne shared with another girl since there was such a large cast: they were now into their eighth week with "no time for ourselves…. Well, we have to earn a living, and it seems to take every day, all day." The demanding week before the show had premiered on November 30th with all night and all day rehearsals made opening night "such a nervous strain." Many old friends had attended the show, and then had come backstage to visit them, always wanting after the show to go to a nearby restaurant to talk and eat. Lillian wrote that they had had no time to go Christmas shopping except to buy a few gifts for family and a delicious roasted turkey for the holidays, which lasted them almost two weeks. "As I said to Jeanne, 'Well, we've gotten through another big opening of a big show and are alive.' But I do not know whether I can take many more," wrote Lillian.

Lillian's exhaustion and nervousness were mitigated by the rave reviews that Jeanne had received for her stunning performance in gorgeous scenes: "This time Jeanne was the acknowledged STAR of the big cast, and it was terrific, the Radio loud speaker telling about her all day on the Radio," she wrote. "Well, it is stupendous, and terrific, but very enervating, and after a few weeks, one is so worn out." While still on the West Coast, they hoped to secure a movie contract with a stellar dancing role for Jeanne. So far they had had no time to do any sightseeing and needed to move to another apartment.

Although Jeanne was making a decent salary, her expenses were considerable and cash flow always tight. If the show were extended until April 1st, Lillian wrote Bill, they would be digging out of their financial hole with the prospect of beginning to pay him back his loan. However, after deducting expenses from Jeanne's salary they were never able to "collect huge sums," but only hoped to "get a little ahead." "It will feel grand to get a few extra dollars between us and the wall again," she wrote. "We need a working capital because we always have to lay out so much—before we can get anything in." On February 6th Bill wrote he was pleased that they had received his Christmas gift box and he had enjoyed receiving his customary fruitcake, which was already stored for future edible pleasure on a high shelf in his room. He had been stunned by the recent news that his rent at the YMCA was being increased from $17 a month to $26 as a result of high demand for cheap lodgings by the military during wartime. Since his friends and clients were familiar with his longstanding address at the Y, he had decided to remain there and work harder selling his advertising products to pay the increased rent.

Jeanne and Lillian focused on their work. After a twenty-week run the *Folies Bergère* closed in San Francisco in February 1944, and it was then booked for twenty-six weeks on the road. In her March 20th letter to her father Jeanne wrote that this "show takes

Jeanne Devereaux in a promotional photograph for Clifford C. Fischer's *Folies Bergère*, November 1943–February 1944. Jeanne's ballet pose features her famous vertical arabesque, which she perfected under her mother's guidance for her sensational vaudeville act soon after she arrived in New York in early 1927. She claimed to be the first ballerina to master this difficult position, now part of the standard ballet repertoire. Courtesy Jeanne Devereaux Perkins Collection.

up more time than five shows a day," since in addition to her performances they had kept her busy doing thirty-two radio broadcasts, advertisements, selling war bonds, or being a spokesperson for the Red Cross—wonderful experiences for Jeanne since she had a natural talent for public speaking and envisioned that later in life she might have her own radio show.

As usual Jeanne and Lillian's life was primarily in the theatre, and the rare occasions they would have for sightseeing on Sundays between shows were highly valued. Before leaving on tour for their ten-day booking at the Civic Auditorium in Seattle, friends drove them to iconic San Francisco sites. After Seattle the show was scheduled to travel to Portland, Oregon, and then Vancouver during the lovely spring season. Eight days later in a postcard to her father from Portland, Oregon, where they had a four-hour stopover on the train to Seattle, Jeanne waxed poetic about the natural scenery outside her train window: "Have been riding thru Oregon's wonder forests all day. Snow capped peaks reflected in mirror lakes, and giant piles of logs ready to slide down, into the rushing streams. Its been a tantalizing day. Memories crowded in, of when we wandered liesurely thru this country. Now we are cooped up, and cant even smell the mountain air."

Wartime rationing was affecting the country, even Jeanne's supply of toe shoes. The United States Office of Price Administration (O.P.A.M.), created in May 1942, froze prices on everyday consumer goods, issuing war ration books and tokens to every American family, including equal share rationing and that based on need. One month Jeanne's toe shoe maker informed her that he only had enough material to make her twenty-five pairs of toe shoes, which she ordered immediately since now the O.P.A.M. had demanded equal share ration points for all toe shoes. She had to scrounge around for points in order to purchase the toe shoes, and even had to send them the ones that she and Lillian were allowed as civilians for street shoes. In her March 20th letter Jeanne asked her father to send her any shoe coupon that he wasn't using: "Of course I dont want it, if you are getting a new pair of shoes with it. Only if you werent going to use it before it becomes void."

14

Hollywood and Summer Operettas

No one could have anticipated the unfortunate fate of the *Folies Bergère* tour after the run in Seattle at the Civic Auditorium. Audiences had enjoyed the show: a reviewer in the *Seattle Times*, March 30, 1944, enthusiastically praised the spectacular "Rose Ballet" featuring Jeanne and the chorus of show girls in the midst of the other variety acts. However, Lew Wasserman, the powerful head of the Music Corporation of America that booked the show, had a disagreement with the producers and abruptly cancelled all future bookings. In addition to being out of work, Jeanne's prospective movie career was adversely affected by this sudden cancellation, for her agent with the International Theatrical Corporation in Hollywood, being uncertain as to how long the *Folies Bergère* was to run, had not been able to arrange a deal for her with Paramount or Metro-Goldwyn-Mayer. Now that the show had been cancelled, on May 12th her agent aggressively began marketing her for motion pictures by contacting an agent in Beverly Hills, saying that he is "handling JEANNE DEVEREAUX at the moment certainly the best prima ballerina in the States." Jeanne continued throughout her career to audition for the few movies that featured ballerinas.

Though unemployed and finances tight, Jeanne appeared in benefits for charitable causes as she had done throughout her long dancing career. She was particularly fond of the annual police show benefits in Los Angeles, and for a run of ten nights from June 15 to 26, 1944, she performed in the tenth annual police show benefit at the Shrine Auditorium, with proceeds to help underprivileged children take vacations. *Variety*, May 25, 1944, reported that the LA Police Relief Association wanted to produce an annual professional show comparable to commercial entertainments judged on "showmanship merit along." The "presentation" was in the form of a revue called "Koppers' Kapers," consisting of four parts: "Dude Ranch Days," "Minstrel Days," "Circus Days," and the "The Melting Pot." The patriotic themes of the comedy, singing, and dancing also characterized the band and choral numbers, and the scene "The Melting Pot" had a tableau of the various Allied nations. The wartime program featured guest stars Bob Hope, Jack Benny, Bing Crosby, Jimmy Durante, and Jack Carson, performing and acting as master of ceremonies on different nights, as well as the dancing Kaperettes, the Ballet Ensemble, the Glamorines, the singers James Wilkenson, Martha Tilton, and Teddy Lynch, and "Premiere Danseuse" Jeanne Devereaux. The equestrian Cristianis and juggler Truzzi, Jeanne's fellow troupers from the *Folies Bergère*, were also on the bill.

Although he is not mentioned in the program, Jeanne remembered Danny Kaye among the guest stars.

The reviewer of opening night in *Variety*, June 16, 1944, concluded that the show had successfully stood on its own merit "without the benefit angles." The patriotic prologue "For God and Country" included impressive comedy, dance, and song and production numbers. "Dude Ranch Days" featured the obligatory thirty-six scantily-clad beauties, Jeanne Devereaux, and the Cristiani family of equestrians; "Minstrel Days" showcased a tap trio, Selika at the Hammond organ, singer and actress Lillian Randolph, and the line dancing Kaperettes; "Circus Days" brought back Jeanne Devereaux and the Cristianis with the juggler Truzzi. The excellent pit orchestra, directed by Stan Myers, was an unusual addition to a benefit show bill. A review of the show in the *Los Angeles Times*, June 16, 1944, included a large picture of Jeanne performing her famous balloon dance with a caption that read "Jeanne Devereaux, one of the performers of the annual Police Show which thrilled crowd of 6000 persons last night": moreover, "the remarkable pirouettes of Jeanne Devereaux were warmly applauded while the Cristianis equestrians were a big hit," the reviewer added.

Jeanne Devereaux in a promotional headshot for Clifford C. Fischer's *Folies Bergère*, November 1943–February 1944, wearing her costume for the highly praised "Rose Ballet" dance number. This was her husband Tom Perkins' favorite professional photograph of Jeanne. After Jeanne died Tom put this photograph on the kitchen table in his American Craftsman house so he could enjoy it until he retired at night. Photograph by Gabriel Moulin Studios, San Francisco, California. Courtesy Jeanne Devereaux Perkins Collection.

On opening night and for the following two nights Bob Hope was the guest star and performed several comedy routines with musician Tony Romano and singing comedian Jerry Colonna, both of whom had been members of Hope's USO Camp Shows tours during the early 1940s; Colonna had also been one of Hope's zany sidekicks on his popular radio shows and films. Hope was succeeded by other guest stars. Jeanne remembered one night when Danny Kaye was the guest star act: after he had finished his act "in one" in front of the curtain, he took a final bow, the curtain went up, and the ballet began. Prior to Jeanne's entrance, when the corps de ballet were dancing onstage, Danny came onstage in the middle of the ballet and picked up one of the ballerinas, holding her up high over his head while he danced around the stage, much to the amazement and amusement of both the dancers and the audience. As Jeanne finally made her entrance, she felt that she had been "upstaged" by Danny's antics with the corps de ballet, and shook her head in disbelief when she remembered this incident.

Bill did not write them for a couple of months since he had lost their Hollywood address at 1744 North Wilton Place, and finally asked them on June 15th if this address would be permanent for a while. Two months later on August 20th Lillian wrote from Hollywood that they had been forced to postpone looking for work while Jeanne recovered from her second surgery on her nose by a plastic surgeon. Not only did the second surgery improve her physical appearance, but it also corrected a deviated septum resulting from the childhood sledding injury that had made her breathing difficult over the years, particularly when dancing. Although Jeanne's nose was still swollen and she was unable to work immediately, they were constantly trying to line up bookings since it took lead time "even before she could take it," wrote Lillian. Their days were filled with Jeanne's mandatory two hours of practice in a nearby studio, contacting agents, keeping up with the current trends in the entertainment industry, shopping for food, preparing meals against the rules in their one-room apartment, scrubbing the dishes and clothes in the bathroom sink, ironing clothes with no ironing board, and just keeping clean. Jeanne and Lillian also spent time listening to the radio and reading the newspapers for war news. Jeanne undoubtedly composed her poem on "NOSES" during her recovery (see Appendix One). Turning painful life experiences like having her nose fixed into poetic expression was another of Jeanne's natural talents that helped her navigate the tumultuous life of a trouper.

Although Jeanne was always practicing when unemployed, she and her mother were able to spend some time with the Pasadena family, which mitigated their anxiety when looking for work. When they took a tour of the nearby Lockheed Airplane company with their friend Helen Lewis, they went to dinner at Helen's mother's house for a delicious meal—"We appreciate those kind of meals, at her house, and over in Pasadena at Aunt Ida's too, because we have a tiny Silex electric stove to cook on (just a little) to make teas or coffee or boiled eggs, or heat up a can of something," wrote Lillian in her August 20th letter. To celebrate Grandpa Lane's ninety-third birthday, they attended a family picnic in Griffith Park in Los Angeles, and Jeanne and Lillian joined Aunt Ida and Uncle Orville to go peach and cherry picking and share Aunt Ida's picnic dinner. These pleasant outings were over now when Ida and Orville used up their gas rations. The following year on July 9th they were able to celebrate Grandpa Lane's ninety-fourth birthday in Los Angeles by having a nice picnic in Long Beach with the family despite the scarcity of gasoline. Most importantly, Jeanne was able to spend time with handsome Tom Perkins, who came to visit her on Wilton Avenue in Hollywood. While they were walking in Griffith Park, they continued their stimulating conversation on politics and public affairs begun years ago in Pasadena's Junior Town Meeting. Although it was often years between visits, Jeanne was attracted to this young engineer and enjoyed being in his company; he was obviously infatuated with her.

Since Jeanne and Lillian did not have a car, they were dependent on the street cars and walking, which often caused Lillian to have tired feet. Lillian felt fortunate to have enjoyed relatively good health—"I seem to be able to keep from being a liability"—and can still walk fast and put in a day's work: "We are compelled to lay off now and then, for this reason or that, but after that we always get work again, and manage to keep going. Jeanne has something definite to sell, so we always get work, sooner or later. In this business we have to wait for our jobs, and no amount of torment is worse than waiting, keeping up the practice, costumes and music—all ready to work," she wrote. Lillian never doubted that there would always be a market for Jeanne's extraordinary dancing talent.

The sensitive issue of Bill's loan for $300 once again dominated the family letters in the fall of 1944. Having waited until August 20th and in the midst of their financial hardship with no work on the horizon, Lillian responded to Bill's contentious letter two months earlier demanding immediate repayment of the loan. Jeanne had kept his letter "hidden for awhile, as she didnt want me to be hurt, but I came across it," she wrote. Since Lillian had exactly $300 on hand right now and may have to use some of it to get "into the saddle again," she reminded Bill once more that he had previously agreed to allow her use of the money unless he definitely needed it. Lillian exercised great restraint when summarizing their "precise agreement":

> I cannot believe you could forget so easily, what we talked over again in 1943, last summer. You said then that it would be no different to you, if it were in the bank, and if it helped us, to have it, to draw on occasionally, when times were rough, that it would be your contribution to the family...
>
> Sharp words are hard to bear, and I could say them too, but what good to say them. We do the best we can, and it is a hard world to live in at best. None of us drink or chew, or gamble, so I feel it is no good to berate each other. I think we have done a noble job. Havent done a thing wrong, and are alert, and ready to take every job we can get. Who can do more?
>
> But if you are sick and tired of us, and do not want to help in any family arrangements at all, I will do my best to hurry your money back to you. We will then call it a day...
>
> I realized [when I read your letter] that you had simply forgotten again. It was simply clear out of your mind. You have always been paid back, every cent, so far, and you surely cant complain, or be scared. It didnt hurt you any, and it helped us, in pinches.

Not one to carry a grudge and always attempting to connect with Bill as family, Lillian ended her letter on a positive, caring note: "Are you eating plenty of raw vegetables, and fruits this summer?"

Jeanne and Lillian's efforts at finding work paid off, and by the fall Jeanne was once again employed and earning money. In early October she was appearing in a cabaret in the Ramona room at the Hotel Last Frontier in Las Vegas. According to Jeanne, at this time Las Vegas was an unpretentious, small town with only the Golden Nugget casino and on the road leading to Los Angeles the El Rancho and the Last Frontier hotel casinos. People were aware of the encroaching Mafia presence; one day in a Las Vegas restaurant someone pointed out to Jeanne a gangster from Chicago. While she was performing in Las Vegas, she also danced in benefit shows at a nearby secret army base and at the local Lion's Club. In an article in the *Las Vegas Lion Tamer*, October 14, 1944, Jeanne, looking "up from under a big brimmed chapeau cocked over one eye and to the Las Vegas Lions last Monday noon," described her command performance before British royalty:

> Jeanne is a good looking gal, as attractive all dolled up in her diner finery as in the diaphanous shorts she wears whilst whirling dervishes all over the stage floor of That Certain Hotel. Flanked by two wolves in Lions' clothing, Lion Harold Case and Lion Jim Down, she sat down at the table and talked quietly about how during the year in London a long list of acceptable artists is tabulated, then narrowed by the Lord Chamberlain down to a few who are chosen to play before the crowned heads.

This was the only recorded performance for Jeanne in that desert entertainment city, which later in the 1940s and 1950s became one of the last venues in America for spectacular revues and vaudeville acts.

In 1944, like most of the years since Jeanne and Lillian had left home to go on the road, the family was separated for their birthdays and the Christmas holiday but continued giving each other cards and gifts. For his June birthday that year Jeanne and Lillian had sent Bill a card and a new pair of shoes, and when he thanked them he also noted that the shoes were unfortunately too short. On October 27th, now calmed down and not so paranoid about his financial instability, he wished Jeanne a happy birthday and asked if she wanted more of the printed gummed labels as her birthday present this year. He reported that despite the federal limitations on the amount of lumber the American Manufacturing Concern could use to produce their yardsticks and rulers, he had managed to get a little business. Most likely the contentious personal loan had taken an emotional toll on the family, for Lillian and Jeanne did not write Bill again since August 20th until they sent him his Christmas gifts in December. When he responded to Lillian on December 13th, after first complaining that there "seems to be a lag in the family correspondence," Bill's focus was on shopping for gifts.

Bill spent Christmas again this year with his friends at the St. Louis "Y." Writing on December 20th before he had received any response to his recent letter, Bill thanked them for their Christmas gifts—a box of candy and some ties that he mentioned were a little too loud for him since he wore more "sedate" colors at his age. He had mailed his Christmas cards that year to the same list, signing them as always "The Helman Family." He wrote that he had spent one night helping to install and decorate a couple of Christmas trees in the lobby as he had done over the past years with his "little gang." He had been "surrounded with the Xmas spirit, as I have my window decorated with a little line of electric globes, and some other red decorating," A few months before he had injured his side and promised to give them a health update soon: "Anyway you 'still' have someone at this end, that you can write to occasionally," he wrote, "instead of saying, 'Yes, he WAS' a pretty nice fellow, wasn't he. And 'he got to be sixty five years old.' etc."

Throughout 1945 bookings in show business were scarce except for the operettas that had provided Jeanne with steady employment during the spring and summer months. The few remaining vaudeville theatres and movie presentation houses, lacking air conditioning, were closed during the summer. While living in Hollywood during this year, she continued to audition for movies despite one of the worst labor strikes between studio unions and the producers in Hollywood history that would last for five years.[1] Although they were on the road on the operetta circuit during the spring and summer months, Jeanne and Lillian followed the progress of the Hollywood strikes throughout the year.

With the family letters diminishing, Bill often had to rely on mutual friends like Helen Lewis for news of his family. He wrote to Helen on January 21, 1945, that since she occasionally received a letter from Jeanne, she was "luckier than I am." Finally receiving a letter from Jeanne, Bill wrote on February 6th that he now understood they had a new Hollywood address—5156 Marathon Street—and noted that Jeanne had some good prospects for a movie and a play in February. Two weeks later after receiving a letter from Lillian describing their new, improved living quarters, Bill's March 4th reply consisted of a description of his injured rib resulting from a fall and his hospital stay.

In the spring of 1945 Jeanne's fortunes changed with her appearance at Detroit's Civic Light Opera at the Masonic Temple Auditorium in *The Great Waltz*, a Broadway revival about the historic rivalry between Johann Strauss, Jr. and his father. The press release noted that Jeanne would star in the role of Kathie Lanner and that Managing Director Max Koenigsberg "specially selected her for the Kathie Lanner role on his trip to New York last week and secured her release from the Radio City Music Hall for the Detroit engagement." There is no record, however, of her having performed at Radio City at this time. The reviewer for the *Detroit Free Press*, March 28, 1945, wrote that "Prima Ballerina Jeanne Devereaux was the show-stopper, with her dazzling display of turns, pirouets and arabesques in the opening of the last act"; the *Detroit News* for the same day said that the ballet number "in particular, is a real honey; 16 pretty, light-footed girls who have been trained to virtual perfection. They compose a lovely frame for Jeanne Devereaux, who comes to town as prima ballerina and does a lot of breathtaking fouettés in the big ballet number."

Jeanne wrote on March 30th that the "show has opened, and is a terrific success" despite her having had a terrible cold during rehearsals that resulted in her having to "stagger straight to bed" every night: on opening night she had received "a real rousing Ovation. The applause roared like Niagara Falls, and when the sheaf of Red Roses—(sent by the management) were handed over the footlights—They went wild and wouldn't let me off the stage." The Detroit newspapers included "beautiful" reviews, but since the newspapers were sold out, she asked her father to go to the local library and send her some copies. Since Jeanne had the next week off before beginning rehearsals for the operetta *Balalaika*, they planned to sightsee in Detroit and visit Windsor, Canada. On April 1st Bill wrote he was pleased that opening night had exceeded their expectations and "that you almost had to wear 'ear-muffs,' to keep the applause out."

Beginning in the week of April 17th Jeanne danced in a production of *Balalaika* in Detroit that featured singers Wilma Spence, Lansing Hatfield, a sixty member singing and dancing ensemble, and a thirty-piece symphonic orchestra. In the program she was included in a section titled "America's Foremost Opera and Operetta Stars," with a note saying that she "will be recalled for her marvelous ballet dancing in the production of 'The Great Waltz.'" Praising her amazing artistry, the *Detroit News*, April 18, 1945, observed that Jeanne's dancing in *Balalaika* "turns the crowd upside-down." In an article in the *Detroit Civic Light Opera Preview* for April 19th, titled "Favorites of 'Great Waltz' Return in 'Balalaika': Wilma Spence and Jeanne Devereaux Again Shine in Operetta at Masonic Temple," the reviewer waxed effusive about the "dark, graceful" ballerina who, having danced all over the world, has been "acclaimed the world's high priestess of the pirouette and her *eleveé* is astounding."

With her Detroit engagement over and en route back to Hollywood with a layover in Chicago, Jeanne wrote her father that she would perform in St. Louis this summer only if the price were right. Not hearing from his family for a month, he wrote Jeanne on June 2nd that he wanted to hear "something about yourselves. If I wasn't interested, I wouldn't ask." He wanted to know if she were going to Dallas in the summer, and also if any progress had been made on her "'picture' proposition": he felt encouraged about her prospects since he had recently seen movies featuring some ballet. His marketing business had been slow, and the "Y. wanted me to have my picture taken, at their expence, and they are going to have a large frame down in one of the halls, with individual spaces in it, entitled some of the 'old timers' of the Y. I guess, I am probably the oldest member," he wrote, "as I believe I told you that we 'buried' one of the real old timers a few months ago, and I was pall bearer. Its been rather a long time, since that September of 1930 when I 'took a chance' and landed here."

Jeanne and Lillian's days in Hollywood were long, spent looking for bookings in theatres and movies in Los Angeles. On June 2nd Lillian explained to Bill that the movie strike was in its twelfth week, so they had practically given up on Jeanne appearing in a movie; however, Jeanne was practicing intensely every day and was on a sparse liquid diet to control her weight for any future opportunities. This was her eighth day of strict dieting, and she had gone to see a film to keep from eating. Lillian told Bill that auditioning for movies was time consuming and expensive:

> Yesterday Jeanne had an interview with a director for Paramount about the Irving Berlin movie, to be called Blue Heaven. To be done as soon as the strike ends. Hence—the strenuous dieting will be necessary. They were "very very" interested in her "Moth and Flame" which she did in London—for this picture. But that does not mean that we have the contract. The producer has to be sold also—on the idea. (Twas the director who asked Jeanne to come and present the idea) and, then she will have to give a demonstration, and explain further. There is no end to all these things, and they are very very expensive (auditions, or showings). We dropped about $25.00 all told, for the audition at Warner's.

Auditions also required taking a taxi to the movie studios and bringing along costume cases, sheet music, and make-up, as well as hiring the same pianist for a week so he would be familiar with the speed and tempo of Jeanne's music. Lillian wrote that complicating their prospects further was the fact that the producers now favored hiring dancers from the big ballet companies like Balanchine's New York Ballet Society and Lucia Chase's Ballet Theatre, but Jeanne still could not survive on the meager salaries these companies paid their members:

> If we could just afford to go into a Ballet Company for awhile. The pay is so little in them, we have not been able to go into them, and as Jeanne is much more wonderful than they are, she has been able to do solo work—at a big salary. However many producers give its members of Ballet Companies the first chance at everything. As they are not good judges themselves, they think if one is, or has been in one of the big Ballets Companies, one is just naturally more great than anyone else. Yet how to afford it!

Over the years Jeanne "has been so bitter about all this," since she "can surpass on every point of dancing," but these ignorant producers "who know nothing rely on ballet company members, when they want people for shows and movies. Just because they must rely on something besides their own judgement."

Since auditioning at Hollywood movie studios proved unsuccessful primarily because of the continuing strikes, Jeanne and Lillian focused on securing work back east where there were more paying jobs. Jeanne was now scheduled at the Starlight Operetta in Dallas on August 6th to begin rehearsals for the operettas *Maytime* and *The Three Musketeers*. Transportation during wartime was difficult with so many soldiers on the move. On July 12th Jeanne sent Bill a postcard explaining that they are "frantic once more over tickets to Dallas. Transportation is so tight we don't know whether we can get back to N.Y. or back here [Hollywood]. Packing and sorting and storing from Morn till night. Leave around the 30th of July if we can get reservations. How I'd like a few Roots—instead of Uproots, all the time." The next day Lillian wrote that they had to get to Dallas either by train, bus, or licensed auto, and since the strike was still on in Hollywood, after Dallas it would be easier to go back east.

Bill was pleased that during their sojourn in Pasadena and Hollywood they had been visiting the beaches and taken rides in the country with the family. He finally showed his best friend and accomplished poet Bert Loewnstein a copy of Jeanne's poem the "Traveller's Lament," where she contrasted the comfort of vicarious travel with the addictive, exhilarating fatigue of visiting strange lands (see Appendix One). On July 26th Bill wrote that Bert thought her poem worthy of publication, suggesting that Bill send it immediately to *The Saturday Evening Post*. Bill, however, to avoid any "misunderstanding," thought it best that Jeanne send it in herself directly to the editor of the poetry page and provided her with the address. He was delighted that she had some viable prospects for future bookings, and would address his future letters to her at the downtown hotel in Dallas called the Adolphus.

Jeanne's engagement in August 1945 at the Fair Park Casino at the Texas State Fair in Dallas was a great success. She opened in the Starlight Operetta's production of Sigmund Romberg's *Maytime*, playing a character named Lizzie and performing her "Clair de Lune" number to Debussy's music as well as an exuberant can-can with the corps de ballet. She also appeared in the last show of the Dallas summer season, Rudolf Friml's *The Three Musketeers*, where she was the featured prima ballerina performing the classical ballet *Swan Lake* and a court dance in the final act. Lead singing roles were played by Harold Patrick, Marguerite Piazza, and Dorothy Sandlin. The reviewer in the *Dallas Morning News*, August 21, 1945, said Jeanne had performed *Swan Lake* in "notable classic style. Not once was anybody reminded of Fannie Brice's Swan." When recollecting this production of *The Three Musketeers*, Jeanne described how the singer playing D'Artagnan, known as the fourth musketeer in Alexandre Dumas' novel, held her to his chest as he belted out his aria; unfortunately, the garlic-laden dinner that he had ingested before the show infused each note.

Following Jeanne's career became more difficult for Bill. He was forced to go to the local library to read the Dallas newspaper, where he learned for the first time that Jeanne was billed at the Starlight Operetta, concluding on August 22nd "everything must have gone alright so far. Thought maybe you would have sent me one of the papers, showing same, but you, eh?" He wondered about her future plans and whether she would return to the West Coast after the Dallas booking; he was interested in whether or not she had received any positive response from the USO for performing in a Camp Show. He also wanted to know if she were interested in publishing her poem.

Jeanne wrote her father on August 26th telling him how she had enjoyed performing in the two operettas in Dallas, adding that in a few days when the season ended they would take the train back to Hollywood. *Maytime* had been a huge success and *The Three Musketeers* was the "height of Operetta." She had particularly enjoyed her performance in the latter, for "it encompasses all the ingredients that thrill people. Swashbuckling, Fighting, Ballet. Beauty and Romance. The costumes are an eyefull, and I get a kick out of it, every night." Last week in *Maytime* she "played the role of a very talkative woman who takes the conversation, and keeps chattering, a mile a minute, almost without breath for about four minutes. It was a good part, and I wore an adorable old-fashioned bustle dress of the 90's. First time I have gotten to wear one, and I enjoyed it." She loved performing *Swan Lake* in *The Three Musketeers*: "It's the dance Pavlova made famous, and has been mutilated by most dancing school pupils, than the census could count," she wrote. "However, good dancers have avoided it long enough, so I am going to revive it, and make it a permanent part of my repertoire, as it has a story, and can be acted without too strenuous dancing, when I have to do two numbers together."

Lillian wrote Bill two days later on August 28th, reflecting on the pros and cons of their Dallas booking while on board a Southern Pacific train bound for Los Angeles. Success in the theatre was never without sacrifice, since performing in the sweltering summer operetta open-air Midwestern theatres could be difficult: "We had a very hot but successful two weeks, in Maytime and the Three Musketeers," she wrote, "and have been assured they will want her back next season." Lillian complained in her letter how the sacrifices for this success were stressful and exhausting:

> One waits for everything. For eats and street cars and elevators, and cabs, and all things. The rehearsing is done in a big auditorium out in Fair Park, 20 minutes away from center of town. But the evening shows are given at the Open Air Casino, in a different part of the large park. And they rehearse one whole day, out in the blistering sun—on the stage—and open the new show that same night. If that isnt sumpin!! But that is the way they do it. Under those circumstances it is a miracle that anyone can give decent shows—but they do. With the Thermometer up to 107 TOO.!.

As for their future plans, Lillian was fearful that if they were booked for a USO Camp Shows tour to the Pacific, they might contract some deadly disease, so she was not in favor of going. She wondered whether the movie strike in Hollywood was over, since Jeanne was "dickering with Paramount for a 'short' as you know." She thanked Bill and Bert for their encouraging suggestions about publishing Jeanne's poem, saying that they would attend to that when back home in Hollywood, and enclosed a roll of newspapers with Jeanne's recent clippings from the Dallas booking. Unfortunately, Paramount was not one of the few movie studios that was willing to bargain after the March 1945 strike, so the short film that Jeanne was "dickering with" was never made.

Without the paralyzing movie strikes Jeanne would likely have appeared in more films while living in Hollywood. Since bookings in vaudeville and other forms of variety entertainment were still scarce, despite some initial misgivings Jeanne finally accepted the offer to entertain the troops in the Pacific on a USO Camp Shows tour beginning in December 1945. The family letters and postcards over the next seven months are filled with the arduous preparations for the tour—the many painful inoculations, purchasing of appropriate military-like clothing, and long rehearsal sessions and tryouts beginning in October—and the high drama of the tour itself as they flew to Hawaii, the Philippines, and finally Japan in two C54s, returning to New York in April 1946.

15

A USO Camp Shows Tour to Japan

During her dancing career Jeanne participated in hundreds of benefit performances at military bases around the country, and now she was eager to be part of a USO Camp Shows tour to entertain the troops. President Roosevelt had formed the United Service Organizations, commonly known as the USO, in February 1941, to provide services and entertainment to the troops at home and abroad. As the demand for entertainment increased, a USO subsidiary called Camp Shows, Inc., was created in October of the same year to organize and manage the professional tours. During the war years of the mid–1940s inexpensive radio and feature length movies had dominated the American popular entertainment field, and vaudeville flourished in these USO Camp Shows that traveled around the globe. Although she was working at a reduced military salary, Jeanne was thrilled to be among the many talented troupers of her era performing in one of these patriotic touring shows. For her performances in the Pacific front she received the rank of "Honorary Captain."[1]

Jeanne considered her USO Camp Shows tour to Japan in 1945–46 the culmination of the many military benefit performances she had given for veterans and soldiers to serve her country. Later in life Jeanne described the hardships of these free performances, while simultaneously under contract to perform in the commercial theatres to make a living:

> I danced for soldiers at all the military camps back East and even at a secret base near Los Vegas—all before my USO tour to Japan at the end of World War II. Performers had to rush to get their music from Orchestra leaders, pack costumes and shoes and then get a cab to the benefit show. You had to get ready fast, do your act, reverse rush to get back to our theatre, and be ready for our next show. I doubt if the benefit people ever realized what a strain we were under to not be late for our performances at our own theatres doing four and five shows a day. If people give money they are thanked all over the place, but if you give a performance to raise money, then there's hardly a thank you of any kind. I feel that it's unfair to the performers. I gave literally hundreds of benefit performances for worthy causes in every city we toured all over America. My first was for wounded soldiers at the Jefferson Barracks in St. Louis.

As a precocious nine-year-old dancer, Jeanne had performed in front of World War I veterans at the VFW hospital—the Jefferson Barracks—in her hometown and had a close view of the ravages of war. She remembered looking down into the haunted faces of recovering soldiers while she danced: "I could clearly visualize the poor, wounded men of WWI, some lying in coffin-shaped wicker baskets placed on auditorium chairs." For the rest of her career she strongly felt that the beauty of her exquisite dancing provided for these soldiers a welcome distraction from the horrors of war.

Since the 1930s Jeanne and her father had engaged in a spirited, ongoing dialogue in their letters about the ravages of war. On September 11, 1940, Jeanne had written about receiving a letter from her friend Bert Rose in London who told her "as much about the war as is possible I guess to write as the censors read all letters going out as well as going in. He told how high the morale was and illustrated it by telling the story of an old man 90 and his Son 60 who went out rabbit hunting in the middle of a terrific air battle overhead. However, that letter was written three weeks ago and the terrible bombings had'nt started then over London." Five days later she wrote about the ongoing war in Europe, lamenting the destruction of her beloved London: "What do you think Englands chances are now? It seems a shame that she cant defend London and prevent the invasion at the same time for the city is being utterly ruined. Such wanton destruction of famous land marks and relics is criminal as what possible military objective could Museums, Schools, Hospitals, and homes be."

While dancing for soldiers at an anti-aircraft artillery training center near Riverside, California, a caption under her picture in the *Seattle Times*, July 20, 1941, noted that Jeanne and other dancers had taken time from Hollywood's *Earl Carroll's Vanities* to perform at the camp: Jeanne found "kicking above Pvt. F. L. Andrews' rifle an easy job. Needless to say, the soldier boys enjoyed the Hollywood show." Months later on December 7, 1941, Pearl Harbor Day, Jeanne was performing in *Earl Carroll's Vanities* in a theatre in Columbus, Ohio, and late that night she wrote her father an emotional account of the moment when she learned that the Japanese had bombed the American fleet in Hawaii:

> Today has been filled with noon day shock and drama. We listened to the usual Monday news at the hotel, then packed up the radio to take to the theatre to get the Sunday programes.
>
> After our second show began, the rumor began to spread among the cast that Japan had started to bomb our ships and possessions. We flew up to the dressing room between dances, to listen in, and get the news pieced together.
>
> One by one the facts were stated and all rumor dispelled. Thus even the doubt as to whether the Tokyo Govt was in on it, was dispelled.
>
> I stepped onto the stage in a daze. Hardly conscious of what I was doing I went thru my numbers. The lights were rosy, and the people seemed so close to me, I almost wanted to say to them "Do you know whats happening at this moment? Do you know your whole lives are being changed, and while you sit here and we smile at you, and perform our entertaining tricks, we're thinking what fools you are to have let this happen. The blame is on you, for with interest and knowledge, and influence, you could have stopped 'aggression' and Japan in Mansuria [sic] eight or nine years ago!"
>
> The kids in the show came in to hear the broadcasts, sitting on the couch and floor. We all felt a numbing shock at the suddenness of the attack. Danny (our singer) is a gorgeous specimen, and only 22 years old, so he knows its just a matter of time. Pete, (our carpenter) has a son in the navy and one in England, making planes. Fay Carroll's brother is in Manila. Angela Wilson's Dad, in Hawaii, and everybody will understand, really understand what WAR means by this time next year.

With America entering the war, they planned to purchase some new clothes and other necessities and urged Bill to do likewise before everyday commodities became expensive, of inferior quality, and scarce. When Bill answered her letter four days later, he declared that the war would "change the lives of the WHOLE WORLD, and no one can see the finish."

After Pearl Harbor Jeanne and Lillian listened to the radio and read newspapers daily to keep up with the national war news, a practice they continued for the next three years. By the summer of 1944 it was obvious that the Allies were winning the war against the Axis on the European front. On August 15, 1944, Jeanne wrote from Hollywood that during these "war days of inadequate housing" she and her mother were grateful to have a roof over their heads and not be forced to "sleep in the park." They had encountered an explicit symbol of American military power on a Sunday afternoon two weeks ago when their good friend Helen Lewis, who worked at the nearby Lockheed Airplane company "where they make the P 38's bombers," gave them a tour of the plant: "It was so interesting, and we walked miles and miles seeing all the operations and gadgets, great and small, plus the terrific big molding presses, and the amount of things that go into one of those big bombers is just inconceiveable."

After the bombs that decimated Hiroshima and Nagasaki in the summer of 1945, Japan surrendered on August 15th and the war was over. On September 2nd Emperor Hirohito signed the instrument of surrender in front of General MacArthur on the battleship *Missouri* in Tokyo Bay. Jeanne and her mother celebrated the end of the Pacific front and World War II in Dallas, Texas, during the run of *The Three Musketeers* in August 1945 at the Texas State Fair. While all the performers were backstage preparing for the show, a little boy who had been selling popcorn up and down the aisles in the open-air theatre every night suddenly sang out to the audience, "Get your post–War peanuts here!" So that is how the cast and some of the audience learned that the war was finally over.

After the final show ended that night, on their way to the Adolphus hotel Jeanne and her mother were astonished when they stepped off the streetcar to see what looked like snow all over the street. To celebrate the war's end, people in the hotel had ripped open all the white goose down pillows, scattering them out the hotel windows, feathers floating down to the street like snowflakes. The entire town of Dallas was celebrating and the restaurants were packed; they had a long wait for a table at a restaurant across from their hotel. Finally, when their fried chicken dinners arrived at their table, the frenzied kitchen workers had not had sufficient time to pluck the chickens completely, so on the ends of the chicken legs were little curls of French fried feathers. Writing Bill from their hotel on August 24th with only three performances left before the Dallas booking was over, Jeanne asked: "Can you realise the war is over. We cant 'feel' it even yet. Of course Dallas went wild, as did every little town, big town, City, and Hamlet in the country. The center of Dallas is right under our window so bedlam reigned all night at full tilt."

While Jeanne was performing in Dallas she received a telegram from the USO Camp Shows office in Hollywood asking her to lead a six-month tour to the Pacific. The USO tours included four circuits: the Victory circuit that brought performers and Broadway revues and concerts to larger stateside military installations; the Blue circuit that brought smaller vaudeville touring companies to stateside Army and Navy installations; the Hospital circuit that brought performers and graphic artists to stateside and overseas military hospital wards and auditoriums; and the Foxhole or Overseas circuit that brought performers to overseas military fields and camps close to the front lines. Jeanne was offered to lead a tour on the Foxhole or Overseas circuit.

15 • A USO Camp Shows Tour to Japan

The over 7,000 performers—the "Soldiers in Greasepaint"—who participated in these camp shows on the various circuits between 1941 and 1947 included movie and theatre actors, radio and concert performers, vaudevillians, and other lesser known entertainers. Units sent overseas included variety, concerts, plays, musical comedies, sketching artists, all–Negro, sports, and all-girl. At its peak in 1945 USO performers presented nearly 700 shows a day overseas and in the United States. Discontinued in 1947, USO Camp Shows, Inc., was then revived in 1951 at the beginning of the Korean War, eventually dissolving in 1957 when the USO again directly managed the military's worldwide entertainment needs.

Jeanne's negotiations with USO Camp Shows, Inc. for leading a tour to the Pacific front began during the late summer of 1945 and continued into the fall, when Jeanne was asked by Harry Krivit, one of her former agents and now Director of the USO Camp Shows, Inc., to lead a six-month tour. Lillian was invited to accompany her. Jeanne received two contracts on the very same day: one from Rio at the Copacabana where she had played in 1939 and another from the USO Office asking her to lead a "Copacabana Night Club Revue" to the Pacific, the show title taken from New York's famous Copacabana nightclub. "How ironic," she reflected in a later interview, "two shows with the same name but entirely different." Responding on August 24th to Bill's query about the USO Camp Shows, Inc., Jeanne admitted that the adventure lured her, but common sense said, "Whoa, Stop Look and Listen," for she was afraid that she would be "just the one who would get malaria, and crash into sea—at the very least." Wanting to remain stateside, she wired back asking for an American Hospital tour first. In her August 28th letter Lillian, writing on a train back to Hollywood, also feared the tour would be dangerous, with "Fevers, Malaria, and 'what-not,'" so for the moment they rejected the offer.

Later they overcame their fears, and Jeanne signed a contract to entertain the troops in the Pacific on one of the first postwar USO tours to Japan, from December 1945 to March 1946, following on the heels of Danny Kaye's highly successful performance in Japan that October and before Bob Hope's highly publicized postwar tours. Jeanne, featured as the famous Radio City prima ballerina, led a talented troupe of forty beautiful dancers in the "Copacabana Night Club Revue from New York" to the Pacific front—Hawaii, Guam, the Philippines, Okinawa, and finally Japan. It was the largest USO show ever sent to this region. According to Jeanne, the military had been so depleted in the Pacific region that the American troops were not able to use their points and come home after the war, resulting in a rebellion in the Philippines. Wanting to stem this rebellion and not let it spread to Japan, the military realized that the occupying soldiers craved popular entertainment and hired performers like her and the Copacabana girls to entertain their troops. The boys "'would look at you and go cross-eyed.... Well, the girls were pretty ... and there were feathers,'" Jeanne later said jokingly in the *Pasadena Star-News* article for January 20, 1994.

In an October 11th postcard Jeanne wrote her father that they were departing from Hollywood on the train for New York to arrive for rehearsals beginning a week later with her troupe of forty dancers. Jeanne sent another postcard on October 21st informing him that hotel rooms in New York were scarce, since there were "30,000 extra men here for Navy Week in a town already so crowded a mouse would have to diet." After having checked eleven pieces of luggage and shipping seventeen, they arrived in New

Jeanne Devereaux in a USO Camp Shows tour, "Copacabana Night Club Revue from New York," Tokyo, Japan, February 1946. Jeanne is wearing a classic ballet tutu performing an arabesque. The title of the show was taken from the famous Copacabana nightclub in New York, known for its spectacular chorus girls. Jeanne was invited by her former agent Henry Krivit, now the director of the USO Camp Shows, Inc., to lead a three-month tour from January to March of forty glamorous performers to the Pacific. She most likely was the first performer after the war had ended to lead a large USO Camp Shows tour to this region, following Danny Kaye's solo tour in October 1945 and well before Bob Hope's postwar USO tours. Courtesy Jeanne Devereaux Perkins Collection.

York and immediately reported to the USO, who had "washed their hands of hopeless situation" with accommodations, forcing them to walk 110 blocks up and down every street until they managed to rent a room at the Hotel Belle Claire at 77th and Broadway—a run-down "dump" far too expensive at $6 a day.

There was only four days' notice before they had left for New York, resulting in "days and sleepless nights of packing," yellow fever shots, passport pictures, and answering questionnaires for the FBI. "So tired of questionnaires almost answered druid for religion," Jeanne wrote. She told her father that they had been driven in a chauffeured limousine to the station for their train to Chicago, and then had two roomettes on the second train from Chicago to New York: "The U.S.O. got us the best they could," she wrote. Right now "Bob White is asleep in a state of complete collapse," and since Lillian needed a copy of their marriage license so she could go on the tour, she asked her father to "shoot us a copy as soon as possible." On October 22nd she wrote that they had moved to the Marseilles Hotel at 103rd Street and Broadway for the time being: on the same day she sent a postcard to her Grandma Lane in Pasadena saying, "Rehearsals started today—so honeymoon is over & 'shots again.'"

On October 24th Bill answered Jeanne's postcards. His curiosity was aroused by their twenty-eight pieces of luggage, and he was pleased that they had located a hotel room. He wanted to know all about the rehearsals and whether or not he should address his correspondence to the USO Camp Shows at 8 West 40th Street. As usual, he focused on her birthday gift for that year, and was planning to fill a box with small items that she might use on the military tour. He claimed to be still solvent financially: "Glad to state that I am getting a little business, now and then, from a few old customers."

Preparations for the tour were extensive. Lillian confirmed on October 28th that she would be accompanying the tour as wardrobe mistress: "WE'RE IN THE ARMY NOW. WE'RE IN THE ARMY NOW! Not quite, but a U.S.O is under army jurisdiction entirely," she wrote. She had to claim that she was fifty-five years old—not sixty—to be eligible to travel with the show, and was relieved when she passed the physical; since returning to New York, they had been immersed in rehearsals, attending meetings, filling out papers, being finger printed, and opening a bank account. They already had received multiple inoculations in both California and New York and would have more aboard ship. They both had come down with fevers and had sore right arms, and to avoid getting sick, they planned "to eat-light, eat only army food, and drink army coffee, powdered milk, and boiled and chlorinated water and—observe curfew." Lillian needed Bill to send her a copy of their marriage license so she could go on the tour; after delaying for a couple of weeks Bill finally confirmed that he had obtained a copy of the marriage license at City hall and had mailed it to her.

On November 3rd Jeanne wrote her father that since "they were flying in B[-]20s" they were limited to around sixty-five pounds of luggage, requiring "judicious packing and selection to cram ones needs for 6 months—and for two climates, Tropical and cold." Because they had had so little time to pack before leaving California, they had stored some boxes with relatives, but had to bring along everything else including "tons of theatrical paraphernalia." Their arms were still sore from the inoculations, and it had been raining so hard that Jeanne had fallen down an iron stairway in the New York subway, scraping off layers of skin.

Two days later Jeanne wrote about having gone to Abercrombie and Fitch to buy some sensible, brown walking shoes and a brown leather belt "to give a little class and support to my slacks and skirt. The uniforms are military, and that's all one can say. Glamorous? No No No." With swollen glands throughout her body and the inoculation site on her arm festering, Lillian had had a delayed reaction to her smallpox vaccination. Jeanne had been in rehearsals at Victory Hall, and the USO Camp show opened at Camp Monmouth, New Jersey, "before an audience of Army-Brass hats, in charge of entertainment and army," she wrote. After telling her father that she had had to purchase sixty pairs of toe shoes and Lillian a new pair of eye glasses, she warned him that their letters would be censored: "While we are away we shall be subject to censorship 'in everything we say' Rigid Political censorship is in force now, that the war is over. If

I want you to read between the lines—I shall add 'As Shakespeare used to say' so you can freely translate that into his famous quote from Hamlet 'There is something rotten in the State of Denmark' Can you remember that and not be baffled if it crops up three or four months hence." On November 10th Bill noted what she had said about censorship, promising to "be on my guard" for the duration of their tour.

To break in the USO Camp Shows tour, Jeanne performed on the East Coast at Camp Yaphank and several other army camps before going to Bolling Air Force Base and on to San Francisco. Writing from Camp Kilmer, New Jersey, aboard a subway train, Lillian briefly noted that they were "still alive.... Two more army camps, and then we leave next Thur and Friday for Frisco. Just in time to have my teeth fixed. Thats a relief." Bill was uncertain about their route, and once again, the family was separated on the Thanksgiving and Christmas holidays, and had to rely on letters and gifts. On November 26th Bill described the delicious Thanksgiving dinner he had enjoyed at his good friend Bert's house. Later, on the back of a New Year's card on December 14th, he informed them that he had once again taken the "liberty of including the words, from the Helmans" on most of his New Year's cards. He had also sent them his mailing list of old friends that "may come in very handy," since "one cant look into the future, very far, they tell me."

On December 16th while sitting on the side of her bed in the barracks at Hamilton Field, which was about forty miles outside of San Francisco, Lillian wrote that they were now on high alert for their imminent departure, which she was constantly reminded of by the "drone of motors" of the "big Flying Fortresses and C 54's leaving and arriving" that she heard from her window. Although she still felt the trip was unsafe, this USO Camp Shows tour was Jeanne's best option for work during a protracted Hollywood movie strike and a depressed popular entertainment market:

> But you know Bill, how hard it is, now-adays for an artist dancer, unless they can get into some "movies" which was just what we were waiting around Hollywood for, but the strike held on and on, and finally forced us to recouprate our money by this means.
>
> It is a 6 months contract, and we can come out ahead, if no accidents occur, so keep your "fingers crossed" for our safety over the vast reaches of the Pacific. 12 hours in the air, then 2 hours to re-fuel—then 12 more hours in the air. Plus re-fueling and more hours in the air.
>
> You can see it will be no "lark" even in a C 54. We have all sorts of things, besides canteen of water hanging on us, plus a parachute apiece (In Case).

Most of their stops at Johnston Island, Midway, Kwajalein, and Guam would be refuelling stops. After Hawaii, they were scheduled to be in the Philippines for two months before traveling to Japan via Okinawa: "Remember we may not hear from you for 2 months, altho you can hear from us," Lillian wrote. "Again I say, Take care of yourself, and let us know you received the money we sent. There is a little more we will send by money order." This money was most likely the first installment of their reimbursement of the contentious $300 loan.

A day later on December 17th Jeanne wrote her father from the Hamilton Field barracks outside of San Francisco before departing for Honolulu, Hawaii, in which she described their final preparations. Lillian was still recovering from the flu, and every day they were at Hamilton increased her chances of going on the tour. Having been briefed on proper hygiene in the tropics, they intended to follow instructions "explicitly, as we don't want to get any weird diseases." That night most of the performers had gone to the Post theatre, but Jeanne had stayed behind to complete some washing and clean their canteens; they had bought a few more light weight shirts at the Post Exchange (P.X.), had purchased a watch to wear on tour (the first watch that Jeanne had worn in years), and still needed to get their wooden clogs for the showers to prevent foot fungus. Life at Fort Hamilton over the past weeks had been a memorable experience, wrote Jeanne:

> The "Retreat" at sun down was beautiful, as the bugle call rang over the hills. Of course we all jumped a mile when the cannon was fired.
> This is beautiful. Outside my window, down the hill are the various Fort Buildings. Then the Field itself, with the giant C 54's like silver gulls.
> At night, the lights on the field and the lights in the Bldgs from up here look like glittering jewels from a Sultan's Jewel box.
> The roar of planes is so constant, one takes it for granted.

The leather bookmark that Bill had given her last year was on its way to Japan in one of her favorite books. She promised to notify him "pronto" when they arrived in Manila and obtain their new A.P.O. number, but until then he should use the current one for sending his correspondence. "This will probably be the last letter for awhile," she concluded. "If we don't go-in wee hours—will write again."

This Christmas the family was nearly half a world apart. On Christmas Eve while living at Hickam Field in Hawaii Jeanne managed to send Bill a short message on a postcard, telling him that they had been three days on this gorgeous island—"hope we come back for a longer stay"—and that they had seen the bomb damage at Pearl Harbor; they would be leaving for the Philippines in the dawn of Christmas morning. Conditions in the Pacific islands were difficult during those early months after Japan's surrender, and Jeanne's troupe of dancers had to adjust to many privations and inconveniences. In an interview she described how performers were forced to "put up with the most primitive conditions like giving shows in airplane hangers with no dressing rooms, so spaces to change costumes were made by pinning army blankets on ropes to form walls." At one military base they were taken "to a ship and climbed up a rope ladder to use the Captain's bathroom with a sailor standing guard outside; and another where washing facilities were metal helmets kept upright with coiled towels under it, and water in it and a tiny cake of soap." Jeanne felt grateful that the "lads did the best they could to help us."

On that same Christmas Eve from cold, slushy St. Louis Bill wrote his final letter of 1945 from the warmth of his room at the Y, presuming they had already departed and his letter would "have to chase you about one third around the World." He assured Lillian that he would cross his fingers "while you are soaring the Pacific.... You are no doubt soaring RIGHT NOW" and if you read this letter "you must have landed safely on the other side of the EARTH." He would follow the instructions in Jeanne's last letter not to send them any packages or copies of their letters, as was his normal practice, but would file them in his room for now. Since they were not able to receive packages, he was going to send his faraway family gift certificates for their Christmas gifts this year that they could use when they returned to the mainland. He planned to join Bert again for Christmas dinner, and Bert had suggested that Jeanne send in her poem

"Traveller's Lament" to *The Saturday Evening Post* from some foreign port in the Far East to enhance her chances of publication.

Until Jeanne and Lillian's return to the mainland in April 1946, most of the surviving family letters are from Bill, some of which were never delivered. From Bill's letters it was clear that Jeanne and Lillian were able to write him while on the tour. On January 3, 1946, Bill wrote that he would be pleased to have "a report of your trip and your safe arrival, as soon as you can spare the time." He noted that since she could read a few things that could be "slipped into an envelope for 'digesting,'" he was taking a chance and sending a few little booklets on topics "that may fill in a little time for you, when you may have some [time] for reading." He had received a Christmas card from Jeanne's cousin Jeannette in Pasadena, with a note informing him that Uncle Orville, Aunt Ida's husband, had died about a month before, so he will send a few "consoling words." He wrote that "Everything going along 'as usual' and nothing strange or unusual has happened." On January 1, 1946, Bill commented on a letter from Jeanne, written from Honolulu on January 1st, in which she described how they had toured the tropical island and enjoyed a Christmas turkey dinner complete with native coconut and pineapple sides in the army mess hall, where they had the best opportunity to interact personally with the soldiers.

When Jeanne and Lillian arrived in the Philippines just north of Manila, they were horrified to see the wartime destruction of this once beautiful city. On January 7th Jeanne wrote her father from the military headquarters in Manila to tell him that Captain Ellery, having obtained a jeep and driver, gave them a personal tour of Intramuros, the devastated historic core:

> It WAS the Walled city, and a real "walled fortress." It was with walls and a height and thickness to rival the Great Wall of China. Within, are the wrecked remains of the main business section. A church is about all that is intact. (Other churches werent spared at all) We bounced and jounced past the Gaspig Gardens. A night club that the Japs converted into torture chambers. McArthur, or the collaborationists. Their property is still intact. It is an open scandal, that Gen. McArthur preferred to lose countless thousands of men—rather than use heavy artillery on his property, and he reportedly owns between 65% and 90% of property of Manilla. His apartments, Hotel and Brewery, are hardly a bit damaged yet hospitals, Universities, Federal and Civic buildings and private homes are pathetic wrecks and ruins. Manila general Hospital with large Red Cross on roof is gutted to a bed husk.

Historians have corrected this popular misconception of General MacArthur, proving that he never owned property in Manila and refused to allow the bombing of the walled city of Intramuros to protect the remaining Filipinos still living there.[2]

In her January 7th letter Jeanne describes how she and her mother climbed to the top of an apartment building left in Manila, seeing a panoramic view of the city's harbor, which "must be something to navigate, because the sunken hulls of ships, with funnel or mast above the water." They also visited the unscathed suburbs at Santa Pinas, where they saw the world-renowned Santa Pinas bamboo organ in the ancient Catholic church. They also saw "such sights of crowding, filthy conditions, pig, chickens and naked children, all rooting in the dirt, that one wonders how they can live, and I guess that the average life isnt too long, because it is a rarity to see old people."

When they visited the fascinating Chinese Cemetery and Temple, with its ornate, jeweled decorations and elaborate mausoleums, which miraculously were untouched by the bombing, they unexpectedly noticed "on a peacefull rise ... a 105 MM gun with muzzle pointed upward skyward. Perhaps some water buffalo grazing near its base." In a later interview Jeanne said that to visit this Chinese shrine they had to "walk across a river to what was left of downtown ... and walk on planks suspended on ropes. It swayed like a swing and one held a rope on each side. It was a one-person side." While in Manila, they still wanted to visit the Chinese House, Santa Tomas Concentration Camp, and Bilibid prison, "where our boys were interned so many years," and a lake inside a volcano.³

In Manila, Jeanne and Lillian were always unsure of their schedule, as they depended on a manager who never had complete information. At one point their orchestra leader had a fight with the manager and failed to show up for their rehearsal. "The orchestra here is made up of army boys from some little High school bands, with no great musical backgrounds," wrote Jeanne in her January 7th letter, so "they must rehearse hours to read our music, and not let us down in a pinch.... I'm dead on my feet. Climate and too much social life when we get no sleep." Thousands of soldiers on the island had not danced with an American woman for one or three years, so they "literally" begged the performers "to dance upstairs each night," wrote Jeanne, and "since I love to dance anyway, it's a pleasure." Having been warned that the Army nurses would hate us because the boys would like us better, we were not surprised when six nurses arrived in our barrack early in the morning and made "as much noise as possible." Another reason the boys favored the attractive dancers was that the nurses were often officers who were not allowed to date the enlisted men. Since Captain Ellery had joined an Officer's Club, Jeanne needed to socialize with him "untill the dancing stops at midnight again tonight, as I must repay with companionship, for the grand sight seeing trip we had yesterday. Has invited us to a Native party, sometime soon, if we're here, with whole roast pigs, and reliable native food. We are not supposed to eat 'out' anywhere, unless [we are] sure it is Army vouched for. Dysentery is rugged."

A month later they left Manila for Okinawa, Japan's fifth largest city, en route to Tokyo on two planes, each carrying twenty performers. Days later the flight from Okinawa to Tokyo was filled with high drama. The pilot in the first plane had invited Jeanne to sit next to him in the cockpit, surprising her when he said that they were ahead of schedule. He asked, "Would you like to see Hiroshima?" "Why yes," Jeanne replied. He then quickly dropped his altitude from 12,500 feet to 1,000, causing the dancers in the cabin to be sick and throw up. As Jeanne looked out the cockpit window she could see the famous tall curved dome of the Hiroshima Prefectural Industrial Promotion Hall, now called the Genbaku Dome, one of the only buildings left standing in Hiroshima: "The destruction below was mind-bogling," Jeanne wrote her father. As they proceeded toward Tokyo, she saw firsthand how the twenty miles between Yokohama and Tokyo "was burned out by the American bombing. The only thing left standing were the brick chimneys of the bath houses."

Bill's letter of February 3, 1946, was a welcome respite from the life in these war ravaged Pacific islands. He enclosed newspaper clippings for Jeanne about how America was filled with labor strikes and influenced by Britain's new experiment with socialism. "How are things getting along at that end? Presume that you are still in Japan, and 'company' matters are improving a little. My <u>best wishes</u>, for your <u>welfare</u> at that end," he wrote. A month later on March 3rd after having received two letters from them about a week before, giving him "a nice little 'peep' into Japan's back yard, and a bird's eye view of the island," Bill noted that they had seen a "preponderance of Bow legged people" in Japan and that the plumbing conditions are horrible, especially the "toilet facilities."

Jeanne remembered only a few of her performances in Japan, and there are almost no references to specific shows in her letters. In an interview she emphasized that she had not created any new dances for the tour, but had used her standard repertoire. The author of an article in Jeanne's scrapbook described the show scheduled for Japan's Tachikawa Army Base Hangar, located in a city forty kilometers west of Tokyo's center, as a "top notch musical show, featuring eighteen curvaceous girls fresh from the states." The revue "is hailed by audiences in the Tokyo-Yokohama area as one of the best entertainment features to play the Pacific in many months," wrote the author. The program featured "Songs, ballet, dancing, and the fast line of patter." The Yokota Air Base's newsletter for February 15, 1946, praised the show as "outstanding ... [one that] compares with any current Broadway show in humor, dancing and singing": the cast consists of forty-nine performers including eight "gorgeous gals know as the Copa Sirens, whose performance of the 'Gretchen' and 'Baia' numbers have wowed GI audiences all over Japan. The classical touch is added by the Cheena De Simone dancers under the direction of Jeanne Devereaux."

Jeanne remembered a special performance in Tokyo at the Hibiah Theatre for General MacArthur, named by President Truman to govern in Japan as the Supreme Commander of Allied Forces in the Pacific. Jeanne wrote about MacArthur attending one of her performances: "We were asked to be ready on stage at exactly 8 PM. We were, and we waited and waited backstage in that cold theatre for the word that he had arrived and we could begin. Finally a little after 9PM the orchestra struck up a march and as the curtain rose, he and his aides strode down the aisle to their reserved seats and we began our performance. Halfway through he got up and left, but the grateful Guys we were sent to entertain stayed cheering until the end." In a later interview Jeanne explained how most of the occupying American soldiers—kids who were inducted and trained shortly before or after the surrender of Japan—had not participated in the heroic Pacific battles, but were fighting off homesickness and the boredom of occupation. They craved anything American, particularly entertainment; they craved beauty. In an article in the *New York Herald Tribune*, titled "A Ballerina's Visit to G. I.'s In Japan," November 17, 1946, she was quoted as saying, "Wherever she went, the ballerina said, she was surprised how much the men were interested not only in the popular-styled elements of the revue, but also in those examples of 'classic' ballet which she gave, despite the fact that most of the boys knew nothing of actual stage productions, let alone the subtle points of the dance. Actually, she reports, ballet was cheered by them more than anything else. Hungry for beauty, they gave it their highest praise by calling it 'Stateside,' meaning 'like America.'"

Jeanne and Lillian sent a short note to Bill on March 19, 1946, telling him that they were en route to New York via Seattle: "We crossed on General Pope—largest Pacific troop ship. 5.265 persons aboard. It was 'murder'! We're quarantined four days in Puget, on suspicion of typhus aboard. Write us % Camp Shows, 8 W 40th N.Y.C." Bill replied to his "tribe" the next day that he hoped they would be able to find suitable accommodations in New York, since he knew there was still a housing shortage. He wished they could see the "Y's" lobby "with discharged soldiers, not being able to find accommodations, lying in every conceiveable position, in the chairs, asleep, and on the floors of the lobby." On April 1st Jeanne wrote Bill that they were grateful to find accommodations in the Hotel Columbia at 70 West 46th Street, although it was an expensive "10th rate hotel," and they were "both still sick from the terrible pneumonia colds, we had. We think the 21 shots—-had a great deal to do with our Lowered resistance. Those injections aren't easy on people, especially the fever ones like Typhus, Typhoid, Small pox, and Bubonic Plague." They had recently sent him a pair of Japanese flying boots, an army sweater, a few wool gloves, a muffler, and a fine poplin shirt. Writing the next day with his characteristic lack of appreciation, he confirmed that he already had a closet full of similar articles, most of which they had given him in the past. On April 12th Bill asked Jeanne if she were "still with that Govt Company [the USO], or whether that has disbanded."

Jeanne's historic USO Camp Shows tour made a lasting impression on her and deepened her understanding of the futility and destruction of war, the loneliness of occupation, and the frustrations of reconstruction. The *New York Herald Tribune*'s November 17th article, published five months after she had returned to Radio City Music Hall after her USO Camp Shows tour, emphasized that Jeanne's current dancing role in the patriotic stage show "United We Stand" was inspired by her firsthand experience of war and reconstruction while performing in Japan. She had returned to the mainland with "vivid impressions of the consequences of the war and of American efforts to recondition the 'Land of the Rising Sun'":

> To the Music Hall dancer, Japan was a startling composite of an exquisite, dreamlike beauty and stark, cruel realities. She speaks of the enchantment of ancient temples of Kyoto and the magic of a bamboo forest in the snow, and then the horror of Hiroshima and Nagasaki, from the air—still great areas of seared, red-brown earth from atom bombing. What's more, she told of the continued need which American soldiers, stationed now in Japan, have for entertainment and of the fine work which the USO is still trying to carry on for those Army men.

She now believed, the article concluded, that it was the duty of all Americans to help the occupying soldiers, who are "just a lot of normal, healthy American fellows and Japan is as foreign to them as a post on the moon might be."

Later in 1951 during the Korean War when Jeanne and Lillian were living again in New York Jeanne had another opportunity to perform in a USO Camp Shows tour. On October 18, 1951, Jeanne wrote Tom Perkins about a letter she had received from a fellow performer who was on a tour to Korea: "Ray wrote us again from Korea—He was north of the 38th Parallel and told of the life in front lines—When the men get too beat they bring them back—Put on a show, give them coffee & doughnuts & after a couple of hours send them back to the battleline." Once again the USO Camp Shows tours were providing many unemployed performers a steady job: "Now there are plans to send out 82 U.S.O. shows to our bases all over the world—It's the first time since 1946 that U.S.O. shows have been planned on such a large scale," she wrote, "So Ray will be happy as it will undoubtedly assure him at least three months of work." Given her current passion for Hindu dance, Jeanne said that if they were planning to send a USO Camp Shows tour to India, she would definitely be interested.

Jeanne Devereaux in Radio City Music Hall's stage show "United We Stand," October–December 7, 1946. A patriotic salute to the United Nations and world peace, the revue was part of the four-part spectacle "All in a Day." Jeanne is performing her silk flag waving routine with the Corps de Ballet called "Banners in the Breeze." Jeanne's recollections of the lonely soldiers she had visited on her USO Camp Shows tour inspired her performance in this postwar revue at Radio City. Having made her début at Radio City in "Dawn of a New Day," on December 29, 1938, Jeanne performed on Radio City's magnificent stage throughout the 1940s. Courtesy Jeanne Devereaux Perkins Collection.

Jeanne realized how financially profitable these USO Camp Shows tours were given that other opportunities for performing in New York at her age were practically nonexistent. On November 16th she wrote Tom Perkins that Ray and another friend had repeatedly tried to recruit her for their unit: "They even went so far as to request me from the U.S.O. office—I haven't been into the U.S.O. but they are reorganizing that Korean unit for the middle East—They play our Airforce bases in Labrador, Greenland, Azores, N. Africa, Greece, Turkey & Triests." Having promised that she and her mother would go visit the man organizing the tour at the USO office, Jeanne wrote that she hated "the thought of shots & flying & Army etc—but the twelve weeks tour would take me to a few places I've always wanted to see &, and, and, and, And, I would have about $3,000. at the end of the trail."

Having visited with the man at the USO office the very next day, she learned that it would take too long to obtain her FBI clearance to go on the Far East tour leaving on December 7th. When the man asked her if she would be interested in touring in Korea or Alaska, she "gave him a flat 'No,'" so he registered her personal data to begin the clearance process, and would let her know when the next Far East tour was scheduled to deploy. However, she was nearing the end of her professional dancing career and never performed in another USO Camp Shows tour.[4]

16

Radio City, Summer Operettas and the Milton Berle Television Show

Five weeks after she returned from Japan and arrived in New York, Jeanne took pen in hand and wrote to her father on April 23, 1946, to give him the good news that they were still alive. She had not resumed performing: "We have had practically no time to do much of anything, for I have had to practice very hard every day to get back in practice," she wrote. They had been looking for an apartment, shopping, organizing their clothes, making new hats, paying their income tax, and visiting agents to push for future bookings in a show biz market where jobs were scarce. She described one of her rare days off—a mild Easter Sunday afternoon after a windy March—enjoying visiting the sites of New York with a friend: "So Easter was a great day, for it was mild, and not a single saucy bonnet blew off. Everyone looked wonderful—and the Avenues were jammed with Easter Parade Strollers." On this same Easter Sunday Bill, lonely, missing them, and not knowing if they were still with the USO tour, wrote that he had once again spent another family holiday with his good friend Bert.

Over the next few months the family letters diminished. Frustrated by not hearing from his "Tribe" in almost a month and uncertain of their address, Bill wondered in his May 20th letter if they had sprained wrists, were out of ink, or no longer enjoyed receiving his letters. Hoping that Jeanne might get a booking that would bring them to St. Louis, he filled his letter again with information about the Muny Theatre's summer season. On June 8th he tersely asked for verification of their current address, ending his letter with a plaintive "Why the silence?" When Lillian finally wrote Bill on June 10th, she told him that she believed President Truman and his postwar administration were providing "poor leadership," avoiding any kind of reasonable rationing of goods and nationalizing the railroads, mines, and merchant marine, much to the detriment of the American citizens. Jeanne and Lillian's funds were so tight that they could only send Bill a $20 bill this year for his June birthday gift. They were, however, sending the final reimbursement for the loan: "It has been a while, and the figures escape me now, so if it isnt right, advise," wrote Lillian.

While they were in Japan, bookings for ballerinas at the Muny and at Dallas for the summer operetta season had been set. Jeanne's rival Patricia Bowman had been booked for two weeks at both places, as "she is known to the producer, and got them

16 • Radio City, Summer Operettas and the Milton Berle Television Show

'set' early in the year." Reduced salaries ruled out working even "an isolated week, either place, as traveling expenses are too great, even when Jeanne's ticket is paid for, by them," she wrote. They hoped for a booking at Radio City Music Hall, but would have to wait for the current motion picture to finish. Bill replied on June 19th that he was disappointed that Jeanne would not be playing the Muny this summer—maybe next. In a September 21st letter he chastised them again for not writing more often, and threatened them that if they "want to hear from me more in details, go into details a little yourself."

Jeanne and Lillian's standard of living and Jeanne's prospects for employment as a prima ballerina in theatres and movies were diminished by the postwar stock market crash of 1946, which had resulted in a 20 percent drop in value between August and October, taking four years to regain the loss. One evening on October 3rd when Jeanne was out dining and dancing with a beau at a nightclub, Lillian described in a long letter to Bill the hardships of living in postwar New York, where there was little heat, no soap, no meat, a scarcity of groceries forcing them to shop in many different stores, and general inflation. As for show business, "we heard of all the theatrical activity which would begin right after Labor Day, yet now the whole 'house of cards' has fallen," she wrote, "for it seems all the rich old Angels who used some of surplus money, to back shows, in other years, have had it snatched away from them by the recent crash of the Stock Market." It was particularly difficult for ballerinas in show business, who had many expenses to keep physically fit and attractive in addition to the necessities of daily living. Continuing her letter two days later when Jeanne was out on a date with a different beau, Lillian, worried again about finances, stressed that it "is quite a life, trying to keep the WOLF from jumping in our window, and requires much-doing," she wrote.

Since bookings were practically non-existent, they explored Jeanne's earlier entrepreneurial efforts in 1940 to produce filmed dance lessons. Lillian wrote that she was enthusiastic about their current concept for dance instructional films and how she would need investment capital. She calculated they would need to raise $5,000 to cover their start-up expenses, and believed that the market for these kinds of instructional dance films would be huge. She knew that thousands of dancing teachers travel every year to New York to attend the expensive Dancing Masters of America Convention, but if they stayed home and used the educational films, they could learn more about dance than by attending these conventions. "We knew the idea was a gold mine, and so during these war years we kept it right tight to ourselves, because, most people now-a-days can get the 'backing' of [if] they can only get a fool proof thing in a new field," she wrote. Indirectly dismissing her husband as a financial failure, she said that since she had "no men folks, and no connection," someone else might trump their idea and their opportunity would be gone.[1] Lillian wrote Bill soon again on October 6th that they had attended a delightful party with friends who lived in Flushing, New York, where Jeanne was "so honored for her magnificent dancing by everyone." On October 24th Bill suggested that they look in the "Business Opportunities" section of the daily newspapers for possible financial backers. The educational film project never materialized, and Lillian was distressed when years later she learned that other dancing teachers had executed her original concept.

On October 14th Jeanne proudly wrote her father that she was now under contract to open at Radio City Music Hall for the usual three or four weeks performing the same flag dance that she had presented there over four years ago. She hoped that the run would last five or six weeks. Writing on October 26th, Lillian described how they had been overwhelmed with rehearsals and preparing for opening night at the "nation's greatest theatre," but now that the premiere "is over, and our nerves quieted down, we pick up threads of daily living—once again." Jeanne was performing four shows on weekdays and five on Saturday in a patriotic salute to the United Nations called "United We Stand" that was part of the lavish four-show spectacle "All in a Day," produced by Leon Leonidoff with settings by Bruno Maine, featuring the Corps de Ballet, the Rockettes, among others. Charles Previn directed the Music Hall's Symphony Orchestra. A playbill for Radio City Music Hall, November 14, 1946, advertised Jeanne as performing on the great stage in "an inspiring pageant" that was "dedicated to the United Nations and the Cause of World Peace," with more than 100 artists, including "thrilling dances by Jeanne Devereaux, prima ballerina, and the Corps de Ballet." One of her specialty dances with the Corps de Ballet was called "Banners in the Breeze"; the stage show shared billing with the movie *The Jolson Story*, starring Larry Parks and Evelyn Keyes. Jeanne and Lillian had visitors backstage all day long between shows, and would occasionally join the cast for a mid-night supper.

In her October 26th letter Lillian described Jeanne's hectic schedule while performing at Radio City and the deprivations caused by the recent truckers' strike and subsequent rationing. Jeanne had to arrive at the theatre for the first show an hour and a half before show time in order to make up, put her costume on, and get down on the stage ready to dance, "so she cant do a great deal in the morning, but take care of getting in the daily supply of milk, which, by the way, is so scarce in New York, we have to return the empty bottles, to get a bottle of milk," she wrote. The recent trucking strike was about settled, so Lillian hoped that the rationing would end, and the long lines at the neighborhood markets and supermarkets would soon shorten from being nearly three blocks long. "People here are desperate for shortening, sugar, and soap chips or Oxydol, Super Suds, or anything at all. Thanks again, for the soap," she wrote. "You certainly saved our lives." Unfortunately the trucker's strike also prevented her from buying sixteen millimeter film for her camera; otherwise, she could have taken some fast black and white photos of Jeanne's scene and dance at Radio City.

Although Jeanne was vigilant in her attempt to keep in the best physical shape possible so she could perform, like world-class athletes, star dancers have their share of injuries, and until 1946 Jeanne had been miraculously free of any serious physical limitations. Now at age thirty-four after dancing professionally for twenty-five years her body was more vulnerable to the strenuous physical demands of ballet, but she usually managed to perform through any pain. On November 13th, the fourth week of the show at Radio City, Jeanne, now back at the hotel and exhausted after so many performances, wrote to her father at two o'clock in the morning that she had a bad case of bursitis in her left foot, as well as a pulled Achilles tendon in her heel: "Its dreadfully painful, but as long as there is a day's work in the air,—I'll hobble through somehow. And so far, I have managed to do darn fine performances in spite of the 'Miseries,'" she wrote.

The stage show "All in a Day" in the *New York Times*, December 6, 1946, included

Jeanne among the "stars." When the show closed the next day, Jeanne was ecstatic to learn that her employment at Radio City was being extended until Christmas. On December 9th Jeanne and Lillian wrote on a postcard that they were working "terribly hard" preparing for the Christmas show, "but glad of it." The Christmas show featured a Nativity spectacle based on biblical scenes and was usually attended by entire families; the set featured live animals including the standard feature of bringing a live camel onstage. During the Christmas show Jeanne danced in a huge, colorful revue called "Good Ship Holiday," starring the Music Hall Choral Ensemble, the Symphony Orchestra led by Charles Previn, the Nonchalants, the Shyrettoes, the Corps de Ballet, and the famous Rockettes. She performed as a soloist in front of the Corps de Ballet in "Skiing Under Northern Skies"; the Technicolor movie was *Till Clouds Roll By*, a musical biography of the composer Jerome Kern starring Judy Garland, June Allyson, and Van Johnson.

As 1946 drew to a close the family was separated as it had been since 1927 for the winter holidays, which were celebrated as usual by letters and gift giving. Bill had once again spent Thanksgiving with his friend Bert and had already sent Jeanne a book and

Jeanne Devereaux in Radio City Music Hall's Christmas stage show "Good Ship Holiday" performing as a soloist with the Corps de Ballet in "Skiing Under Northern Skies," New York, December 1946–January 23, 1947. Jeanne is elevated in the center wearing a white costume. Courtesy Jeanne Devereaux Perkins Collection.

some bars of soap for her birthday. On December 20th Bill sent them a Christmas package containing a mélange of knickknacks. Management at the Y had just informed him that the fire inspector had declared his room, along with others, to be hazards, and he would have to clean out his clutter to meet the fire code. He unexpectedly enclosed a copy of his New Year's card as well as a list of his friends and their addresses in case they would ever have to contact any of them. Once again, he spent New Year's Eve celebrating with his good friend Bert.

On New Year's Eve Lillian wrote Bill to thank him for the Christmas gift box and to wish him a Happy New Year "with many orders in 1947." The holiday schedule for the Christmas show at Radio City was tough—five shows daily and on New Year's eve a midnight show too—but after that they would resume the four shows a day policy. Unfortunately, they had had no time to do any Christmas shopping. Lillian wrote that she was hoping that Jeanne's show would be extended until January 23rd to make "a nice long run here," leaving "the wolf scared a long way away from our door at present." She wished for some solid bookings in 1947 "to keep us from the worries one can have in our line of business."

Moving living quarters was on the family's mind in January 1947. Bill called a few of the smaller downtown St. Louis hotels, and was shocked by the daily rates ranging from $3.50 to $5 per day. To increase his chances of remaining at the Y, he spent early January anxiously cleaning up his cluttered room. His family on the East Coast executed an exhausting move during the current housing shortage: "WE HAVE MOVED! ! !," Jeanne wrote on January 16th. It had been a "titanic ordeal to move, betwixt four shows a day during a two day blizzard": since she was performing at Radio City, Lillian managed the move to the Hotel Belvedere. Reacting to Dad's shock at the St. Louis hotel rates, she wrote, "Where, by the way, may I inquire, have you been all during the war, not to read or hear of the acute housing and hotel shortage, and price gouge. Or did you think we were all kidding, when we wrote you of our problem?" She advised him to "play 'Nice Doggie' around the Y," since he had "a cheap Bonanza there, and we all realized it, even if you didnt."

Along with the prospect of possibly being evicted from the Y, Bill's business was tenuous, since his manufacturers were not able to purchase enough metal or lumber for their rulers and yardsticks. On March 5th Bill received a letter from the President and General Manager of the American Manufacturing Concern, informing him that the company, due to the high demand and supply during wartime, was retiring from the ruler business, and all their ruler machinery equipment and inventory had been sold to American Manufacturing Company, Inc. Bill was devastated. He was instructed to forward his future orders to this new company. On April 9th he complained that the sale of the business had left the sales force a mess. None of the commissions had been paid since last summer, and the new company had not communicated with anyone their new prices or delivery dates. Increasingly estranged from her husband, Lillian focused on Jeanne's bookings and making a livelihood in tough economic times, and barely responded to Bill's letters about the impact of the company sale. On May 2nd she wrote that she was "certainly surprised to hear the American Mfg. had sold out. Will it help to get your orders filled? Now? Everybody and every business is changing all the time. Its just about all I can do to remember who I am."

16 • Radio City, Summer Operettas and the Milton Berle Television Show

Meanwhile, injury forced Jeanne to cancel a major booking for the first time in her professional career. On April 3rd Jeanne informed her father that after the previous show had closed on January 23rd she had been required to rest her injured Achilles tendon for four-and-a-half weeks with no dancing, and had to cancel her next engagement at Radio City. While recuperating, she and Lillian had spent most of their time making props, jewelry, head dresses, and costumes for future bookings: some of these costumes were elaborately beaded, requiring them to spend almost eighteen-hour days sewing on the beads. "Hollywood has educated peoples tastes until elaborately beaded and sequined gowns costing from $850.00 to $2.000.00 each, are what the managements expect, (though of course they dont want to pay for them)," she wrote. Jeanne, having been on a strict diet, reported that she had lost twelve pounds.

Bill needed the emotional support provided by their letters. On March 10th he pleaded that he very much wanted to receive a letter from them, even "if it is just a few lines, to relieve the 'silence'": he had a few things "to write about—but first want to hear from YOUR end.... When I hear from you—will write further." Pleased that they had finally broken "the silence," he thanked Jeanne on April 9th for her recent letter. He persisted in keeping the communication alive, writing them a short note on April 30th and enclosing some imitation pearl necklaces "for your theatricals" that he had purchased on sale.

Jeanne inherited good genes from her two grandfathers, who both lived well into their nineties. Grandfather Helman had died at ninety-two, and the death of Grandpa Lane at the age of ninety-five in Pasadena on May 1st sent shock waves throughout the immediate family. On May 2nd Lillian began her letter with the sad news about her father's passing, whom she was certain would have probably lived many more years if he had not contracted bronchial pneumonia: in fact, her sister Lenore had written recently about how he had "decided it was time for spring, and so changed his underwear for lighter weight." Lillian then focused on Jeanne's career and their preparations for her summer bookings. "We have signed contracts [for] three weeks in 'The Great Waltz' and 'Three Musketeers' for Pittsburgh's Civic Light Opera at the Pittsburgh stadium, and have two or three operettas on the fire. Also a couple of shows may cast—for summer opening, we hear, so it is highly imperative to keep on tap." Since the manager of the Pittsburgh Civic Light Opera wanted partner dancing as well as solos, Jeanne was practicing with her new partner James Starbuck on some adagio routines. After Pittsburgh they had a booking for summer operettas in Atlanta, Georgia, and a pending offer to perform in Australia.

After the family conducted memorial services for Grandpa Lane in Pasadena, Lillian joined them for the official funeral in Doniphan, Nebraska. Jeanne wrote her father on May 6th that when Lillian had left that night on the train for Doniphan, she had felt "quite lost without her." On short notice, Lillian had only a couple of days to purchase new clothes for the trip, especially an appropriate black dress; she sat up all night on the train ride to Chicago, and then the next night on another train to Grand Island, Nebraska. "That's rough!" Jeanne wrote, hinting to her father that Lillian would probably be pleased to hear from him. Bill, taking the hint, responded to Jeanne on May 9th that he had sent a letter "to one of your parents, out west somewhere, and asked her to give my regards to the members of the tribe, out there, and extend my sympathy also."

On June 18th Lillian again complained to Bill about her financial woes and exhaustion from their time-consuming preparations for the three-week engagement in Pittsburgh, followed by a two-week one in Atlanta with a week in between. They worked on the beaded costumes for *The Great Waltz* and *The Three Musketeers* in Pittsburgh and *Balalaika* in Atlanta, purchased new street clothes and summer practice outfits and cleaned old ones, packed the trunks for storage downstairs at their New York hotel, ordered reproductions of old publicity pictures for every "Tom Dick and Harry" who "'wants a picture' in every place we go," got dance orchestrations costing hundreds of dollars, paid for the rehearsal hall and pianist, and did the daily cooking, washing, and ironing. For the Pittsburgh engagement alone there were nine new dances to be created and practiced. "All of these operettas require plenty of outlay ahead of time, and yet every dancer is fighting for them and Envy Jeanne her chance to play them," she wrote.

In the wake of Grandpa Lane's death, Lillian and her sisters inherited a modest amount of land in Nebraska. That June Lillian and Bill began a five-month acrimonious battle about money. Enclosed in Lillian's June 18th letter was a transcript of a deed in both of their names for her one-fourth share of 160 acres of land in Nebraska left to her by her father. Since her sisters wanted to sell their "undivided ¼ part" interest in this land, she had agreed to sell her share worth $2,000 and needed Bill to sign the quitclaim deed, have it notarized, and then send it back to her in New York immediately before she and Jeanne left for Pittsburgh on July 13th for the new booking.

On June 30th Bill wrote that he would delay signing the deed of trust until they "can come to some understanding on" this inheritance. Although he was not "given to weeping on other people's shoulders" even when he "could use some financial aid nicely," he proposed to Lillian that if she would divide the payment of $2,000 for the land with him and send him a check to cover his share, then he would agree to signing the deed of trust. Lillian's heated response to Bill's letter was one of the few times that she openly confronted the reality of their strained marriage, emphasizing that Jeanne had really been the family's financial support for twenty years. "Your letter has completely flabergasted me," wrote Lillian despondently on July 7th, for after "twenty years of total non support, and after keeping your own inheritance [$5,000 from Uncle Henry and $1,500 from his father] entirely for your own whims and follies, and reminding me eternally it was 100% YOUR inheritance, I fail to see on what grounds you think you have any interest what so ever in this little acreage my father left to me." She angrily confronts Bill about his lack of ambition, squandering of money, and irresponsibility in not supporting his family:

> During the years when it was easy for you to make nice large commissions you squandered your time and money on vacation after vacation, and stamp collecting, saying always that "umbrellas were for a rainy day" and now I see that you want us to give you our umbrella.
>
> You have waited so long to get out of the advertising business, that you are now grasping at straws, instead of getting some job you can do with your hands.
>
> You have very low rent in the Y.M.C.A. and most any job with a regular salary will cover your expenses, if you live there, as you are very capable with your hands.
>
> You know well that WE have never had a moments security, and Jeanne's dancing engagements have supported us for 20 years, during which time you have not had to contribute one cent.
>
> She has been supporting YOUR wife, altho we have never chided you about it. I have remained true and faithful to you all these years, while you assumed no responsibility for me or Jeanne in any way.

When Jeanne was born in 1912 Grandpa Lane had given the family money from one of his profitable investments and "'this' you squandered, even during the times when It was easy for you to make a living," she wrote. Of the two pieces of land that she had recently inherited, only the larger one was saleable, representing everything that she has in the world to sell, which "was not given to you in any way at all."

Although most of the family correspondence had avoided these dark issues, Lillian's letter confirmed that Jeanne's extraordinary professional success had required years of hard work and personal sacrifice. Since Jeanne had worked as a young girl at the St. Louis' vaudeville, Garden, and Muny theatres, she alone had paid for most of her dancing lessons and later was the sole support of herself and her mother:

> She has been dancing and making a living for us both, for almost 20 years and is a Nationally known name, in the dancing public, but now has had to cancel an engagement at the Music Hall because of inflammation in the small bones of her toe.
>
> This may put an end to her dancing, and I intend to give her this $2.000 so that she can have just a little chance to get into something else.
>
> I want her to get one moment of freedom from the fear that she has had every moment these 20 years. HARD years and no one but me to help.
>
> You had a wonderfully GOOD time untill you were close to 50 years. Jeanne is now 34 years old, and has never married because there are few men today who can take on the support of her, plus your wife too.
>
> Just what moral right have you to one half of that little legacy left to me? Look the facts squarely and honestly in the face and you will realize you havent a leg to stand on. Here's hoping you land a job with your hands, and get off the worry seat. I'm sure you will be much happier there.

Underneath Lillian's firm loyalty and love for her husband, there was hurt and resentment.

Before the Pittsburgh booking Jeanne returned to Radio City Music Hall in June to dance in a stage show called "Merry-Go-Round," also featuring the Rockettes, aerial feats by Janet and Paul, baritone Robert Shanley, dancers Lucienne and Ashour, and the Corps de Ballet. The stage show shared billing with the movie *The Ghost and Mrs. Muir*, starring Gene Tierney, Rex Harrison, and George Sanders. "Merry-Go-Round" was the last stage show in which Jeanne performed in this iconic theatre. She then opened in July in *The Three Musketeers* at Pittsburgh's Civic Light Opera open-air stadium, where she danced three duets with James Starbuck on a very slippery stage. According to the *Pittsburgh Press*, July 22, 1947, "Jeanne Devereaux and James Starbuck were featured dancers and the ballet corps give a good account of themselves in spite of the slick stage." Jeanne's biography in the program said, "Jeanne Devereaux (Premiere Danseuse of the Court) has stopped so many shows with her exquisite Classic Ballet and unbelievably phenomenal pirouettes, and has captured such rave notices from the press all over the world that she finds herself starring not only in Musical Comedy and Revues, but in Operettas."

Ending the Pittsburgh operetta season in July in *The Great Waltz*, Jeanne performed again with James Starbuck one of her lovely Strauss waltz dances. According to the *Pittsburgh Press*, July 29, 1947, "Jeanne Devereaux and James Starbuck again demonstrated their art effectively and merited the acclaim bestowed upon them"; the *Pittsburgh Post-Gazette* for the same day praised the singing and dancing: "Any evening would be that with such lovely waltzes by Johann, Sr. and Jr., and such good people to sing them,

Jeanne Devereaux backstage with unidentified cast and crew in her costume for an operetta at the Pittsburgh, Pennsylvania, Civic Light Opera, Pittsburgh Stadium, late July 1947. While in Pittsburgh she performed in the classic operettas *The Three Musketeers* and *The Great Waltz*. Courtesy Jeanne Devereaux Perkins Collection.

and a corps de ballet, superlatively sparkled by Miss Jeanne Devereaux, that has apparently reserved its collective best foot forward for the farewell." Jeanne's personal scrapbook of newspaper articles and reviews and official programs and playbills ends with this July performance in Pittsburgh.

Having returned to the Hotel Belvedere in New York, Jeanne soon signed a contract to perform for a season at the Tivoli Theatre in Melbourne, Australia, with an opening in Sydney for two shows daily in November. She and Lillian had reservations aboard the steamer *Marine Phoenix* leaving San Francisco on October 21st. However, on September 17th Jeanne sent David Martin, the Managing Director in Australia, a cablegram informing him that she would have to cancel the contract since she "PULLED LEG MUSCLE BADLY SECOND TIME SPECIALISTS WARN REQUIRES SEVERAL MONTHS COMPLETE REST HOPE TO PLAY AUSTRALIA IN FUTURE." Martin replied that when she had sufficiently recovered they would inform her about rescheduling, and if she were available, they would be "only too happy to avail ourselves of your services." Meanwhile, he expressed his sincere wishes for her speedy recover.

They also had to cancel the Australian engagement because the management could not pay in dollars, but with only British pounds used in Australia.

Bill's feelings were deeply wounded from Lillian's heated July 7th letter about his financial irresponsibility during their marriage, so he took a hiatus from letter writing. It was not until shortly before Jeanne's birthday on October 31st when Bill answered Lillian's accusations: "Guess you are wondering why you havent heard from me recently—so I will be frank in telling you that I didnt like the 'contents' of your last letter Mrs. and the way you are willing to stretch FACTS to suit your own convenience, or rather mis-state facts, for that purpose," he wrote. In his last letter he had told her about his dire financial situation, hoping that he "could come to you, for some help," but all he received was criticism of my "'past life'": no mention of what he "'HAD DONE,' only my failures." So now he had to remind her again of his financial contribution to their marriage by itemizing a year-by-year list of his earnings from 1911 to 1925 totaling nearly $41,000.

Their cancellation of the Australian booking left them with no immediate prospects for employment. As "there is at present the worst slump ever experienced in the show business it takes some time to get good engagement," Lillian wrote Bill on December 18th. They had heard that "acts" performing in England could now bring back to America "about 50% of their salaries," so they would investigate performing in London again. If they were successful at securing another booking, they still needed to face the reality that at age thirty-five Jeanne's body was experiencing the wear and tear of her long dancing career. To keep her tender feet in better shape, they had all her street shoes corrected so that her "toe bones" did not "ride up-hill all day long" in bunched up soles. Lillian frequently massaged Jeanne's legs until her hard calf and thigh muscles softened. They realized that from now on they would have to devote more of their time to maintaining Jeanne's physical fitness, "as her muscles had gotten so hard from controlled leg extensions."

After nearly twenty years Bill was finally forced to leave the security of the St. Louis Y and move to new living quarters at the La Salle Hotel. In her December 18th letter Lillian had wondered why he was not living at the YMCA anymore and now at this hotel address: "Send a card or letter by return mail, so we can send your gift, as Xmas is very near. Don't send us anything," she wrote. "P.S. what became of the barrels of silver and china, at the Y.M.C.A." Bill's 1947 Christmas letter provided details of his move from the Y to his new hotel room. Still wounded by Lillian's accusations about his financial irresponsibility, on December 20th Bill described his new housing arrangement—"to relieve the tension, will send you a few lines"—despite his dislike of "the tone –of your previous letter of last July, with nothing but 'incriminations' in it, and nothing but fault finding, and not one 'kind' word in same." Two months previously the YMCA had changed their rules and informed their older residents that they had to find other living quarters. He and an old acquaintance—a compatible, white-haired, eighty-three-year-old "chap"—had found a large room in the old La Salle Hotel. He had mailed his New Year's cards, and had learned from Jack Leigh in St. Louis that Aunt Kate was dead as well as other friends: "it seems as tho people keep on dying, eh?" he grimly reflected.

The family correspondence for 1948 diminished in quantity and substance to the point that often Jeanne and Lillian did not even know where Bill was living and vice versa. Having not heard from Bill since Christmas, Lillian wrote him on February 12, 1948, that in her last letter she had enclosed $10 for him to buy a Christmas gift. She and Jeanne were once again living at the Hotel Belvedere in New York, enduring the harsh, snowy winter weather, and for a month she had had a lung infection and Jeanne a terrible cold. Due to continued postwar inflation and rationing, times were tough in the show business industry in 1948: "95% of all entertainers in the show business are out of work here, and all over the country," she wrote. "Many reasons. Mainly the people who went to places of entertainment cannot afford to go now, since food and rent is taking every cent they make. So a slump is sure to come, in the show business." Later, on July 8th, Lillian wrote how she believed that America was in the midst of another Depression, although the press avoided using this inflammatory term.

Jeanne had received an offer to return to London for a four-week engagement in a first-rate nightclub, but they had asked her agent to get a booking for the London Palladium instead, as that show would begin in October and last nearly eight months. They had been busy with "the eternal sewing," for there were always rehearsal and old performance costumes to refurbish. More out of touch with Bill than ever before since leaving St. Louis in early 1927, Lillian asked him to write more often, and tell them if he were still in the advertising business.

Once again Lillian's small inheritance from her father dominated the family correspondence. For most of 1948 Lillian and her remaining sisters attempted to sell the parcel of Nebraska farmland that they had inherited. In May Lillian traveled by bus to Grand Island, Nebraska, to manage the sale of the property, and Jeanne was emotional about finding herself alone in New York. On May 26th Jeanne wrote to Lillian: "When I waved good bye on the platform I tore thru the station to wave again from the sidewalk but I was too late so raced to the corner on the wild hope the traffic light would hold you up a min & good luck with me it did!—Then the light changed and off you went following your little nose pointed west.... I turned & walked from the corner with my eyes so blurred with tears.... Every few min I think where you must be by now—I'm just glad it was a modern up to date clean bus." Fortunately, Jeanne could not dwell tearfully on her mother's absence, since she was currently practicing with handsome, young Ken Spaulding on a partner dance, which she had choreographed and was designing the costumes for their benefit performance.

On June 9th Bill received a letter from B.J. Cunningham, Lillian's lawyer in Grand Island, Nebraska, asking him to sign the enclosed quit claim deed and have it notarized to avoid any litigation costing $200, for Lillian would rather pay him this money than spend it on court costs and attorney's fees. Since Jeanne had had no bookings for a while, having to pay anyone $200 was an extreme hardship for Lillian at this time, for their income from show business in these tight economic times was minimal; she had even been forced to borrow money from her family to finance the trip to Nebraska and to offer Bill the payment. For the next two weeks Bill and Lillian's contentious letters and telegrams overlapped, so Lillian was unaware when she left Grand Island for New York that he had signed the quitclaim deed and had sent it along with an invoice for the $200 to her lawyer.

On June 21st Jeanne wrote her father telling him how scarce jobs were in show business, and complaining how the competition for getting bookings was fierce. She admitted "I'm very unhappy over not playing St. Louis this summer," she wrote. "The man promised me some nice shows there this summer, when I saw him last year, but then he had no shows for me when the time came." Jeanne had created some new dances with her current partner Ken Spaulding, but since he was injured, they were unable to audition for eight weeks, and in the meantime all bookings had been given to others. "So we lost out all the way around," Jeanne wailed, concluding that "when things are tough with us, they are 'tough'!!!" After paying their hotel rent and fees for a rehearsal hall and pianist, Jeanne and Lillian barely had enough funds to pay for food, telephone calls, and bus fare. Obviously aware of the contentious communication between her parents about the pending land sale in Nebraska, Jeanne diplomatically asked her father why he had delayed "sending that paper back? You held Mom out there [Grand Island, Nebraska] waiting, paying hotel bills, and finally she had to come home, or go broke," she wrote. "What was the matter?"

Lillian and Bill's acrimonious negotiation of the Nebraska land sale continued to dominate their letter writing. On July 8th Lillian informed him that the attempted land sale had never closed, so she had only succeeded in correcting the title; however, she did not begrudge him having received his $200: "I have never in all these years played a trick on you at any time, and have always, in every way, been fair and honorable," she assured him. Her plan now was to pay off her debt to her family and recoup Bill's $200 by selling the other piece of her inherited land—an arid parcel in western Nebraska that had been for sale for years and was a tax drain on the family. Anxious to settle her debts, she asked Bill to write her "at once, if you are still living at the La Salle Hotel," so they could send him a quitclaim deed for the second property to sign immediately.

On July 12th Bill wrote that he had thought that the land sale business was settled; he would need more information about the new land sale before he would sign a second quitclaim deed. Lillian explained that after the sale of the arid land she would receive about $1,000, which was the amount of her current debts, so there is "not a penny in it for you naturally." On July 21st Bill heatedly replied that he would sign the quitclaim deed but with a significant condition. Greatly offended by the line in Lillian's letter—"There's not a PENNY in it for you NATURALLY"—he adamantly defended his right to a percentage of the $1,000 legacy. He repeatedly emphasized that he had spent about sixteen years of his early married life, which were his "MOST PRODUCTIVE YEARS," supporting two people who were on the "'receiving end' of his earnings. Also, if he had "no interest" in these land sales, she would not "NEED" his signature, so her accusation that he had no interest was "a poor way of showing your hand, when you used up your full shares of the two legacies left me." On August 16th he was surprised when two days later Lillian informed him that the second Nebraska land sale had been cancelled, since the prospective buyer did not have enough money and her sisters refused to take any mortgage. Although the subject of the land sale was never discussed again, it had significantly fueled the ongoing tense dialogue between Lillian and Bill since 1927 over money matters.

Lillian believed that the entertainment industry was "at its lowest ebb" in August 1948. Although theatre was "dead as a door nail at present," she wrote, a producer wanted Jeanne to head a small show playing big hotels. Their employment woes were compounded by a recent flood in their room at the Belvedere Hotel. About everything they owned was ruined, including shoes, clothes, piece goods, costumes, toe shoes, and suitcases. Fortunately, they had taken pictures of all the damaged costumes, and having immediately contacted a lawyer, they hoped for a quick settlement and wanted to avoid any court charges. Bill could empathize with their recent misfortune, since he had also had a flood in his room at the La Salle Hotel about the same time.

During these final months of 1948 the family letters, continuing to diminish in quantity and length and now often only short notes, became even more impersonal and disinterested. Since Bill did not have a "route list," he took his chances in sending them any correspondence. On September 14th he thanked them for the nice lounging robe they had sent him, making his usual sarcastic quip that he would add this one to his collection of robes that they had sent him over the years. He noticed that the return address on their package was Chicago's Edgewater Beach Hotel, indicating that Jeanne must have a booking there on her hotel tour. He was not writing much except to thank them for the present, hoping "that things will go to your satisfaction, in any new venture that you may be indulging in. Anyway lets hear from you with anything of mutual interest, that you have to offer." Still remembering that her birthday was on Halloween, although he usually got the date wrong, he wrote briefly on October 29th that he had just sent her a birthday package. For the first time in all their correspondence for over two decades on November 7th Jeanne corrected her father about her birthday: "P.S. Haloween is Oct 31st/not 30th."

Once again Jeanne and Lillian were back in New York spending long days pounding the pavement looking first for adequate housing and then for bookings. They finally returned to the affordable Hotel Belvedere, which was so well-located that they could walk to their appointments, averaging close to four miles a day. Since the insurance company had only offered them $500 for their flood-damaged goods that were probably worth a couple of thousand dollars, they were forced to sue: "Heaven knows where the witnesses or we will be by the time the court gets around to our case." In addition to all the time-consuming tasks required to deal with the insurance company, as well as working to find bookings, they had been busy making new hats from morning until night.

Bill's letters were now much briefer than usual and were filled almost exclusively with small domestic details and requests to hear from them more often. On November 16th he described how in order to save money he went to the market a few times a week, and then prepared meals for himself and his elderly roommate in his room. On December 3rd he wondered if Jeanne wanted those couple dozen postcards with the old photographs for her advertising. Obviously looking forward to the coming year, he described a calendar for 1949 that he planned to hang on the wall in his room. Although there was no specific hint that he was suffering from a terminal illness, in this December letter he offered them his Christmas mailing list of sixteen to eighteen people, adding that "you may wish to have a little list of those you may wish to notify, in case of my death, as, of course, it is just a question of not 'if I die' but 'when I die' so let me know whether you want same," he wrote.

Bill's final letter to his family on December 27th was devoted to his favorite topic of gift giving, which had been a large part of the family dynamic for over two decades. Having not received a letter from them since November, he thanked them for their Christmas card and box of candy. Their Christmas gift this year from him had been some shelled Texas pecans. He had also added a few newspapers and a little holiday ornament that they could give to one of their elevator operators at the Belvedere if they did not want it. He reported that he had sent his New Year's cards to his "usual list," and that he had "quite a lot more to write about, but not this evening." Then on January 15th of the following year he passed away.

After being notified of Bill's death, Jeanne and Lillian took the first train from New York to St. Louis. There was no public funeral, since Bill had no other living family but them, and Jeanne was relieved that the family funeral had occurred in between her professional engagements. When Lillian applied in February 1949 to the Social Security Administration regarding her claim to benefits based on the wages of William D. Helman, she received a letter informing her that she was not entitled to any payment since Bill's wages were not fully or currently insured. He had primarily worked over the years as an independent contractor, not as an employee, and had neglected to pay any social security taxes. When the will was probated in April 1949, Bill left an estate comprised of postal savings notes, a U.S. savings bond, a commission check for $293.97 from the American Falcon Manufacturing Corporation, and a shotgun worth $30. According to the Administrator, when his will was probated and after his debts were paid, Lillian and Jeanne both would receive the sum of $1,044.30; Lillian also would receive $1,600 as a "Widows Allowance and Absolue property, as per order of court." They also finally retrieved the remaining family heirlooms that Bill had managed to store since 1927—the china, silver, and other sentimental valuables that Jeanne so passionately wanted for posterity.

Jeanne eventually gave her good friend and fellow dancer Jimmy Givens her father's prized watch, who often used it in the dance studios on the ships where he would be working. She claimed that Bill's elderly roommate at the La Salle Hotel had stolen her father's beautiful diamond stickpin right after his death. Bill had been a collector of valuable antique coins, and when his estate was probated, Jeanne and her mother went to see the attorney, who informed them that Bill's billfold had contained only a few dollar bills and some coins, duping them to think that this money was just out-of-pocket change. Thus, Jeanne and her mother waived their rights to it, only later to learn that the coins were from his valuable antique coin collection.

Jeanne had never visited her father in that St. Louis La Salle Hotel room that he had shared with his aged companion from the Y. In a later interview she said that she naturally mourned his death but really did not miss him, for she had been on the road for twenty-six years and had rarely been in his presence since she was fourteen years old. She had written him so often, because she felt sad for him being in St. Louis all alone: "He was such a smart, amusing man, a wonderful conversationalist with a terrific sense of humor. It was a tragedy." Although she emphasized that the few times she had seen him over the years he "always seemed wonderful," she knew that the times in between visits had been tough. Later after she had been happily married Jeanne admitted that her father could have been bi-polar, but he was never officially diagnosed because Freudian psychology was not as popular in his time as it is today. Neither

Jeanne nor her mother ever knew the exact cause of his death, or had ever suspected that he was terminally ill during that last year of his life; Lillian left no written record of her feelings about losing her husband after so many years living apart. The only real legacy Bill left them were the family letters that he had so faithfully typed up and diligently sent back to them for safe keeping. It is in these family letters where Bill inscribed his love for his family, his fears and insecurities, his loneliness and pettiness, his resentments and disappointments, and his determined and often humorous struggle to remain emotionally stable so he could survive the perils of everyday living. Ultimately unable to accept and understand her father's mental illness and limitations, throughout her long life Jeanne perpetuated her childlike myth of him as a Renaissance man—her intellectual muse with whom she had engaged in a long epistolary dance until the curtain finally fell on him. So similar to him in appearance and personality, Jeanne often referred to her father's many talents and personal tragedy in her remaining years. She always prominently recorded his birthday in her calendar journal entries from 1993 to 2008.

With the family past now fading into memory, Jeanne and Lillian again focused all their time and energy on getting work. Lillian had correctly predicted in her July 8, 1948, letter that "television is in its infancy, but will probably revolutionize the show business." Jeanne had already made her successful European television debut in London in 1935, and now she was on the verge of débuting on American television. According to Andrew Lee Fielding in *The Lucky Strike Papers*, a Gallop poll published in June 1949 revealed that only 44 percent of the American population had ever watched a television program, and many people still did not own a television set and visited local department stores like Macy's and local bars to watch their favorite shows.[2] Television was gaining in popularity, however: approximately one million television sets were sold at the beginning of 1949, with another three million sold by the end of the year. Most of the programs were performed live from New York studios and broadcast on the existing four television networks. By 1951 programming was available to the entire country via cable when direct television from coast to coast was inaugurated on September 4th. Vaudevillians, like Milton Berle, Sid Caesar, Imogene Coco, and Groucho Marx, were the first television stars, and the early intimate television dramas and variety shows had more affinity with the live Broadway stage than with Hollywood cinema.

In May 1949 Jeanne was booked by the William Morris Agency to appear on television in the *Texaco Star Theatre* comedy variety show, which had premiered as a television show on June 8, 1948, and was hosted by Milton Berle, affectionately known to later television audiences as "Uncle Miltie." In Berle's personal interview in the 1970s included in Bill Smith's *The Vaudevillians*, the comedian described his new television show as the result of his deep roots in vaudeville: "It was a vaudeville show. That's the way it was billed—*The Texaco Star Theater Vaudeville Show*—on circulars we gave out to the studio audiences."[3] The public still craving variety, Andrew Lee Fielding reported that at "the end of 1949 ... TV's most popular program was Milton Berle's *Texaco Star Theatre*. Other popular shows at the time [were] *Arthur Godfrey's Talent Scouts*, *The Goldbergs*, and Ed Sullivan's *Toast of the Town*."[4] Telecast live from a studio in New York, the *Texaco Star Theatre* eventually became the most popular show in the history of television, running from 1948 to 1956. In 1953, changing sponsors, it became known as *The Buick-Berle Show*; a year later it was called *The Milton Berle Show*.

Jeanne appeared on the *Texaco Star Theatre* show on May 17, 1949, and her contract, which was sent to her at the Belvedere Hotel, stipulated that she would be compensated $100. She would supply all her music; would attend all necessary rehearsals; would not perform on any other television show for eight days following her appearance; and would guarantee that she had not appeared on any television show for three months prior to the date of their engagement. For her dance number Jeanne impersonated the famous dancer and singer Marilyn Miller, who had trademark blonde tresses and had been a big star on Broadway in the *Ziegfeld Follies* in the 1920s and the star of Ziegfeld's blockbuster musical comedy *Sally*. Having investigated the cost of purchasing a blonde wig, Lillian, in her characteristically frugal fashion, decided that it would be more economical to just bleach Jeanne's dark hair for the performance, and Jeanne continued to be a blonde for many years. At the end of the show when the cameraman pointed the cameras at each star's face as they signed off, the stars were instructed to look straight into the camera and hold their smile. Although performers like Jeanne, used to stage productions, when dancing live in front of a television camera usually felt some tension and anxiety, her American television début was flawless.

Whenever Jeanne heard or said the name "Milton Berle" she giggled. Jeanne had worked several times in vaudeville with Berle. Since the number of acts in a vaudeville bill usually were determined by the size of the theatre, in the 1930s, when she and Berle were stars in vaudeville, they shared a billing at a small, vaudeville theatre in New York, located at 81st and Broadway, with only three acts on the program: Red Donahue and his Mule, Milton Berle, and Jeanne Devereaux and Company. After the first matinee on opening day Jeanne remembered hearing Berle talking on the pay phone next to her dressing room, furiously reprimanding his booking agent at the William Morris Agency for misleading him about his star billing: "You promised me that I'd be next to closing, the choice spot on the bill. Now I'm in the deuce spot." After a short pause, she heard him say "Huh! I am in the deuce spot and next to closing. There's only three acts!" She also remembered Milton's mother, another "stage mother," whom she first met when riding in the same car on a train returning back to New York from a vaudeville tour. The legendary Mrs. Berle was famous for her hearty laughter when her son was performing, and she believed that if she sat out in front as a member of the audience and laughed loudly, her son would be even more successful than he already was. In Berle's tongue-in-cheek column in *Variety,* July 8, 1942, titled "The Berle-ing Point," he joked that his "mother got so hoarse from laughing through four shows a day," at New York's Loew's State where he was headlining that "she had to go out and get her voice retreaded."

After her television appearance and into the early 1950s live show business continued to be tough and jobs scarce. Jeanne and Lillian migrated between living on and off with relatives in Pasadena and their apartment at the Belvedere Hotel in New York. On January 19, 1950, Jeanne signed an exclusive contract with the agent Herman Friedman for all her future appearances on television and in "kinescope film and general motion picture activity." Jeanne had recently tried her hand at writing an autobiographical movie script and had been marketing it for months. The script featured two distinct images of professional women dancers based on a wager by a well-known agent and a concert manager as to whether talent or glamour make a star. After attending a concert featuring a balloon dance to the music of "Clair de Lune," a saucy French can-can, an Afro-Voodoo dance, and a classical ballet with spectacular arabesques and pirouettes that was the obvious crowd-pleaser, the agent and manager agreed that all the glamour and publicity in the world could never trump amazing dancing talent; however, to be a star, talent needed enhancement to be sensational. There is no evidence that Jeanne's movie script was ever produced.

As this final year of the decade of the forties drew to a close, Jeanne sensed that a significant phase of her life was coming to a natural end with a new one just on the horizon. Approaching forty years of age and with some hard-earned savings and her father's inheritance providing financial security for a couple of years, she had the luxury for the first time in her life to relax and consider the possibility of marriage. Sometime in the late fall of 1949 while living in Pasadena with her Aunt Lenore Jeanne called handsome Tom Perkins, now an engineer at the William Miller Corporation, and asked him if he were still single. Since Tom had not been financially able to consider any serious relationships with the opposite sex leading to marriage during the Great Depression years and World War II, he was still an eligible bachelor, so they started dating, enjoying romantic shopping trips from Pasadena to fashionable Beverly Hills. When Jeanne was visiting Pasadena again in the summer of 1950, they decided to get engaged and be married in the fall of the following year. Reflecting back on their final courtship days in Pasadena that year, Jeanne wrote to Tom a year later on July 23rd: "Darling I am so glad that we were in Calif. long enough so that I could get to know you in a different way than I ever did before, and grow to love you because I needed someone worth loving, to love. Everybody does but they don't quest long enough and settle for someone other than Their Love." It was during that summer and fall in 1950, as Tom later wrote his half-brother Basil on February 5, 1953, "we finally lost ourselves to each other completely."

Although deeply in love, they still faced some challenges in their relationship. Since Tom needed to save money for their marriage, they agreed that Jeanne would spend the rest of the year in New York making her final attempt at earning a living from her dancing career, as well as becoming a student of ethnic and character dance to prepare for her career as a teacher. Difficult as it would be, they could endure a year's separation to lay a solid financial foundation for the rest of their lives as a married couple. Jeanne also wanted more time to adjust to the reality that New York, with all its glamour, art, culture, and her theatrical friends, would no longer be at the center of her life, and she still had reservations about moving permanently to smoggy, arid, pedestrian Pasadena, where Tom's roots were deep and his job secure. Given their preference for different living environments after marriage, Jeanne needed this final year in New York to do some soul searching and confidently prepare herself for her future as Tom's wife.

17

Final Year in New York

Jeanne, unlike stars who eventually fall into oblivion, kept shining brightly as she re-created herself for life after marriage. All of Jeanne's future plans—her hopes, dreams, frustrations, and disappointments—are documented in a series of personal letters that she wrote her fiancé Tom Perkins during her final year of living with her mother in New York from June 1951 to June 1952. Once again, as she had with her father, she engaged in an epistolary dance with her beloved Tom, to feel emotionally connected as family despite their living on opposites coasts during their engagement. Jeanne and Tom had agreed from the beginning of their courtship to be totally honest with each other, aspiring to be a liberated modern couple engaged in an equal partnership.

Although Jeanne and Tom had planned to be married in the fall of 1951, financial difficulties delayed their marriage. Jeanne's final year in New York would be different than the ones before, for she was recovering from a foot injury and had some money to live on. On July 13, 1951, Jeanne described for Tom her new sense of personal freedom: "Can you put yourself in our place and realize how utterly, devinely, soul soaringly luxurious it is to read late, sleep late, read in the bath, come and go as we wish, and to answer to on one. We are FREE!!!!! We can listen to our favorite programs and listen to soothing music whenever we like. S'wonderful!!! ... Our liberty goes on but the time will get hectic."

Tom Perkins—handsome, charming, and highly intelligent—came from a family of engineers. He was born in Salt Lake City, Utah, on March 15, 1913, to an Irish mother and a father who was the brother of the feminist writer and lecturer Charlotte Perkins Gilman. Although Tom had a half-brother twenty-three years his senior named Basil who was also an engineer, he rarely saw him, and like Jeanne, Tom grew up as an only child and was primarily self-educated, having been forced by economic reasons to drop out of the middle of the eleventh grade. Tom spent his first ten years living in Idaho before moving to Pasadena in 1923. He began working in 1939 as an engineer for the instrument manufacturing company the William Miller Corporation, where he stayed until 1960 when he became an independent contractor with Cal Tech's Jet Propulsion Laboratory working for a year on the 1969 Mars flyby. He then started his own business called "Perkins Development Engineering," which included designing and constructing museum cases, exhibits, special scientific instruments, and equipment for medical and aerospace researchers, where he worked until his retirement in 1985. During the war years he had had a deferment because he was involved with a highly secret project involving instrumentation for aircraft for the William Miller Corporation.

After first meeting Jeanne in 1933, Tom had dated other girls over the years, but no other girl seemed very interesting to him. Although he emphasized in an interview that he had not spend those twenty years always pining for Jeanne, for he was far too busy doing his creative, complicated work, it is difficult to believe that Jeanne was ever far from his mind. Tom wrote his half-brother Basil on February 5, 1953, shortly after he and Jeanne were married, that he had always had an enduring attraction to Jeanne: "It seems a little late in the day to forsake single blessedness, but I've known Jeanne for many years, and have developed an inclination to marry her every time I saw her, which hasn't been very often, usually several years between meetings." Before he married her, he had seen her dance only once in Hollywood until she was teaching in her ballet school, and he thought her better than most of the celebrated Russian ballerinas. In that same letter to Basil he boasted that Jeanne "has been in the theatre all her life, one of the eight or ten best ballerinas in the world, so she never stayed home very long at a time."

Jeanne's letters to Tom beginning in June 1951 and ending on her last transcontinental trip across America in June a year later en route to Pasadena are love letters between an engaged couple. Jeanne reveals her feelings about being an artist, her fears about losing her identity when she retired from performing, her desire to express herself professionally even as a married woman, her need for stimulating and intelligent conversation, her passion for nature, her excitement about finding an affordable way to furnish a new home with the exquisite objects she had long admired in shop windows, quaint antique shops, and glossy magazines, her constant quest for beauty in all of its forms, and her enduring love for Tom. She only mentions her father once in these letters to Tom, filling them instead with vivid descriptions of her immersion in New York's vibrant, diverse neighborhoods and show business culture.

After bidding a tearful farewell to her beloved Tom, Jeanne left Pasadena with her mother for New York on June 20, 1951, in Aunt Lenore's Ford loaded with their precious cargo. They reached St. Louis by the end of the month. The floods of June and July 1951 in the Lower Missouri River valley were the greatest in that region for over a hundred years, so Jeanne and Lillian were delayed for a week after arriving in their former hometown. In a July 1st postcard Jeanne was understandably nostalgic during this short six-day visit in St. Louis, writing Tom that every time she heard "a Bob White Call across the meadow," she expected "to see my father come into sight." To avoid passing through St. Louis "like strangers in our native land," they attended the operettas at the Muny with a friend of a former ballet classmate of Jeanne's and his cousin Angel from Spain. One night she went dancing with Angel and their Paso Doble, a dance that Jeanne had never done before, and now with Angel teaching her, brought loud applause from the audience.

In spite of all this socializing, however, on July 5th Jeanne wrote Tom how terribly she missed him and how postcards—her only vehicle now for "imagined conversations"—were inadequate to express her elusive thoughts and strong emotions. Suddenly her life had meaning only in their shared moments together: "All my life I have looked over each new hill with excited interest wondering what new & delightful bits of life were waiting for me to see & make into rich memories. Now for the first time I am looking back and my thoughts go streaming back to you like a banner in the breeze," she wrote.

17 • Final Year in New York

Jeanne and Lillian arrived at dawn on July 8th in New York at the Belvedere Hotel, exhausted and hot from the long drive through Pennsylvania. Jeanne was elated to be back home. They were swamped with messages from their theatre friends like fellow dancer Jimmy Givens, who came over that night to see them and stayed until midnight; they called their good friend Ference Piroska, since he would be leaving for Chicago soon to dance in the fairs. None of Jeanne's friends except Piroska knew that she had fallen in love and was engaged to marry Tom Perkins. Much of their time was taken up with getting settled. Since they knew their way around the hotel, they could get things done quickly: "Permanents who want things clean and nice have to do it themselves," she wrote Tom, "so you see they pay for the privilege of helping the Hotel cut down on Hotel Services." Used to the high humidity of New York summers, they nonchalantly swatted the mosquitoes flying around their hotel room from the open windows.

When Jeanne was not either practicing or taking a dance class, they immersed themselves in their normal New York lifestyle. They window-shopped along New York's most sophisticated avenues and visited their favorite discount book stores, purchasing books on dance. They enjoyed the many inexpensive neighborhood ethnic restaurants, and often on Sunday after reading the *New York Times*, they would visit a favorite museum and then stroll in Central Park and sometimes visit the zoo. Their days and nights were filled with seeing popular and art films, Broadway musical comedies like *The King and I* and dramas like *Streetcar Named Desire*, a few vaudeville shows, and some television, as well as listening to their faithful radio and attending performances by the touring Sadler's Wells Ballet Company.[1]

Radio had been a big part of their life since the 1920s, and they loved listening to the news and filling their hotel room with beautiful music from the radio or their Dynavox phonograph machine. In October they tuned into Barry Gray's early morning radio program with Walter White of the NAACP relating the sensational inside story of the Josephine Baker Stork Club incident. The night before when Baker had ordered dinner in the Stork Club's famous "Cub Room" and had to wait for an hour for her food, she abruptly left with her entourage, claiming that the Stork Club was racist; the NAACP filed a formal complaint against the famous restaurant, but the case eventually was decided in favor of the Stork Club. They were just becoming members of the growing audience for television. They enjoyed watching shows at their friends' hotel rooms and apartments, and since color television was the new invention, they often stopped at the RCA building to see if there were a color television exhibit.

At the few remaining movie presentation houses they saw a vaudeville bill followed by a film. On July 27, 1951, Jeanne wrote that they had gone to the Palace Theatre to see "a very good Vaudeville Bill with several mutual friends appearing." On September 3rd Jeanne described how they had been at the Roxy to see a "grand show—Beautiful costumes, scenes, talent, & a Super 'Must See' picture." In December they enjoyed the revival of big-time two-a-day vaudeville at the Palace with Judy Garland headlining in a production supervised by her manager and later husband Sid Luft. The first half of the bill featured acrobats, dancers, singers, and the old time comedians Smith and Dale, with Judy Garland presenting a solo act in the second half to loud applause and glowing reviews. On December 19, 1951, Jeanne described how the previously closed Palace theatre had "reopened all pristine & refurbished with white walls—gilt trim & scarlet velvet drapes," and how thrilling it was "to see the old theatre ringing with applause for good acts, a marvelous Star—pretty scenery & lights & a real Orchestra," she wrote. "We enjoyed it very much—Judy is really a talented girl & deserves every success—She doesn't bluff & her audience therefore gets that old thrill & tingle of pleasure that just doesn't come up your spine when overpublicised mediocrity tries to fool you with nothing to give." In January of the following year they saw the beautiful, talented Beatrice Kraft at the Roxy perform her jazzy Hindu dancing along with the movie *The Marriage Broker*, starring Thelma Ritter.

Jeanne's dancing career was too early to reap the benefits when the American Ballet Theatre and New York City Ballet Companies emerged in the 1950s into major cultural attractions reaching large American audiences. The only ballet company that she and her mother saw during their final year in New York was the touring Sadler's Wells from England. On December 6, 1951, Jeanne wrote Tom that they had gone to City Center to purchase tickets for performances for both weekend nights. Jeanne wanted Tom to increase his understanding of ballet and what it meant for his future wife to be a "Prima Ballerina" by familiarizing himself with the language of classical ballet. She was eager for him to attend the Sadler's Wells' touring company's performance in Los Angeles, emphasizing that it "should be a delightful experience … with music color & beautiful movement all happily married," she wrote. Although Jeanne felt that the "tired old" Ballet Russe "with its ancient tottering Prima Ballerina Danilova" was inferior to the more dynamic Sadler's Wells, she also wanted Tom to see the Ballets Russes when in Los Angeles, so he would be familiar with their classical repertoire. When they saw the Saddler's Wells' New York production of *Coppelia* in 1952, Jeanne wrote on April 7th that they "were glad that we saw it as we havent ever seen the complete 3 Act Ballet, as excerpts are all that are ever given in America."

Jeanne's dancing was always at the heart of her lifestyle in 1951, so she immediately resumed her daily ballet dance practice to keep in shape and develop her skills. Since she had taken six weeks off for only the second time in her career with their trip to Pasadena, she needed to put in long hours to make up for the time missed. She especially needed to rehearse for her only professional performance that year—a benefit for the Crippled Children in the luxurious ballroom of the Plaza Hotel. Her former dancing partner Billy had arranged for them to dance together in November 1951 at the Plaza. On July 17th she described for Tom her first rehearsal with Billy after a thirteen-month hiatus:

> We started to work without music as I havent had time to plow through the storage trunks for the Dynavox yet and none of the studio machines were any good. We hummed snatches of Swan Lake to ourselves and tried to remember the routine we set. Almost with fear and trembling we started to work and miracle of miracle our bodies and timing were so well tuned that everything went so well we were puffed with pride. We tried the difficult bits and they were smooth as could be, so we looked at each other and without a word went into our most difficult step the long finger-pirouette that we do for the climax of the dance, and did 49 before we finished because I got so dizzy and we were on such perfect balance that we were going too fast for me to see. Ah happy day, happy day!!! Billy and I just gloated, and he said "there is only one thing I have to worry about. Not doing the steps, but getting the endurance to get through them all."

Although Billy had been asked to perform a simple dance with one of his ballroom class teachers, he had insisted on performing with his favorite partner who had just returned to town. On October 25th Jeanne wrote Tom that Billy "underplayed it for all he was worth & is mentally enjoying their pop-eyed amazement when they see the dances in this other field [ballet] that he can do—Isnt life fun!" Jeanne was never happier than when performing, and after practice she and Billy would usually go to the LaSalle Cafeteria to meet their fellow dancers to discuss New York's dance world and exciting cultural scene.

Now approaching forty years old Jeanne could not take her dancer's body for granted, and throughout the year she was plagued with a chronic foot injury. A few days after rehearsing with Billy she injured the arch of her right foot so was unable to rehearse, asking him for the name of a good foot doctor whose specialty was treating dancers. Still plagued by the foot injury, which now required regular visits to a podiatrist and daily soakings in the bathtub, on July 31st Jeanne wrote Tom that by continuing to practice at the studio with Billy she kept repeatedly straining the arch of her foot and had to cancel working out for a week. On September 3rd she informed him with great relief that her foot was much improved, and she could finally "stride with my usual speed again," although she still had to wear a compression stocking when she walked long distances; later in the month she took off the support stocking for the first time so she could put on her black boots for her Russian character classes.

Although her foot continued to hurt until the end of the year, causing her to limp again, Jeanne was accustomed to dancing through pain throughout her career. She saw the podiatrist regularly and still managed to rehearse with Billy and continue her classes. On December 30th she wrote Tom that a specialist masseur well-known to the dancers could keep her in good enough condition with his heat lamp treatments to warm up her icy feet and an hour foot and leg massage. He would also treat her tense back "because a big tendon that turns all the way up thru pelvis & connected with spine or something has been troubling me for years." She searched for a plausible diagnosis for her chronic sore foot, and in early 1952 an X-ray revealed an old injury, but it did not seem adequate to explain the foot pain. By February she was seeing a chiropractor three times a week and the foot was feeling better, but she still was not able to resume her ballet practice until March 12th, when she carefully practiced her relevé on her good foot, not yet putting the sore foot to the test. In her last report at the end of April 1952 before leaving for Pasadena, she stated that her sore foot had slowly improved despite the constant setbacks whenever she over-exerted or when it rained.

Despite the foot injury she continued rehearsing in the fall of 1951 with Billy for the benefit performance on November 2nd at the Plaza Grand Ballroom. On October 24th she described the rehearsals at the Plaza, adjusting to keeping their footing on the slick dancing floor, as well as the costume fittings for the black velvet leotard she would wear for the performance. An all-night rehearsal with the orchestra was scheduled for her birthday on October 31st, and they were "meeting ourselves going in circles—Costumers, rehearsals, Shoe dyers, Music Rehearsals—Chiropractor for a slight twinge in a vertibrate—Make a headress etc. etc. etc," she wrote. On the way to her final rehearsal she opened her birthday gift from Tom, which was a beautiful green silk scarf with gold thread.

On November 5th Jeanne announced that the benefit performance had been "spectacular!" and had been attended by 3,000 beautifully attired women and men, seated on three sides of the huge ballroom with crystal chandeliers "ablaze":

> The show followed an hour of dancing and awarding of diplomas & Medals—We were last and when the Master of Ceremonies announced my name there was such a burst of applause it drowned out the Introduction & I had to watch the Conductor's arm to tell the music had begun. Billy looked wonderful in a Mess Jacket-Cummerbund -tux trowsers—Several times the audience broke into clapping during the dance—The orchestra played so slowly it would have been disasterous if we weren't both old hands at adapting ourselves instantly—We were so elegant we could have taught royalty how it's done—But that is the only way to fill in slow music—We got thru without any feared disasters like slipping on a slick floor—and falling down—During the finger turns at the end when we hit about 20 they started to applaud & it thundered on till we finished amid cheers—They applauded so long we had to take 10 bows & could have gone back for more—It was a real Ovation & repaid us for all the hard work—Afterwards Hundreds of strangers crowded back to tell me how they had enjoyed us & how thrilling the experience had been—One handsome young man said: "I was completely hollow when you finished—It was so beautiful I gave every bit of response in me to the beauty you created." Those things are what repay the artist for the dreary hours of hard work & nervous tension.

Jeanne loved performing in front of an applauding, appreciative audience, and wrote Tom on November 19th that when she later talked with her Russian character class teacher about becoming a dance teacher, they had both lamented having to give up actual performing in front of a live audience and would never be truly happy again "unless there is a good substitute for the mental and emotional stimulation of creating beauty for the world and getting to see the beauty others created for us."

Tom only visited Jeanne once during this final year in New York, but it was a memorable reunion. Jeanne first mentioned the prospect of Tom's visiting her on July 11, 1951, but both her fear of flying and her thought that the $500 in expenses could be used for their future home made her hesitate initially to urge him to take his weeklong vacation across country to visit her. Although Tom had a steady job, he was still struggling to save enough money so they might possibly be married that fall. Since Lillian did not regard the impending marriage "with glee" given Tom's modest finances, Jeanne wrote Tom on July 19th that she had resolved not to tell her mother about the possibility of having to delay their wedding plans. She would focus on the best way to spend her time in New York—dancing professionally to earn money or primarily taking classes to prepare for teaching—until she was certain that they would be financially able to get married: "I don't like to have to write like this but I must be truthful and let you know exactly how important it is that I know where we stand so I don't waste money & time doing one thing when I should be doing the other," Jeanne wrote. She eventually convinced herself that no matter what the cost her darling Tom needed a vacation in New York.

A week later Tom called to report that he would be coming to New York on August 11th. Ecstatic and breathless, on July 27th she replied that she could "trill like a canary" at this good news and will reserve him a room at the Belvedere, although with the itinerary she had planned for them he would not be occupying it often. She was excited about introducing him to her theatre friends, and was consumed with planning their time together. "Darling—I'm just not making sense—Everything I write turns out incoherent when it stares back at me—Surely love is a form of insanity & yet I'd hate to be cured," she wrote. Wanting her handsome Tom to be a dapper dresser, she reminded him that he should only bring his blue suit, gray and tan slacks, and a sports jacket, since they could shop for some new clothes while he was in New York. She would take him to all the obligatory tourist sites they must see together, including in her long list the Palace, the Roxy, and Radio City Music Hall.

Since no letters exist for the period of Tom's visit, one can only presume that Jeanne, with all her energy, creativity, and curiosity, managed to show Tom most of these iconic sites in her adopted hometown. In subsequent letters she referred to their visits to all the famous museums and how they rode the Staten Island ferry for a nickel. They saw the Broadway musicals *Two on the Aisle* and *South Pacific*. After Tom returned home to Pasadena Jeanne wrote in an undated letter how lost she had felt when she waved goodbye to him as his plane took off like a "tiny bird flying west into a clear sky." The next day "life again became daily," and she rested her sore foot to prepare for the week ahead.

On October 24th Jeanne reflected on Tom's recent visit and regretted that she did not have a chance to show Tom "how" they lived their daily life in New York. She was frustrated that despite their deep love for each other they favored different living environments. She wrote that it would have taken weeks in New York for him to have experienced "the feel of the endless variety of outlets for curiosity in every field. Every time she was in California she was only marking time until she returned to New York's artistic world," she wrote, "so to be happy in Pasadena she would need to substitute another form of beauty ... [with] a dear home—flowers—birds & music." She dreaded losing "a delight & feeling of oneness with the people who talk ideas—who paint, create ... the ideas that the rest of the country accept on radio, in newspapers, in magazines, fashion, decoration, cooking—in short almost everything & phase of our life in America first has its birth of creation or production here [New York] & that spirit is abroad." She was just not at heart a domestic woman "who had never achieved anything nor looked higher than dishes, laundry & a husband," so she felt that her leaving New York would be a major personal sacrifice. She reminded him that they both needed to soul search how they could happily blend their lives together.

Jeanne called the many letters that she wrote Tom during her last year in New York her "wailing" letters. She had grandiose plans for her dancing school and tried to persuade Tom to relocate to New York or St. Louis, where she believed there would be more opportunities to have a first-rate school with national attention than in smoggy, drought-ridden Pasadena. She told him about her circus performer friend the aerialist Elly and her husband Eddie, who had just purchased beachfront land in Florida for a housing development. She wished they could also live in a city with clean air and an adequate water supply. "We said before I left any move or change on your part would have to be very well considered, hashed, rehashed & slept on—but I do wish we could be where the air is sweet & the water supply assured," she wrote on July 13th. When Tom replied that he had sent her a positive article on California's water supply, she still wondered how the long-term projects described in this article would solve the immediate problems.

Over the following months Jeanne continued to persuade Tom to re-locate either to New York or St. Louis. Most of her July 23rd letter, however, was devoted to reassuring Tom that her reservations about California were always superseded by her love for her soul mate:

> I want to be with you and once more have our eyes meet with deep understanding and appreciation, or shared glee or bitter irony. Sunday when we walked through Central Park I saw with new vision the "Alone" people who sat on the benches alone with nobody to share their dreams or thoughts with. Just sitting waiting, for what? ... The thought of marriage sometimes frightens me but it is not because I think you aren't the right one. On the contrary to know in my heart that you are my love—a different half of me, and that in this hit and miss world that we should find each other is rather wonderful. Its just that the problems are the outside ones that will be presurring us inside sometimes. Then too that oft discussed difference in invironment and needs for individual expression, will often rear its head and cause misunderstandings but somehow I realize that my love for you can recognize all of these things and still not be altered by them. Darling I wouldn't trade you for anyone I've ever known.... Don't pop your buttons off.... You see I cant express what I want to say when it is about my own inner feelings, but then I never tried to.

All her life Jeanne had been focused on her work and earning a living, but now love had opened her heart.

In her September 8th letter Jeanne admitted that starting a dancing school was a risky business no matter what the geographic location, but she had great confidence in her talent and experience. She knew that the key to getting Tom to re-locate was to overcome his resistance at leaving the Miller Equipment Company and finding another job. However, she also knew that Tom would most likely remain with his company. "Everything beckons & lures except Calif. which I really don't like—and there you are enscounced four square," she wrote on October 4th. Jeanne ended the year on December 31st with a long "wailing" letter in which she asked Tom if he would have to work for Mr. Miller on Saturdays, with no time to pursue inventions, or retail or mail order business ventures, to supplement their income. Throughout the year Jeanne had suggested various inventions and projects with possible commercial appeal for Tom to consider pursuing on his own.

In 1952, Jeanne reiterated that contrary to his opinion, her current interest in opening her dancing school in St. Louis was not a nostalgic "whim to return to the scenes of a happy childhood and old friends." In answer to Tom's emphasis on the importance of his work since he needed to "feed her," she stressed that they were not defined by the menial tasks of daily living but by the quality of their minds shaped by their education and environment. After marriage they would have to support both themselves and their mothers "with a few of the beauties as well as the basic needs." She would continue working not only to fulfill her essential self, but also they would need two incomes to afford the beautiful rose bushes for their home's new landscaping, as well as "that glowing log in the fireplace." Although he felt secure financially at the moment, she wanted to prepare them for all future contingencies, including her being their sole support. Jeanne believed that both the man and woman needed to enter marriage faced with the possibility of role reversals, for she could eventually be as responsible for feeding him as he was for her—a weighty responsibility that she had experienced for her parents, especially her mother, since she was thirteen years old.

Jeanne was at heart an artist and needed to hold on to her dreams: she not only needed to work, she loved to work. She wrote Tom that her ultimate argument for locating in St. Louis was that she loved her art:

> I love dancing. I love shows, and I want to be somewhere where those loves plus all my training and experience can be utilized and not lie fallow until I rust out inside. You see people who have been disciplined by an Art, like work and arent thinking of ways to avoid it. Naturally I don't

mean work for work's sake, I mean the kind that creates something beautiful to give the world, that inspires a new generation to carry on a real Art instead of cynically trying to bluff for financially attractive reasons.

On February 6th she wrote that while he had a right to his desire to stay in Pasadena, and to his fears at starting over, he did not have a right to characterize her life and professional career as "unreal." Only people content with their status quo live their whole life with no dreams or aspirations to grow and better themselves; she has had a unique and extraordinary life very different from ordinary people, because she was an artist and will need to continue being one after marriage. On February 13th she described what she had wanted Tom to say to her in his letters: "I know you are dedicated & trained to giving beauty thru dance & you love it, And I never want you to feel that marriage will chain you or rob you of artistic freedom."

Tom's financial situation began improving over that final year in New York, so instead of looking for professional bookings Jeanne focused most of her time and energy on her ballet practices, ethnic and Russian character dancing classes, sketching and sewing costumes and hats, and purchasing props, to prepare herself for her future as a dance teacher. She had enrolled in classes in tap, ballroom, ethnic dancing like Hindu and Thai, and Russian character folk dancing. Although she had seen the famous Isadora Duncan dance at the Odeon Theatre in St. Louis around 1924–25, modern dance was still unappealing to her, as the dancers had to get down and roll around on dirty floors. After classes Jeanne and her classmates and friends would go to the automats and cafeterias to share ideas about teaching in a world of unscrupulous entrepreneurs starting national chains of dancing schools.

Jeanne knew that to be an excellent teacher she needed to return to the basics. She had learned ballroom dancing automatically by dancing with good partners, but when she would be required to teach young and mature students who might not know their right foot from their left, she needed to understand basic rhythms and dance patterns. Her ethnic Hindu and Russian character dance classes presented new challenges to her ballet trained body. She studied Hindu dance with the celebrated dancer, teacher, and writer Russell Meriwether Hughes, a woman known as La Meri, who had founded in 1940 the School of Natya Ethnologic Dance Theatre. On September 26, 1951, she described her first Hindu class of the six she had pre-paid: the class comprised fourteen dancers equally divided by gender. All the dancers in the class sat cross-legged on the floor and did "hastas," the elaborate hand gestures in Indian classical dance, followed by a half-hour coordinating the hand movements to the traditional Asian semi-squat positions. Since her muscles had been used to many years of ballet training, she was sore from head to toe, groaning even when doing the knee bends and having to cancel her Russian character class that afternoon because of sore knees. On September 30th she explained that Hindu dancing did not require "the terrific coordination & strength" of ballet and "character," so the instructor was very pleased to have a ballerina like Jeanne in the class, since she "will make every effort to relay the mental picture into physical exactness." Totally enamored by exotic Indian dance, she would often put on her Hindu ankle bells and finger cymbals and chime around her hotel room.

After her second Hindu class she was able to attend her first Russian character class, describing how she had danced with the instructor, who had ignored the rest of the class while they entertained all the curious spectators:

> I danced Mazurkas & Chardas until I was scarlet & BW. [Lillian] Looking in the door thought I had apoplexy!—So few people know how to draw true correct body lines, & let The proper feeling show even in a shrug that the door was jammed with watchers, & the teacher & I almost got applause as we worked—When I came out they parted & let me pass through staring as if I were royalty—It was fun alth' I was perspiring so I couldn't dress for ¼ hour & my face didn't fade out for an hour—each leg felt as if I were dragging a hundred lb. ball & chain when I went downstairs.

This was the first day that she had taken off her foot support to dance, since she needed to fit her foot into the black boots. She regretted that her foot had been injured during Tom's visit, for she would have loved for him to have seen her dance in her boots in these spirited character classes, so he could have experienced "a different phase of the Art." In December she had a new pair of comfortable Russian boots made—red leather with a white leather lining and cuff—to last her for many years as a dance teacher.

After her fourth Hindu class, wrote Jeanne on October 10th, "the Teacher came up to me afterwards & said I should specialize as I have a great feeling for it!!! It tickled me because he has the reputation of being tart as a lemon." By the seventh lesson with a new teacher she had totally overcome her initial intimidation and was now leading the class, with the more experienced Hindu dancers watching her every move. She had to miss her Hindu class at the end of the month because of the benefit performance at the Plaza Grand Ballroom and sometimes other classes because of the recurring foot injury. By December her schedule was tighter than ever, filled with taking and viewing classes at various studios. On February 2, 1952, she wrote Tom about how her strong work ethic and love for dance had helped her make significant progress with her Hindu dance classes to the point that she had already become a teacher, for she had faithfully practiced every day to master the basic training.

Jeanne also spent an inordinate amount of time sketching and getting photocopies of ethnic costumes, musical instruments, stage settings, and dance poses and purchasing dance books that she would need for her dancing school. She went to decorators' supply stores to sketch baskets used for primitive dances. She traced by hand the 200 Indian "hastas" and full figure poses from the dance book that she had borrowed from fellow dancer Jimmy Givens. On April 29, 1952, she wrote Tom about having spent two days in the library copying some dance poses in a rare Swedish book with color plates of the "Temple Dance of Bali," and by mid–May she had completed copying the Bali pictures. Also in May she purchased an illustrated book of Indian love poems called "The Garden of Kama," to inspire future dances for her students.

For most of the year Jeanne and Lillian were busy making ethnic costumes. The year before they had purchased seven yards of percale to make either an Indian sari or the pants styled dhoti, and went down to Greenwich Village to have a woman fit a choli or Indian bodice pattern for Jeanne's costume. On April 29, 1952, she described for Tom how they had sewed gold thread around the twenty yards of hem of her new sari, although she preferred the dhoti for dancing since it revealed "the line of the body better." She bought a pair of the little slippers that Japanese girls wear with their best kimonos: "If I want to do a dance sometime at a recital in my kimono I need them," she wrote him on May 14, 1952. She also bought a dancer's fan at the same Japanese Shop, which had the sticks spaced far apart so that the fingers could be inserted to twirl the fan.

Jeanne spent long hours acquiring authentic music for her dances. She purchased dance records, especially for the ethnic Hindu and Russian character dances. Her Hindu classes had been accompanied only by native drums, and she was thrilled that she now had recordings of the reedy wailings of true Indian music. Once she moved from New York it would be difficult to find authentic records for oriental dance, and since people today have access to wonderful dance books and authentic music, a good teacher needs to be well equipped.

In mid–October 1951 Jeanne and Lillian began the arduous process of sorting through their storage trunks in the dark, damp hotel basement to decide what to bring to Pasadena. Standing on her injured foot for hours in the basement sorting and packing made it worse, but their departure date for Pasadena was looming and the packing needed to be completed. On June 15, 1952, in her last "wailing wall" letter to Tom Jeanne described how they had to write tags for all the eighteen boxes, cases, and trunks to be hauled by truck to Pasadena, including all the boxes they were taking in their car. Since they would not able to "ship the tape recorder, phonograph, silver, records, [and] glassware," they would be heavily loaded in their reliable old Ford.

Both the gas shortage and extensive flooding in the Midwest that spring delayed the trip to Pasadena until late June, a delay that had pleased Jeanne since she wanted to finish her Thai dance course at the end of May and complete the stick figure drawings of the ethnic Hindu and Russian character dances in her teaching notebook before heading west. She hated the thought of leaving New York and dreaded the quick ten-day trip to California to be there when the moving truck arrived at Aunt Lenore's house. She wrote Tom on June 19th that her "Chinese Coolie hat" was making "its 5th transAmerican trip. I tilt it against sun & wind & endure the hair snagging for the protection."

A few days later Lillian and Jeanne finally loaded up their old Ford for their final trip across country to Pasadena. They averaged about 300 miles per day; they spent only one night in St. Louis, and "didn't call any one or look around," Jeanne wrote Tom on June 24th. The next morning they had nostalgically stopped "at our old summer cabin site. The Trees, giant green Monarhs [sic], & wonderful grass just thrilled us anew!" Then they came across Kansas during the summer heat, got back on Route 66 at Tucumcari, stopped at trading posts along the way, and admired the Indian jewelry in Albuquerque. They arrived in Pasadena at Aunt Lenore's house exactly ten days after their departure, using her garage as a temporary storage depot.

18

Marriage and Four More Careers

Before returning to New York in 1951 Jeanne and Lillian had toured a large, American Craftsman house at 897 North Holliston Avenue in Pasadena for sale, and then suggested to Tom that he inspect it immediately. The house was soon taken off the market for a year, and a few months before their wedding Tom fulfilled Jeanne's lifelong passion for a family home by purchasing the grand house on Holliston. Now Jeanne had a permanent place where she could display beautiful objects that dazzled her talented collector's eye, and from that moment on she and Tom furnished their dream home in Pasadena with purchases from estate sales. Within weeks after marriage she officially opened her dancing school.

Still sporting her glamorous blonde tresses from the Milton Berle television appearance and wearing a practical hunter green silk dress, Jeanne married Tom on November 6, 1952, in a Pasadena Judge's chambers, followed by a dinner at a fancy restaurant.[1] The announcement in the *Pasadena Star-News* on November 7th, titled "Jeanne Devereaux Weds Here," emphasized that the bride was an "internationally-known ballerina" who had performed at Radio City Music Hall and in two command performances before royalty. Jeanne explained in an interview that since she had spent her entire life wearing beautiful, expensive costumes and had only a few friends in the Los Angeles area, her wedding did not need to be "a big, white dress event," so she chose a dress that she could wear more than once. They moved immediately into their new American Craftsman home. None of Jeanne's fellow troupers in New York except Firenze Piroska knew that she was married. When Jimmy Givens and the Sullivan twins received her wedding announcement a few days after the ceremony, the news came as a "thunderbolt," and they told her that Tom must always share her with her old friends from her performing days.

Jeanne's close friend Cath Esler, the Australian dancer with whom Jeanne had toured the provinces in England in *George Ahoy!*, was her maid of honor. Now living on Wilshire Boulevard in Los Angeles, Cath was looking for work in the movie business. Among the other guests attending the wedding dinner at "The Stuffed Shirt," chosen by Lillian and located on Pasadena's tree-lined Green Street, were Lillian and her two remaining sisters Ida and Lenore, various cousins, Helen Lewis' mother from St. Louis, and the movie actress Ida Moore, who lived in a hotel on Highland street north of Hollywood Boulevard and who maintained a close friendship with Jeanne and Lillian until

Jeanne Devereaux Perkins and Tom Perkins cutting the cake at their wedding dinner reception in Pasadena, California, November 6, 1952. In 1949 Jeanne had dyed her hair blonde for her television performance on Milton Berle's *Texaco Star Theatre*, and continued to be a blonde until she closed her dancing school in Pasadena in 1964. Eschewing an expensive white wedding dress since she had worn so many elaborate costumes during her dancing career, Jeanne chose a modest hunter green silk dress for her wedding. Jeanne and Tom knew each other for over twenty years before their marriage. Courtesy Jeanne Devereaux Perkins Collection.

Jeanne and Tom's American Craftsman house at 897 North Holliston Avenue in Pasadena, California. After retiring from her dancing career and marrying Tom, Jeanne finally had the dream house that she had longed for since age thirteen when she started her career on the vaudeville circuits. Built ca. 1910 by real estate developer Guy Bliss, it was the largest and one of the most expensive houses in Pasadena's oldest official historic neighborhood Bungalow Heaven. Courtesy Archives, Pasadena Museum of History, Flagg Collection (1909–40) 3-49-361.

her death in 1964. Jeanne and Tom meticulously planned the seating chart for the guests attending their wedding dinner, and Jeanne, with an impish gleam in her eye, described how she and Tom sat "sourpusses" next to "jolly people." The head waiter, however, mixed-up the seating plan and sat all the "sourpusses" at one end of the table and the "jolly people" at the other. Jeanne and Tom laughed about this mix-up ever after.

"Of course Lillian wasn't too keen on Jeanne marrying," said Tom, for "she had been Lillian's sole source of support for most of her married life, so having Jeanne marry was obviously very threatening for her." Fortunately, Tom Perkins welcomed both Jeanne and her mother into his life, and they lived together for the rest of their lives in Pasadena in their spacious American Craftsman house. A few months after his marriage Tom wrote to his half-brother Basil on February 5, 1953, that Jeanne and he "both feel pleased & smug about the whole thing [falling in love and getting married] and are ridiculously happy." Unlike her parents, Jeanne and Tom had an extremely affectionate relationship that pleased both of them and made them very close.

Now that Jeanne was married, she became more assertive when she felt exploited by anyone, including her mother. Though Lillian had a bossy temperament, Jeanne was used to working with her as a team. Tom, on the other hand, seeing how Lillian could manipulate Jeanne, sometimes thought of asking his mother-in-law to move, but he had promised Jeanne that he would not raise an uproar about Lillian's overbearing, possessive personality: "At times it was hard not to get mad at Lillian, but I kept my promise," said Tom. The only direct confrontation Jeanne remembered ever having with her mother after her marriage was one time, when they were standing by the kitchen sink and Lillian was bossing her, she became angry and reprimanded her mother: "Look, you were married at twenty-six and you thought you knew enough to be married and take care of a family; I have waited to get married until I was forty, and I do know that I am old enough to do exactly as I want to do." Jeanne's former student and close friend, Patrick Purdy, however, remembered various spats Jeanne had with her strong-willed mother. They would both pout, eventually make-up, and all would be forgiven.

Delicious food being a high priority in the Perkins' household in Pasadena, Tom was now the main beneficiary of Jeanne's culinary skills. Jeanne remembered what a good cook her mother had been both during her childhood in St. Louis and her professional years on the road whenever they had access to a sink and stove. Although from the time she was thirteen until forty she had spent most of her time living in hotels, Jeanne also loved to cook, but to maintain her slim ballerina figure, she had to monitor her eating carefully. She had never eaten breakfast and during her performing days—days of fast pirouettes and back bends—she ate very sparingly. "You didn't want to have much food in your stomach when dancing," Jeanne said. She remembered nights in New York when she and her mother would often go out about midnight with other cast members for a bite to eat after the show.

Jeanne was proud of Tom's blood relationship to the famous Perkins/Beecher family, which indirectly related her to two amazing, unconventional women. His great-great-aunt Harriet Beecher Stowe, who hailed from a Connecticut family dedicated to reforming America's gilded but "corrupt" nineteenth-century society, was the author of the best-selling, anti-slavery novel *Uncle Tom's Cabin*, published in 1852. His aunt was the radical thinker Charlotte Perkins Gilman, a famous writer, social critic, and world-renowned lecturer in the early twentieth century, who wrote the feminist classic novel *The Yellow Wallpaper*, which depicted her "traditional rest cure" in an isolated room to clear her mind of all career thoughts after a bout of depression. Tom inherited his aunt's autographed books from his father along with all but one issue of Charlotte's radical monthly periodical *The Forerunner* (1909–16) that validated the monetary value of women's work both inside and outside of the home.[2]

When Jeanne was diagnosed with breast cancer in 1984 she opted for a cure—a double mastectomy and the removal of seventeen lymph nodes, followed by chemotherapy and radiation treatments—remaining cancer-free ever after. While recovering from the surgery Jeanne took her first and last airplane trip since the USO Camp Shows tour in 1945, accompanying Tom to Hartford, Connecticut, for a Stowe family reunion, which was held on the lawn in front of the big Victorian Gothic cottage style house on Forest Street known as the Stowe house, located directly behind the famous Mark Twain house.

Jeanne and Tom were inseparable after marriage. Tom's quiet strength and orderly intelligence complemented Jeanne's more theatrical, romantic personality. Her aggressive, business savvy stimulated stable Tom to think more creatively and entrepreneurially.

Spacious living room of Jeanne and Tom's American Craftsman house at 897 North Holliston Avenue in Pasadena, California, decorated with antique treasures from the Los Angeles area estate sales, January 1966. Jeanne's artistic taste formed by visiting hundreds of museums and reading decorative arts books during her dancing career created the elegant décor of her special home. She was informally qualified to be a professional appraiser of fine antiques and oriental rugs. Photograph by Fred Murphy, who was the best friend and later brother-in-law of Pat Purdy, one of Jeanne's favorite dance students and good friends. Courtesy Pat Purdy.

They both had a sophisticated and often childlike wit that charmed their family and friends. They loved filling their Pasadena home with beautiful objects acquired at the local estate sales and maintained a close circle of stimulating and entertaining friends. They continued their lively debates over the controversial public issues of the day. They delighted in nature's flora and fauna, maintaining a beautiful garden on the grounds of their home and adoring the cats that shared their home. Jeanne grew to love Pasadena's arid Mediterranean climate, with its smoggy air virtually cleaned up by the 1980s.

The Perkins' dream home, built in the American Craftsman style popularized by the Pasadena architects Charles and Henry Green, who in 1906 designed and built the famous Gamble House following the architectural principles of William Morris' arts and crafts movement and Japanese design, was built ca. 1910 by real estate designer Guy Stanley Bliss. It is one of the largest houses in Pasadena's oldest historic neighborhood called "Bungalow Heaven."[3] On February 5, 1953, Tom had written to his half-brother Basil: "We have bought us a great big old house, I guess about 3,000 sq. ft. of it, on an 80 × 208 lot, of which we are very proud & are having no end of fun & hard work fixing up." It had eleven rooms, an exquisite eighteen by thirty-eight living room; both the upstairs and downstairs had wonderful maple hardwood floors. "Its one of those California type things, with five foot eaves & shingle siding.... We are tickled to death with it," Tom wrote. Alida Cervera, a former ballet student of Jeanne's in the mid-50s to the early 1960s, remembered when Jeanne invited all her dance students to a Christmas party at her "fabulous" American Craftsman home: "I could go on about that house forever!" Alida recalled. "As a child all I knew is that it was huge and 'really neat.' Now, as an adult, with a full appreciation of that style of architecture, I am at a loss for words." Writing to Jeanne and Tom on July 13, 1965, the dancer Harry Woolever, one of Jeanne's good friends from her New York days who had just visited the Perkins's in Pasadena, raved about their antique-filled American Craftsman house: "Everything in it is so 'special' having been chosen with such loving care," he wrote. Ginger Paul, the daughter of Jeanne's good friend Kay Bennett Paul, used the words "absolutely mesmerizing" to describe Jeanne and Tom's dream house, which was filled with "a lot of stuff around the large rooms from the estate sales." The boxes and stacks of books everywhere, Jeanne later said in an interview, were her second love next to Tom.

Although Jeanne had never been formally tested, she obviously had an extremely high IQ, an opinion confirmed by her husband Tom who believed that she would have been extremely successful in any endeavor: "She would have been good at anything—surgeon, detective, attorney, artist, or what have you—whatever she wanted." But Jeanne was born to be a ballerina, for as Kevin McKenzie said in his "Foreword" to Nancy Upper's *Ballet Dancers in Career Transition*, "I think most dancers would agree that the art of ballet chooses the dancer, not the other way around." Later in life to "give up the identity of oneself as a dancer is an awful thing. On the other hand, though, a dancer's ability to find a new identity can be truly awe-inspiring."[4] So it was a logical career transition for Jeanne to put aside her fears and frustrations and open her dancing school in Pasadena, teaching classes and conducting dance festivals for twelve years after her marriage.

Jeanne opened her dancing school in her new home's thirty-eight-foot living room, applying all the knowledge and experience about dance that she had acquired during her professional career and her studies during her final year living in New York. Jeanne was the artistic director and Lillian was the business manager and piano accompanist of the Devereaux Ballet Arts School. Once again, Jeanne and Lillian were a tight team. No longer the sole financial support of her family and no longer having to choreograph and perform short, specialty dances that emphasized theatrical tricks to please audiences, Jeanne returned to her artistic roots in classical ballet and ethnic dance. Opening a ballet school not only fulfilled a dream Jeanne had had during most of her professional life, but also contributed to the financial support of her mother since Tom had responsibility for his own aging mother. Writing on December 23, 1952, from New York, Jeanne's good friend the dancer Eileen O'Connor told her about the joys of having a dance school: "I love teaching, Jeanne; it is more rewarding and more exhilarating than show business (though most of my friends disagree.) Will you be doing any teaching now that you are settling down in California? I hope you try it, if for no other reason than to keep up with your own first love, which can never really be put aside."

Because of a zoning law prohibiting a home business in her neighborhood, she was forced to move first to a small studio on Colorado Boulevard and then to the historic Spaulding House at 164 North Euclid Avenue, originally built by the Spaulding Sporting Goods family and located behind Pasadena's monumental city hall and next to the renowned All Saint's Episcopal Church. According to Alida Cervera, the Spaulding House "was lovely. Set back from the street, there was a circular driveway leading up to it and upon entering the building there was a long sweeping staircase (think Gloria Swanson's home in 'Sunset Boulevard') to the second floor where the studio was located. The dark wood door had a set of tiny porcelain ballet shoes and a small card with the name of the school in a brass holder." The studio was located over the American Bible Society's offices on the first floor, but the building was so well constructed that no sound traveled between the floors. Having such a beautiful dance studio was a great relief to Jeanne when she remembered the hours she had spent in the unpleasant, run-down rehearsal halls in New York's Times Square neighborhood.

An advertisement for the opening of her dancing school at the old Spaulding House promoted it as "Pasadena's Newest and Finest Studio of Classical Ballet and Authentic Character Dances of Around the World" geared toward students from "beginner to Professional Through all Ages from Kindergarten to College," and even offering evening classes for business women and men. Her students knew that Jeanne had been a world-class professional dancer, but the majority of them had no awareness of vaudeville, particularly of a "toe dancer" performing on popular stages in vaudeville theatres and movie presentation houses. However, they were aware, as Alida Cervera recalled, of elite ballet companies, and Jeanne kept them all informed about upcoming performances in the Los Angeles area by the Bolshoi Ballet, the Royal Ballet, and the Moiseyev Folk Dance Company.

Jeanne designed her new dancing school with the same meticulousness and devotion to beauty that she had displayed during her dancing career. The design highlight of her studio were the unique twenty-three feet mirrors and white maple barres that she had specially made for the historic space. Alida Cervera described the layout of the "bright and airy" studio:

> It had floor to ceiling mirrors all along one wall to the right as you entered and large windows on the opposite wall, where the barre was located. The walls were a kind of powder blue and I think there were venetian blinds on the windows. The barre was a double one, to accommodate both children and adults—it was a light wood, secured with black scrolled iron brackets. At the far end of the studio was Jeanne's "station." … At the opposite end there was a dressing room and a pink tile bathroom with a pedestal sink.

Next to the entrance on one side was an outer office where Lillian sat at her desk. Alida remembered that Lillian was "bright, smiling and energetic," and warmly greeted all the students when they arrived for their lessons. On the other side of the entrance was a small seating area for the parents to watch the classes. On the wall next to the seating area was a blackboard "flanked by lovely black and white framed photos of Jeanne in various dance poses" where Jeanne "would draw illustrations to clarify what she was trying to teach" her students. These wall photos were also mounted around the studio, offering the public the best of her hundreds of professional promotional photographs.

Jeanne designed her ballet school to introduce students not only to classical ballet but also to diverse forms of ethnic dances worldwide, such as Russian czardas and

Interior of the Devereaux Ballet Arts School on the second floor of the Old Spaulding Mansion at 164 North Euclid Avenue, Pasadena, California, early 1950s. Jeanne's students are practicing in front of her two-level white maple barres and are reflected in her custom-made twenty-three-feet mirrors. Photographs of Jeanne from her dancing career are hung on the walls. Jeanne said that her studio was considered one of the most beautiful in America. Courtesy Jeanne Devereaux Perkins Collection.

mazurkas, including the music and costumes that accompanied these dances. Her completed brochure featured classes in ballet, toe, adagio, character, and Hindu. Jeanne knew the history of almost every dance imaginable from all the races and ethnicities of the world. In 1952 when accomplished ballroom dancer Peggy Almquist wanted to learn ballet she discovered in Pasadena's yellow pages the recently opened Devereaux Ballet Arts School; she became Jeanne's first ballet student at the small studio on Colorado and later at the Spaulding House. When Peggy first encountered Jeanne in the small studio demonstrating her world-class fouettés, she was astounded, later describing Jeanne as thin, cute, and very charming.

Jeanne believed that dance could help to overcome the racial and economic barriers that divided American society. Since she was thirteen she had lived in the integrated world of vaudeville where African American performers were substantial contributors. When a little African American girl named Chantal Gaffney applied to Jeanne's ballet school, she signed her up with no hesitation. Shortly thereafter another dancing teacher in Pasadena since the 1930s, having just seen Jeanne's advertisement for her new ballet school in the local telephone book, called her up and said, "I hope you will join me in not having any black students." Jeanne proudly replied, "Oh, I'm sorry because I already have two excellent black students whom I like very much." Jeanne was never going to allow the racial bias of those days to interfere with her personal and professional values. If a student were poor, she would provide scholarships.

Alida Cervera's memories were shaped by Jeanne's total commitment to her students, her extensive knowledge of dance history, her remarkable discipline and professionalism, her beautiful artistry, and her ability to make extraordinary sketches of the classical ballet poses. Given Jeanne's mastery of dance and her excellent teaching skills, there was "no chance to be bored in her class!" said Alida. She attended classes every Saturday and at least once during the week. "Classes were intense and Jeanne was exceptional at making sure every line was correct. Legs had to be turned out, arms curved and no 'broken wrists,' no 'sickeled' ankles. Posture was paramount!" Alida recalled. At the end of class the students "in turn, as though coming out for a curtain call, went to the center of class, bowed (reverance) and got to pick a piece of candy from this HUGE jar of individually wrapped candies that waited at the end of every lesson." Even now when Alida hears certain pieces of music she still creates "the choreography" and imagines herself on a wooden stage "superb and perfect, creating the illusion of grace and light that it's all effortless—just as Jeanne taught me and making her proud." She believed that Jeanne "was the best ballet teacher anyone could have asked for. She didn't just teach, she inspired. She respected herself, ballet and her students enough to demand the best from all of us and she never gave any less than her absolute best to all of us. Her approach was decidedly no-nonsense, but we knew she cared. She cared deeply for ballet, for her students and for getting it right." The principles that Jeanne instilled in her ballet students "are sadly lacking in today's world," said Alida, "but they are timeless and apply to all walks of life and what a wonderful gift she gave to all of us who were privileged to have been taught by her."

Jeanne was a natural networker and had good marketing instincts for both herself and her students. After classes she would often invite her students to her home for good food, fellowship, and networking. Her student Frank Bourman had been a dancer before he studied with Jeanne, and eventually he and his wife Rosalia went to Australia to dance with the Australian National Ballet. When they departed for Australia they had no money, so Jeanne, advising them to make a good impression or they would not be treated with respect, gave them her beautiful, ivory wardrobe trunk in mint condition as a farewell gift, instructing them to "put all your clothes, ballet shoes, and costumes in it and then send it to the theatre so everyone will see it, be properly impressed, and treat you correctly." Frank and Rosalia were a great success in Australia, and eventually returned home to open a ballet school in Santa Monica and direct their own professional ballet company.

As a dance teacher, Jeanne was well known and respected in the Pasadena community and contributed to many of its revered cultural institutions. In 1954 she loaned dance materials to the Pasadena main library for their exhibit "Dancing Around the World." According to an article in the *Los Angeles Times*, February 7, 1954, "Ballerina Jeanne Devereaux has loaned an unusual array of books, ornaments and items of attire

Jeanne Devereaux Perkins rehearsing her students for a dance festival in Pasadena, California, early 1950s. Jeanne choreographed all the dances, designed all the costumes and sets, and personally performed in all of her dance festivals. Courtesy Jeanne Devereaux Perkins Collection.

used in the art of terpischore, all of which have been neatly packaged in showcases to illustrate the theme" of the exhibit. She "has accumulated a collection of books which include dance dramas of ancient Japan and Sumatra."

When she had performed ballet on the commercial stages of popular entertainment, teachers from dancing schools all over the country would send their students to watch her, and her attention to technical excellence carried over to her teaching and festivals. Alida Cervera remembered how Jeanne had "a reel-to-reel tape recorder with various music selections" in her studio to which she choreographed her dances, and when Jeanne listened to a piece of music she instinctively knew what "the music says" for physical movement. Almost every year after she started her dancing school she produced elaborate student dance festivals. Not only did Jeanne train all the dancers in the festivals, but also she selected the music, choreographed the dances, designed all the elaborate costumes and sets, and often performed in the program. Her surviving color sketches for her gorgeous costumes and sets reveal how meticulously she planned these festivals and her extensive knowledge of the history of fashion in world cultures. After

Jeanne Devereux Perkins' color sketches for costumes in one of her dance festivals, Pasadena, California, 1950s. Starting clockwise in the upper left hand corner are sketches for a Hindu dancer, a faun, Russian mazurkas and czardas, and a dragonfly. The costumes are based on elaborately detailed color sketches she made from dance books during her last year in New York. Courtesy Jeanne Devereaux Perkins Collection.

the dance festival Jeanne received congratulations from many of her New York theatre friends. On June 19, 1955, Louise and Alice O'Sullivan—the Spaulding twins from Jeanne's vaudeville days—wrote Jeanne about the festival, hoping that all the "ignorant mothers didn't add to the usual nerve wracking confusion." Jeanne also received a letter two days later from her dancer friend Jimmy Givens who wrote that his Pasadena cousin had attended the festival and said, "your show was simply great."[5]

Alida Cervera remembered another exciting dance festival held at the Pasadena Civic Auditorium most likely in 1959, which required, like all the others, months of extensive planning and rehearsal: "I remember the countless hours of rehearsals, the theatre dressing room that looked just like the ones in the movies and the incomparable excitement of performing on stage before a live audience—nothing like it!" Jeanne had designed every gorgeous costume "down to the last detail—every embellishment, every accessory—they were gorgeous!" Alida recalled. Jeanne would give each student "an exquisite drawing of the full costume complete with fabric requirements—and the parents made the costumes!"

In the spring of 1960 Jeanne staged a three-act ballet recital with her students at Pasadena's Civic Auditorium that was widely covered by the local press. According to the *Pasadena Independent*, May 30, 1960, Jeanne's ballet company, called the Pasadena Regional Ballet, "hopes to give ballet a life of its own in Southern California by gathering the region's talented artists to perform in a professional manner." Described as the "driving force behind the ballet's quest for recognition in Southern California," Jeanne was quoted as saying, "When I started out in ballet in the United States, any show that would take a ballet act—vaudeville, a high school variety show, anything, that was the place you tried to find a public.... We want this ballet group to gather the talented artists who are ready to graduate out of ballet schools and to offer these dancers and the region an organization of professional competence." Many dancers and their supporters throughout the Los Angeles area joined forces for this pioneering effort: "Garages and living rooms have become workshops for the Sunday performance, according to Miss Devereaux." Among the many supporters Jeanne's then elderly mother Lillian researched magazines that included information and sketches of Versailles ballroom costumes, while also managing the more than a hundred costumes used for the performance.

The *Pasadena Star-News*, June 3, 1960, contained an article entitled "Ballet Sets Styles Says Miss Devereaux" that was a clever promotional plug by Jeanne for the pervasive cultural influence of ballet. "Even if you've never seen a ballet performed in your entire life, chances are that you have been indirectly affected by it. Most of us have," claimed Jeanne proudly. Moreover, clothing fashions were directly influenced by ballet: "Ballerinas, who were the darlings of the public long before radio, television or motion pictures, did more to change and color women's fashions and behavior than any other group. Skirts were shortened an inch or so a la Camargo, hair was dressed a la Salle, heels were Lowered or left off entirely, corsets were abandoned, panties invented, all because dancers led the way—sometimes against the shocked protest of a public who soon followed suit." She ended by describing how ballet was popular with merchants— "Many of the buyers have never had a ballet lesson, but like the look of ballerinas"— and how "ballerina-length" evening and bridal gowns "especially show the influence of the 'dance of royalty.'" Even Cecil Beaton and other famous photographers "were quick to direct their subjects into graceful, dance-like poses."

In 1961 at the El Capitan Theatre in Hollywood, the Greater Los Angeles Chapter of the American National Theatre and Academy presented its fourth annual Children's Theatre Festival. The program included the Pasadena Regional Ballet Foundation in association with The Devereaux Ballet, featuring its junior division in ballets and divertissements in a program entitled "The Reception at Versailles," set in the year 1760 at a party given by the Dauphin of France for the court's noble children. Jeanne choreographed, created, and directed the pas de trois to old French airs, the musette, the passé pied, and the gavotte, and she also designed all the period satin costumes complete with white curler wigs. The program noted, "Learning the formalities of Court Life began early for Royal Children. They dressed as young adults and were expected to behave as miniatures of their parents." The purpose of the Children's Festival was "to bring together the various cultural and entertainment activities of this great community of Los Angeles."

In 1964 the Spaulding House was torn down to make way for a parking lot next door to All Saint's Episcopal Church. In a letter to Jeanne, dated April 22, 1964, the Rector of All Saint's Church gave notice that they must vacate their rental space within ninety days, since the church had decided to convert the building for church use. Jeanne and Tom searched for an alternate space in Pasadena, but were unsuccessful, so she closed the dancing school in that same year. When Jeanne later reflected on how she had felt about having to close her business, she first mentioned how expensive it had been to run the ballet school: "It took too much money to rent a studio or auditorium or to make costumes. And I was too busy with all aspects of the school and festivals to look for outside support. At that time in America there was not that much financial support for the arts, and what money that was donated usually went to museums and maybe opera companies, certainly not to the ballet." She then described the personal liberation she had felt: "I had worked my entire life and for once I had the responsibilities removed for my shoulders. Being free of these responsibilities gave me time to pursue other interests." Within weeks Jeanne donated fifty pairs of new toe shoes, costumes, bolts of silk chiffon, beads, and lace to the newly formed Los Angeles Civic Ballet Company. She also stopped bleaching her hair blonde, and when her natural brown color started to grow back, she discovered many strands of gray.

Although Jeanne officially retired as a ballet teacher, her passion for dance never waned. The wonderful floor to ceiling mirrors with specially-made iron brackets for the ballet barres, which Jeanne and Tom had stored in their garage, were later purchased by Elly van Dijk for her ballet studio known as the Pasadena Civic Ballet, located on the second floor of a building on Sierra Madre Boulevard. A native of Holland where she had had a successful ballet school for many years, Elly had moved to Pasadena with her husband in 1973, and a year later opened her ballet school. In a short article that she wrote about Jeanne for the *Sunday Star*, November 25, 2001, Elly recounted how after her school opened she "received a memorable call from a lady who said: 'My name is Jeanne Perkins. I saw the write-up about you in the [*Pasadena*] *Star-News* and since I am a former prima ballerina and teacher, I would like to welcome you to our city and offer you my help, if needed.'" Elly and Jeanne soon became fast friends: Jeanne occasionally was a guest teacher in Elly's studio, gave her much of her music, and even made costumes and headpieces for some of her shows. "She was inspirational," said Elly, a "unique woman whom I admired very much." When Elly moved her school in the early twenty-first century, she told the new owners of her former school to cherish the majestic mirrors and custom ballet barres that she had purchased from Jeanne Devereaux Perkins, the famous prima ballerina.

In that same newspaper article Elly van Dijk applauded Jeanne for her resilience, for "it takes courage and perseverance to start new projects." She also admired Jeanne and Tom's curiosity, for "they are great role models, who live their lives with gusto. With the much longer life span we enjoy today," she wrote, "it is encouraging to learn that not one but many more careers are real possibilities as long as one stays open to change and keeps the mind active." At age fifty-two Jeanne looked forward to new challenges. She relished working with Tom from 1965 through the mid–1980s as a consultant and designer in their custom museum exhibit case business called "Perkins Development Engineering." In her interview for the *Pasadena Star-News* on January 20, 1994, she jokingly reflected that after closing her dancing school "for the first time in my life I thought 'I don't have to do anything but be plain people…. That lasted a year and a half.'"

Jeanne used all her experience in designing and sketching her own costumes when she partnered with Tom in their museum case venture.[6] She was an aggressive marketer, and contacted all of the museums located in the Los Angeles metropolitan area, as well as those in nearby states and owners of private collections. Over the years their custom exhibit cases were installed in many major museums around the country.[7] They often worked from scratch with the museum staffs throughout the night preparing for grand openings. On September 1, 1977, in a letter to her Aunt Lenore Jeanne provided a snapshot of the demanding life of the museum case business. Jeanne and Tom had worked long, arduous hours to finish the cases for the Page Museum at the La Brea Tar Pits in Los Angeles: "Tom is exhausted with these 12 to 16 hour dys [days] for over a year now, really it is closer to two years now. As the official opening of the Page drew closer we worked day and night at the Museum driving home at dawn, feeding the cats, catching 4 or 5 hours sleep, and right back to do it all over again, till we were ready to drop." Admitting that her back had been painful and troublesome for the past twenty-five years and that she had been seeing a chiropractor for relief, she stressed her need to be back on her feet to help Tom finish their big order for museum cases for Los Angeles' Getty Villa Museum. "Some way or other I have to get on my feet to stand and cover the case floors for the eight Greco-Roman cases," Jeanne wrote. They had just shipped a huge case to the Warm Springs Indian reservation in Oregon: "It was 8' × 10' and was a monster to build, crate and get safely shipped," she wrote her aunt.

In January 1971 Tom was hired over other competing bidders to design an electronics museum in a new building constructed specifically for that purpose in the Space Science Center on the campus of Foothill College in Los Altos, California, where they lived for the year. Jeanne had joined Tom voluntarily as a co-curator of the new museum. When they arrived at the empty building, Tom had to classify all the electronic equipment stored in hundreds of enormous boxes in the basement; Jeanne then had to design what was going to be exhibited in the circular museum space and how it would be displayed. They worked tirelessly on the project for nearly a year, but even Jeanne's optimism and incredible work ethic could not guarantee success: much to their disappointment the project was prematurely terminated when the Foothill College administrators, most likely because of inadequate funding, commandeered the museum building for their own use. About twenty-five years later the college moved the electronics collections to a new venue in San Jose.

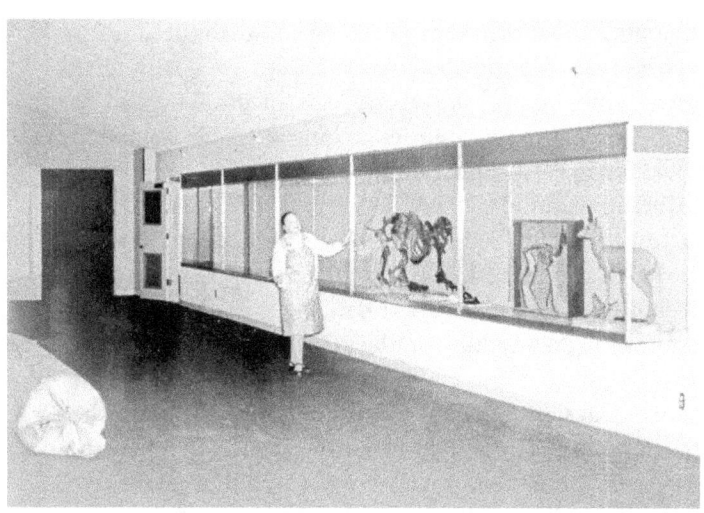

Jeanne Devereaux Perkins standing in front of the custom exhibit cases at the Page Museum at the La Brea Tar Pits, Los Angeles, California, created by the Perkins Development Engineering Company—makers of museum cases, exhibits, prototypes, scientific instruments, and research equipment in the 1970s–80s. Jeanne designed the cases, and Tom built them in their three-car garage. Having visited most of the major museums in America and Europe during her dancing career, Jeanne had learned what museum curators needed for their exhibitions. Courtesy Jeanne Devereaux Perkins Collection.

During Jeanne and Tom's yearlong residency in Los Altos the indefatigable Lillian, who was now eighty-six years of age, suffering from the aches and pains of old age and in need of a hearing aid, wrote them at least weekly, imparting the daily minutiae of maintaining the big house and yard on Holliston. Throughout her letters Lillian occasionally mentioned her arthritis and chest pain. In early 1972 a few months after Jeanne and Tom had returned to Pasadena, Lillian had a massive heart attack and died four days later. Although Jeanne was saddened by her mother's death, she was not devastated. In an interview she explained that since they had closed the dancing school, she and her mother had not had the intense close working relationship they had had since she was eleven, and now they related just as family. "When life changes, your close daily involvement even with your loved ones can also change," Jeanne said. She stressed how all-consuming her professional dancing career had been and the need she had felt all her life to support her mother financially, stoically never allowing herself to analyze her feelings about being exploited from a young age by such a demanding responsibility: "It was my work that earned the money. We were in it together like a team and had no discussions about it. She never thanked me later in life. It didn't bother her." In her letters to Bill, however, Lillian admitted her regret that she was such a stressful financial burden on her daughter, forcing her to delay marriage and having a family of her own. When asked if it bothered *her*, Jeanne refused to elaborate her feelings, as she had done during most of her professional life. Her former dance student and devoted friend Patrick Purdy, however, felt that Jeanne mourned her mother's death very intensely for at least two years: her dampened spirits were very obvious to those close to her. Whatever her feelings, in the wake of her mother's death, Jeanne coped by immersing herself in work and planning for the future.

As they grew older by the mid-1980s Jeanne and Tom retired from the business of making exhibit cases. Jeanne's love of books, antiques, and the decorative arts, as well as her natural talent for public speaking, easily translated into her next career as a popular public lecturer in the Los Angeles area. As early as 1944 when she had participated in thirty-two radio broadcasts advertising the *Folies Bergère*, as well as selling war bonds and talking for the Red Cross, she had been praised by the radio announcers and interviewers for her oratorical skill. Although Jeanne never did pursue a career in radio, she prided herself on using the correct vocal pitch and volume while speaking extemporaneously to various groups in the Los Angeles area. Tom described her as "a natural communicator," unafraid to perform before audiences small and large, so he was never surprised by her exceptional oratorical ability.

Jeanne's public lecturing career was closely tied to her membership in an organization called the Questers El Molino, a restoration and preservation study group dedicated to collecting and restoring antique furniture and other collectibles, preserving and restoring historic fine architecture, and promoting good fellowship.[8] In January 1978 Jeanne suffered a bout of pneumonia and agonizing sciatica, which confined her to bed until April when she could walk again with the assistance of two canes; by July she could cautiously sit in a chair. In late 1978 she immediately accepted with pleasure an invitation to become a Reader at the Huntington Library to use research materials there to prepare a lecture and paper on the history of tea for the Questers El Molino, describing in her Christmas letter for that year how she filled out the questionnaire required to become a Reader. Although Huntington Readers usually have graduate degrees and are experienced researchers and writers, Jeanne knew she had already transcended the limitations of her eighth grade formal education with her extensive traveling and visiting museums and her lifelong habit of voracious reading and writing. In her 1979 Christmas letter she described how the Huntington was "a new world" to her of international scholars who usually met in groups at the Rose Garden Café for lunch: their conversation could be as "'Hammy' as a burlesque comedian, but on a very high plane." At first she just listened to their learned dialogue until after five or six months she had the confidence to engage in "quietly throwing out a 'Yes, but don't you think that something or other should be considered.'" After a few weeks the scholars on the grounds and in the hallways warmly greeted her: her wit, charm, and quality of mind had earned their respect and she belonged.

Over the years, using the vast resources of the Huntington Library, she developed fifteen lectures for the Questers El Molino, usually illustrated with slides prepared by Tom, that showcased her love of learning, natural curiosity, library research skills, and oratorical talent. Jeanne told others that her main motivation for lecturing was that she "wanted people to enjoy the information and learn; I spoke to them as an educator, not an egoist, sharing my lifelong curiosity and love for information." She always spoke from memory—no notes: "If you use notes you're always looking down and dropping your voice at the end of every sentence," she explained. Her research strategy was to read hundreds of books on a subject while scribbling "a cryptic word or two on the

Top: Jeanne Devereaux Perkins, Reader at the Huntington Library in San Marino, California, ca. 1978–1980. Jeanne's first research at the Huntington was for her public lectures for the Questers, an international organization dedicated to the study of architectural and antiques restoration and preservation. Later Jeanne dedicated almost twenty-eight years of her life at the Huntington researching a biography of Grace Nicolson, an early twentieth-century entrepreneurial woman who collected and sold rare Native American basketry and Asian art and antiques. In 1924 Grace designed and built her famous "Chinese Treasure House of Oriental and Western Art," which became the Pasadena Art Museum, then the Pacific Asia Museum, and now in partnership with the University of Southern California the USC Pacific Asia Museum. Courtesy Jeanne Devereaux Perkins Collection. *Bottom:* Jeanne Devereaux Perkins and Tom Perkins at the Huntington's Rose Garden Café, San Marino, California, late 1980s. Lunching with Jeanne and Tom at the Rose Garden Café was an enjoyable and stimulating experience. Courtesy Jeanne Devereaux Perkins Collection.

back of an old envelope or grocery tab," to trigger her "internal computer" so that when she opened her mouth "the memories flow out." In addition to the hundreds of books that she had read over the years, she now spent months at the Huntington, which she called "a researcher's Paradise." She spent five days a week from nine to five reading books and loved every minute of her work; she then transformed her research into an interesting lecture. "To make the story flow one must digest the material so completely that you can mentally move through the places, times, and know the people's lives and current events so well that it is like visiting old friends, or your ancestors lives," Jeanne said. With this method the speaker could be free of notes and could use the information in another context if needed.

Now popular on the lecture circuit, Jeanne delivered her lectures not only to her fellow Questers but also to other important local civic and cultural organizations in the Los Angeles area. "Revolution in a Teacup," probably her favorite lecture, described all the industries that had evolved from the importation of tea in England from Holland in the late seventeenth century. Jeanne designed a creative flyer to accompany this lecture, featuring objects from all the industries over the centuries related to drinking tea. Elly van Dijk remembered hearing Jeanne's lecture on tea: "Fascinating! I mentioned it to all my friends." In 1980 Jeanne delivered "Revolution in a Teacup" at the Questers' National Convention in Los Angeles, and received many notes from admirers praising her intelligence and skilled oratory. Jeanne calculated that for the next ten years she had presented about four to five paid lectures a year on topics such

Jeanne Devereaux Perkins holding her promotional headshot from Clifford C. Fisher's *Folies Bergère* **at the Huntington's Rose Garden Café, San Marino, California, late 1980s. This was her husband Tom's favorite professional photograph of Jeanne from her dancing career. Promotional headshot by Gabriel Moulin Studios, San Francisco, California. Courtesy Jeanne Devereaux Perkins Collection.**

as history, the decorative arts, conservation, and antiques, earning an average of $150 per lecture.

In the early years of the twenty-first century when invited to speak to groups in the Pasadena area, Jeanne lectured primarily on Grace Nicholson, the subject of her research for nearly twenty-eight years at the Huntington Library (see Appendix Three). During the first half of the twentieth century Grace Nicholson had become one of the foremost collectors and dealers in America of Native American baskets and Asian art and antiques. Jeanne's interest in Grace Nicholson began when she worked as a popular docent at the Pacific Asia Museum—formerly Nicholson's Chinese Treasure House of Oriental and Western Art and now in partnership with the University of Southern California the USC Pacific Asia Museum—where she was known for her entertaining and informative tours. David Kamansky, the museum's Director, called her one morning and asked in a wheedling voice, "Jeanne, will you do me a favor?" Jeanne replied, "Sure David, what do you want?" and David asked her "to write Grace Nicholson's biography." When Jeanne exclaimed, "Why, I don't know a thing about her!" he said, "That's alright. Just go to the Huntington Library and get busy. All of her papers are there." Over the years Jeanne read and examined every item in the extensive collection of manuscripts and photographs making up the Huntington Library's Grace Nicholson Collection, daily deciphering Grace's illegible handwriting, with the goal of reconstructing the life of this extraordinary, unconventional woman.

Soon after Jeanne had begun her research she developed a passionate affinity with Grace Nicholson. Like Jeanne, Grace was a highly intelligent, pioneering woman who had pushed the boundaries of acceptable narratives for women of her generation to achieve a high level of professional success and distinction. Jeanne admired her open and friendly personality, trustworthiness, and extraordinary achievements based on natural talent and hard work. Neither Jeanne nor Grace had experienced motherhood and were able to devote their lives to their work and extended families. They had both been "orphaned" at age thirteen and forced to earn a living: "We were both orphaned—Grace literally and me figuratively by my father's devastating illness," Jeanne reflected in an interview.

From the outset all her research notes were written in longhand on cards and in notebooks. Over the years her desk in the Huntington's Rothenberg Reading Room was covered with books, photocopies of journal articles, and her handwritten notes. When younger scholars with a project in California history that included Grace Nicholson passed through the Huntington and encountered Jeanne, they were not only charmed by her charismatic personality, but by the depth of her knowledge about Grace's extraordinary life. Jeanne's research project on Grace Nicholson is primarily an oral history, supported by her voluminous, handwritten notes, which she always intended to donate to a California library.

In January 2007 at age ninety-five Jeanne impressed the members of the Questers El Molino with an hour-and-a-half long erudite lecture on Grace Nicholson, delivered extemporaneously with no notes, never dropping her voice while looking her audience directly in the eye. She made each historic moment of Grace's life come alive for her attentive audience. Once again, Jeanne was rewarded with the loud applause that had validated her outstanding public performances on theatre stages and now in an antique armchair. Her long, colorful dress almost reached the floor, and throughout her lecture she could not resist smiling when gently petting the hostess's darting Siamese cat during its momentary pauses on her lap.

In October 2007 Jeanne was the featured speaker at another meeting of the Questers El Molino, where she skillfully narrated the amazing story of her twenty-nine-year professional dancing career, which one listener described as the cultural history of America in the first half of the twentieth century. The flower arrangement on the coffee table directly in front of Jeanne contained a spray of the beautiful, yellow "Dancing Girls Orchid," purportedly named after Jeanne by the renowned botanist Dr. Pring of St. Louis. Although her official birthday was not until Halloween, she was feted that night with a birthday cake and heartfelt rendition of "Happy Birthday" to celebrate turning ninety-five. Despite the strength of her voice and mind and animated expression, she remained seated in a comfortable, upholstered armchair throughout the evening, and her increasing fragility was evident to some of the Questers who had known her for more than twenty years.

Epilogue

In her twilight years Jeanne advocated the strong relationship between creativity and a well-lived life, especially how the mental and physical discipline of the arts shapes morals and character. When she was asked what message she would like to share with America's youth, her voice took on a sharp, deliberate quality, her eyes became even more intense, and her mouth edged with barely perceptible lines. Having lived the disciplined life of a ballerina, she encouraged America's youth to pay attention to the arts: "The self-discipline of doing art correctly—whether you are balancing on your toes, learning lines for your part in a play, painting a picture, playing an instrument, or designing a costume—stays with you all your life. All comes together in art and life, like fingers spread apart and then joined tightly into a strong fist. Children need the discipline of art to do things right and correct and to develop good character." Jeanne's own life of excellence in five careers epitomized her lifelong value of the disciplined creativity essential to achieving success.[1]

Continuing her public legacy in 2005, Jeanne proudly deposited in Britain's Royal Archives some written anecdotes of her 1935 and 1938 performances before British royalty. During one of his annual visits to the Huntington Library, J. Marc Meltonville, Esq., project coordinator of the Historic Kitchens at Hampton Court Palace in Surrey, England, encouraged Jeanne to allow him to send these anecdotes to The Royal Collection Trust at Windsor Castle for deposit in The Royal Archives. A letter dated December 30, 2005, addressed to Mr. Meltonville from Miss Pamela Clark, Registrar for The Royal Archives, thanked him on the Queen's behalf for sending these interesting "items relating to Jeanne Devereaux's performances before members of the Royal Family," asking him to thank "Mrs. Perkins for her kind thought in sending these items."

Due to old age and increasing infirmity Jeanne retired from the Huntington Library in September 2008. She had always said, "Cheery pip" with a slight British inflection each afternoon to her colleagues when she left the Huntington Library, and would continue to say it as she bid her friends farewell after lunch at the Huntington's Rose Garden Café or on the telephone. This was her creative conflation of the dual expressions "Cheery O" and "Pip pip!" At her ripe old age, forever a "prima ballerina," whenever someone wanted to take her picture, she would strike a graceful, doll-like ballet pose and smile, her eyes laughing, momentarily experiencing the sublime joy of performing in her dancing days. Continuing the birthday party tradition begun at the Huntington in 2006, after her retirement Jeanne and Tom gathered with friends at a local Mexican restaurant in Pasadena to celebrate her ninety-sixth birthday, and in the following two years most of her remaining friends in Pasadena attended her birthday lunch or dinner. In a 2011 interview when they were both ninety-eight Tom summed up Jeanne's life as meaningful and joyful: "She had the dancing career of her dreams, she got the man she wanted, she got the house she wanted, and she had the four more careers she wanted. She had a wonderful life. She's surely one of a kind!" Always the consummate trouper bringing joy each day to those who have had the privilege of her friendship, "she ran between the raindrops" in her lifelong quest for art, beauty, and learning and survived every obstacle put in her way.

Jeanne made her final appearance in a professional theatre in December 2009 when she attended a holiday matinee of the biblical nativity story set to the Beatles music at the Open Fist Theatre in Hollywood. My husband was in the cast, and he had arranged for the artistic director to introduce Jeanne to the audience before the show began. With the roar of her final standing ovation ringing in her ears, Jeanne, who was seated in the front row, slowly rose from her chair with the assistance of her cane, turned toward the audience, gracefully raised her hand, and bowed. Enthralled by this elderly trouper of the vaudeville era, many of the actors eagerly pursued her as she made her way to an awaiting car on the arm of a trusted friend.

Jeanne Devereaux Perkins entering her ninety-fourth surprise birthday party on October 31, 2006, in the Footnote Lounge at the Huntington Library in San Marino, California. This was the second birthday party that Jeanne had ever had in her long life. Photograph taken by her biographer Kathleen Menzie Lesko. Courtesy Jeanne Devereaux Perkins Collection.

During the final year of her life Jeanne was in and out of the Huntington Hospital and convalesced for four months in a nursing home in Pasadena before passing away on July 28, 2011, with her beloved husband Tom at her side. She was wearing the colorful, glittering bracelets given to her by friends who had brought a momentary twinkle to her visibly weakening eyes. With Jeanne's passing the vibrant voice of one of the last vaudevillians has been silenced except for her legacy that lives on in the hearts of family and friends and the pages of this book.

In October 2011 her friends and colleagues held a celebration of Jeanne's life at the Huntington Library, and for this special occasion Sarkis Badalyan, the security guard for the library, wrote a heartfelt commemorative poem in her honor (see Appendix Four). Living alone in the Pasadena house during the year after Jeanne was gone, Tom became increasingly resigned to what he called "her return to her ancestors," and on October 15, 2012, Tom passed away peacefully in the same nursing home just a few weeks before Jeanne's 100th birthday. During his last month of convalescence he said that they had enjoyed almost sixty years of happily married life on earth, and he was now quite curious about reuniting with his beloved Jeanne in the life beyond.

Afterword by
Jeanne Devereaux Perkins

During a 2011 interview with Jeanne I asked her how she felt about having her life story recorded for posterity. She told me that for many years after she closed her dancing school in Pasadena in 1964 she had always intended to write her autobiography, but other fascinating opportunities and challenges always distracted her. After she became a Reader at the Huntington Library in late 1978 until her retirement in 2008 she had shared the highlights of her life story in entertaining conversations with staff members and scholars there, many of whom eventually became her good friends, but she had never met anyone whom she trusted to write down her story until she met me. Here in her own words is Jeanne's answer to my question:

When I was a child learning interesting things and fortunate to have had intelligent and talented parents, I had no way of knowing what the future held. So during my unusual childhood I just lived life without analyzing it. No one can foresee how things will turn out, and when I took my first ballet lesson I didn't know what the future held for me in ballet or what wonderful opportunities to see the world it would provide. I could not anticipate how my ballet career would also include visiting the great cities of America and Europe and their museums—experiences that would eventually be part of my later life in the museum world.

In my day, performers in vaudeville, musical presentations, or Broadway shows did not hire press agents to make themselves household words or get themselves on the glossy covers of magazines. Their reward was the acceptance and approval of the live audience, which was shown by rounds of applause, many curtain calls, and occasional cries of "Bravo!" So many well-known performers of the World War I period and the 1920s and 1930s are now totally unknown to the public because they didn't have press agents promoting them. Many famous stars are now totally forgotten, and if you mention their names to a friend, you get a blank look. Unfortunately, these talented performers are gone and forgotten, whereas far less talented people today are known far and wide. So I feel that this biography will be a tribute to the thousands upon thousands of now unsung performers of the past.

Working with Kathleen on my biography has dredged up long forgotten memories of many careers. Although I never dreamed of having this written legacy, I am pleased that this book will educate the public about the everyday life of a performer in between the two World Wars of the twentieth century, and the ways the experiences and rewards of my professional dancing career carried over into the other careers of my long life. When one is as old as I am, one reverts to this early training, which was based on learning and discovery, so that each new career could be successful and intellectually rewarding.

Having had a successful and happy marriage of fifty-nine years to a talented and creative man who shares my memories and values is my greatest reward. Sharing my life with Tom Perkins as I grew older has given me daily companionship with someone from my own generation. So many of my friends say to me that growing older is particularly hard when one has lost so many close family members and friends. Losing people one loves really hurts. In 2006 I lost one of my fellow performers and dear friends—Kenny Spaulding—who performed in the Folies Bergère in 1943 with his partners Alice and Louise O'Sullivan and later was a featured dancer and performer in many television and Broadway shows. Of all of my old theatre friends, he was the last performer except for Louise to live until now. The curtain has been lowered on all of the others.

Appendix One

Sample of Jeanne's Poetry

Throughout her life Jeanne wrote poetry for her family and friends and often recited poems she had read since childhood. Many of her parents' friends thought that some of Jeanne's poems were even worthy of publication. Having a natural passion for poetry, Jeanne often clipped out favorite poems from magazines and newspapers to include in her many personal letters.

When Jeanne was hospitalized in Paris with diphtheria in 1938 a month before her performance in the Chateau Bagatelle in the Bois de Bologne before King George VI and Queen Elizabeth, she composed the following humorous verses.

Witty Verses

Imprisoned am I because a germ lit upon my epiderm.
Oh he was smart and he was wary so picked a quiet sanctuary.
Safely ensconsed behind his moat, my throat he pained, my tongue did coat.
This pampered pet of Docs & Nurses justly earned my heartfelt curses.
He raised a family vastly numbered that got me down while thus encumbered.
Injections rotate from side to side and how I pray his horde has died—
I've gargled this, am sprayed with that—Am pampered like a Persian cat.
He shows he's licked in Sunday's Culture—Monday revives this tiny vulture.
Yes on he lives thru every test, this hateful little tyrant pest.
He cares not how I twist and squirm—How I resent this sickroom term.
The only pleasure that I glean from grappling with this germ unseen
Is—If I die and am interred he goes along without a word
And if I live (let's hope I may) He meets the same end anyway.
It means he's dead and dead to stay—

In 1944, after Jeanne had surgery for her deviated septum and cosmetic damage done to her nose from a childhood sledding accident, she waxed poetically about noses.

Noses

I go I find
Noses fill my sight and mind.
I'm victim of a nose complex
I tabulate noses, concave and convex.
Noses, pert or retrousee
The Pug type, or lump of clay
There are noses sonnets are written of
Shaped to kindle the spark of Love.
Or Proboscis, that by sheer size and shape

Fascinate, and make one gape!
Others puffed, as if stung by bees
Or saucy ones tilted at forty degrees.
I recollect noses of every clime
Most preposterous, some sublime!
Wouldst know if a person married for love
Just peek at the beak of his Turtle Dove.

After a lifetime of incessant travel, Jeanne wrote the following poem in 1945 about the hardship combined with the addiction of adventurous traveling and consumption.

The Traveller's Lament

Happy is the Land Lubber
Terra Firma, Country Clubber
He neither utters sea-sick groans
or "tips" untill his bank-roll moans.
He stays at home, in peace and quiet
Eating his usual homey diet.
He never shuts his eyes to try
Flying fish, or Octopi.
His throat has never had to swallow
Food that made his stomach hollow.
Snails Eeels and Arab Kus
Would promptly kill his palate's goose.
He jaunts and journeys in his mind
Without leaving Home behind
By book he visits Borneo
Shivers with Bird, in Arctic Snow.
Thru printed word, and photograph
he meets and sees the Veldt's giraffe,
Or haggles in the Arab Sukes,
Or gapes at England's reigning Dukes.
Tho his is an adventurous life
He glides thru it without much strife
While we misguided Masochists
Who dash about with guides and lists.
Just wear ourselves into a lather
To spongelike facts and figures gather
Buy odds and ends, to drag thru "customs"
And then for years must clean and dust 'em.
O what fools we mortals be.
To take a ship, and set to sea.
Yet, six months later, by the clock
I'm packed and waiting at the dock.

Appendix Two

Jeanne's World War II Legacy

In 2003 at the Huntington Library in San Marino, California, Jeanne became acquainted with Diana Selig, an assistant professor of history at California's Claremont McKenna College, and began her official public legacy. In that same year Laura Marrone, a student in Professor Selig's "World War II History" class, conducted an oral interview with Jeanne. A copy of the audio cassette and a typewritten transcript of the interview entitled "The Jeanne Perkins Collection" were deposited by Professor Selig in the Veterans History Project Archives at the Library of Congress' American Folklore Center in Washington, D.C. (AFC/2001/001/11146). Many of Jeanne's recollections about her performances for veterans and soldiers and observations on wartime America are documented in this primary source.

In 2012 Jeanne's green army trench coat and hat that she had worn during her USO Camp Shows tour to Japan in 1945–46, both of which have the red, white, and blue "USO Camp Shows" insignia attached, as well as a story summary and a few surviving photographs relating to her USO touring show called "Copacabana Night Club Revue from New York," were deposited at the USO San Diego Center in San Diego, California. These items are the first that the USO San Diego Center has collected to archive and display in their new space at San Diego's USO Neil Ash Airport Center. According to John T. Dooley, former President and CEO of the USO San Diego Center, his organization "is privileged to be in possession of such treasured memorabilia" of one of the first and largest shows sent to this region after the war ended. To display Jeanne's memorabilia, Mr. Dooley and his project team commissioned the construction of a special glass exhibit case for the coat and hat and attractive professional framing with interpretive brass labels for the story material and photographs.

Researching Jeanne's USO Camp Shows tour has been challenging. Over the years the USO Office, now located in Washington, D.C., had two natural disasters that destroyed the majority of its archives. A few photographs and documents relating to USO Camp Shows are archived in the Billy Rose Theatre Collection at the New York Public Library for the Performing Arts at Lincoln Center, the National Archives, and in private collections. At the end of 2015 the USO discontinued its historical "USO Camp Shows" timeline on its website that listed no performance records between Danny Kaye's solo tour to Japan in October 1945 and the following March 1946. I will be sending the USO a copy of Jeanne's biography for their current archive.

Appendix Three

Jeanne's Research on Grace Nicholson

This account of Grace Nicholson and her famous Chinese Treasure House in Pasadena is based on Jeanne's interviews, her handwritten research notes written while in residence at the Huntington Library, and her public lectures. Approximately 90 percent of the Grace Nicholson Collection at the Huntington Library consists of Grace's business correspondence along with some personal letters. Jeanne was always quick to point out that even the business letters have a personal flair because Grace had become friends with her colleagues: letters to Grace beginning with "Dear Miss Nicholson" would soon become "Dear Grace." The collection also includes nearly 2,000 photographs of Grace's collecting trips to the Indian tribes and the various stages of development of her Chinese Temple building, now know as the USC Pacific Asia Museum.

Grace Nicholson was born in Philadelphia on December 31, 1877, and her mother died that same week; her father died in 1891, leaving her orphaned at age thirteen. Using a small inheritance from her grandparents, Grace moved to Los Angeles in 1901, probably because of her incipient tuberculosis, and she obviously thrived in its Mediterranean climate. Immediately seeking employment, Grace initially worked as a freelance secretary downtown on Spring Street. One day another typist came running into her tiny office and said, "I'm in a terrible fix. I have promised this man that I would have his lecture ready at 6:00 PM and there is no way that I can get it all done. But if you do half and I do the other half, we'll have it ready." Grace agreed, and when the client, who was the famous lecturer George Wharton James, came to the office to edit the typescript, he was formally introduced to Grace. Quickly discovering that she had no relatives, family, or friends in Los Angeles, he introduced her to the Charles Fletcher Lummis circle, which included many Los Angeles artists and intelligentsia, particularly those interested in the history of Native Americans and the Southwest. Lummis was an accomplished writer, photographer, and Native American historian and activist, who in 1907 established the Southwest Museum in Los Angeles, which officially moved to a new building in Mt. Washington in 1914.

The Lummis circle met at Lummis' house in Highland Park, known as *El Alisal*, which was decorated with Native American baskets and artifacts, and Grace admired these native works of art. The famous writer Mary Austin, a member of the Lummis circle, encouraged Grace to start collecting Native American baskets herself at the regional missions in the Los Angeles area, and Grace subsequently visited these missions to find native weavers who had beautiful baskets for sale. When the curator of Anthropology of the Smithsonian Institution visited Los Angeles, he contacted the Lummis Circle, and members urged Grace to show him her impressive basket collection. Admiring them, the Curator bought the entire collection of ten baskets for $60, and from this point on Grace made a conscious career change, resolving to convert her basket collecting into a profitable business.

In 1902 admirers of her growing collection of Native American baskets encouraged her to open a store at 41–43 South Raymond Avenue in Pasadena, which she called the Old Curio Shop. She shared the space and rent with the famous artist Frank Sauerwen. One of the walls was devoted to Sauerwen's paintings, and the other featured Grace's Southwestern Native American basket collection. The displays in the front windows enticed wealthy visitors from the neighboring, fashionable Greene Hotel on their way to the shops and restaurants on Pasadena's Colorado Boulevard.

A year later Grace was making collecting expeditions to the basket making centers of the Native American tribes of California and the Northwest. During this era of the Arts and Crafts movement in America, Grace's hand-woven baskets were widely sought after by collectors for both their moral and decorative qualities, and although not a trained anthropologist, ethnologist, or photographer, Grace realized the cultural value of her Native American artifacts and documented the history of the pieces she acquired both in photographs and her business and personal writings. Over her long career as a collector and dealer, with the assistance of her longtime friend and business associate Carroll S. Hartman, she meticulously recorded the origin and authenticity of her purchases. She eventually became a member of the American Anthropological Society and the American Folklore Society.

In 1904 Grace rented Dr. George S. Hull's house and office at 46 North Los Robles Avenue, designed by Pasadena's famous Greene brothers, converting the buildings to display her Native American art objects and provide her with living quarters upstairs above the shop. As the years passed, she developed a growing interest in Asian art and antiques, which soon superseded her specialization in Native American art. Soon after she had arrived in Los Angeles, Carroll S. Hartman had introduced her to his employer F. Suie One, the most successful Asian antique dealer in the area and the great grandfather of the successful novelist Lisa See. Under F. Suie One's tutelage, Grace had learned about Chinese art, jade, porcelains, and history, and when she could afford it, augmented her collection of Native American baskets with Asian art and antiques. To accommodate the wealthy women who wintered in Pasadena, who wanted fancy silk dresses in many beautiful colors, Grace contacted the leading Chinese silk merchants to supply her with the largest selection of silks in America. She also contacted leading Chinese antique dealers, who would send Grace crates of art and antiques on approval, which she would sell in her shop. Each room of her shop featured different types of Chinese art and antiques, such as a jade room, a carved ivory room, and a porcelain room.

Having purchased in 1907 the Greene and Greene house at 46 North Los Robles Avenue where her business and home were located, Grace had the old house moved in 1924 a block north across the street from the Congregational Church, so that she could begin construction on a new, monumental commercial building, designed by the prestigious architectural firm Marston, Van Pelt, and Maybury—the Chinese temple building known as "The Chinese Treasure House of Oriental and Western Art" for which she is now famous. Completed in 1925 at the Los Robles Avenue location, the new building included cultural, intellectual, and social spaces: a garden courtyard, public and private galleries, a public research library, a 200-seat auditorium, and two private apartments, one for herself and the other for visiting artists and museum curators. Many of the women artists, collectors, and writers whom she patronized were often in residence in the guest apartments.

In 1929 she took her first and only trip to China, Japan, and Korea, accompanied by Carroll S. Hartman, shipping home many new treasures for her inventory. When she returned to Pasadena in November 1929, little could she have predicted the imminent stock market crash followed by ten years of the Great Depression and five years of world war. A remarkable business woman, she was able to sustain herself for ten years under these financially challenging conditions until back income taxes forced her to put her precious Chinese Treasure House on the market, only managing to sell the adjacent south lot. In 1943, being close to foreclosure and in very poor health, she donated her Chinese Treasure House to the City of Pasadena as a home for the Pasadena Art Institute. She continued to live in her private apartment, but moved her business to 35 South Euclid Avenue. During her final illness Grace was carried down the steps from her private apartment in the Chinese Treasure House on a stretcher to be taken by ambulance to the hospital, but she wanted to stop so she could look at her beloved building one last time before she left the premises.

At her death in the hospital in 1948 the Grace Nicholson Gallery officially became the Pasadena Art Institute, which soon became the Pasadena Art Museum specializing in modern art. Grace willed her Native American collection to her longtime salesperson, Miss Bynum; most of her Asian collection remained in the Chinese Treasure House, with some of it eventually sold at the Curtis Auction House ironically located at the same location as her Old Curio shop. Grace was primarily self-educated by books and travel, having educated herself with books about the Pacific Coast Native Americans and Asian art purchased from Dawson's bookstore in Los Angeles and then working around the clock educating customers about the items of interest to them. After her death Mr. Dawson was disappointed that her library had been sold, since he had lost a chance to buy back the special books that had been in Grace's possession.

Soon thereafter the Board of the Pasadena Art Museum, deciding that the beautiful Chinese Treasure House was not a suitable venue for displaying modern art, began construction on a new museum at a new location. However, they were financially unable to complete the building, and the project was taken over by the business entrepreneur and art collector Norton Simon, who created the now famous Norton Simon Museum in Pasadena. At this time many of the small business owners on adjoining Colorado Boulevard wanted Grace's Chinese Treasure House demolished for a parking lot, but citizen activists were able to save the landmark building, which eventually became the Pacific Asia Museum, retaining most of the spaces of the original design. In 2013 the museum affiliated with the University of Southern California to form the USC Pacific Asia Museum—a partnership that will expand its role for education and cultural heritage to new audiences.

Appendix Four

Sarkis Badalyan's Commemorative Poem Written for Jeanne's Celebration of Life at the Huntington Library, October 2011

To Jeanne

when I am alone
My memories take me
To the recent past—
I see that face and twinkling eyes
And remember fondly
A gracious lady ...
Today, I want to bow
In front of her image
And say thanks—
Thanks, because I learned
From her to enjoy this wonderful life,
To be positive, generous, and kind.
She was amazing
And I will never forget
That lovely gracious lady.

Chapter Notes

All quotations from Jeanne Devereaux Perkins, her husband Tom, her friends, and former students are taken from her handwritten notes, personal letters, and interviews in the Jeanne Devereaux Perkins Collection. The majority of the dates for the personal letters are those typed or written at the top of the first page; otherwise they are from the postmarks on the envelopes. All quotations are documented in the text. Newspaper references in the text from Jeanne's scrapbook are unpaginated. *Variety* references in the text are from clippings in her scrapbook and from the trade newspaper's online archives. All other quotations are cited in the "Chapter Notes."

Chapter 1

1. Travis D. Stewart, *No Applause—Just Throw Money: The Book That Made Vaudeville Famous* (New York: Faber and Faber, 2005), 284.
2. Lucile Iverson South, *On Toes of Gold: A Story of the Dance and the Dancer* (Cliff, New Mexico: Blusage Studio Designers & Publishers), 19.

Chapter 2

1. Reva Howitt Clar, *Lollipop: Vaudeville Turns with a Fanchon and Marco Dancer*, ed. Mimi Melnick (Lanham, Maryland: Scarecrow Press, 2002). In 1921 Reva was "overwhelmed with admiration and awe" when as a young girl her mother took her to see Pavlova perform in Stockton, California. Three years later in San Francisco when she performed as an extra in the ballet *Don Quixote* with the great Pavlova, Reva observed the international star ballerina in the chilly backstage wings "dressed in a practice shift and an old gray roughneck sweater, her hand on a kitchen chair." She was surprised to see "the great prima ballerina, doing elementary warm-up *barre* exercises." Reva regretted that she never purchased an autographed picture of Pavlova (13).
2. Buster Keaton with Charles Samuels, *My Wonderful World of Slapstick*, new intro. Dwight Macdonald and new filmog. Rayment Rohauer (1960; repr., New York: Da Capo Press, 1982), 171.
3. Tamara Karsavina, *Theatre Street* (1931; repr., New York: Dutton, 1961), 68.
4. Walter Ware, *Ballet Is Magic: A Triple Monograph: Harriet Hoctor, Paul Haakon, Patricia Bowman* (New York: IHRA Publishing Co., 1936), 44.
5. Nancy Upper, *Ballet Dancers in Career Transition* (Jefferson, North Carolina: McFarland, 2004), 40.
6. Ultimately, according to contemporary dancer/choreographer Twyla Tharp in *The Creative Habit: Learn It and Use It for Life* (W.A.T. Ltd., 2003; New York: Simon & Schuster, 2006), "dance is governed by passion and skill and the "*ur*-skill ... is *discipline*," 171.
7. In *The Creative Habit* Twyla Tharp describes the choreographer's work as encountering an empty room that "symbolizes something profound, mysterious, and terrifying: the task of starting with nothing and working your way toward creating something whole and beautiful and satisfying." For the choreographer the "black space can be humbling"; it becomes the artist's "identity"; it becomes her "home," 5–6.

Chapter 3

1. Thelma White with Harry Preston, *Thelma Who! Almost 100 Years of Showbiz* (Lanham, Maryland: Scarecrow Press, 2002), 34. When Thelma was an eleven-year-old member of the singing White Sisters on the B. F. Keith vaudeville circuit her mother was issued a summons by the Gerry Society. The head man told her they had received several hundred letters complaining about the White Sisters performing: "There was one from Sarah Berle who said that her son Milton was a talented child performer and if the White Sisters were allowed on stage, why wasn't he?" Thelma's mother forced her father to obtain a fraudulent birth certificate that stated Thelma had been born in 1904 instead of 1911, which Thelma's mother used in court to get the case dismissed.
2. In 1930 *Manhattan Mary* was adapted into a film called *Follow the Leader*, with Ed Wynn and Lou Holtz making their first talking picture, and featuring Ginger Rogers and Ethel Merman in their film débuts.
3. Russell Markert produced, staged, and

choreographed the Rockettes' spectacular productions at Radio City Music Hall until his retirement in 1971. His obituary in the *New York Times*, December 3, 1990, noted that in "the era when the Music Hall played to full houses every day of the year, he trained and rehearsed 2,500 Rockettes." Beginning in 1939 and throughout the 1940s Jeanne performed numerous times in the spectacular stage shows at Radio City. She had fond memories of sitting with Russell Markert in his spacious office between shows for long conversations about their beginnings in St. Louis and now on the world stage. In 1934 a troupe of the Roxyettes performing at Radio City were re-named the "Radio City Music Hall Rockettes," and have continued performing four shows a day for six days a week and five on Saturdays since their smashing début. There are currently forty-six dancers in the famous Rockettes troupe but only thirty-six perform at a time. In 1955 the Rockette Alumnae Association was founded to organize programs for many charitable causes, and in August 2007 four hundred Rockettes converged on Radio City Music Hall to celebrate their seventy-fifth anniversary. When Jeanne scrutinized the list of attendees, she recognized the name Demler, an original Roxyette from St. Louis, whose sister had also danced at that time but was not on the list.

4. As Twyla Tharp observes in *The Creative Habit*, "All dancers lead the same life; the lowliest corps member and the megastar still have to go to the same class at 10:00 A.M. to stay in shape.... Prima ballerinas work as diligently and carefully at the barre as any novice. (Actually they work *more* diligently on basics that lesser dancers might consider beneath them.) The great ones never take fundamentals for granted," 166.

Chapter 4

1. *Are You There?* was revived at the New York Film Festival in 1969 and premiered to appreciative audiences in New York at the Museum of Modern Art (MOMA) on August 1, 1971. Author Kathleen Menzie Lesko arranged for a special showing of the film at MOMA in New York City to determine if Jeanne's dance were included in the film, discovering that it had been cut.

2. *Kiss Me Again* was first released in late 1930 with the title *Toast of the Legion* and then re-released in early 1931 with a new title and some cuts. The film survives only in black and white. A DVD of the film with a separate DVD of Jeanne's solo dance is in the Jeanne Devereax Perkins Collection. Unfortunately, her solo is not on YouTube, but the film's acrobatic "Ballet Medley" is available for viewing at http://www.youtube.com/watch?v=o1rK-a_8EyM.

3. Gladys Hall, quoted from *Dance Magazine* on back of Jeanne's promotional picture. I have been unable to locate the primary source for this quotation. Gladys Halls high praise is significant. In his book *Inside the Hollywood Fan Magazine: A History of Star Makers, Fabricators, and Gossip Mongers* (Jackson: University Press of Mississippi, 2010) noted theatre and film historian Anthony Slide praises Hall as a writer who was not only "good" but also "incredibly prolific," 35. In 1928 Gladys had been a founding member of the Hollywood Women's Press Club, and during the 1930s was at the height of her career in Hollywood.

4. According to Reva Howitt Clar's daughter in her mother's memoir *Lollipop*, by 1932 "the Ideas were replaced with versions of Broadway musicals and general variety shows, with fewer of these in production as time passed. Fanchon and Marco managed to keep their hand in show business in one form or another into the 1950s, but their career never again reached its former heights," xvii. Fanchon ended her show business career by staging dance numbers for movie musicals for studios like Paramount and Twentieth Century-Fox, while Marco produced several of the Academy award shows.

5. An itinerary in the Jeanne Devereaux Perkins Collection for the last half of a "Fanchon & Marco Tour 1931" documents that Jeanne performed in theatres from the Northeast to the South, including the Palace in Springfield, the Palace in Worcester, the Capitol in Hartford, the Palace in New Haven and Bridgeport, the Fox in Brooklyn, the Academy and Audubon in New York, the Fox in Philadelphia, Washington, and Atlanta, and the Loew's State in Memphis, New Orleans, and Houston.

6. Simon Fanchon and Marco Wolff, *"Love Letters" Newsletter*, 1. The Fanchon and Marco Collection of Photographs and Ephemera, Approximately 1917–1940, Call Number PhotCL 487, at the Huntington Library, San Marino, California.

7. *Ibid.*, 1.
8. *Ibid.*, 1.
9. *Ibid.*, 1.
10. *Ibid.*, 1, 4.
11. *Ibid.*, 3.

Chapter 5

1. Michelle Vogel, *Lupe Vélez: The Life and Career of Hollywood's "Mexican Spitfire"* (Jefferson, North Carolina: McFarland, 2012), 125.

Chapter 6

1. On November 7, 1935, Jeanne and other performers from the cast of the London Palladium's "Round About Regent Street" were featured in a program at the Royal Opera House, Covent Garden, for the Infants Hospital Ball under the patronage of H.R.H. the Princess Royal, the eldest daughter of the reigning monarch. The Embassy Orchestra, directed by Jack Harris, played until midnight when the cabaret show commenced with acts by the J. Sherman Fisher's London Palladium Girls, the Streamline Girls, Jack Taylor's Shout for Joy Girls, the dance team Harrison and Fisher, the African American dance team the Four Flash Devils, the singing cyclist Joe Jackson, the Four Whirlwinds, and a spectacular finale titled "La Caprioca" starring Jeanne Devereaux and the Harmony Rev-

eller—all appearing by Mr. George Black's permission.
  2. Frederick Ashton, interview by David Vaughn, 1973, New York Public Library for the Performing Arts Research Collections, the Jerome Robbins Dance Division, MGZTL 4–517, audio disc #6.
  3. *Ibid.*
  4. David Vaughan, *Frederick Ashton and his Ballets*, 2d ed. (London: Dance Books, 1999), 119. Vaughn used *The Tatler* review in his interview with Ashton, where Jeanne was described as having "'twirled with exciting rapidity on her toes.'" There are numerous periodicals named *The Tatler* in the library databases, but this one is *The Tatler: An Illustrated Journal of Society and the Stage*, published in London from 1901 to 40. I have been unable to obtain a copy of the September 11, 1935, issue.

Chapter 7

  1. Sophie Tucker and Dorothy Giles, *Some of These Days: The Autobiography of Sophie Tucker* (Garden City: Doubleday, Doran, 1945), 270–72. When Sophie had sailed to London she received a radiogram from her agent Harry Foster informing her that she had been selected to sing at the Royal Command performance at the Palladium Theatre on May 9, the same night when she was opening at both the Holborn Empire and Café de Paris. After the second show at the Holborn, Sophie took a taxi to the Palladium: "It was a rainy night, but all around the theatre the street was black with people, waiting for a glimpse of the King and Queen. It was as much I could do to get to the stage door.... With hardly time to realize that this was the event of a lifetime, I went out on the stage." Sophie was limited to the two songs selected by the Lord Chamberlain, so she was unable to sing an encore: "I bowed and bowed.... I looked up at the royal box. King George was smiling broadly. Queen Mary, looking so regal in a silk coat of peacock blue embroidered with Chinese dragons, smiled at me encouragingly," she wrote. While attempting her second curtsy to the royals, her heel got caught in the lace hem of her dress, causing her to wobble, so she "straightened up, gave Their Majesties a good American salute, and left the stage, while the royalties and the audience howled with laughter." She then took a taxi in the rain to the Café de Paris for her third opening that night.
  2. After purchasing a fresh chicken from a grocery store in Montmartre on the Rue Lépic close to the Moulin Rouge, in a flash a member of a band of thieves reached into Lillian's big purse hanging over her shoulder, emptying it of its valuables. By the time Lillian realized the items were missing, the band of thieves had already disappeared into the crowd. Jeanne ran across the street to a corner policeman whom she thought might have been a lookout, frantically telling him that her mother had just been robbed. He answered, "*Je suis fini.* [I'm off duty]." When she later told her story to the chief of police at headquarters, he asked. "How much will you pay me to look for these thieves?"

Chapter 8

  1. Jeanne and Lillian followed the enfolding royal drama of King Edward's abdication of the throne and his subsequent marriage to Mrs. Simpson. Jeanne's first mention of the Simpson scandal was in a letter to her father on September 26, 1936, where she noted that Mrs. Simpson accompanied the King everywhere and was reputed to be "very witty." In early November while performing in Newcastle-on-Tyne Jeanne shared with the cast the American magazines and newspapers that Bill had sent her, and they all particularly enjoyed the scandalous stories about the Mrs. Simpson and King Edward affair. In early December while in Glasgow, Scotland, everyone in the cast was distracted by the exciting prediction in the newspapers of the King's imminent abdication, even missing their cues during performances. Everyone was still upset over the King when they traveled to Sheffield for their next engagement, where they first learned the news of the King actually abdicating.
  2. Ten years previously when they had arrived in New York from St. Louis, Lillian purchased a clock that they had dubbed "Big Ben." "Well, it has never been cleaned, oiled, or re-timed," Jeanne wrote her father on January 13, 1937, "so yesterday when we heard it grinding, we decided its valiant and loyal 'time-keeping' deserved a good overhauling. Believe me, the Big Ben people should hear the adventures of that clock. We'd simply be lost without it." Symbolizing Jeanne's nomadic life as a trouper over the past ten years, the invaluable clock has "lived in suitcases and been all over America, England, Scotland, France, Switzerland, Italy, and Liberia. Has sailed the ocean, and flown over the channel, and due to the faithfulness in the ten years of constant use in traveling, we've never missed a train, boat, or plane," she wrote. Two days later Jeanne wrote in her diary that their "faithful clock" was back from the Leeds repair shop and should last for another ten years.
  3. During the Dublin engagement Jeanne was sitting on a stone bench under the equestrian statue of King George III in Phoenix Park, reading a copy of *The Saturday Evening Post* that her father had just sent her. She rushed off to the theatre to be on time for her next performance. Later that afternoon she learned that a bomb had been placed under the bench where she had been sitting. This was followed by another harrowing experience when she was with her mother in Phoenix Park, when they were surrounded on one side by a large elephant and on the other by an enormous tortoise. All she could think to do was to slow down, back up, and avoid being trampled to death.

Chapter 9

  1. *International Night Life*, the New York magazine of night club activities, dedicated its first issue to the International Casino's premier production that "will depict in stage pictures the most beautiful girls of the world and lighting and costuming that have set a new standard of magnificence in stage

productions." In this production Joseph H. Moss, Louis J. Brecker, Pierre Sandrini and Jaques-Charles "enrapture with spectacles and ensembles, specialities and dances," with the music of George Olsen and His Music of Tomorrow and Yascha Bunchuc and the Continental Orchestra. The magazine claimed that modern "restaurants providing night entertainment" such as the International Casino were even more luxurious than the feasts and festivals of the Greeks and Roman celebrating the Greek Dionysius and Roman Bacchus, the mythological gods of wine, and that the ancient entertainments did "not compare with present-day restaurant revues." One could drive cheaply to and from modern venues in the same day, as opposed to many days of travel in ancient times. Mechanical problems with the stage unfortunately had marred opening night.

as the Music Hall's director general; he was in the hospital and not consulted when the Music Hall Board of Directors combined an abbreviated stage show revue with a motion picture beginning on January 11, 1933, featuring *The Bitter Tea of General Yen* starring Barbara Stanwyck. Radio City thus turned into another movie presentation house that continued to lose money over the years. Tired of the restrictions the Board placed on him, Roxy left the Music Hall management in 1934 and died on January 13, 1936, never realizing his vision for the spectacular theatre he had created. Radio City Music Hall kept the combined vaudeville and film presentation format long after other vaudeville theatres, with the program alternating feature films and lavish stage shows up to the final performance on April 12, 1978. The next year Radio City became primarily a concert house.

Chapter 10

1. Designed by John Price in the Art Deco style, showcasing new decorative materials like transite, aluminum, vitrolite, and stainless steel, Radio City Music Hall was the largest indoor theatre in the world seating nearly 6,200 people, suitable for spectacular stage show presentations. Its massive stage was divided into three elevators that could be raised or lowered, with a sectional revolving stage. It housed the "Mighty Wurlitzer" organ, the largest pipe organ built for a stage and movie theatre.

For its grand opening night on a torrentially rainy December 27, 1932, Roxy devised what Charles Francisco calls in *The Radio City Music Hall: An Affectionate History of the World's Greatest Theatre* (New York: E.P. Dutton, 1979) "the biggest variety or vaudeville show in history," 17. Roxy elevated the program by including opera and ballet. The opening act was the "Symphony of the Curtains" to showcase the spectacular contour stage curtain, and the "Orchestral Interlude" allowed the audience to view the Radio City Symphony Orchestra's spectacular rise in its pit elevator to stage level. Among the vaudeville entertainers on the program were the flying Wallendas aerialists, the Radio City Music Hall Ballet with soloist Patricia Bowman, German opera singer Fraulein Vera Schwarz, London Music Hall dancers Kirkwhite and Addison, the Tuskegee Institute Choir, the headliner Ray Bolger, who later starred in *The Wizard of Oz*, a mini ballet by the in-house company, excerpts from Bizet's *Carmen*, and comedian "Doc" Rockwell, with a finale featuring the entire company. The Radio City Music Hall Roxyettes performed Russell Markert's "With a Feather in Your Cap" on the same program with Martha Graham and her modern dance company, who performed "Choric Dance for an Antique Greek Tragedy."

Because of the rainstorm, the audience arrived late, delaying the show's opening for an hour. Many in the audience left early and missed the second act. The reviews praised the acts with large casts that filled the immense stage, but deemed the venue unsuitable for the individual performer. Roxy collapsed the following morning and never regained his status

Chapter 11

1. A leading architectural historian, Dr. Robert Winter, a retired professor living in the famed tile maker Ernest Batchelder's American Craftsman house in Pasadena and publisher of numerous books on California architecture with an emphasis on the Los Angeles area, identified Frederick Roehrig as the famous architect of Aunt Lenore's house. Roehrig not only designed her American Craftsman house in the style of the low buildings connected with the mission churches, but most likely designed much of the original furniture for his famous client Eddy. For an excellent description of the historic "Eddy House," see George Stickley, ed., "A Modern 'Mission' Dwelling," *The Craftsman* (November 1906): 208–21.

2. Later in 1971 when Aunt Lenore sold her historic house, the new owner speciously promised to be a good steward. However, the new owner immediately violated its landmark status and had the building torn down, replacing it with a large condominium that still stands on the corner of the two prominent Pasadena streets. Whenever Jeanne passed the intersection where Aunt Lenore's historic house had so proudly stood, she felt the loss of this family home. Dr. Robert Winter tried to save this Frederick Roehrig house from the wrecking ball. He considered Aunt Lenore's house to have been a treasured city monument, and he is still angry about its demolition. He believes that this tragic architectural event ignited Pasadena's preservationist movement. Winter keeps a river rock that he salvaged from the ruins as a paperweight on the desk in his living room. At Aunt Lenore's estate sale, impressively organized and managed by Jeanne, Winter noted that most of the original Eddy furniture was sold at top market prices to collectors. Winter himself purchased nine Craftsman lamps from the Eddy era and the andirons now placed in his beautiful Batchelder tiled fireplace. He gave one of the lamps to the curator of the historic Gamble house in Pasadena, who later sold it for thousands of dollars; he also gave a lamp to a friend, who placed it in Pasadena's Castle Green, another of Frederick Roehrig's famous buildings.

Chapter 12

1. In the first half of the twentieth century variety entertainers, a category that included vaudeville performers, were unprotected and their attempts to unionize ineffective. Their primary grievances included the theatre managers' unchallenged right to cancel an act before the third performance, low salaries, the excessive commissions performers were required to pay to the monopolistic booking offices and to their own agents, extra charges demanded by their agents for favors, the unsanitary conditions in the theatres, and the grueling schedule of four and five shows six or seven days a week. They also complained that they had to perform on Sundays with no pay. The American Guild of Variety Artists (AGVA) was founded in 1939 to protect the performing artists and stage managers against the theatre managers. The AGVA was the successor to the American Federation of Actors (AFA) organized by Sophie Tucker and friends in the mid–1930s that dissolved because of financial irregularities. Some AFA members subsequently joined the Actors' Equity Association (AEA), which had been founded in 1913 to protect the rights of legitimate theatre actors. The AGVA and AEA were both affiliated with the American Federation of Labor (AFL). Sometimes it took the political clout of the AFL to solve disputes.

Chapter 13

1. Vaudevillians Jack Donahue and William Frawley, who later played Fred Mertz on the hit television show *I Love Lucy*, along with French actress Lili Damita, starred in the original Broadway show *Sons o' Guns*. The later film version in 1936 featured Joe E. Brown, Eric Blore, and Joan Blondell.

Chapter 14

1. The labor strikes were precipitated by a dispute between the Conference of Studio Unions (CSU), which represented the rank and file carpenters and painters who built the movie sets, and its rival the International Alliance of Theatrical Stage Employees (IATSE), whose members assembled the sets and whose union leaders favored the studio moguls. The Hollywood labor strike began in March 1945 when over 10,000 workers went on strike for seven months protesting negotiations between the unions and the studios, drastically reducing the number of new films, delaying several major films, and causing the studios to rely on their backlog. On October 5, 1945, known later as "Hollywood Black Friday," strikers picketed in front of Warner Bros. main gate, preventing the replacement workers from crossing the barricades, resulting in violent clashes between the strikers, Warner security guards, and the police.

Chapter 15

1. Jeanne Devereaux, interviewed by Laura Marrone, 2003, oral history interview and transcript, Jeanne Devereaux Perkins Collection (AFC/2001/001/11146). Veterans History Project, American Folklife Center, Library of Congress. Much of the content in this interview was repeated and expanded in personal interviews conducted with Jeanne by Kathleen Menzie Lesko from 2006 to 2011, many of which were preserved on audiotape in the private Jeanne Devereaux Perkins Collection.

2. For a graphic description of the destruction of Manila by the Japanese, see William Manchester's *American Caesar: Douglas MacArthur 1880–1964* (Boston: Little, Brown, 1978), 413–44. Manchester emphasizes that the "catalogue of myths about him [MacArthur] is endless. Men who fought in the Pacific and are skeptical on every other topic will swear that some or all of these stories are true, though research exposes every one of them as a lie," 6. Also see George C. Kenny's *The MacArthur I Know* (New York: Duell, Sloan, and Pearce, 1951), 98–100, where Kenny, the head of the air force in the Philippines in 1945, says that MacArthur was never a property owner in the Philippines.

3. In 1945 before the fighting in Manila had ended, a distraught Macarthur demanded to see the newly liberated prisoners of war, many of whom had been his soldiers in the brutal battles of Battan and Corregidor lost to the Japanese in 1941. In his autobiography *Reminiscences* (1964; repr., Annapolis, Maryland: Naval Institute Press/ Bluejacket Books, 2001) MacArthur describes how his first stop was at Santo Tomas prison, where he was "immediately pressed back against the wall by by thousands of ... [men]" wearing "ragged, filthy clothes, with tears streaming down their faces"; then he went to Bilibid, where he saw many of his former soldiers "bearded and soiled ... with ripped and soiled shirts and trousers, with toes sticking out of such shoes as remained, with suffering and torture written on their gaunt faces.... It made me ill just to look at them," 247–48.

4. When Jeanne was in her 90s she said that she knew that Pearl Harbor and World War II had changed American history, only to be repeated with the massive, single day of destruction of New York's Twin Towers on September 11, 2001. She and her husband Tom were watching television in their living room when they saw the airplane hit the second Twin Tower: they were horrified by such a blatant act of violence. Jeanne feared that her dear friend and fellow Broadway dancing partner, Ken Spaulding, who lived on West 16th Street, had been affected; she also thought about her husband's cousin, who lived next to Washington Square. Having lived through the horror of Pearl Harbor, Jeanne was astonished that 9/11 took more innocent American lives than the disastrous day in Hawaii.

Chapter 16

1. Lillian wrote in her October 5, 1946, letter that their concept was "to teach the exact way, to do every Ballet step, which most dancing teachers guess at. And all other Oriental dancing, Character dancing, National dancing, such as Russian, Roumanian, Peasant dances and ballroom. Then finished dance routines, and groupe, etc." They

believed that the potential market would include dancing teachers, dancing students, and even parents for their children; the films could be sold directly to schools. She wrote that 999 dancing teachers out of 1,000 "are in doubt about the exact 'right way' to do every ballet step," and with the films "they will get it, but quick." Start-up costs would be expensive, since they would need to rent a studio "with big lights so that every move of whole body can be seen distinctly. And then doing the illustrating of all these things in front of the camera"; then they would need to print hundreds of films and hire advertising salesmen to contact the dancing teachers. Since this would be a "foolproof thing," they wondered why some "smart enterprising business man hasn't stumbled onto this before now," emphasizing that "artists have no money, and business men do not think about the arts, as having big profits in the persuance of teaching them, so they have so far never started it": because of the recent stock market crash, they would need a backer "with plenty of money they made during the WAR!!!"

2. Andrew Lee Fielding, *The Lucky Strike Papers: Journeys Through My Mother's Television Past* (Albany, New York: Bear Manor Media, 2007), 31.

3. Bill Smith, *The Vaudevillians* (New York: Macmillan, 1976), 73.

4. Andrew Lee Fielding, *The Lucky Strike Papers*, 57.

Chapter 17

1. On March 22nd Jeanne wrote Tom that they had seen the film *Streetcar Named Desire*, and she was moved by its unforgettable truth: "It should win the Oscar this year and everyone should see it. It has something in it that will almost tear you to pieces with the awful truth of them—Williams who wrote it can do anything in the world with words & not glib, nor trite, nor clever things—but deep to the roots of life honest things with words that almost make one ache." Their year's highlight was seeing the Broadway production of *The King and I*.

Chapter 18

1. In *The Creative Habit* Twyla Tharp included a set of questions that make up one's "Creative Autobiography," 45. In an interview in 2007 when posed with Tharp's question "What is the best idea you've ever had?" Jeanne unhesitatingly answered, "Marrying Tom"—a decision that defined her life for over half a century.

2. After being diagnosed with incurable breast cancer in 1932, at the end of her life Aunt Charlotte moved to Pasadena to be near her daughter and her family. Her nephew Tom Perkins visited her, discovering that she also had a severe case of abdominal shingles. Two weeks later on August 17, 1935, she committed suicide by taking an overdose of chloroform.

3. Juliana Delgado and John G. Ripley, *Images of America: Pasadena's Bungalow Heaven* (Charleston, South Carolina: Arcadia, 2012), 33–34. This book contains photographs of the Perkins' American Craftsman house, Jeanne and Tom in their house on their wedding day in 1952, and a promotional picture of Jeanne from 1935.

4. Nancy Upper, *Ballet Dancers in Career Transition* (Jefferson, North Carolina: McFarland, 2004), 1–2.

5. An advertisement in the *Pasadena Independent* for May 27, 1955, for the Devereaux Ballet Arts School's dance festival the following evening at Pasadena City College's Auditorium had a professional picture of Jeanne with the caption "Jeanne Devereaux of Radio City Music Hall will appear with dancers" of her school. The ambitious program featured a variety of ethnic dances, with Jeanne dancing the "Doll Fairy" in "Fantastic Doll Shop"; "Geisha Harusame 'Spring Rain'" in "Japanese Children's Party"; "Variation" in "Coda Deuxieme Quadrille"; "La Demoiselle" in "In the Park, in Paris, in the Spring—1898"; "Mother Goddess" in "Hindu Legend"; and "Russian Dance." Jeanne designed the costumes, scenery, and props and most of the choreography. The program for the Devereaux Ballet Dance Festival held on June 22, 1957, at Pasadena City College's Auditorium featured forty-five students in a three-Act program. An advertisement in the *Pasadena Independent*, June 20, 1957, described the upcoming dance event as "A WONDERFUL EVENING OF COLORFUL SPECTACLE, MUSIC, BALLET AND AN EXCITING MAGIC CARPET TOUR OF MANY LANDS," including a picture of two young dancers in costume holding props. In the final act, titled the "Magic Carpet Travel Agency," Jeanne was the village storyteller and celestial elephant in "Gauba's Journey to Paradise," based on a folktale by Babe Trinco, as well as the gypsy fortune teller in "Italy." She created, designed, and choreographed the entire production, and Lillian was the general manager and head of special props and effects, while Tom directed sound, recording, and scenery construction.

6. In 1966 Bob Wark, the director of the Arts Department at the Huntington, asked Jeanne to help him design shelving for exhibiting a collection of cream pitchers in the Huntington Mansion House. She suggested that broken pediments instead of straight shelving was the answer to his problem. Later, the Director of the Huntington hired Jeanne and Tom to design special cases for the old bookstore that would properly show off its prints and postcards. Wark then recommended that Jeanne and Tom attend the Association of American Museums (AAM) conference in Chicago to learn more about the museum business and its needs. As they drove to Chicago, they stopped at twenty museums interviewing museum curators, who all wanted more secure, functional, and attractive exhibit cases for displaying their treasures. When Jeanne and Tom returned to Pasadena, they began the complicated process of designing a revolutionary museum exhibit case that met all their criteria. Tom then built the new cases in their three-car garage. Jeanne used her experience in designing and sketching her own costumes when she partnered with Tom in their museum case venture.

7. Jeanne and Tom installed exhibit cases in many

prestigious venues, including the Norton Simon Museum in Pasadena, the USC Pacific Asia Museum in Pasadena, the Huntington Library's Mansion House, the Griffith Park Observatory in Los Angeles, the Alaska State Museum, and the Air Museum in San Diego.

8. In 1944 when a group of women led by Bess Barden in Philadelphia were wrapping bandages for World War II soldiers, Bess put something in the middle of the work table and said: "I fell in love with this object, I purchased it, but I don't know what it is. Can any of you tell me?" When no one recognized the object, Bess suggested that they form a group to study art and antiques. From those few ladies the Questers evolved into an international organization dedicated to historic restoration and preservation with 900 chapters in America and Canada. In 1972 Jeanne was a founding member of the Questers El Molino Chapter in Pasadena, and in 1979–80 she was also the vice-president of the California State Chapter. She remained an active Quester well into her nineties when she became an honorary member.

Epilogue

1. Twyla Tharp's inspiring message about creativity in *The Creative Habit* echoes Jeanne's: "When creativity has become your habit; when you've learned to manage time, resources, expectations, and the demands of others; when you understand the value and place of validation, continuity, and purity of purpose—then you're on the way to an artist's ultimate goal: the achievement of mastery," 240.

Bibliography

Affron, Charles. *Lillian Gish: Her Legend, Her Life.* Berkeley: University of California Press, 2001.

Allen, Robert C. *Vaudeville and Film, 1895–1915: A Study in Media Interaction.* New York: Arno, 1980.

Aloff, Mindy. *Dance Anecdotes: Stories from the Worlds of Ballet, Broadway, the Ballroom, and Modern Dance.* New York: Oxford University Press, 2006

Alter, Judy. *Vaudeville: The Birth of Show Business.* New York: Franklin Watts, 1998.

Anderson, Chuck. "Foothill Gets Museum Bargain." *San Jose Mercury,* March 25, 1971.

Aschenbrenner, Joyce. *Katherine Dunham: Dancing A Life.* Urbana: University of Illinois Press, 2002.

Ashton, Frederick. Interviews by David Vaughan, 1973. New York Public Library for the Performing Arts at Lincoln Center. The Jerome Robbins Dance Division. MGZTL 4-517, Audio Disc #6.

Aylesworth, Thomas, and Virginia Aylesworth. *New York: The Glamour Years, 1919–1945.* New York: Gallery, 1987.

Balaban, Connie. *Continuous Performance.* New York: A. J. Balaban Foundation, 1964.

Baronova, Irina. *Irina: Ballet, Life and Love.* Gainesville: University Press of Florida, 2005.

Berger, Robert, and Anne Conser. *The Last Remaining Seats: Movie Palaces of Tinseltown.* Pasadena: Navigator Press, 1997.

Berkowitz, Edward D. *Mass Appeal: The Formative Age of the Movies, Radio, and TV.* Cambridge Essential Histories. Cambridge: Cambridge University Press, 2010.

Bret, David. *Joan Crawford: Hollywood Martyr.* New York: Da Capo Press, 2006.

Caffin, Caroline, and Marius De Zayas. *Vaudeville.* New York: Mitchell Kennerley, 1914.

Churchill, Allen. *The Great White Way: A Re-Creation of Broadway's Golden Era of Theatrical Entertainment.* New York: E. P. Dutton, 1962.

Clar, Reva Howitt. *Lollipop: Vaudeville Turns with a Fanchon and Marco Dancer.* Ed. Mimi Melnick. Lanham, Maryland: Scarecrow Press, 2002.

Csida, Joseph, and June Bundy Csida. *American Entertainment: A Unique History of Popular Show Business.* New York: Billboard, 1978.

Cullen, Frank, with Florence Hackman and Donald McNeilly. *Vaudeville Old & New: An Encyclopedia of Variety Performers in America.* 2 vols. New York: Routledge, 2007.

Davies, Marion. *The Times We Had: Life with William Randolph Hearst.* Ed. Pamela Pfau and Kenneth S. Marx. New York: Ballantine, 1977. First published 1975.

Davis, Lee. *Scandals and Follies: The Rise and Fall of the Great Broadway Revue.* New York: Proscenium Publishers, 2000.

Delgado, Julianna, and John G. Ripley. *Images of America: Bungalow Heaven.* Charleston, South Carolina: Arcadia Publishing, 2012.

Dijk, Elly Van. "Retirement Not an Issue for 89-Year-Old." *The Sunday Star,* November 25, 2001.

Dimeglio, John E. *Vaudeville U.S.A.* Bowling Green, Ohio: Bowling Green University Popular Press, 1973.

Drez, Ronald J. *Twenty-Five Yards of War: The Extraordinary Courage of Ordinary Men in World War II.* New York: Hyperion, 2001.

Eliot, Karen. *Dancing Lives: Five Female Dancers from the Ballet d'Action to Merce Cunningham.* Urbana: University of Illinois Press, 2007.

Fanchon, Simon, and Marco Wolff. *"Love Letters" Newsletter* and Photograph Album, 1931. The Fanchon and Marco Collection of Photographs and Ephemera, Approximately 1917–1940. Call Number PhotCL 487. Huntington Library, San Marino, California.

Fielding, Andrew Lee. *The Lucky Strike Papers: Journeys Through My Mother's Television Past.* Albany, New York: Bear Manor Media, 2007.

Fields, Armond. *Women Vaudeville Stars: Eighty Biographical Profiles.* Jefferson, North Carolina: McFarland, 2006.

Fisher, Barbara Milberg. *In Balanchine's Company: A Dancer's Memoir.* Middleton, Connecticut: Wesleyan University Press, 2006.

Francisco, Charles. *The Radio City Music Hall: An Affectionate History of the World's Greatest Theatre.* New York: E. P. Dutton, 1979.

Freedman, Russell. *Martha Graham: A Dancer's Life.* New York: Clarion Books, 1998.

Garrett, Betty. "Naughty and Nice." *Los Angeles Times,* May 27, 2009.

_____, with Ron Rapoport. *Betty Garrett and Other Songs*. Lanham, Maryland: Madison Books, 2000.
Gilbert, Douglas. *American Vaudeville, Its Life and Times*. New York: Dover Publications, 1963. First published 1940.
Gilbert, Martin. *The Second World War: A Complete History*, rev. ed. New York: Henry Holt, 1991.
Gish, Lillian. *Dorothy and Lillian Gish*. Ed. James E. Frasher. New York: Charles Scribner's Sons, 1973.
Gomeroy, Douglas. *Shared Pleasures: A History of Movie Presentation in the United States*. Madison: University of Wisconsin Press, 1992.
Green, Abel, and Joe Laurie, Jr. *Show Biz From Vaude To Video*. New York: Henry Holt and Company, 1951.
Hall, Ben M. *The Golden Age of the Movie Palace: The Best Remaining Seats*. New York: Clarkson N. Potter, 1988. First published 1961.
Hayes, Helen, with Katerine Hatch. *My Life in Three Acts*. New York: Harcourt Brace Jovanovich, 1990.
Heilbrun, Caroline G. *Writing A Woman's Life*. Foreword Katha Politt. New York: Norton, 2008. First published 1988.
Henderson, Mary C. *The City and the Theater: The History of New York Playhouses*. Back Stage Books, 2004.
Homans, Jennifer. *Apollo's Angels: A History of Ballet*. New York: Random House, 2010.
Karsavina, Tamara. *Theatre Street*. New York: Dutton, 1961. First published 1931.
Keaton, Buster, with Charles Samuels. *My Wonderful World of Slapstick*. New introd. Dwight Macdonald and new filmog. Rayment Rohauer. New York: Da Capo Press, 1982. First published 1960.
Kennedy, David M., ed. *The Library of Congress World War II Companion*. New York: Simon & Schuster, 2007.
Kenney, George C. *The MacArthur I Know*. New York: Duell, Sloan, and Pearce, 1951.
Kibler, M. Alison. *Rank Ladies: Gender and Cultural Hierarchy in American Vaudeville*. Chapel Hill: University of North Carolina Press, 1999.
Laurie, Joe, Jr. *Vaudeville: From the Honky-Tonks to the Palace*. New York: Holt, 1953.
Lee, Carol. *Ballet in Western Culture: A History of Its Origins and Evolution*. New York: Routledge, 2002.
Lesko, Kathleen Menzie. "Jeanne Devereaux Perkins: International Ballerina." *Pasadena Star-News*. August 14, 2011.
_____. Personal interviews on tape with Jeanne Devereaux Perkins and Tom Perkins. 2006–2011.
_____. "Thomas Gardiner Perkins, March 15, 1913-October 15, 2012." *Pasadena Star-News*. January 13, 2013.
MacArthur, Douglas. *Reminiscences*. Annapolis, Maryland: Naval Institute Press-Bluejacket Books, 2001. First in 1964.
Manchester, William. *American Caesar: Douglas MacArthur 1880–1964*. Boston: Little, Brown, 1978.

Marsh, John L. "Vaudefilm: Its Contribution to a Moviegoing America." *Journal of Popular Culture* 18, no. 4 (Spring 1985): 17–29.
McCabe, Maureen. *Moon Over Vaudeville*. Bellingham, Washington: Moon Over Vaudeville LLC, 2011.
McLean, Albert F. *American Vaudeville as Ritual*. Lexington: University of Kentucky Press, 1965.
Miller, Terry. "Pasadena Prima Ballerina and Vaudevillian Passes Away in Relative Obscurity." *Pasadena Independent*. August 11, 2011.
Murray, Williamson and Allan R. Millett. *A War to Be Won: Fighting the Second World War*. Cambridge: Belknap Press of Harvard University Press, 2000.
Naylor, David. *American Picture Palaces: The Architecture of Fantasy*. New York: Van Nostrand Reinhold, 1981.
_____. *Great American Movie Theaters*. Great American Places Series. Washington, D.C.: Preservation Press, 1987.
Nielsen, Mike, and Gene Mailes. *Hollywood's Other Blacklist: Union Struggles in the Studio System*. London: British Film Institute, 1995.
O'Connor, Jane. *The Cultural Significance of the Child Star*. New York: Routledge, 2008.
"Jeanne Devereaux Weds Here." *Pasadena Star-News*. November 7, 1952.
Jeanne Perkins. Jeanne Devereaux Perkins Collection. Laura Marrone, Interviewer. Collection AFC/2001/001/11146. Veterans History Project, American Folklife Center, Library of Congress, 2003.
_____. Jeanne Perkins Collection. Private Collection of Documents and Photographs in the Estate of Jeanne and Tom Perkins, Pasadena, California.
Playbills for "*Manhattan Mary*." 1927 and 1928. "Belnap Playbill and Program Collection" in the Belnap Collection for the Performing Arts of Theatre Playbills and Programs from the Late 18th Century to the Present at the George A. Smathers Libraries. University of Florida, Box #62.
Renton, Edward. *The Vaudeville Theatre: Building, Operation, Management*. New York: Gotham Press, 1918.
"Russell Markert, 91, the Founder and the Director of the Rockettes." *New York Times*. December 3, 1990.
Safer, Jeanne. *Beyond Motherhood: Choosing a Life Without Children*. New York: Pocket Books, 1996.
Samuels, Charles. *Once Upon a Stage: The Merry World of Vaudeville*. New York: Dodd, Mead, 1974.
Scott, Harold. *The Early Doors: Origins of the Music Hall*. London: Nicholson & Watson, 1946.
Seidel, Andrea Mantell. *Isadora Duncan in the 21st Century: Capturing the Art and Spirit of the Dancer's Legacy*. Jefferson, North Carolina: McFarland, 2016.
Seymour, Maurice. *Seymour on Ballet*. Foreword Leonide Massine. New York: Pellegrini and Cudahy, 1949. First published 1947.

Short, Ernest Henry. *Fifty Years of Vaudeville*. London: Eyre & Spottiswoode, 1946.
Simonson, Mary. *Body Knowledge: Performance, Intermediality, and American Entertainment at the Turn of the Twentieth Century*. Oxford: Oxford University Press, 2013.
Slide, Anthony. *Hollywood Unknowns: A History of Extras, Bit Players, and Stand-Ins*. Jackson: University Press of Mississippi, 2012.
_____. *Inside the Hollywood Fan Magazine: A History of Star Makers, Fabricators, and Gossip Mongers*. Jackson: University Press of Mississippi, 2010.
_____. *The New Historical Dictionary of the American Film Industry*. Lanham, Maryland: Scarecrow Press, 1998.
_____. *Selected Vaudeville Criticism*. Metuchen, New Jersey: Scarecrow Press, 1988.
_____. *The Vaudevillians: A Dictionary of Vaudeville Performers*. Westport, Connecticut: Arlington House, 1981.
_____, ed. *The Encyclopedia of Vaudeville*. Westport, Connecticut: Greenwood Press, 1994.
Smith, Bill. *The Vaudevillians*. New York: Macmillan, 1976.
Snyder, Robert W. *The Voice of the City: Vaudeville and Popular Culture in New York*. Chicago: Ivan R. Dee, 2000. First published 1989.
Sobel, Bernard. *A Pictorial History of Vaudeville*. New York: Citadel Press, 1961.
South, Lucile Iverson South. *On Toes of Gold: A Story of the Dance and the Dancer*. Cliff, New Mexico: Blusage Studio Designers & Publishers, 2001.
Spitzer, Marian. *The Palace*. New York: Atheneum, 1969.
_____. "The People of Vaudeville." *Saturday Evening Post*. July 12, 1924.
Steeh, Judith. *History of Ballet and Modern Dance*. New York: Galahad Books, 1982.
Stein, Charles W., ed. *American Vaudeville As Seen By Its Contemporaries*. New York: Alfred A. Knopf, 1984.
Stewart, D. Travis. *No Applause—Just Throw Money: The Book That Made Vaudeville Famous*. New York: Faber and Faber, 2005.
Stickley, Gustav, ed. "A Modern 'Mission' Dwelling." *The Craftsman* (November, 1906): 208–221.
Stratyner, Barbara. *Ned Wayburn and the Dance Routine: From Vaudeville to the Ziegfeld Follies*. Studies in Dance History, No. 13. Madison, Wisconsin: Society of Dance History Scholars, 1996.
Taylor, William R., ed. *Inventing Times Square: Commerce and Culture at the Crossroads of the World*. Baltimore: Johns Hopkins University Press, 1996. First published 1991.
Tharp, Twyla. *The Creative Habit: Learn It and Use It for Life*. New York: Simon & Schuster, 2006. First published 2003.
Time Magazine. "Rockettes to Paris." *Time Magazine*. June 21, 1937.
Tucker, Sophie, and Dorothy Giles. *Some of These Days: The Autobiography of Sophie Tucker*. Garden City: Doubleday, Doran, 1945.
Toll, Robert C. *On with the Show: The First Century of Show Business in America*. New York: Oxford University Press, 1976.
Upper, Nancy. *Ballet Dancers in Career Transition*. Jefferson, North Carolina: McFarland, 2004.
Valentine, Maggie. *The Show Starts on the Sidewalk: An Architectural History of the Movie Theater, Starring S. Charles Lee*. New Haven: Yale University Press, 1994.
Valentine, Martha. *The Show Started on the Sidewalk/ S. Charles Lee*. Los Angeles: University of California Press, 1987.
Variety. New York: Variety Publications Company. Multiple copies from Online Archives. Dates included in the text.
Vaughan, David. *Frederick Ashton and His Ballets*, 2d ed. London: Dance Books Ltd., 1999. First published 1977.
Vogel, Michelle. *Lupe Vélez: The Life and Career of Hollywood's "Mexican Spitfire."* Jefferson, North Carolina: McFarland, 2012.
Ware, Walter. *Ballet Is Magic: A Triple Monograph: Harriet Hoctor, Paul Haakon, Patricia Bowman*. New York: IHRA Publishing Company, 1936.
Watts, Jennifer A. "Let Us Entertain You: Fanchon and Marco's Big 'Ideas' Revolutionized the 1920s Theater World." *Huntington Frontiers*. Fall/Winter, 2015.
Wertheim, Arthur. *Vaudeville Wars: How the Keith-Albee and Orpheum Circuits Controlled the Bigtime and Its Performers*. New York: Palgrave MacMillan, 2006.
White, Thelma, with Harry Preston. *Thelma Who! Almost 100 Years of Showbiz*. Lanham, Maryland: Scarecrow Press, 2002.
Wilson, Lee. *Rebel On Pointe: A Memoir of Ballet & Broadway*. Gainesville: University Press of Florida, 2014.
Williams, Janette. "Ballerina to Biographer." *Pasadena Star-News*. January 20, 1994.
_____. "Jeanne Perkins Dies at Age 98." *Pasadena Star-News*. August 10, 2011.

Index

Numbers in ***bold italics*** indicate pages with photographs.

Academy of Music 60
"Acceleration Waltz" 66
Achilles tendon 196, 199
adagio 24, 26
Adeline Rotty's Ballet School 20
Adler, Larry 79, 88, 98
Aeroplane Girls 49
agents 34
Albee, Edward R. 8
Albee theatre 65–66
Albertieri, Luigi 42
Alexandra Palace 117
Alhambra 87–88
"All in a Day" ***192***, 196–197
Almquist, Peggy 229
American Ballet Theatre 9, 214
American Expeditionary Forces 162
American Guild of Variety Artists (AGVA) 144, 146, 259*ch*12*n*1
American Manufacturing Company 198
American Manufacturing Concern 14, 158, 175, 198
American Musical and Dramatic Academy 162
American National Theatre and Academy 234
amphitheatre, Roman 89
Anderson, John Murray 44; *see also* Greenwich Village Follies
ankle 110
Apollo Theatre 37
arabesque, vertical (split) 28, ***67***, ***169***
Ardelty, Elly 166, 217
Are You There? 45, 256*ch*4*n*1
Argas, Getulio 126
Argentine (ship) 127
Ashton, Frederick 72, 82, 257*n*4
Aubrey, Will 49
audiences, apathetic 101
audition 34, 36, 47, 53–54, 55, 56, 76, 120, 161, 171, 175, 177

Australia 202–203, 230
autographs 81

Badalyan, Sarkis 244, 254
Baker, Josephine 126, 213
Bal Tabarin 112, ***113***, 113–114
Balalaika 164, 176, 200
Balanchine, George 177
Ballerina 141
ballet: fundamentals 20, 22, 27–28; influence on women's fashions 233–234; perfection expected 30, 230
ballet companies 9, 177, 214, 228
ballet mistress 36
balloon dance 30–31, 107–110, 115, ***116***, 157, ***163***, 164, 168, 172
bangs ***59***, 64
"Banners in the Breeze" ***192***, 196
Barto, Dewey, ***165***, 166
Bayes, Nora, 18
Beaton, Cecil, 234
Belle, Ida, 68, 107–108
Belvedere Hotel 73, 151, 159, 164, 202, 204, 206, 207, 209, 213, 216
benefit performances, 8, 53, 54, 69, 70, 71, 113, 171, 174, 180, 214, 216, 256–257*ch*6*n*1
Bennett, Mrs. 39, 59
Bennett family 39, 70, 72, 106
Benny, Jack 171
RMS *Berengaria* 69–70, ***70***, 71, ***71***
Berle, Milton 17, 208, 209, 222
Berle, Mrs. 209
B.F. Keith Memorial Theatre 41
B.F. Keith's Eighty-First Street Theatre 41
Billy (dancing partner) 214–215
Biltmore Hotel 161

birthday: of Bill 175, 194, 208; of Grandpa Lane 15, 173; of Jeanne 25, 61, 97, 140, 159, 175, 185, 198, 206, 215, 241, 243–244; of Lillian 151, 152
Bitter Sweet 162–164, ***163***
Black, Alfie 80, 81, 100, 120
Black, George 65, 66, 72–73, 76, 80, 81, 86, 94, 118, 120
Black, George, Jr. 80, 81, 98, 99, 100, 103, 105, 106, 108
Black, Mrs. 80, 100
Black, Pauline 80, 81, 87, 100
Bliss, Guy Stanley ***224***, 226; *see also* dream house: Jeanne and Tom
Bloom Chicago ***59***
Bolling Air Force Base 186
Bolm, Adolph 42
bomb scares 150, 151, 156, 159
Boop, Betty 107
Bourman, Frank 230
Bourman, Rosalia 230
Bowman, Patricia (Patsy) 28, 34, 94, 98, 119, 155, 194
"Bravo" 107–110
Brazil, tour in 124–127
Brice, Fanny 22
British Broadcasting Company (BBC) 117
Broadbent, Aida 166
Broadway 32–33
Brockton Fair 158
Brown, Gilmore 54, 55
Brown, Helen 82
Brown, Lew 36
Brown Palace Club 57
bubble dance *see* balloon dance
Bungalow Heaven 226; *see also* dream house
burn 74
bursitis 196
"Buster Shaver with Olive and George" 143, 144, ***145***, 151–152
"Buy My Cherries" 76, 84

265

Caesar, Sid 208
Camille at Roaring Camp 54–55; *see also* Pasadena Community Playhouse
Camp Kilmer 186
Camp Monmouth 185
Camp Yaphank 186
camping 12, 13–14
cancer 225
Cannes, France 88
canoeing 13–14
El Capitan Theatre 234
Capitol theatre 62, 129, 132, 147, 156, 157
Caron, Leslie 42
Carroll, Earl 2, 32, 124, 132, 133, 142, 143, 144, 146, 147–148, 151, 152
Carroll, Faye 144
Carson, Jack 171
Casino de Urca 125, 126
Caton, Eddie 42
censorship, of letters 185–186
Cervera, Alida 30, 227, 228, 230, 231, 233
Chalif, Louis Harvey 42
Charisse, Cyd 42
Charles, Jacques 108
Chateau Bagatelle 83, 114–115, *116*
"Cherry Ripe" 76, 78, *78*
Chester theatre 60
Chevalier, Maurice 79
Chevrolet touring car 68, 70
Chicago Theatre 110, *111*
child employment laws 37–38
Children's Theatre Festival 234
Chinese Cemetery and Temple (Manila, Philippines) 188–189
Chinese Treasure House of Oriental and Western Art 1, *238*, 240, 251, 252–253
The Chocolate Soldier 136, 137
chocolates 86
choreography 30–31, 54–55, 73, 75, 82, 113, 125, 155, 204, 231, 234
Christensen, Lew 137
Christmas 33, 62, 80, 98, 99, 112, 120, 129, 142, 150–151, 159, 160, 168, 175, 187–188, 198, 206–207
circuits, tours of 9, 10, 40–42, 44, 47–53, 57–68, 106–107, 143–152, 168–171
Civic Auditorium 170
Clair-Guyot, J. *113*
"Claire de Lune" 31
Clare, Ina 38–39
Clarke, George 94, *95*, 100, 103
coats, fur 100
Cobb, Lee J. 53
Coco, Imogene 208
coin collection 207
Colonna, Jerry 172

"Copacabana Night Club Revue from New York" 183–190, *184*, 250
Coppelia 214
costumes: *21*, *23*, 30, *35*, *48*, *49*, 69, *77*, 92, 105, 115, 124, *135*, 162, *163*, *165*, *167*, *169*, *172*, *184*, *192*, *197*, 199, *202*, 204, 206; for balloon dance 108, *109*, *116*, 144; beaded 199; bird, for Rose Pageant 54; black lace *59*, 61; black velvet leotard 215; for "Cherry Ripe" 76, *78*; designed by Jeanne for dancing school 231–233, 234; ethnic 137, 220–221; Hungarian 137; for "The Lady in Red" 73, *77*, 97; for "The Moth and the Flame" 73, 74, *75*; patriotic 155; sheer net 64; of Sixteen Sunkist Beauties 50; sketches for 107, 220, *232*; white feathery *59*; white pompoms 129
Coudy, Doug 24, 33
courtship 210
The Crazy Gang 73, 84
Cristiani family (equestrians) 171, 172
Crosby, Bing 171
Cunningham, B.J. 204
Curt Fox LA *48*, *49*

"Dancing Girls Orchid" 16–17, 241
"Dawn of a New Day" 121; *see also* World's Fair
defense business 155, 156
de Mille, Agnes 42
deMille, Cecil B. 154
destruction, from war 181, 188, 189, 191
DeSylva, Buddy 36
Detroit Civic Light Opera 176
Devereaux, Ida Belle 149
Devereaux, Jeanne *17*, *21*, *23*, *29*, *35*, *43*, *46*, *48*, *49*, 50–51, 55, 58–59, *59*, *67*, *70*, *71*, *72*, *75*, *77*, *78*, *85*, *109*, *116*, *135*, *145*, *163*, *165*, *169*, *172*, *184*, *192*, *197*, *202*, *223*, *231*, *238*, *239*, *244*; on art and self-discipline 243; character 20; childhood 11–14, 16–19; dance school 133–134, 138, 139, 141, 218–221; death 244; final professional appearance 244; financial freedom 210, 211, 216; honored as outstanding TV performer 117; in love 58, 210; marriage proposal 61, 90, 98, 106; oral history 6, 250; overview of career 8–10; pastel portrait 131; performance before royalty 83–87, 114–115, *116*, 174; relationship with father 12, 51, 70, 101–102, 122–123, 132, 136, 137, 139, 140, 141, 150, 178, 181, 207–208; relationship with mother 18, 55, 60, 62–63, 80, 93–94, 97, 131, 174, 199, 204, 224–225, 236–237; thoughts on biography 246–247
Devereaux, Ray 149
Devereaux Ballet Arts School 227–234, *229*, *231*
diphtheria 114
Disney, Walt 123
"Dive In" 53
Dixon, Harland 36, 44
Dodge touring car 44
Dolin, Anton 84
Dollar, William 24, 33, 60, 110
Dorchester hotel 93, 117
dream house: Aunt Lenore 138–140, 142; Jeanne and Tom 222, *224*, *226*, 226–227
Duke of Kent 83
Duncan, Isadora 219
Durante, Jimmy 171
Dwyer, Norah 94
The Dying Swan 22

Earl Carroll's Vanities 32, 40, 143–152, *145*, 154, 155, *165*, 181
Easter 123, 154, 194
Eddy, Arthur Jerome 139
Eddy, Wesley 58
Eddy House 139, 258*ch*11*n*1,2
E.F. Albee Theatre 41
Ellery, Captain 188, 189
Empire Park theatre 103
Empire theatres 96
England: tour in 94–104, 117–118; travel to 70–72
Errolle, Martha 164
Esler, Cath *95*, 102, 106, 222
Europe and North Africa, tour in 87–92
exhibit at San Diego USO Neil Ash Airport Center 250
eye-black 79, 125

Fair Park Casino 162–164, 178
Fairbanks, Douglas, Jr. 79
Fairbanks, Douglas, Sr. 18
Fanchon and Marco 47, 56
fashions, women's, influenced by ballet 233–234
Fays (Providence, Rhode Island) 131–132
feet 30, 196, 203, 215
festivals (Los Angeles) 231–233, 260*n*5
Fields, Gracie 79
finances: Bill's 38, 122, 128–129, 141, 198, 203; cars and 44, 159; dancing lessons and

27; Great Depression and 82, 91; house prices and 138, 139; inheritances 200–201, 204, 205, 207; insurance 206; money from Bill 38, 112, 121, 125, 129, 130, 131, 134–135, 153, 156–157; money from Bill, repaid 114, 186, 194; preparatory to marriage 210, 216, 218; rents 121, 151, 152–153, 159, 165, 168, 198; savings and 97, 100; of shows 121, 144, 146; television payment 209; unemployment program and 134, 137; upset letters about 122, 128–129, 130–131, 134, 136, 137, 139, 141, 153, 156–157, 158, 174, 200–201, 203, 204, 205; weekly income 10, 25, 26, 51, 69, 106, 107, 122, 131, 133, 158, 161, 165
The Firebird 54
Fisher, Clifford C. 108, 159, 164, **167**, **169**; see also Folies Bergère
flag 154, 155
"The Fleet's In" 57–58
flooding 26, 206
Fokine, Michel 42
Fokine ballet company 60
Folies Bergère 164–171, **165**, **167**, **169**, **172**, 237, **239**, 247
foot 215
Foote, Horton 54
Foothill College Science Center (Los Altos) 235–236
Ford cars 159, 212, 221
Fort Hamilton 186–187
Fortunato, George 54
Foster, Gae 49
Foster, Harry 87, 93
fouetté 8, 28, **29**, 54, 60, 76, 87, 95, 99, 176, 229
Four Flash Devils 76, 78
Fox, Will 61
Fox theatre 148
Foy, Bob 59
Frawley, Paul 36
French Casino Follies 108
Friedman, Herman 209
fruitcake 150, 168
furniture 139–140

Gabriel Moulin Studios **172**
Garden Theatre 24–25, 26, 27
Garland, Judy 213–214
General Pope (ship) 190
George Ahoy! 94–104, **95**, 117
Gerry Society 37, 255ch3n1
Getty Villa Museum 235
Gil Maison and Company 154
Gilbert, Gloria 82
Gill, Chas 76
Gilman, Charlotte Perkins 225, 260ch18n2

Ginsberg, Dr. 55
Givens, Jimmy 26, 108, 207, 213, 222, 233
Glen, Cynda 157
"Glory of Easter" 123
"God Save the King" 83
Golden Gate Theatre 143–144
Good News **135**, 136, 137
"Good Ship Holiday" **197**
Grace and Niko 149
Grand Hotel 60
Great Depression 39, 45
The Great Waltz 176, 199, 200, 201–202, **202**
Green, Charles 226
Green, Henry 226
Greenwich Village Follies 40, 44
Grosvenor House hotel 117
Gutchrlein, Eleanor 90
Gutchrlein, Karla 90

Haakon, Paul 127, 128, 155
Hall, Gladys 47
Hamilton Field 186
Hansel and Gretel 25
Harrison and Fisher (dance team) 78, 84, 127
Harry Foster Agency 34
Hartman, Carroll S. 252; see also Nicolson, Grace
Hawaii 186–187
heirlooms 122, 141, 207
Hellzapoppin Company 148, 149
Helman, Amanda Lillian Lane **15**, **16**; ancestors 12–13; death 236–237; inherited land 200–201, 204; on Jeanne marrying 216, 224; musical talent 14–15; nicknamed "Bob White" 18; researching costumes 233; travel to Nebraska 138, 199, 204; work at dancing school 227, 228
Helman, Grandpa 199
Helman, Jean see Devereaux, Jeanne
Helman, William "Bill" Douglas **13**, 13–14, **16**, 18, 26, 39–40, 51, 70, **71**, 111, 122, 125–126, 137–138, 152–153, 176, 203; death 207; emotional needs 128–129, 195, 199; mental health issues 25, 26–27, 44, 51, 129; New York 38, 61–62, 63, 68, 70; suicide attempt 32
Henderson, Ray 36
Henry, Dick 66, 106
Hibiah Theatre (Tokyo) 190
Hickam Field 187
Hindu dance 219, 220
Hines, Elizabeth 37
Hippodrome (Birmingham) 95–96

Hippodrome (Brighton) 73, 74, 94, 101
Hippodrome (Portsmouth) 95
Hippodrome (Shea's) 41, 60
Hiroshima Prefectural Industrial Promotion Hall (Genbaku Dome) 189
Hoctor, Harriet 82
Holborn Empire theatre 96–97, 102, 117
Hollywood restaurant-theatre 132, 143
Holman, Jane 19
Holtz, Lou 36, 38
"Honorary Captain" rank 180
Hope, Bob 171, 172, **184**
Hotel Last Frontier 174
Houck, Florence and Dick 16
house see dream house
Hughes, Russell Meriwether 219
Huntington Library 1, 237–239, **238**, **239**, 243, **244**, 246
Les Hures Sont Belles 113–114
hurricane 118
Hutton, Barbara 114
Hyde Park 80, 93

"Idea" stage shows 47, 256ch4n4; see also Fanchon and Marco
income tax 100, 102, 153
inheritance 27, 141, 200–201, 205, 207
inoculations 179, 184, 185, 191
International Casino 107–110, **109**, 257–258ch9n1
Ireland 103
Ivanov, Lev 28

Jackson, Helen Hunt 139
Jackson, Joe 78, 84, 111, 117
Japan, tour in 189–190
"Jeanne Devereaux and Company" 59, **59**
Jefferson Barracks 180–181
John Tiller girls 40
Johnson, Chic 148; see also *Hellzapoppin* Company; Olsen, Ole
Junior Town Meeting of Pasadena 53, 57

Kamansky, David 240
Karsavina, Tamara 28
Kaye, Danny 172, **184**
Keaton, Buster 22
Keith, B.F. 8, 41; see also B.F. Keith Memorial Theatre
Keith-Albee Coliseum Theatre 41
King Alphonse 83, 88
The King and I 213
king and queen of Siam 83
King Edward VIII 98–99
King George V 83–84

King George VI 2, 83, 103, 114–115, *116*
King Gustav of Sweden 83, 114
Kiss Me Again 45–47, *46*, 256
kittens 164
Knight, Irene 49
Kobeleff, Constantin ("Kobie") 42, 106, 111
Koenigsberg, Max 176
"Koppers' Kapers" 171–172
Korean War 191–193
Korman, Murray *67*, 68, *77*
Kraft, Beatrice 214
Krivit, Harry 40, 183

La Meri 219
Laddie *13*, 18–19
"The Lady in Red" 66, 68, 73, *77*
Lali, Dat so 12
Lamb, Bob 60, 68, 106; dated Jeanne 58, 61, 65, 66; proposed elopement 107; proposed marriage 106
Lanchester, Elsa 79
land 200
Landseer of Regent Street (London) *72*
Lane, Althea 15, 16, 132–133
Lane, Blanche 15
Lane, Edith 15
Lane, Eldoras 15, 136, 159, 173, 199
Lane, Ida 15, 16, 173, 222
Lane, Jeanette 15, 53, 133, 136, 159
Lane, Lenore (Marsh) 15–16, 57, 72, 138, 139, 142, 222
Lane Brothers 157
Lane family reunion 112
Laughton, Charles 79
laws, labor 37–38, 52, 62, 107, 146
Le Barron Studios *35*
Lebrun, Madame 115
Lebrun, President 115
lecturer, public 237, 239–241
Lee, Anna 144
leg muscle, 202
Legnani, Pierina 28
Leigh, Jack 16, 120, 203
Leigh, Kate 16, 120, 203
Leonidoff, Leon 121, 123, 196
Le Seyeux, Jean 166
lessons, dancing 20, 22, 27, 42–44, 106; ethnic 219–220; filmed 138, 195, 259–260*ch*16*n*1; by Jeanne 227–234
letters, from fans 81–82
Lewis, Helen 140, 173, 175, 182
ligament 118
Lillie, Beatrice 45
Lincoln theatre 42
Loew's Capitol Theatre (Washington, DC) 129–130, 132

Loew's State Theatre (New York) 9, 61, 151, 152, 209
London City Council 74
London Palladium 2, 69, 72, 76
loneliness 7, 40, 63, 80, 106, 120, 128, 150, 194
Longchamp Racecourse 92
Los Angeles Civic Ballet Company 234
Lou, Anito 149
Love Letters 47–53, *48*, *49*
Lowenstein, Bert 13, 178, 187, 197
Lucia Chase's Ballet Theatre 177
Lucienne and Ashour (dancers) 201
Lugano, Switzerland 88
Lummis, Charles Fletcher 251; *see also* Nicolson, Grace

MacArthur, Douglas 188, 190, 259*nn*2,3
Mahoney, Will 2, 84
Maine, Bruno 121, 196
Malcia 166
Manhattan Mary 34–38, 255*ch*3*n*2
Manila, Philippines 188–189
Mann, George *165*, 166
March, Frederick 79
Marcus Loew's Orpheum 26
Markert, Russell 40–42, 119, 127, 255–256*ch*3*n*3
marriage 222–224
Marsh, Roy 138, 139
Martin, David 202
Marx, Groucho 208
Maslin, Marsh 166
Masonic Temple Auditorium 176
The Master Thief 54; *see also* Pasadena Community Playhouse
Mayfair hotel 92, 93, 117
Maytime 177–178, 179
McBride, Patricia 28
Meltonville, J. Marc 243
"Merry-Go-Round" 201
Metropolitan Opera Theatre *see* Muny theatre
Metropolitan theatre (Boston) 107
MGM Loew's tour 44
Mille, Agnes de 42
Miller, Marilyn 82, 209
Minnelli, Vincente 121
mirrors 228, *229*, 234
Missouri (ship) 182
Missouri Botanical Garden 16
Mistinguett 126
M N Pubx *46*
mob 100
Moore, Ida 222, 224
Mordkin, Mikhail 42
Mordkin Ballet Company 34

Morgan, Kenneth 147
Morosco, Bill 41–42
Morosco, Ray 41–42
Morris, William 226
Morris Creative Agency 107
"The Moth and the Flame" 73–76, *75*, 117
Mount Royal Hotel 74, 80, 92, 93, 96, 98, 102, 103
movie script, autobiographical 209–210
movies, Jeanne in 45–47
Mrs. Clark's Dancing School 20, *21*, 24
Munson, Ona 37
Muny theatre 25, 26, 27, 129, 132, 135, *135*, 155, 162
Murphy, Fred *226*
Murphy sisters 157
Murry, Vera 30
museum exhibit cases 235–236, *236*
music 30
Music Corp of America 114
Mussolini, Benito 89

name, stage 18, *23*
Native American crafts 12, 251–252
Natya Ethnologic Dance Theatre 219
necklace, wampum 12, 140
Nell Gwyn 38–39
Nelson, Billy 49
New Palace Theatre 41
New York City Ballet 9, 24, 214
Nicholson, Grace 240, 251–253
Normandie (ship) 66, 112, 118
nose 12, 55, 112, 173

O'Connor, Eileen 227
Office of Price Administration 170
Olive and George 143, 144, *145*, 151–152
Olsen, Ole 148; *see also* Hellzapoppin Company; Johnson, Chic
One, F. Suie 252; *see also* Nicholson, Grace
Open Fist Theatre 244
operettas 25, *135*, 136, 137, 162–164, 175, 177, 178–179, 199
orchid 16–17, 241
Orpheum circuit 27
Orpheum theatre 57, 59, 147, 148
O'Sullivan, Alice 166, 222, 233, 247
O'Sullivan, Louise 166, 222, 233, 247

Pacific Asia Museum 240, 251, 252–253

Page Museum at the La Brea Tar Pits 235, *236*
Palace Theatre (New York) 2, 8, 9, 22, 34, 37, 65, 72, 79, 165, 213–214, 217
Pantages theatre 54
Paramount theatre 57, 130, 142, 147, 161
Paris 87–88, 91–92, 112–114
Parnell, Val 94
Pasadena Civic Auditorium 54, 233
Pasadena Community Playhouse 53–54
Pasadena Regional Ballet 233, 234
Paso Doble 212
Paul, Ginger 227; see also Bennett family
Paul, Kay Bennett 39, 70, 106, 123–124, 135, 136; see also Bennett family
Pavlova, Anna 22, 75, 83, 127, 179, 255n1
Pearl Harbor 150, 181
Pepper, Jack 53, 57, 58
Perkins, Basil 212, 224, 226–227
Perkins, Thomas 53, 142, *172*, 173, 212, 222, *223*, 224, *238*, 247; courtship of Jeanne 210; custom museum exhibit cases 235–236; death 245; short bio 211–212; visited Jeanne in New York 216–217
Perkins Development Engineering 211, 235, 260–261nn6,7
Petipa, Marius 28
philatelists 13
Philippines 188–189
Pickford, Mary 114
pickpocket 91
"Piquant Perfume" 127
Piroska, Ference 213, 222
Pittsburgh Civic Light Opera 199, 201, *202*
Plaza Hotel Grand Ballroom 135, 214–216
pneumonia 191, 237
poetry 173, 178, 187–188, 248–249, 254
Poggi, Grace 166
police show benefit 171
Popeye 107
Previn, Charles 196
Price, Vincent 136
Pring, G.H. 16–17, 241
Prival, Bert 45
program, souvenir 84, *85*
Purdy, Patrick 225, *226*, 236–237

quail 18
Queen Elizabeth 83, 114–115, *116*
Queen Mary 2, 83–84, 86
Queen Mary (ship) 105–106
Queen Maud of Norway 83
"The Quest" 54
Questers El Molino 237, 240–241, 261n8
Questers' National Convention 239

racial bias 229–230
radio 213, 237
Radio City Music Hall 119–121, 123–124, 127–128, 151, 154–155, *192*, 196–197, *197*, 198, 201, 217, 255–256ch3n3, 258ch10n1
Radio City Rockettes 40, 255–256ch3n3
Radio Exhibition at Olympia (Radiolympia) 117
Radio Keith Orpheum (RKO) tour 40–42
rank, "Honorary Captain" 180
rationing 160, 170, 196
"The Reception at Versailles" 234
Red Donahue and his Mule 209
respiratory disease 164
"Revolution in a Teacup" (lecture) 239
Reynolds, Eugenia 50
Rio Brothers 107, 117
Rio de Janeiro 124–127
Riverside Theatre 148, 149
RKO theatre 148, 150
Roberta 162, 164
Rockefeller brothers 123
Roehrig, Frederick 139; see also dream house
Rogge, Florence 34
Romano, Tony 172
Rose, Bert 181
Rose, Harry 131
"Rose Ballet" 166, 171, *172*
Rose Pageant 54
Roseland building (rehearsal hall) 130
Rothafel, Samuel Lionel "Roxy" 33
Rotty, Adeline 22, 24
"Round About Regent Street" 72, 73–80, *75*
Roxy Theatre 33–34, 57–58, 213, 217
Roxy Theatre Roxyettes 40
Royal Archives, Windsor Castle 243
Royal Bath hotel 117
Royal Command performance 83–87, *85*, 257ch7n1
Royal Opera House 103
rulers 14, 152, 158, 175, 198
rumba 73, 76
Russian character dances 219–220

Sadler's Wells Ballet Company 213, 214
Saint George theatre 60
Sam Jack Kaufman House Orchestra 157
Sam S. Shubert Theatre 36
Sandrini, Pierre 108, 112, 118
Sands, Hal 59, 60, 62, 66, 69, 71, 74, 106–107, 112, 121, 124, 160
Savoy hotel dinner club 103, 105, 117
School of Natya Ethnologic Dance Theatre 219
Seabold, Miriam 137
Seeley, Blossom 57
Selig, Diana 250
Seymour, Jack 59
Seymour, Maurice *109*, *163*
Shakuntala 55; see also Pasadena Community Playhouse
Shaver, Buster 143, 144, 151, 152; see also Olive and George
shoes, toe 30, 76, 82, 87, 152, 170, 185
Shrine Auditorium 171
Silverman, Sime 8
Simpson, Wallis 98–99, 257ch8n1
Sisters G 90
Sixteen American Rockets 40
Sixteen Russell Markert Girls 40–42, 119
sketches 31, 220, *232*
"Skiing Under Northern Skies" 198
Skouras, Spyros 40
Slate Brothers 144
Smith and Dale 213
Social Security Act 134
Social Security Administration 207
Sons O' Guns 162
South, Lucile Iverson 17
Spanish Civil War 91–92, 99
Spaulding, Kenneth 31, 166, 204, 205
Spaulding House 228, 234
Spaulding Trio 166; see also O'Sullivan, Alice; O'Sullivan, Louise
Spence, Wilma 176
Spring Maid 25
Springman, Fague *157*
stairway 185
stamps 13
Stanley theatre 148, 150
Starbuck, James 199, 201
Starlight Operetta 177
"Stars on Parade" 117
Stencel, Mildred 50
Sterners sisters 149
stock market 195
storage 122, 141

Stowe, Harriet Beecher 225
Stowe family reunion 225
Stratford Empire theatre 117
Streetcar Named Desire 213
strikes 91, 175, 177, 259*ch*14*n*1
student dance festivals 231, 233
Sunday, prohibition against dancing on 52, 62, 107, 146
Sunkist Beauties 49, *49*, 50
Swan Lake 54, 178, 179, 214
"Sweet Georgia Brown" 59

Tachikawa Army Base Hangar 190
tap dance 40, 41, 50
Tarasov, Ivan 42
tea set 80, 98
teeth 91, 102
television 117, 208–209, 213
Terrace room 161
Texaco Star Theatre 208–209, *209*; *see also* Berle, Milton
Texas State Fair 147, 178
Thanksgiving 110, 140, 148, 186, 197
The Three Musketeers 177–178, 179, 182, 199, 200, 201, ***202***
Three Swifts 99, 131
Tivoli theatre (Australia) 202–203
Tivoli theatre (New York) 60
"To the Colors!" 154
Todd, Wilson (Todd Studios) ***23***
toe tapping 82
Tokyo 190
Tournament of Roses coronation pageant 54
Tower theatre (Kansas City) 147, 148

"Traveller's Lament" 178, 188
Tripoli, Libya 89–90
Troizky, Vera 108
Truzzi (juggler) 166, 171
Tucker, Sophie 87, 257*ch*7*n*1
tummy button 108, ***109***

Uaddam Hotel and Casino 89
unemployment insurance 134
United Service Organizations 180
United States Office of Price Administration 170
"United We Stand" 191, ***192***, 196
SS *Uruguay* 125
USC Pacific Asia Museum 253; *see also* Nicholson, Grace; Pacific Asia Museum
USO Camp Shows 155, 156, 179, 180, 182–193, 250
USO San Diego Center 250

Valentinoff, Valya (Paul Valentine) 129–130
van Dijk, Elly 234–235, 239
Variety Artistes' Benevolent Fund 83–84
variety shows 69, 72–73
Vasilieff, Nicholas 127
vaudeville: circuits for 9, 10 (*see also* circuits, tours of); overview of 8–10
Vélez, Lupe 63–64, 65, 66, 93
"Victory Revue" 157

Waller, Fats 117
Ward, George *48*, 49, *49*, 50; *see also Love Letters*
Wasserman, Lew 171

Watts, Hannah 78, 84
wedding reception ***223***
weenies 33
Weissmuller, Johnny 63–64
Weldy, Max 36
Wells, William K. 36
West, Mae 60
White, George 34, 36, 61
Wiere Brothers 144
Wiesfeld, Mr. 149
William Miller Corporation 211
William Morris Agency 208, 209
William Randolph Hearst Collection 152
Winchell, Walter 128
Winkler, Bill 24, 105
Winter, Robert 58*ch*11*n*1
Winterland Theatre 164, 165, 166, ***167***
Woolever, Harry 162, 227
World War I veterans 180–181
World War II 89, 127, 150, 181–182
World War II legacy 250
World's Fair 119, 124, 127
wrist 25
Wynn, Ed 36, 38
Wynn, Keenan 38

YMCA 19, 122, 141, 152–153, 168, 177, 198, 203

Ziegfeld, Florenz 32, 38, 143
Ziegfeld Follies 18, 32, 34, 36, 38, 40, 209

www.ingramcontent.com/pod-product-compliance
Lightning Source LLC
Chambersburg PA
CBHW081545300426
44116CB00015B/2763